ALSO BY TED WIDMER

American Speeches:

Political Oratory from Abraham Lincoln to Bill Clinton

(as editor)

American Speeches:

Political Oratory from the Revolution to the Civil War

(as editor)

Martin Van Buren

Campaigns:

A Century of Presidential Races

(with Alan Brinkley)

Young America:

The Flowering of Democracy in New York City

ARK OF THE LIBERTIES

Insula hyspana

ARK OF THE LIBERTIES

AMERICA AND THE WORLD

TED WIDMER

for Nina Houghton,
with fond memories
of Chestertown,
best wishes,
Ted

HILL AND WANG

A DIVISION OF FARRAR, STRAUS AND GIROUX

NEW YORK

(copy #1!)

Hill and Wang
A division of Farrar, Straus and Giroux
18 West 18th Street, New York 10011

Distributed in Canada by Douglas & McIntyre Ltd.
Printed in the United States of America
First edition, 2008

Library of Congress Cataloging-in-Publication Data
Widmer, Edward L.
Ark of the liberties : America and the world / Ted Widmer. — 1st ed.
p. cm.
Includes bibliographical references and index.
ISBN-13: 978-0-8090-2735-4 (hardcover : alk. paper)
ISBN-10: 0-8090-2735-6 (hardcover : alk. paper)
1. United States—History. 2. United States—Politics and government. 3. Liberty—United States—History. 4. Democracy—United States—History. I. Title.

E183.W545 2008
973—dc22

2008004446

Designed by Jonathan D. Lippincott

www.fsgbooks.com

1 3 5 7 9 10 8 6 4 2

For a family of explorers:

Eric Widmer

Ellen Widmer

Matt Widmer

And for Freddy Widmer and all the places he is going

You must have plenty of sea-room to tell the Truth in; especially, when it seems to have an aspect of newness, as America did in 1492, though it was then just as old, and perhaps older than Asia, only those sagacious philosophers, the common sailors, had never seen it before; swearing it was all water and moonshine there.

—Herman Melville

CONTENTS

PREFACE

Caliban: Freedom, high-day! high-day, freedom! freedom, high-day, freedom!
Stephano: O brave monster! lead the way.

—Shakespeare, *The Tempest*

In 1850, Herman Melville dashed off an adventure story, *White-Jacket*, to make a little extra money. Amazingly, he wrote the entire thing in about two months. He denigrated it as a mere "job," but it sold well, introduced the terms "squeegee" and "wine cooler" to the English language, and gave him the confidence to contemplate something more ambitious. Like all of his books, it was based on his own life, and recounted the story of a young sailor traveling around the world on a ship. In the novel, Melville called that ship the *Neversink*, but in real life, he had sailed on a naval vessel named after his country, the *United States*. It was the only time he sailed in a military expedition, in this case at the outermost point of America's expanding presence in the Pacific. Appropriately, he was full of feeling for his country, and in one passage he gave vent to a grand vision of America's destiny that is read far more often than the rest of the book. It was the sort of grand declamation that nineteenth-century audiences thrilled to:

> And we Americans are the peculiar, chosen people—the Israel of our time; we bear the ark of the liberties of the world. Seventy

> years ago we escaped from thrall; and besides our first birthright—embracing one continent of earth—God has given us, for future inheritance, the broad domains of the political pagans, that shall yet come and lie down under the shade of our ark, without bloody hands being lifted. God has predestinated, mankind expects, great things from our race; and great things we feel in our souls. The rest of the nations must soon be in our rear. We are the pioneers of the world; the advance-guard, sent on through the wilderness of untried things, to break a new path in the New World that is ours.

That passage has been widely cited by admirers and critics alike as embodying a typical American confidence in the right to expand indefinitely, offering liberty to all who desire it (and perhaps a few who do not). But like everything Melville ever wrote, it's more complicated than meets the eye. He spent most of *White-Jacket* arguing that a U.S. naval vessel was anything but an ark of the liberties, and was better described as a holding pen where sailors were flogged mercilessly for the slightest infraction. He suggested that only rank disobedience to a captain's mindless order had saved the *Neversink* from the humiliation of sinking. Melville even came close to saying "our Revolution was in vain" and "our Declaration of independence . . . a lie," but pulled back before crossing that heretical line. Still, he was disturbed by America's failure to live up to her ideals, and he poured some of that frustration into the masterpiece to come, *Moby-Dick*.

Today, that frustration is a global phenomenon. Approval of the United States is at record lows in nearly every nation on earth. But still, without a doubt, deep wellsprings of hope persist for this extraordinary nation as it completes one chapter of its history and begins another. *Extraordinary* is the right word, for a sweeping look at our history shows that nothing was ever ordinary about the discovery of America and the growth of political institutions destined to travel around the planet. By definition, the New World was different from the Old, and from that elemental fact came five centuries of shock, awe, and gradual enlightenment. The journey that began with a single voyage—by Columbus—continues to this day.

For all these reasons, I was attracted to Melville's passage and to the phrase "ark of the liberties." It is resonant for any student of early American history, recalling the arrival of the *Ark and Dove*, the first vessel to arrive in Maryland, one of the most tolerant places on Earth when it was founded. It conjures Noah's ark—an apt metaphor for America, with two of everything coming by boat to establish a new society. And it hints at the Ark of the Covenant, the legendary container of the Ten Commandments, and suggestive of the idea, still palpable in the ether, that Americans possess the key to religious truths that are unavailable to others.

I also like the word's versatility; to me, *ark* conveys both venerability and motion; the pitch and heave of a crossing, the arc of a pendulum, a constant inconstancy. I was taken with the image of a vessel that steadily takes on more passengers, stopping here and there in remote locations. I also thought it accurate for the fact that boats rarely float in a straight line, but tack from one course to another, testing the prevailing winds, going as far as currents and weight and food supply will allow before taking new measurements and correcting course again. Last, the word *ark* faintly suggests *arc-en-ciel*, or "arc in the sky," the French term for a rainbow. For what idea has been more powerful in our history than the hope that something wonderful—a pot of gold or simply a new beginning—waits over the next horizon?

All these arks bear upon a very old American idea that I would like to explore in this book. As Melville hints, our nation's journey is no simple commute from Point A to Point B. The ark of the liberties has always been interpreted by Americans as a voyage on behalf of all humanity. At its essence, it is a voyage in search of freedom, defined in a thousand different ways, to be sure, but still understood to be a destination we are searching for so that we can make its coordinates known to the rest of mankind. As politicians from Thomas Paine to Woodrow Wilson to George W. Bush have told us, we have nothing less than a mission to redeem the world. The urge to be free—so basic as to barely need expression—infuses the eternal language of the Declaration of Independence, the still-astonishing orations of Abraham Lincoln, and the great statements of American purpose offered by Franklin Roosevelt during the darkest days of World War Two. It also can be reduced to cardboard simplicity, as in New Hampshire's terrifying license-plate motto, "Live Free or Die." My hope was that a more thorough inspection of the American ark—its origin, destination, and manifest—would help all passengers.

For some time, I had wanted to write an expansive book about America's engagement with the world—not a history of U.S. foreign policy, exactly, but a reflection on the ideas that we Americans carry around like iPods, barely conscious of their weight. True, it's an inexhaustible topic, and it may be a fool's errand to try to capture it within a single book. But I miss the sweeping histories of the 1940s and '50s, when Americans thought nothing of trying to express big national ideas at a time when everything American suddenly had global ramifications. I thought that a series of discrete chapters on different moments from our past would allow me to cover a lot of ground without having to write about *everything*.

One of my goals was to give back to Americans a sense of how vast our history truly is. We think of Jefferson as an early figure, but even he was amazed at how old America was. He never admitted that the last mastodons had disappeared from the interior, and went into raptures when the fossilized toenail of a giant sloth, the "Great Claw of Megalonyx," was discovered at Big Bone Lick in Kentucky, proving that enormous creatures had once stalked North America. I knew that I wanted to take the story back to its beginning, but I had no idea how far back it went. I'm not sure that I've found it yet.

It may surprise readers to encounter a book about the ideas inside American foreign policy that begins with Columbus. Most accounts go back to Vietnam, or possibly World War Two. But I believe it a worthy enterprise to read more deeply in the obscure texts of the distant past than is the norm. After all, extremism in the defense of liberty is no vice. These older voices tell a remarkable story of one part of the world awkwardly integrating itself with the rest, often in the face of dogged refusals to accept its existence. Slowly, amazingly, a fantasy evolved into a nation, which then grew into a superpower. Besides, Columbus is not so irrelevant; even his mistakes were visionary, and billions of dollars flow every day on his assumption that Asia and America are near to each other. We have been global from the start.

Another travel advisory: as I wrote this book, I tried to avoid the Scylla and Charybdis of excessive adulation and criticism of the United States. So many people seem to occupy one extreme or the other. My preference was to explore the story with respect for its epic grandeur, but also with a sense of humility. *The Tempest*, Shakespeare's most

American play, describes the "sea change" that can put everything in a sparkling new light on a beautiful island (islands abound in this book). But Prospero also says, "this thing of darkness I / Acknowledge mine." I see no reason not to explore our mistakes as fully as our triumphs. We have nothing to fear from them; on the contrary, I find a great deal of hope by consulting the oracles of the past.

In fact, the past is everywhere, if only we open our eyes to see it. With a little imagination, it is possible to go back to our origins in just a few leapfrog steps. One could argue that the Iraq conflict is traceable to the peace negotiations at Versailles, led by Woodrow Wilson in 1919. The U.S. entry into World War One was distantly related to the Mexican War (Americans were enraged when an intercepted German telegram promised to return to Mexico all the territory we had won from her in 1848). The Mexican War was distantly connected to the Reformation and the fear that a Catholic nation was a threat to America's southern flank. Traces of that fear of papal authority lingered at least until the Kennedy administration.

The Mexican War had just finished when Melville wrote his greatest novels. It remains a most important conflict, despite the fact that it receives little attention north of the border. It was our first large-scale foreign intervention, it brought California and half of the West into the Union, and it gave an early indication of the matchless military prowess that Americans would show the world. But as any honest historian has to admit, it was fought on shaky moral grounds, and Americans paid dearly for its unfocused ambitions. Undeniably, the questions created by this conflict led to the Civil War—the greatest tragedy in American history. Ulysses Grant later wrote that the Civil War was divine retribution for what the United States had done to its neighbor.

During and after the war with Mexico, Americans were roiled by an acrimonious debate that involved two questions simultaneously. Does the United States have the right to go to war to promote liberty? And should we not resolve some of our own imperfections before claiming it? In *White-Jacket*, Melville gave his optimistic answer. In *Moby-Dick*, a year later, he gave a darker response. Today, those questions are still before us, and they beg new answers.

As someone who has both taught history and written presidential speeches, I wanted to show respect for the immense power of language to shape ideas. *Liberty* is one of the biggest words in American history—so vast that it is difficult to fix its precise coordinates. In 1864, Abraham Lincoln put it perfectly: "The world has never had a good definition of the word *liberty*, and the American people, just now, are much in want of one. We all declare for liberty; but in using the same word we do not all mean the same thing."

That problem is still with us. *Liberty* is so ubiquitous in American history as to be nearly without meaning, ranging freely across the spectrum of political expression, from the American Civil Liberties Union on the left to Jerry Falwell's Liberty University on the right. It includes gun nuts, peace nuts, and wing nuts of every political persuasion. It covers entities that have nothing to do with liberty, such as a professional women's basketball team (New York Liberty), a sports utility vehicle (Jeep Liberty), and Gerald Ford's pet golden retriever. Purveyors of junk food, fighting against studies that tell us their food makes us fat, have been lobbying that Americans should never give up the right to "food liberty" that the founders fought for.

There is no better way to see how confusing *liberty* can be than to consult other peoples—often the exact peoples we are trying to bring liberty to—whose languages do not include near equivalents. They literally have no idea what we are talking about. In China, the word for liberty is a cognate of the word for oil—a comment not on our petroleum but on the oleaginous way in which we tend to talk about our values. In Arabic, as the historian Bernard Lewis has argued, the word for freedom—*hurriyya*—means nothing more complicated than a specific legal status (in this case, not being a slave). When Napoleon invaded Egypt in 1798, "in the name of the French republic, founded upon the principles of liberty and equality," those concepts were deeply confusing to local people. It was not until decades later that the confusion was resolved, at least partly. In 1834, an Egyptian scholar, Sheikh Rifa'a Rafi' al-Tahtawi, brought out a book that suggested Europeans mean "justice" when they say "freedom."

Without a doubt, great things have been done by Americans to advance liberty. There is a glorious arc—America's true *arc-en-ciel*—stretching from the Declaration to the Gettysburg Address to the Fourteen Points to the Atlantic Charter to the Universal Declaration of Human Rights. Generation after generation, we have refined our definition of what constitutes a just society, and expanded its reach to include hundreds of millions of people who live very far from the United States but are still affected by our sense of what is right.

Honesty requires us to admit that we have not always lived up to our high standards. Indeed, scandalous things have been done in the name of liberty. When the American buccaneer Thomas Tew established a pirate community free of all laws on the island of Madagascar, he named it Libertatia (we should never forget how close *liberty* is to *libertine*). We bear a peculiar responsibility for the peculiar institution, slavery, a terrible crime in any country but somehow less forgivable in the land of the free. Samuel Johnson had a point when he complained, "How is it that the loudest cries for liberty come from the drivers of Negroes?" It is likewise bittersweet to contemplate that the greatest step forward for liberty in human history was probably the Emancipation Proclamation, an act of liberation *by* Americans, *for* Americans, and *from* Americans.

I would like to spend time in the gray, between the black and white answers that come too quickly to jingoists and cynics, and between the scary extremes of the New Hampshire license plate. Has America truly been a force for liberty in the world? Or have our imperfections doomed us to irrelevance? I will argue yes to the first question and no to the second, but I would like to do so with more rigor than we get from Fourth of July speeches. The conventional story of our external relations is that we were isolationist until 1898, and that we've been internationalist since then. I think it's much more complicated. We've always been more international than we let on. For starters, there is a deep-seated tradition, centuries old, of expecting the regeneration of the world to come from America. And I believe the second half of that equation is also wrong—we are far less comfortable with our global power than we appear to be, deeply unsettled over the errand into the Mesopotamian wilderness and unsure where it is leading us. In other words, we have always had two traditions in conflict. It is perhaps useful to think of the Gulf Stream that facilitated the exploration of America. At the surface of the water, there is a powerful flow in one direction, and then farther down, the stream flows in the opposite direction.

Let's take a moment to define these two traditions. Both have excellent pedigrees. First, there is George Washington's still powerful idea, articulated in his Farewell Address, that American liberty is precious and unique, and that we imperil it when we involve ourselves in foreign entanglements. Then there is Franklin Roosevelt's equally powerful idea that American liberty at home depends on our solicitous interest in liberty overseas. Both traditions are dedicated to our well-being. But they are utterly opposed to each other.

There is ample evidence to support both Washington and Roosevelt. But the passage of time and the extent of America's global reach have tilted us irrevocably toward the latter. Defying Washington's Farewell Address, the United States is now a party to so many thousands of international obligations that it takes 510 pages of tiny type to list them all in the 2007 edition of *Treaties in Force*. Despite the presence of a huge number of isolationists in both parties, American presidents have led us into conflict no fewer than 105 times in the last century, almost always in the name of defending foreign liberty. We see the same pattern time and time again: a candidate pledges to conduct a more humble foreign policy—only to embark on new schemes beyond the wildest imagination of his predecessor.

I believe that it's an act of patriotism to ask hard questions, rejecting the twin pitfalls of extreme defensiveness and extreme criticism. We've always been better than our detractors claim, and we have never been as good as our most ardent defenders insist. These questions matter not only to us, but to the millions of people around the world who still look to America for guidance, despite the bad press that we have been getting. There has never been a more important moment to get right with our story. If the most powerful nation on earth cannot explain itself to the rest of humanity, problems will originate naturally and persist indefinitely. That's bad for the United States *and* the world. For who else has the capacity to fix the enormous problems still bedeviling mankind? For that matter, who else has the desire?

It can help to take a step back and look at this story from a wider perspective. And American history *is* a story. It is not random movements of people and economic forces. There are ideas at every stage. Americans may be the most intellectual people on earth. We would be stunned if the French launched an invasion on behalf of existentialism, or the Germans did so on behalf of Hegelian metaphysics, but we think nothing of launching huge armies to defend freedom around the world.

It is in fact the official policy of the United States, as defined by President Bush's second inaugural address. I would argue that every time an American G.I. points a weapon at an Iraqi insurgent, or vice versa, it is the end result of a long sequence of ideas dating back centuries in each country.

In particular, I hope to restore our grasp of the startling global ambition that propelled so much American history. Throughout our early history, we see again and again a rash insistence that this provincial society at the edge of the known world was not only relevant, but *essential* to the rest of civilization. Because of the great space taken up by George Washington's Farewell Address in the attic of memory, it has been widely assumed that early Americans took little interest in the rest of the world. That is simply not true. It ignores the audacious claim of the Declaration of Independence to appeal to "the opinions of mankind." It ignores the long history of millennial expectations, especially in New England, but in the other colonies as well. And it ignores the historic link between the very idea of America—an undiscovered new world—and the possibility of redemption. A second chance, as it were.

Everything changed, of course, in 1776. The birth of the United States did not take place in a vacuum—ideas about liberty had been gathering strength for five generations. But it is difficult to overestimate the power of the Declaration's significance. That document signaled the first time that a new government enshrined the basic principles of human freedom in a founding charter. It's right there, in black and white: "Life, liberty and the pursuit of happiness." The power of those words persists in thousands of ways, from the mundane (the 1974 film *Life, Liberty and Pursuit on the Planet of the Apes*) to the inspiring (the clear chain connecting the Universal Declaration of Human Rights, and by extension all human rights arguments, to Jefferson's language). The language is so powerful that every nation is forced to use it. We have the ridiculous spectacle of a nation named the Democratic People's Republic of Korea (every word a lie except the final one). Iran now claims an "inalienable right" to develop nuclear weapons.

The Declaration is so familiar that it is difficult to reread it in a new way. But clearly, this is much more than a document announcing a mere political separation. It is a philosophical document calling for the regeneration of the world. It presumptuously demands the attention of all people. Thomas Paine wrote, "The cause of America is in a great measure the cause of all mankind." But the most amazing thing about the Declaration may be the fact that its bold predictions actually came true. It *did* usher in a new age, against all expectations in Europe, and probably to the amazement of its signers as well. To this day we celebrate the Fourth of July not merely because we need freedom from work and sobriety. Instead, we recognize that 1776 genuinely signaled the beginning of a new time in human history, when a nation came into existence insisting that government is consensual and power flows upward from the people to their representatives. A simple reading of the Declaration, with its calm insistence on rights and their radical possibilities, can provide more fireworks than any pyrotechnic display.

At our best, that simple philosophy continues to guide us. It certainly strengthened the Northern cause during the Civil War, when Lincoln invoked the Declaration to argue that any democracy based on force was no democracy. (The Confederacy grew so uncomfortable with the Declaration that it disavowed it.) It guided the rapid growth of American influence in the world in the nineteenth century through a vast trade network, the creation of American educational institutions overseas, and the steady exposure of foreigners to our democracy at home. It guided leviathan efforts to defeat formidable adversaries in the world wars of the twentieth century, and just as important, to build a better architecture of foreign relations in their aftermath. One hopes that it will guide Americans again as we renew contact with the true wellsprings of our national greatness. As Ronald Reagan put it in his farewell address: "If we forget what we did, we won't know who we are." If we would like an occasionally ungrateful world to act a little more like us, then it will certainly help to know ourselves better.

At our greatest moments, we have done exactly that. Lincoln, more than any other president, articulated the core beliefs that unite us and explain us. Franklin Roosevelt deepened our idea of liberty with the Four Freedoms and the Atlantic Charter, and Eleanor Roosevelt made American liberty comprehensible to the world in the soaring architecture of the Universal Declaration of Human Rights. But none of those documents offers the final word—there is always room for a new and better definition. That's why pencils have erasers.

If nothing else, I mean to make plain the value of history as a guide for a nation that has not always followed the straightest course in its relations with other countries. Our best leaders have always been students of the past. John F. Kennedy's reading about World War One may have kept the Cuban Missile Crisis from sliding toward Armageddon; Woodrow Wilson and Theodore Roosevelt were deeply learned historians; Lincoln and John Quincy Adams knew the story of America as well as anyone alive in their time. That knowledge offered a reliable compass as they guided the ship of state forward.

The Greeks counseled that there is no better way out of a labyrinth than to follow a thread backward. An unblinkered look at posterity can explain not only who we have been, but who we desire to be. For Americans, more than for most, that has always been an act of will rather than a biological necessity. We may invoke "destiny" from time to time, but in fact, the United States has always been a republic of choice.

Arthur Schlesinger Sr. once proposed that American history moves in cycles, bends, and dips that one might recognize with a trained eye, the way a cardiologist reads a cardiogram. By that, he largely meant domestic history, but I believe that rhythms can be detected inside the long history of American foreign policy as well. Every so often, Americans are swept up in a fever of expectation about the future, often tied to moments of conquest. These viral episodes are inevitably followed by self-correcting moments of realism, such as Lincoln's contempt for Manifest Destiny or FDR's rejection of the dreamy utopianism of the 1920s.

These rhythms can be heard as well as seen, for our story has been deeply shaped by the language used to describe it. That's why we celebrate Columbus, who prolifically described what he had beheld, rather than the Basque fishermen who preceded him. Throughout American history, the act of writing down an aspiration, even when it could not quite be realized, was essential to building the rights and liberties that came to distinguish this nation. I am especially intrigued by the long history of presidential language, a ripe subject for exploration. From Washington's Farewell Address to the Monroe Doctrine to the Atlantic Charter, it is in these moments of executive communication, both guarded and unguarded, that we have revealed our innermost thinking about how the United States relates to the rest of humanity. As Franklin Roosevelt said, "All our great presidents were leaders of thought when certain historic ideas in the life of the nation had to be clarified."

If history is a guide, we will move past the present difficulties into a new and better era. But we will do so only if we are prepared to make real sacrifices and genuinely come to terms with the way the rest of the world feels about us—a constellation of fears and hopes roughly equal to our own. Thomas Jefferson, who wrote our greatest charter of liberty in spite of his own manifold weaknesses as a human being, may have said it best when he wrote modestly, "The ground of liberty is to be gained by inches."

ARK OF THE LIBERTIES

CHAPTER ONE

FANTASY ISLAND

> Be not afeard. The isle is full of noises,
> Sounds and sweet airs that give delight and hurt not.
> —Shakespeare, *The Tempest*

When the first American naval vessel sailed into Constantinople in 1800, Ottoman officials had no vocabulary to describe the strange new people and where they came from, so they referred to the United States as an "island kingdom." That was not the worst way to describe the only democracy on earth, but it proved once again that a wide ocean separated Americans from the hierarchies of Europe. This immense intellectual distance was revealed every time a writer from the Old World labored to apply words to places that seemed to exist outside all known realms, including those of time and space.

"In the beginning, all the world was America," wrote John Locke, famously, in his *Second Treatise on Government* (1690). But those words, for all their airy resonance, were hardly complimentary. Instead, Locke was arguing that the Old World was once, near the dawn of history, as barbaric as the New. Even two centuries after Columbus, America conjured little more than a vast vacuity.

Of course, Europeans were fascinated by America, and in the early centuries of exploration, a tiny percentage actually came to live here, but the vast majority of the world's people were as removed from the new realm as they were from the moon. In fact, there *was* something extraterrestrial about the early accounts of this alternative world. America seemed to be a place of half-humans and sea monsters, hastily sketched into the corners and wide-open spaces of maps—more an idea than a location. With the passage of time, topographical detail has filled those spaces, but misperceptions remain. An immense gulf yawns between the way that citizens of the United States perceive the story of America, as the culmination of all prior events, and the way that most foreigners do, as a world that is still deeply new, and more than a little unsettling.

We still struggle with these ancient archetypes. Americans today, weighted down with doorstop biographies of the founders and entranced by war footage on the History Channel, have difficulty fathoming that we are merely one of 194 nations on the planet, and that each has a long history separate from our own. Other nations, no less proud, have trouble explaining the remarkable ascendancy of a people who, only a few centuries ago, were running around an untamed wilderness firing arrows and flintlocks at one another. Too many foreign observers look across the ocean and still expect to see monsters, or failing to see them, invent new ones.

Surely a splash of cold-water realism can help each side to see the other perspective more clearly. An honest look at the origins of the American errand can help to dispel both the notion that we are a divinely anointed people and the opposite premise, that our ascendancy was a nightmare, correlated with the decline of other civilizations—in particular that of Islam, banished from Spain in the same year that Columbus set out to the west. Osama bin Laden has mentioned that historical coincidence to his followers, as if it proves a cosmic enmity between Muslims and Americans. Nothing could be further from the truth, and a deeper reading of history can rebut the extreme claims of both the America-haters and the superpatriots for whom the creation of the United States was only a little less significant than the events of the book of Genesis.

Near the end of *The Tempest*, Shakespeare has Gonzalo report breathlessly on the virtue of the "people of the island" he has encountered, and wonder if they might even be the gentlest, kindest people on earth. Unable to bear it, Prospero responds sarcastically that it would be difficult to be worse than the people of the Old World. That refreshing skepticism helps on a journey into the exaggerated world of early travel literature. Aquariums often enlarge the stature of their occupants, and so it was with the tidal wave of writing that followed in the wake of Columbus.

No matter where you think American history begins, chances are that you are beginning too late. We often date our origins to the birth of the U.S. government in 1789, or the Constitution in 1787, or the Declaration of Independence in 1776. Some intrepid souls even wander back as far as the earliest arrival of settlers in New England (1620) and Virginia (1607). Yet it is clear that American history had been unfolding for some time before that. The extraordinary Spanish empire penetrated deeply into the Americas during the long century that elapsed between the landfall of Columbus in 1492 and the first English settlements. The English and their proxies had explored the eastern seaboard in the immediate aftermath of Columbus, legitimating their future claims to this valuable real estate with their first landing at Newfoundland in 1497. But the earliest foreign contemplation of America went back even further than that—to what T. S. Eliot called "a time older than the time of chronometers." It may disturb some readers of a book on American history to go back to the Renaissance, even to the Middle Ages and before. But what could be more American than to encroach on someone else's territory and start prospecting?

This early history still abides with us, just as a child's features are traceable in the adult he or she becomes. The United States is an older nation now, as experienced as any in the problems of modernity, and in many ways more so, but still, we are connected to those earlier times and geographical circumstances. We inhabit the New World, a designation that persists from the world-doubling discoveries of the late fifteenth century. But the New World is not so new; the oldest living thing on earth is a bristlecone pine tree named Methuselah, nearly five thousand years old, in California. Of course, human beings had been living in the New World a long time before it was unveiled and christened. The recent discovery of an old footprint in Mexico suggests that hominids may have been here as long as forty thousand years—far longer than previously assumed.

Long before Columbus left his own footprint in the sands of Watling Island, Europeans felt a strong intuition that a great land existed to the west. Near the beginning of *Moby-Dick*, Melville uses the word *loomings* to conjure presentiments of the great epic about to begin. That same sense of America's loomings was pervasive long before 1492, and without looking terribly far, one can find throughout European literature a sense that another world was waiting to be discovered. The literature of antiquity furnishes frenzied speculations on what exactly lay past the Pillars of Hercules guarding Gibraltar, none more famous than Plato's riveting account of the great civilization of Atlantis that had perished nine thousand years before: a land that abounded with "kings of amazing power," golden statues, even hot and cold running water.

But Atlantis hardly constitutes the beginning and end of the European daydream. The westward longing seems to have been a perpetual condition from the origin of recorded thought to the explosion of interest that followed the letter Columbus had published at Barcelona in 1493 (quickly republished in many other cities), describing the voyage he had just taken to the ends of the earth. Nearly every European tradition has a story that describes the inclination to sail toward the sunset and what lay beyond it. There were true sightings of land—we know now what we did not for most of our history, that Norsemen were in North America a thousand years ago. And there were hundreds—thousands—of reports from the nebulous and interlocking worlds of mariner gossip, writerly embellishment, and outright fabrication of places that seemed so real that mapmakers routinely listed them, well into the modern age.

The Sunken Land of Buss, for example (an imaginary island between Greenland and Iceland), was soberly reported by Martin Frobisher and Richard Hakluyt at the beginning of English colonization, and lingered on some maps and accounts into the twentieth century. The maps that were used to settle the boundaries between the United States and Canada during the negotiations ending the American Revolution described two islands in Lake Superior that were completely fictitious. A smart lawyer might have challenged the treaty simply on that basis. California was depicted as an island until the late eighteenth century, and in some ways has never stopped being one. It may become an island again if a sufficiently large earthquake pries it loose from North America. Similarly, the fabled Northwest Passage, long dreamed of as a shortcut between Europe and Asia, may actually become a viable shipping lane if global warming can melt enough ice. Sometimes the old mapmakers weren't as ill-informed as we think; it just is taking us a while to catch up to them. When Gertrude Stein complained to Pablo Picasso that she did not look like his portrait of her, he replied, "You will."

Today it takes a mere six hours to fly across the Atlantic, but we should never forget what a daunting barrier the "Sea of Darkness" once presented to the intrepid. Yet even at its darkest, the Atlantic stirred as many imaginations as it terrified. Was there ever a time that explorers did not quest to the west? We believe with reasonable certainty that the Phoenicians sailed far into the Atlantic. Coins from ancient Carthage have been found as far west as the Azores. Roman amphorae have been discovered in the waters off Rio de Janeiro. Norsemen stayed for more than four centuries in Greenland—far longer than the United States has been a nation. The Irish, according to the Book of Lismore (compiled in the fifteenth century, but containing far older information), knew of a Land of Promise, fifteen days' sail to the west. The Book of Lismore tells the story of a sixth-century monk, Saint Brendan, who prayed to the Lord for "a land secret, hidden, secure, delightful, separated from men"—and was then granted an angelic vision of an island in the Atlantic that answered his needs. From the end of the thirteenth century until the time of the first English settlements, "St. Brendan's Island" appeared on maps, beckoning sailors (it may have been Madeira). Bretons and Basques fished far to the west, and one Breton legend described *les Iles Fantastiques*—the Fantastic Islands—a near cousin to television's Fantasy Island, and like it, a place where dreams were believed to come true.

Even the Moors were tied to incipient ideas about America. When they invaded Spain at the beginning of the eighth century, it was rumored that seven bishops fled with their followers across the Atlantic to found "the Island of the Seven Cities," another fabled place that found itself on otherwise reliable maps in the fifteenth and sixteenth centuries. One of these possible places was called "Antillia," and the Antilles in the Caribbean derive their name from it. The Moors also had their own traditions. The great Arab geographer Edrisi described a mariner, Magrurin, who sailed across "the Sea of Darkness and Mystery" sometime before the middle of the twelfth century and discovered a number of islands. Would it not change a few worldviews to find proof that America was discovered by a Muslim?

But my point is not to prove the unprovable. It is merely to suggest that notions of America—and of America's freedom from Europe—were present in history long before America was discovered, and that in many ways we still live in a terraqueous world in which myths about the New World compete with hard-won facts. Legends are important, as I will argue throughout this book. They shape dreams and ideologies ranging from the dream of one young man to defend freedom by enlisting in the service, to the decision of another to migrate here to benefit his family, to another's choice to fly an airplane into a skyscraper.

In 1492, Columbus indisputably encountered terra firma, ending the long era of groundless speculation about the New World. Words cannot convey the magnitude of this achievement, which finally rooted longings about the West in something tangible. But his discovery unsettled the known universe nearly as much as it expanded it. Before Columbus, Europeans retained a healthy sense that there were limits to knowledge. Certain things—the face of God, the distance of the sun, the western edge of the Atlantic Ocean—were simply beyond the ken of mortals. And so the discovery of America was more than a simple advance in geographical awareness. It signaled a quantum leap forward in man's understanding of where he stood in the cosmos. As such, it was a colossal step toward achieving a certain kind of liberty well before specific notions of liberty were ever debated in the New World. On that day, the earth doubled in size, and men realized that there was a place for them to test their limitations—if, indeed, there were any limitations at all. F. Scott Fitzgerald famously ended *The Great Gatsby* with the thought that "the fresh, green breast of the new world" presented man, for the last time in history, with "something commensurate with his capacity for wonder."

The capacity to wonder—and to wander—proved robust following the first glimpses, and the tendency to exaggerate America only intensified after 1492. Europe was seized by a passionate interest in the discoveries and by a desire to read as much about them as possible. But the new reality-based accounts were often as fabulistic as the old.

Columbus himself borrowed ideas from writers whose fantasies had stimulated his imagination—such as the Cardinal d'Ailly, who felt that an Earthly Paradise might be located near the islands of the western Atlantic. He also wondered, in his early confusion, if he might have stumbled on the Terrestrial Paradise—a mythical place in the eastern regions of Asia. At other times, he thought he might be near the mines of Solomon. Of course, he also thought he was sailing toward China and the Indies.

For quite some time America was described as a series of islands, reflecting the way it was revealed to island-hopping explorers and the fact that their knowledge of the continents was so patchy that they might as well have been islands. The first communications from Columbus back to the king and queen of Spain indicated that he had discovered "very many islands." The path across the Atlantic had been marked by the slow discovery of archipelagoes farther and farther away from Europe—the Canaries, Madeira, Cape Verde, and the Azores. It made perfect sense to think of the newest discoveries as the latest link in the chain. Of course, Columbus was not wrong; it just turned out that some of the islands were extremely large.

But some of the islands were extremely small, and if there was something a little insular about this land coming into focus, one reason may be that so much of it barely existed at all. Many geographical features were enlarged through overeager imaginations, but even real ones could be hard to describe. The Sargasso Sea, with its floating seaweed, seemed a place between land and water. Various rocks and sandbars appeared one moment and disappeared the next. Far off the shore of Newfoundland, for example, are the Virgin Rocks, first reported in the early sixteenth century, and legendary both for the wealth they offered (to fishermen) and the danger (the rocks are very close to the surface). Rudyard Kipling described them as mesmerizing in *Captains Courageous*. His little crew, sailing the Atlantic, comes across a veritable city of boats, nearly a hundred of them, all clustered around a seemingly random point in the ocean, their crews speaking in what seems like all tongues ("every dialect from Labrador to Long Island, with Portuguese, Neapolitan, Lingua Franca, French, and Gaelic, with songs and shoutings and new oaths"). Just below them rises the "cap of the Virgin": and the fishermen look down, spellbound, "on the very weed of that lonely rock, which rises to within twenty feet of the surface. The cod were there in legions, marching solemnly over the leathery kelp." That mid-

Atlantic scene, both crowded and lonely, suitably conjures the way the earliest explorers came across the New World and one another simultaneously. The man who named America never came here at all, but would have appreciated that scene—Martin Waldseemüller was a German mapmaker working for a French patron in a tiny village in Lorraine, drawing on the most recent information from Spanish, Portuguese, and Italian sources.

Not all of this information was accidental. Well into the sixteenth and seventeenth centuries, writers combined real geography with pure invention to entertain the masses of readers who had developed a taste for the novelty of the New World. Sir Thomas More's *Utopia* and Francis Bacon's *New Atlantis* were set in places that drew from American travel, and many a political philosopher used a watery locale to conjure up the idea of a commonwealth where humans lived in relative freedom (James Harrington's *Oceana*, for example). It was a rare author who did not pilfer something from an explorer; certainly Rabelais and Shakespeare, two of the greatest, shared liberally in the plunder. *The Tempest* was first performed in the aftermath of the early Virginia settlement. Milton was similarly entranced, and Book Seven of *Paradise Lost* recounts the "great idea," the story of the creation of a new world after the expulsion of Satan. Near its conclusion, he offers a bit of text that might pass for an explorer's tract:

> Witness this new-made World, another Heaven
> From Heaven-gate not far, founded in view
> On the clear hyalin, the glassy sea;
> Of amplitude almost immense, with stars
> Numerous, and every star perhaps a world
> Of destined habitation

Further, many thinkers believed that the New World truly *was* a different world; a widespread belief in the sixteenth century held that there were in effect "two spheres," and that everything about the Americas (land, people, animals, plants) had a different origin, almost as if a new planet had collided with the earth. A long-running scientific argument postulated that there was something quite wrong with the atmosphere in the New World, evident from the fact that insects and amphibians seemed to be too large (huge cockroaches astonished the

Europeans, as they do to this day), while red-blooded mammals seemed too small. A distinguished French scientist, the Comte de Buffon, noticed with royalist pride that no American mammal could compare to the lion, the king of beasts. The nearest contender was the South American sloth, barely able to rouse itself to eat. A disturbing subcurrent of his argument postulated that the feculent air and water of the New World dampened the ardor of the male human for his mate—an argument that Jefferson and Franklin devoted considerable energies to counter.

As a legal consequence of the two spheres, European laws applied indifferently to this nonworld, and certain practices such as piracy were allowed to flourish. The thought that the two worlds were legally different offered a precedent for the powerful idea that Americans would later use to argue that European diplomacy was broken and that its rules did not apply to this hemisphere. It is not so great a leap of the imagination to go from the two spheres to the Monroe Doctrine, America's first emphatic warning to Europe that the New World was developing a foreign policy entirely its own.

Another leap, more recent, took place in 1927, when Charles Lindbergh stunned the world with a feat nearly as surprising as that of Columbus, by flying in a continuous arc, along the Great Circle route, from New York to Paris. But midway through the transoceanic voyage, he experienced delusions straight out of the fifteenth century when he clearly saw land beneath his left wing, "purple, haze-colored hills; clumps of trees, rocky cliffs," and "small, wooded islands" guarding the strange shore. "Land in mid-Atlantic!" he exclaimed. "Something has gone wrong!" He wondered briefly if he had stumbled upon Atlantis. But then it came to him:

> No, they must be mirages, fog islands sprung up along my route; here for an hour only to disappear, mushrooms of the sea. But so apparently real, so cruelly deceptive! Real clouds cover their higher hills, and pour down into their ravines. How can those bluffs and forests consist of nothing but fog? No islands of the earth could be more perfect.

If Europeans did not exactly know *where* America was, then it could also be argued that they did not know *when* it was. Then as now, there was a great inconsistency over America's place in world time. Columbus believed that he was acting out a biblical prophecy and that his discoveries might lead to the Second Coming of Christ and the recapture of Jerusalem (he called himself Christoferens, or Christ-bearer, and devised an elaborate signature that suggested he thought he was the advance messenger). One of his favorite biblical passages was from Isaiah: "Give ear, ye islands, and hearken, ye people from afar." There was a belief in Spain that a "last world emperor" was coming to rule, in fulfillment of prophecy, and that this emperor would fight Antichrist and restore Christianity in the Holy Land. Columbus followed these prophecies passionately, and wrote down his fevered calculations of biblical resonances as if they were geographical bearings. They were no less contested. Sometime in the late sixteenth century, ten pages of his own book of prophecies were cut out by someone who objected to them, on grounds that we know not.

Some writers, such as Bacon, believed that this imagined society was to be ultramodern and futuristic, with technological gadgetry and improved rules of governing. It promised not the end of time but the advent of a new age. Others found in the pristine forests of the New World constant reminders of the deep past. Peter Martyr, one of the earliest translators of the discoveries, compared Hispaniola to the Golden Age of Virgil's *Aeneid*, its inhabitants virtuous, handsome, and nearly akin to classical statuary. In many ways, America was a Renaissance fresco, free for anyone to paint on.

Today we cannot make a cell phone call without revealing our precise GPS coordinates. But in the Age of Exploration, hardly anyone knew exactly where they were, or whose claims encompassed what territory, or what country they were in. Hugo Grotius thought that the native peoples might be from a smorgasbord of different civilizations, the North Americans from Norway, the Central Americans from Ethiopia, and the South Americans from China. Many of the Spanish explorers thought they would find Islamic redoubts, and had orders to destroy any mosques they encountered. Well after Columbus, quasi-fictional islands continued to be "discovered" and given special attributes. Some were very bad places (the Islands of Demons, alleged to be north of Newfoundland), and some were very good (the Saintly Islands, near the tip of Florida). One unusually mobile island, Mayda (its name possibly

Arabic), began its career far to the west of Brittany and eventually moved across the Atlantic, where it settled near Newfoundland before disappearing from maps altogether.

Wherever it was that they had landed, Europeans never tired of the surpassing strangeness of the New World, with humans and plants and animals that seemed to have sprung from the legends of earlier centuries. Mixed in with the science and discovery was a remarkable welter of credulous beliefs and superstitions. Ponce de Leon famously believed that Florida held the key to eternal youth—a longing that still animates millions of retirees. Samuel de Champlain dropped extraordinary claims into his seemingly scientific narratives. In his first book, full of accurate drawings of plants and animals, a winged dragon suddenly appears among all the familiar crocodiles and parrots. At the end of a sober essay about natives, *Des Sauvages*, he introduces the "Gougou," a monster as tall as a ship's mast ("it makes horrible noise in this island"). When Sir Walter Raleigh visited Guiana, he heard about natives with "eyes in their shoulder, and their mouths in the middle of their breasts."

Even the real stories were "rich and strange," as Shakespeare put it. Native Americans were endlessly fascinating to Europeans, and paraded before the royal courts in their finery. Many English settlers thought that the natives' language had traces of Welsh (*penguin*, for example), because of a medieval Welsh prince who had traveled to the west. Language was always a problem; when English settlers came to Carolina in 1584, they named the region "Wingandacoia," which is what they thought the natives called it. It turned out they were mistaken; according to Raleigh, the natives had not understood the question (who could blame them?), and were politely saying, "You weare good clothes, or gay clothes." It was not the worst name for a new country. The land was rich and strange as well, and soon, enterprising scientists realized that the New World's abundant plant specimens offered a dizzying range of new medicines and pharmacopocia. New food products revolutionized the European palate—can anyone imagine steak frites without the potato? Spaghetti without the tomato? More than anything, tobacco signaled the intoxicating newness, excitement, and danger of the Americas. That feeling is still there every time a cigarette is lit.

Of course, America was not the only discovery of the Age of Exploration. Like a map that never stops unfolding, each revelation led to the next. To appreciate the impact of the New World on the Old, it helps to see the full context of the series of intellectual revolutions that ensued in the accelerated half century following 1492. The frontiers of human knowledge advanced in every conceivable direction: toward a better understanding of the past with a lively new interest in archeology (the Vatican Museum was launched in 1523); toward new worlds of faith (and skepticism) with Martin Luther's revolt against the Church in 1517 and the first tussles of the Reformation; toward the microscopic with important advances in anatomy, medicine, and mathematics (Arabic numerals were introduced to Europe in 1494); toward the cosmic with the radical new perspective on the solar system first circulated by Copernicus in 1514; and toward the eternal renewability of these revolutions, thanks to the widespread availability of knowledge itself, building on Gutenberg's movable type and an unprecedented hunger for books and pamphlets. In "Passage to India," his ode to globalization, Walt Whitman saw this as the moment it all came together:

> The medieval navigators rise before me,
> The world of 1492, with its awaken'd enterprise,
> Something swelling in humanity now like the sap of the earth in
> spring . . .

The Americas were connected to all these discoveries in different degrees—because of the vast wealth that flowed back from them and encouraged innovation, because of the unequal way some of that wealth was distributed (benefiting the Church and the Spanish crown above all), and because of the simple excitement that new information was available for people hardy enough to seize it. The expansion of the world that followed in the wake of Columbus revolutionized not only what people knew, but how they thought. The discovery of these vast domains led to a general loosening of intellectual constraints—as if the very knowledge of all that breathing room filtered back across the Atlantic and delivered a blast of fresh air into the stultified confines of European intellectual space.

Inevitably, the ferment led to a new consciousness of liberty, in every sense of the word. It was there in subtle ways from the start, implicit in the story of this enormous new land with no known boundaries, geographical or otherwise. Writers were fascinated by the freedom with which men and women lived their lives in the New World, unfettered by strict rules of propriety in religion, or politics, or the simplest matters of everyday life. This fascination undoubtedly drew on earlier legends—classical antiquity and the Garden of Eden before it—but America now stood before astonished readers in clear anthropological focus, a living example rather than a distant memory. Amerigo Vespucci's letter (1504) painted an idyllic picture of the natives, who "have neither king nor lord, nor do they obey anyone, but live in freedom." Peter Martyr, the source of so much information about the New World, betrayed a similar fascination with the absence of rules in America: "They go naked, they know neither weights nor measures, nor that source of all misfortunes, money; living in a golden age, without laws, without lying judges, without books, satisfied with their life, and in no wise solicitous for the future." These were simple descriptions, of course, and not quite expressions of desire. But they had an immense impact all the same.

It does not take too much effort to perceive an erotic energy pulsing beneath these breathless accounts. Far from thinking the world flat, Columbus likened the earth to a pear shape with a nipple, and throughout the literature of exploration one encounters a relentless emphasis on fecundity, both human and vegetable. In retrospect, the use of the term *Virginia* to describe this land appears to have been somewhat ironic.*

In narrative after narrative, the feeling of liberty was enhanced by the description of unclothed women, eager to do all they could to please the Europeans encountering them, either in person or through the pages of these accounts. Peter Martyr continued:

> When the company approached, some thirty women, all wives of the cacique, marched out to meet them, dancing, singing, and shouting; they were naked, save for a loin-girdle, which, though it consisted but of a cotton belt, which dropped over their hips, satisfied these women devoid of any sense of shame. As for the young girls, they covered no parts of their bodies, but wore their

*The Iranian government blocks access to the website of the University of Virginia, simply because of the word's power of suggestion.

> hair loose upon their shoulders and a narrow ribbon tied around the forehead. Their face, breast, and hands, and the entire body was quite naked, and of a somewhat brunette tint. All were beautiful, so that one might think he beheld those splendid naiads or nymphs of the fountains, so much celebrated by the ancients.

There were countless variations on this theme. In 1742 a pornographic book was written in England that parodied travel narratives to America, and depicted a perfect society "entirely under female government." *The History of Merryland* described geographical features in a way that left little doubt they were being compared to enormous anatomical parts—and no one who bought a house in the boom market of the last ten years would be surprised to hear real estate likened to lust.

That subcurrent of sexual liberation would never entirely disappear from the annals of the New World, despite a powerful countercurrent of religious writing that flowed with equal force from the Americas, and particularly from the chillier precincts of New England. But that impulse, too, was tied to the idea of liberation in its own peculiar way. And through the writings of clerics who found America every bit as fascinating as gold diggers, plant collectors, and booty hunters, a new sense began to emerge that this hemisphere was not only free, but positively redemptive.

CHAPTER TWO

THE AMERICAN MILLENNIUM

And I saw a new heaven and a new earth: for the first heaven and the first earth were passed away; and there was no more sea.

—Revelation 21:1

A NEW HEAVEN AND A NEW EARTH

Long before the United States perceived a mission to spread liberty to the four corners of the world, America was linked to a different kind of global mission, fused with the religious aspirations that drew so many settlers here. We have become so used to hearing phrases such as "God bless America" that we rarely pause to reflect on their provenance. But to restate America's religious origins, as historians are generally loath to do, is to restate a fact that was once so obvious it did not need to be stated at all.

Religion has never been as far removed from our secular government as we claim, and to this day, a low-level insurgency pits the Christian right (which would have us believe that God authored the Constitution) against skeptics on the left (who insist that He has never been anywhere near Philadelphia). It is probably right to minimize the religious fervor of the thirty-nine signers of the Constitution, for the only time they referred to God was in the immortal phrase "the Year of our Lord, one thousand seven hundred and Eighty seven." But when we are talking about the original settlers of the thirteen colonies, and the vast majority of Americans living here in the seventeenth and eighteenth centuries, "Christian" may be too weak an adjective to describe the intense faith that drew them to these shores and colored every choice in their lives. They were extremists in an age that was extreme to begin with; committed members of what Perry Miller called "the Calvinist internationale," quite willing to see all events as part of a global contest against an evil empire—the Roman Catholic Church, and the French and Spanish monarchies in league with it. It could be argued that our original alliance—the Special Relationship above all others—was not with Britain, but with God.

Of course, many other nations identify closely with God; certainly Israel does, and Saudi Arabia, too. On December 31, 2000, Uganda may have set a new standard when its leaders signed a covenant with Him. But in general, it is unusual to proclaim a close connection between state policy and the inscrutable will of the Lord. That is one reason why articulations of American foreign policy can grate on the ears of skeptics around the world. But what they and we should remember is that these sentiments about America's sacred mission—historically felt on the left as well as the right—have a very ancient pedigree. Our critics are free to say what they want, of course, but they run a real risk of going to hell for daring to complain about a nation that has been intimately intertwined with divine will since its, well, genesis.

The United States may seem eternally modern, but still, we are a people with verifiable origins in the seventeenth century, a time of great ferment in Europe over religion, revolution, and war. Despite their obvious separation from Europe, the earliest Anglo-Americans cherished global aspirations from the moment of their arrival. In New England, certainly, but in other places as well, the essential thrust was theological, and a short glance at early American writing is all that it takes to see that our earliest ambitions were not only global, but out of this world.

True, the school of history that interpreted all of American history as an extension of Puritan New England has long vanished, unmourned. Almost no seventeenth-century colonist would have used the word *American* to describe himself, and needless to say, none had a clue that a United States was in the offing. But to ignore the Puritans, which is what we do by refusing to read their ample and expressive writings, seems to me just as shortsighted.

The Puritans annoy people today, as they did in their own time. Alert readers will point out, rightly, that the so-called Puritans occupied only a small part of North America, that they themselves disagreed on a great many matters, and that many non-Anglophone people joined the American alembic that was forming between 1607 and 1776. That is incontestably true. Still, I feel, as Tocqueville did, that the force of Calvinist thinking was such that it flavored the entire experiment, long after its severe theology had withered into irrelevance. It was also paralleled, if not exactly duplicated, by the utopian religious communities that sprang up in all thirteen colonies, nearly all of which fell into the more extreme categories of Protestantism. Doctrinal differences that were heatedly felt at the time seem less important in hindsight, as one contemplates the combined impact of the spiritual energies that drew so many dissenters to these shores. The Quaker William Penn was easily as ambitious as any Puritan New Englander, striving not only for human perfection in his rectilinear townships but for ways to end war among Europeans. Even as religiosity faded in some quarters, it was renewed by the influx of new groups of passionate believers and periodic upheavals such as the Great Awakenings, which distributed New England's ideas to the other colonies, and vice versa. All told, the residue of these intellectual movements left a pervasive distrust of arbitrary authority (wary of popes and kings alike) and a veneration for the principle of local self-government (be it ecclesiastical or political), sustained by written charters that spelled out rights and responsibilities. They also led to North America's first foreign policy: joining loose islands of Englishness in a flexible alliance designed to counter rival European nations, to ensure access to free trade (legal or illegal), and to promote freedom of the seas. All of these ideas would be present at America's "founding" more than a century later.

But before such lofty ideals could be advanced, it was necessary to crush America's enemies. To understand that logic better, I will spend some time with a body of thinking that even scholars of Puritanism have felt uncomfortable with, and for good reason. I'd like to examine the widely held seventeenth-century belief that the final battle with Antichrist was imminent, that it would be a worldwide struggle against a vast and shapeless enemy, and that actions taken in America were essential to its outcome. It is not the most welcoming body of knowledge to investigate, full of locusts and sackcloth and ashes. But it seems to me to deserve more attention than it has received to date. I will not suggest that we still believe in these hoary prophecies and maledictions—to do so would turn the epic of American history into a mere installment of the *Harry Potter* cycle. But the early obsessions of the Puritans foreshadow, to a remarkable degree, a future of struggle in the Middle East, vast difficulties with Islam, and end-of-the-world scenarios centered around the valley of the Euphrates. Few words thrilled Puritan audiences more than *Babylon*, the mythical site linked to the imminent battle expected.

For centuries after its discovery, the New World defied easy description, despite the frantic efforts of Europeans to capture the surpassing novelty of America—including many who never set foot here but knew a good story when they heard one. This newness went well beyond plant specimens and racy travel accounts; it embraced the supernatural along with the natural and ultimately touched upon every aspect of cognition. As such, America inevitably entered the intellectual arena that was of paramount concern to men and women in the sixteenth century: the way in which they contemplated God, and their destiny within God's framework. To anyone who meditated on the spiritual realm—in other words, to all sapient human beings—the discovery of the New World was nothing short of miraculous.

For a thousand different reasons, the Church was quickly enmeshed in the discovery, exploration, and representation of the New World. The vast riches that were discovered in the new Spanish domains flowed to coffers in Rome as well as in Madrid, and the Vatican entered the imperial fray just after the first Columbus voyage, when Pope Alexander VI issued his Line of Demarcation, dividing the new domains between Spain and Portugal (and excluding them from everyone else). But beyond these early efforts to extend the reach of the papacy, there was a sense that the new fact of the Americas somehow altered the underlying assumptions of Christianity. This fact affected not only what people knew, but what they believed, and how. That should not come as a great surprise—all profound advances in human knowledge are followed by adjustments in the way that people worship. The new realms were unveiled at the same time as the revolutionary new astronomical theories of Copernicus and Galileo, advances so disturbing to the Church that until 1992 it did not formally apologize for blocking them.

The discovery of the New World was not nearly as threatening as the new astronomy, and to some extent counteracted it by enlarging the earth just as Copernicus was shrinking it. In subtle ways, the anthropological and botanical revelations that America offered supported the Church's teachings. After all, the Edenic landscapes now coming into focus suggested the book of Genesis and the utopia that human beings had once occupied deep in the biblical past. The presence of Native Americans in these sublime vistas only heightened the excitement, leading some to believe that, at long last, the legendary Lost Tribes of Israel had been found. Skeptics such as Montaigne would complicate the naive fantasy that Native Americans were childlike exemplars of virtue, but the belief took deep hold in the sixteenth century.

The New World was biblical in other ways as well. The book of Revelation is the opposite of Genesis in nearly every respect: it concludes the story that Genesis begins; it describes the future rather than the past; and it paints a dark and moody landscape of fear and retribution that bears little comparison with the luminous landscapes of early Creation. Yet here, too, in the indefinite scenes of days yet to come, biblical scholars and seers found hints of America's relevance to the world struggling to be born.

Specifically, the discovery of the New World, with its Edenic landscapes, encouraged the latent belief that the historic events taking place were in fact extrahistorical. To put it more simply, some believed that a new time was beginning, a time that was outside normal reckoning and was indeed a return to biblical time. Many schools of thought in early Christianity and then throughout the Middle Ages had believed that the events of the Bible were not only real but would be reexperienced when Jesus returned to redeem humanity. These beliefs—outlined in Revelation—had a long history and had fascinated commentators ranging from sage intellectuals to wild-eyed leaders of cult followings.

If America greatly enriched the established Church, it also fueled the opposition. The great drama of the Reformation unleashed by Martin Luther did nothing to reduce the New World's relevance to Europe, and in many ways deepened it. Like astronomy, and relentless advances in printing, a new world of biblical scholarship coincided with the great geographical discoveries of the sixteenth century. That simultaneity was celebrated in the earliest works that we might call American history—the self-glorifying narratives that Puritan New Englanders began to write in the middle and late seventeenth century, boasting that the Reformation, the discovery of the New World, and the settlement of New England were all equal manifestations of divine will. But we hear of the Reformation far less frequently in U.S. history classes today, as if we were embarrassed by the force of the religious winds that blew so many of the earliest Americans to these shores.

During the intensity of the early Reformation, thoughts about the regeneration of the world became especially connected to radical strains of Protestantism. And as that tradition flowered across the next century, it grew to encompass precisely those who were inclined to come to America in the first place. For a significant number of the deeply spiritual men and women who left everything to cross the Atlantic, the New World was something more than a world: it was the New Heaven and the New Earth, the fulfillment of biblical prophecy and the literal answer to their prayers.

Millennialism—the belief in the eventual thousand-year rule of Christ—remains a rather strange pocket of religious history to explore. It is far from empirical—not only are these mere beliefs, they are beliefs that were never converted into reality. Ancient religious prophecies have, at first glance, little to do with the soaring architecture of American history. To the few who study them, these beliefs seem extraordinarily old, and barely American at all. They feel like the rumors of old pirate treasure troves and Indian burial grounds that real estate agents sometimes rely upon to mystify their swampy properties. But there is no doubt that these ancient expectations were real to those who clung to them, just as a suitor's letter, returned undelivered, remains real forever to the person who wrote it.

These millennial dreams and nightmares contributed indelibly to America's intellectual DNA. They can be sensed in the familiar rhythms of a presidential speech, the closing paragraphs that nearly always assure citizens that God is smiling upon the republic (how many, besides Lincoln, have dared to wonder?). They can be heard in the lyrics of familiar songs such as "Onward, Christian Soldiers" and "The

Battle Hymn of the Republic," music that might innocently be heard on a street corner, played slightly out of tune by a Salvation Army band. They can be felt in the widespread belief, shared by evangelicals and nonevangelicals alike, that great things are coming simply because Americans will them to come. And they can be seen by anyone willing to dust off and read the books themselves, the moldy tomes written at the dawn of the American project by the first English men and women to settle these shores.

Millennial thinking was always rooted in the last and strangest of the Bible's narratives, the Revelation of St. John—commonly called the book of Revelation, or more simply, the Apocalypse. A close reading of Revelation can still send chills down the spine, for in addition to the graphic quality of the events described is the clear sense that they are coming soon and will not be pleasant. To say that there is an undercurrent of revenge—even rage—in Revelation would be to state the case mildly. Unlike other prophetic parts of the Bible, the events of Revelation happen on a cosmic scale—on earth and in heaven—and seem to be heading toward the cataclysmic conclusion of all history. These final events appear to be real and connected to the present—they do not exist in a vague future, but are clearly in what we might call real time.

The essential drama is a combat between Christ—now a warrior Christ very unlike his more familiar biblical persona—and Antichrist, a strange and monstrous enemy allied with Satan, sometimes a great red dragon with seven heads who comes out of the sea, at other times a horned monster who lives deep inside the earth. Over twenty-two chapters, the battle unfolds with unremitting intensity. But slowly it turns in favor of Christ and his allies, including angels and archangels, who unleash destruction through the blowing of trumpets, the opening of seals, and the pouring out of vials onto the enemy. There are seven vials in all—a fact that later became crucial to predictions about the Last Events. The sixth vial was poured "upon the great river Euphrates, and the water thereof was dried up, that the way of the kings of the east might be prepared." The "drying up of the Euphrates," interpreted a thousand different ways, has been a prelude to conflict ever since, including in 2003, when Saddam Hussein's dismal irrigation policies acquired intense relevance in evangelical circles.

The final vial, the most dramatic, describes a kind of destruction from above, which gave pause to commentators at the end of World War Two, when it became clear that some biblical scenes were indeed possible to reenact. The seventh angel "poured out his vial into the air; and there came a great voice out of the temple of heaven, from the throne, saying, It is done. And there were voices, and thunders, and lightnings; and there was a great earthquake, such as was not since men were upon the earth, so mighty an earthquake, and so great. And the great city was divided into three parts, and the cities of the nations fell: and great Babylon came in remembrance before God, to give unto her the cup of the wine of the fierceness of his wrath."

Like many folk beliefs, the original belief in a tangible millennium, specific and imminent, was less than respectable at one time. There has always been something a little disconcerting about it. As the historian Norman Cohn put it, "To expect to make the world's City truly righteous is, indeed, an egregious manifestation of pride." It was even a heresy, condemned in 431 by the Council of Ephesus. Augustine believed that it was utterly inconsistent to expect the merger of the City of God and the City of Man—they were by definition separate. He considered the predictions of Revelation to be allegorical and distrusted the impulse to look too closely for earthly confirmation of unearthly ruminations.

But Augustine would not have become a saint if his opinions were widely shared by others. Throughout the long and tortured history of medieval Christianity, countless groups found it difficult to accept his restraint and longed for a chance to enter a great struggle that would somehow hasten the return of Christ and the defeat of Antichrist. Why men and women found these beliefs so entrancing is not easy to say and certainly varied from case to case and century to century. But clearly it originated with some sense that the status quo was inadequate, and the belief that changes *were* imminent must have been connected at some level, whether consciously or not, with the belief that changes *should* be imminent. Some might have felt these longings out of a sense of social justice—while for others it may been genuine religious ecstasy with no reference to justice of any kind. But certainly it is fair to say that beliefs were especially intense at moments of disruption—for example, when large and restless populations lived in regions whose economies or governments were suddenly changing, these beliefs took on a life of their own.

There are too many millennial hiccups in European history to list here but we know of eruptions of expectations in northern France and Flanders in the twelfth and thirteenth centuries, in Holland and Westphalia in the sixteenth, and in England in the seventeenth, just as the first colonists were boarding ships to the New World. Each movement was unique, but nearly all felt that the Last Things were coming soon, in 1186, or 1360, or 1515, or 1655—the list of final reckonings is too long to reckon. Sometimes these movements were inspired by living kings and great warriors, or by the nostalgic memory of long-dead kings such as Constantine and Charlemagne. At other times champions rose up from an obscurity so deep that we still do not know what names to call them by: the "pseudo Baldwin," "the future Frederick," the "Revolutionary of the Upper Rhine."

A far longer book than this one could be written about the political and religious beliefs that propelled these movements, and the complicated social forces that lay close to the surface. At its best, millennialism expressed a longing for a more just world, with oppression defeated, and people free to enter into harmonious social relations with one another. Sometimes this went to the extremes of utopian movements that encouraged free love, egalitarianism, and aspirations for what was called, during one orgiastic sixteenth-century outbreak, "Spiritual Liberty." Even from the deep cover of the Middle Ages, these movements sound pleasingly modern to us—and not all that distant from the impulse that led other brave families, in later centuries, to make the perilous journey to America.

But millennial thinking had a dark side as well. The flagellants and ranters who succumbed most easily to these movements were not always the soundest judges of character and events. Their need to reinterpret history sprang from a deep frustration with the world as it existed. Correspondingly, millennial thinkers often demonized opponents who failed to hear the sounding of the angelic trumpets and divided the world severely into those who were saved and those who were not. Candidates for Antichrist were never hard to find, and by an ancient tradition nearly as old as Christianity itself, Jews were frequently targeted. As early as the second century, a tradition arose that Antichrist would be a

Jew of the tribe of Dan, born at Babylon and raised in Palestine, where he would unite the tribes that had been dispersed and rebuild the Temple. That odious belief persisted well into the twentieth century, and the infamous *Protocols of the Elders of Zion* (1903), the work that spawned so much anti-Semitism in the twentieth century, borrows heavily from early ideas about a Jewish Antichrist.

Beginning in the ninth century, when Muslims made their first incursions into Europe, Islam was easily demonized as well, especially during the Crusades (when Muslims were likened to horned monsters), and then again during the Ottomans' sack of Constantinople in 1453. In an intellectual world where *Babylon* was a catchphrase for everything linked to Antichrist, Islam inevitably absorbed some of the vitriol that also spewed forth from millennial excitements. After all, the ancient city of Babylon was located just outside Baghdad, a city that was perfectly well known to European mapmakers. Even though *Babylon* often meant something quite metaphorical (for Protestants, it was Rome), a real place in Mesopotamia was undeniably considered a focal point of evil centuries before Iraq returned to the forefront of the world's consciousness.

Nor is that the only way in which the long-forgotten yearnings of medieval millennialists occasionally resurfaced in the modern period. Marxists and Nazis certainly echoed elements of the old thinking, with their swaggering claims of future victory, their nostalgia for lost virtue, and their stark division of humanity into the saved and the damned. Some of the same qualities can be detected in the rantings of Osama bin Laden, who likewise claims a great struggle to be imminent and embraces the purifying fire that it offers, harshly denouncing those who follow the cautious road of moderation.

Of course, one danger of accusing others of Antichristian behavior is that the tables may suddenly turn. That is more or less what happened to the Roman Catholic Church with the onset of the Reformation in the early and middle decades of the sixteenth century. As this multiform religious protest movement spread across Germany and northern Europe, it found fertile territory for a new breed of millennialists, perfectly willing to equate the Church ("the old red dragon," according to Milton) with the "great red dragon" of the book of Revelation.

The Reformation and the rise of printing were so linked that it is difficult to say which spurred the other. But clearly the new ability to read and disseminate information allowed unprecedented lay attention to Scripture. Inevitably, the book of Revelation struck this vast new audience as rich for reinterpretation, and throughout the sixteenth and seventeenth centuries, Protestant writers found ample reason to reflect on biblical history through the lens of the angry events happening all around them. The result was a strong sense of parallel with earlier struggles and persecutions, and a feeling that history was rhythmic and repetitive for the People of the Word.

In this ideologically charged context, the discovery and early settlement of America went along with the desire to imitate the example of the earliest Christians and their antecedents in the Old Testament. It was not simply the revelation of a new place of refuge for those seeking escape; it was a place that startlingly resembled some of the landscapes in the Bible, whether described as a forbidding wilderness (as the New England Puritans were inclined to see it) or as a land of milk and honey. As information about America trickled to Europeans, it became clear that this extravagant new continent was tailor-made to support ambitious theories about the millennium. In both its vastness and its apparent simplicity, America fit comfortably alongside preexisting ideas about what a postmillennial world would be like.

In other words, the astonishing facts about the New World that thrilled the scientific thinkers of Europe had an equally dramatic impact on theologians and the leaders of fugitive Protestant movements. The discovery of America inevitably fed the notion that the seismic religious events of the sixteenth century were divinely inspired. It seemed to many that the clouds had lifted and people were suddenly encountering the truth in all things—truths that had not been visible in the long night of the Middle Ages. Luther and Zwingli and Calvin were bringing the light of reason and experience to the study of Scripture. And by revealing the existence of a vast new hemisphere, God had parted the curtain at exactly the right moment.

BY PROVIDENCE DIVINE

> Miranda: How came we ashore?
> Prospero: By Providence divine.
> —Shakespeare, *The Tempest*

As Britain was engulfed by the simultaneous Reformation and Age of Exploration, it produced no shortage of millennial thinkers. Through elaborate "mathematico-mystical calculations" based on Pythagoras, the age of the earth, and the age of Christ, Thomas Browne believed that history had ordained 1588 as a date of immense significance. The defeat of the Spanish Armada that year, dispersed by a "divine wind," only heightened the sense that Britain enjoyed a special relationship with Providence. That island mentality would easily cross the Atlantic to establish the tiny settlements, islands of a sort, that soon dotted the American coastline.

In the early seventeenth century, English Puritans retained a sense of a special relationship, even as they did all they could to flee England. In fact, it was precisely to save the special relationship that they suddenly felt the need to leave. For if England was abandoning God, as so many of them felt, what choice did they have but to try to abandon England? While it is hazardous to generalize about the very different groups of English people who fled to the New World in the seventeenth century, it does not take much reading in the original writings of the Puritans to discern a sense that they were leaving England precisely to save what had once been special—just as, in 1776, the founders argued that they were leaving British sovereignty in order to preserve British rights. In other words, they argued that it was worse to remain in a Britain that had ignored its covenant than to risk everything and try again, in a more biblical place, to rebuild a true Bible Commonwealth. It is difficult to recapture the certainty with which many of them felt that the known world was about to end and corrupt European governments were soon to be obliterated by a vengeful God. Anne Hutchinson revealed a great deal when she arrived in America, depressed by the barrenness of her new surroundings, and said "if she had not a sure word that England should be destroyed her heart would shake."

With that sentence we have, at long last, crossed the ocean into what is conventionally recognized as American history. But despite that long-overdue arrival, I want to make clear that beliefs in America as an exceptional place did not originate overnight—they resulted from generations and even centuries of inherited feelings about a land that no one knew well, but that already excited intensely expectant feelings.

The Puritans—and their near cousins the Pilgrims—have been compressed into a number of stereotypes. A century ago they were lauded as the advance guard of democracy, hardy Anglo-Saxons who introduced the germ of freedom into the primeval forest. More recently, they have been portrayed as dark prosecutors of heretics, disputatious quarrelers, and brutal killers of natives. None of that is exactly inaccurate, but the extremes of criticism strain credulity nearly as much as the earlier extremes of adulation. The Puritans were many things to many people, but more than anything, they were profoundly men and women of their time. As John Robinson, the Pilgrim elder, said to his departing flock, in what may be regarded as the earliest speech in American history, their decision to come to these shores was not an escape from but an extension of European history.

Still, they *were* different, for the simple fact that they came here. And throughout the extraordinary migrations of the seventeenth century, a millennial thrust quickened the hopes of a surprising number of these primordial Americans. It is wrong to generalize about all Puritans, and unwise to extrapolate from the Puritans to summarize the experience of all Europeans in North America. But clearly a significant number of colonists were anything but far-flung wretches seeking a freehold as far from the European mainstream as possible. They were deeply learned men and women, well versed in biblical prophecy, who placed their expedition at the center of what they deemed the course of history. One of the central arguments of this book is that we have inherited an outlook on the world that descends from them, whether we know it or not.

Perhaps the most famous American document of the seventeenth century is John Winthrop's lay sermon "A Modell of Christian Charity," delivered as the Puritans were beginning their voyage to found Boston in 1630. Its celebrated prediction that "we shall be as a city upon a hill" still finds its way into presidential oratory and generally promotes the ahistorical idea that the first immigrants somehow knew that the creation of the United States lay over the horizon. That flabbergasting result was of course completely unforeseeable to anyone who lived before 1776.

A closer reading of Winthrop's sermon shows its tendrils stretch as far into the past as the future. Boston was only the most recent in a long line of sacred cities on a hill—Rome, Constantinople, and Jerusalem being the most obvious precursors. The New Jerusalem they would construct overlooking Massachusetts Bay was built with similar ambition. In the same speech, but less quoted, Winthrop cited the earliest Christians and the twelfth-century Waldensians as role models, and announced that the Puritans enjoyed a special contract with God:

> Thus stands the cause between God and us, we are entered into Covenant with him for this work, we have taken out a Commission, the Lord hath given us leave to draw our own Articles, we have professed to enterprise these Actions upon these and these ends, we have hereupon besought him of favor and blessing.

That may sound presumptuous to modern ears, but to his credit, Winthrop also offered the other side of the same vision. A good lawyer, he knew that the penalty for breaking a contract with God was severe. Quite simply, as Winthrop put it, if we fail "to embrace this present world and prosecute our carnal intentions, seeking great things for ourselves and our posterity, the Lord will surely break out in wrath against us [and] be revenged of such a perjured people and make us know the price of the breach of such a Covenant." Persuasively, before a seagoing audience that was presumably terrified of the venture they were beginning, he promised that if they did not live up to these conditions, they would encounter a "shipwreck" that would make quick work of them.

Of course, Winthrop was speaking in a deeply international context when he spoke those words, and not just because he was near the Atlantic Ocean. He knew exactly what was happening in England, teetering on the precipice of civil war, and in Europe, helplessly roiled over war and religion. Elsewhere, he argued that New England's first purpose would be "to raise a Bulwark against the kingdome of Antichrist, which the Jesuits labor to rear up in those parts"—in other words, to crush the French! The story of the first generation of New Englanders, as Perry Miller observed, is the story of a people who knew they were not on "a mere scouting expedition," but felt their journey to be "an essential drama in the drama of Christendom." These Puritans did not "flee to America," Miller continued; "they went in order to work out that complete reformation which was not yet accomplished in England and Europe." You can dismiss this presumption as arrogance, or even dementia, but to ignore it is to miss a fundamental fact about the origins of American history. There was nothing humble about this errand into the wilderness.

Another way in which Winthrop is often misconstrued is by well-meaning modernists who read his user's manual as an early proclamation that America is going to be a place of political liberty. Winthrop, in fact, denounced liberty, as if he had a sense that it would become the guiding principle of this vast new land, where rules were not easily understood, let alone enforced. In Boston, the freedom to harass dissenters was far more essential than the freedom to dissent. The first line of Winthrop's famous oration reasserts the inconvenient truth that God has organized the world so that "some must be rich some poor, some high and eminent in power and dignity; others mean and in subjection." Throughout he insists on a "due form of Government both civil and ecclesiastical," by which he meant a biblical government, based on a strict interpretation of Scripture. Not long after encountering his first problems with insubordinate citizens, Winthrop issued his considerably sterner "Defence of an Order" (1637), which reasserted his government's right to give and take liberty as it saw fit. That's not quite the same thing as the "shining" city Ronald Reagan liked to unveil to audiences, like an architect showing off a new subdivision.

But at the same time, it is worth pointing out that Calvinism was a deeply political creed, and released nearly as many energies as it suppressed. If the Puritans scoffed at pure liberty, they still believed in self-government. Calvin wrote that man's imperfection made it "safer and more tolerable for government to be in the hands of the many." To worship God *was* to embrace good government. New England was the place "where the Lord would create a new heaven and a new earth, new churches and a new commonwealth together," as Edward Johnson, perhaps America's first historian, predicted. To fight for one meant to fight for the other—and they had little doubt that a fight was coming.

Throughout the first generation, the Massachusetts Bay Puritans paid close attention to the extraordinary events in England that were leading to civil war. If anything, these events only heightened the sense that the Last Days were drawing nigh. Johnson wrote that Christ was "skipping over and trampling down the great Mountains of the Earth" to set up his terrestrial government. New England's most celebrated intellectual, John Cotton, felt the same way. Arguably the most important theologian to come to the New World in the seventeenth century, Cotton is well known to historians for his tortured role in the Antinomian Crisis, and his complicated relationship with the banished freethinker Roger Williams. What is less clearly understood is the extent to which Cotton—and by extension, his many listeners—believed that the Second Coming was imminent as the Great Migration was unfolding.

The second quarter of the seventeenth century was a pivotal time in the history of English millennial thought, and the Puritans were well informed about new theology. A huge number of books had been written on Antichrist between 1590 and 1620, for reasons relating both to religion and to England's foreign policy difficulties (many thought Antichrist was either the pope or the Spanish king). At Cambridge University, where Puritans had strong ties, a theologian named Joseph Mede wrote learned disquisitions on the Apocalypse at precisely the moment of the diaspora. Mede was no crackpot; he had been Milton's tutor, leaned toward Puritanism himself, and by dint of years of hard study had acquired an unusual facility in the languages of antiquity. Through a deep reading of Scripture, Mede concluded that the prediction of a millennial kingdom in the future was not a metaphor but a literal fact, available to living human beings, and closing fast (he even ventured a guess as to when—1666). Mede's findings electrified the faithful. Unlike many millennialists, his writing contained an important note of optimism, a sense that history was improving. Crucially, he gave human beings a role in this millennium and suggested that they could hasten its arrival.

Nothing could have been more pleasing to the New Englanders, who felt they were doing exactly that. Cotton, one of the Puritan leaders in England, continued these efforts from his new perch in Boston. After arriving in 1633 from the English Boston—the American city was named in tribute to him—he was quickly given a central role in shaping the new government. A legal code that he wrote, based on the Ten Commandments, was ultimately not adopted, but it remains fascinating for its suggestion that early Massachusetts was not as distant from Islamic sharia law as we might imagine. Cotton was no proponent of liberty in the modern sense, as his debate with Roger Williams makes clear. But he argued that congregational self-government—the basis of the New England system—was an essential means to defeat Antichrist, always trying to consolidate power in large, shadowy organizations such as the Catholic Church. And he asserted that the reason he had come to America in the first place was to "enjoy the liberty, not of some ordinances of God, but of all, and all in purity."

In the late 1630s, Cotton launched an extraordinary series of Thursday lectures that attempted to explain the book of Revelation to an audience of recent immigrants, hungry to know their place in the world and the afterworld. The result was a sensation. His colleague John Wilson wrote, "Mr. Cotton preaches with such Authority, Demonstration, and Life that, methinks, when he preaches out of any Prophet or Apostle I hear not him; I hear that very Prophet and Apostle; yea, I hear the Lord Jesus Christ speaking in my Heart." Through several works written by auditors who took notes on Cotton's lectures, we have a rough idea of what he was saying. Like most Puritans, he identified the seven-headed beast of Revelation with the Catholic Church, and he expected that Satan would soon be bound for a thousand years, a time that would see the eventual conversion of the Jews to Christianity and the creation of a worldwide kingship for Christ in both church and state. What separated Cotton from most millennialists was that he expected his millennium to begin extremely soon. The methods of calculating are too abstruse to go into in detail, but because the beast of Revelation was expected to reign for 1,260 years, Puritan scribes furiously pored over events of early Christian history, particularly in the fourth century, to prove that Christ was returning soon. Cotton hit the jackpot when he argued that the tyranny of the papacy had begun in A.D. 395, the year the title *pontifex maximus* had first been assumed—with the result that his millennium would begin in 1655.

To a surprising degree for a people clinging to survival in a harsh climate, thousands of miles from the nearest large city, New England millennialists paid close attention to the world situation as they worked themselves into a fever of expectation. Cotton considered New England to be the spark of a global awakening. A follower of his, Ephraim Huit, predicted that the Last Days would begin as soon as the Jews were freed of Islamic domination, which he expected to happen around 1650. Countless other works of the 1640s dilated on Jews and Muslims. Among the many reasons that John Winthrop complained about Anne Hutchinson was that her followers looked at her "as a Prophetess, raised up of God for some great work now at hand, as the calling of the Jews, etc." A great missionary to the Indians, John Eliot, began his heroic efforts out of a frantic notion that they were quasi-Jewish (after all, they were circumcised), and therefore their conversion might hasten the final events. A mere decade into the history of Boston, the Near East was at the center of American foreign policy.

Unfortunately, Cotton's death in 1652 deprived him of the chance to experience 1655, which turned out to be a year like any other. That was not the only disappointment Cotton's heirs would encounter. As the 1640s and 1650s unfolded, it became clear that the revolution taking place in England was more consequential than the one that the New Englanders had hoped to initiate by their shimmering example. Several returned to England for a taste of the action and never returned. One of them, William Aspinwall, urged the English to learn Hebrew as soon as possible because it would be the language of choice once Christ had returned to the throne.

The historian Christopher Hill showed in work after work what a profoundly intellectual struggle the English civil war was, intensely illuminated by the fires of millennial thinking. No longer was the millennium the province of bug-eyed lunatics; great intellectuals such as Milton and Newton shared in the excitement, and large numbers of believers began to feel that the "Fifth Monarchy" of Christ was coming soon—so called to differentiate it from four great empires of earlier history, the Babylonian, Persian, Greek, and Roman (each represented by an animal in the prophetic lines of Daniel 7). This hope embraced new ideas about government as well as religion, for the two were part and parcel of the same revolution. One argument asserted that Antichrist was a force that deprived men of "Christian liberty." Another insisted that Antichrist was simply any foreign enemy of the English people. Yet another insisted that anyone who even moderately enjoyed fashion was "a chaplain of Antichrist." Ultimately, *Antichrist* was tagged to the monarchy itself—the word was always useful for attacks on venerable institutions of centralized power. John Cotton, for example, had cited "kingly governments" in his litany of complaints against Antichrist. These arguments would not be forgotten by Americans a century later.

Of course, history did not turn out as the Puritan millennialists expected, in either New England or Old. Not for the last time, America's desire to reshape the world was uncalibrated with its ability to do so. A sense of disappointment envelops their prose, both at their geographical distance from the great struggle and at its ultimate result, the restoration of the monarchy. One writer, John Davenport, put it bluntly when he said that England had become "the popes ass again." Others were more diplomatic. John Eliot had the misfortune to release his epic celebration of the Fifth Monarchy, *The Christian Commonwealth*, in 1659, just before the British monarchy was restored. But to their credit, the Puritans did not give up; one of the great American virtues is the ability to continue in one's work, cheerful and unmolested, after events have proven you completely wrong. In small but unrelenting ways, they never allowed the flame of their diminished millennialism to flicker out.

On the surface, they had to maintain the fiction of complete happiness with the ruling authorities—despite the meddling of royal officials with the sacred right to self-government that Massachusetts had secured with its original charter. But beneath the surface, like countless colonial peoples before and since, they expressed their truer identity with furtive writings and local rituals, never ceasing to remind new generations that they were in America because of a founding idea. The high degree of filiopiety with which modern Americans remember the eighteenth-century founders—a filiopiety that is unique in the world—bears a close resemblance to the way in which the second and third generations of New Englanders contemplated their own place in the American firmament, and the illustrious ancestors who had led them there.

John Cotton's hopes never entirely vanished and were resuscitated well into the eighteenth century by the Mather dynasty he helped to found. For the Mathers, prophecy was a family enterprise. Throughout his long life, Cotton's son-in-law, Increase Mather, asserted that the millennium was nigh, and that New Englanders would soon hear "the Wo-

Joy trumpets, which with the same Breath sound Wo to Antichrist, but Joy to the Saints of the Most High." For him, the struggle was very much a global contest. His *Ichabod* (1702) lamented the decline of Protestantism around Europe and South America, and the general decline of Christianity in Africa and the Middle East. Like his peers, he strained after the conversion of the Jews and paid close attention to recent victories and losses affecting the Ottomans, whom he disdained as "sarecenical locusts." Cotton's grandson and namesake, Cotton Mather, also pondered the world situation deeply and considered the rise of the Ottomans a harbinger of the final battles to come. The deepest Turkish penetration into Europe, their 1683 approach to Vienna, occurred exactly as the Mathers were contemplating these mysteries. He also followed every tiny development in Spanish and French America, believing, with a touching faith, that secret prayer "does an incredible deal towards jogging the *High Wheels of Providence*, and shaking of Churches and Empires." He even taught himself Spanish and wrote a little book on Protestantism to send into the Spanish territories, wondering if "a little fire may kindle, or whether the time for our Lord Jesus Christ to have glorious Churches in America, be not at hand."

But even if one steps back from the Cotton-Mather dynasty, one can see that a sense of global expectation characterized the entire New England enterprise. One can even see a real foreign policy emerging alongside the imagined contest with Antichrist. The Puritans developed a network of trading partners as soon as they arrived, sending ships up and down the seaboard and especially to the Atlantic islands (Winthrop's son Samuel moved to the Canaries to develop this trade). By 1643, Boston had become an international hub of sorts; Edward Johnson called it "the very mart of a new Land, French, Portugalls and Dutch, come hither for Traffique." Anglo-Americans also participated in Cromwell's ill-fated "western design," an ambitious attempt to seize Spain's colonies in the Caribbean, gain plunder, and poke the pope in the eye at the same time. With similar inspirations, generation after generation of Puritans sent military expeditions to harass the French to their north, who were thought to be in league with the devil as well as the natives.

Even after the disappointments of the first generation and the constant collision between experience and hope, these New Englanders never relinquished a worldview that continues to astonish for its reach. Year after year, election speakers lectured the faithful on their worldwide importance. Top-selling books such as *The New England Primer* instructed children to "abhor that errant Whore of Rome." Edward Johnson's 1654 *History of New England* taunted three nations at once on its cover page: Italy ("the Seat and Center of the Beast"), Spain, and Portugal ("that beastly Whore, who hath made your Nations drunk with the Wine of her Fornication"). Michael Wigglesworth's *Day of Doom* (1662), the most popular work of the imagination to emerge from the first century of settlement, painted thrillingly dark pictures of the end of the world as it raced through sixteen editions. Even Anne Bradstreet, the demure poetess who wrote about chirping birds, entered deeply into the world of prophecy with her longest poem, "The Four Monarchies," a tirade against "Rome's Whore" that urged setting fire to priestly garments and called for the annihilation of Protestantism's enemies. Elsewhere, she urged her readers "with brandished swords to Turkey go." Emily Dickinson she was not!

From the top of colonial society to the dregs, New Englanders lavished attention on obscure bits of Scripture that seemed to favor the wilderness, the West, and the defeat of large powers by small ones. They understood acutely the importance of tactical gains and losses in the global struggle against Rome, a "red" enemy as frightening and diffuse as the Soviet Union in the Cold War. Taking note of every new fortress built by the French in Canada, New Englanders saw themselves as a frontline outpost against evil and a tripwire for the millennium to come. Samuel Sewall, one of the judges of the Salem witch trials, poured his energies into proving that America was to be the actual location of the final battle between Christ and Antichrist. About New England, he asked, "Why may not that be the place of New-Jerusalem?" Sewall predicted, "When Antichrist should clamber up to the top of his imperial Tyranny, by extending it over the New World also; then he was to come to his End."

These religious energies were also quickened by a widespread cultural belief. Countless scholars subscribed to a theory known as *translatio studii*, which posited that learning, religion, and power moved in a westerly direction, carving out a swath of culture that had originated in Greece and passed by Rome on its way to France, England, and ultimately North America. Eighteenth-century schoolchildren memorized Bishop Berkeley's lines about the westward course of empire, and as late as the nineteenth century, John Adams, recalling his youth, said that nothing was "more ancient in his memory than the observation that arts, sciences, and empire had traveled westward, and in conversation it was always added, since he was a child, that their next leap would be over the Atlantic to America."

Nor were these self-important thoughts confined to New England. Millennialists could be found in every region, and by the time of the sprawling revivals of the Great Awakening in the 1730s and 1740s, all of the colonies would be touched by its contagious enthusiasm. That intercolonial solidarity substantially deepened in the middle decades of the eighteenth century, when the people of the colonies were drawn together even more closely because Britain treated them with equal condescension. The word *liberty* was heard far more often then, and with many of its modern, overtly political overtones, but the old millennial thunder would never disappear entirely.

Nathaniel Hawthorne's short story "The Gray Champion" reincarnates a legend that was known to New England schoolchildren for generations, cherished and handed down like an old family Bible. Partly based on fact, the legend told of one of the regicides who signed the death warrant of King Charles I in 1649, then fled to New England after the Restoration. In Hawthorne's conceit, this primeval worthy is reincarnated every time that Americans face a threat to their liberties, and so the hopes of the earliest generations are perpetually present in those of the most recent.

In the chapters ahead, I hope to show that these researches into the seventeenth and earlier centuries are not merely antiquarian exercises, but bear on all subsequent history, from one generation to the next. The Great Awakening could not have happened without the hangover of Puritanism; the Revolution would have been different without the Awakening; and so each age leaves an indelible imprint on its successor. Even as political systems evolve and societies mature, ways of thinking and talking about the world can remain surprisingly stable.

As Hawthorne suspected, the Puritans have never entirely left us, even as we have left them. Mercifully, we do not become enmeshed in their doctrinal differences anymore. But that primal urge to reorganize the world, to fight against a malevolent force, and to denounce those who dare to interrupt our momentum is more deeply rooted in our past than we think. In the current debate about America's place in the world, some insist that we have a mission to save humanity from tyranny, while many of our enemies insist with equal ardor that the United States has itself become "the Great Satan," or Antichrist, or failing that, a great power that must be resisted by the faithful. In these arguments, essentially religious, it is impossible not to hear the faint footfall of the ancients.

CHAPTER THREE

A NEW ORDER OF THE AGES

THE HAPPY EMPIRE OF PERFECT WISDOM

> Can the liberties of a nation be thought secure when we have removed their only firm basis, a conviction in the minds of the people that these liberties are the gift of God? —Thomas Jefferson

The Apocalypse never came, of course. Yet a different kind of seismic eruption *did* take place at the end of the colonial period—the act that ended it, the American Revolution. What Ralph Waldo Emerson would call "the shot heard round the world" was barely audible at first, and on July 4, 1776, King George III famously noted in his journal that "nothing of importance happened today." That same day, the greatest American historian of his era, Thomas Hutchinson, received an honorary degree from Oxford University, a small salve after fleeing his native soil for Tory principles. When Hutchinson heard that Voltaire had anointed Ben Franklin's grandson with the words "God and Liberty" in Paris, he remarked, "It's difficult to say which of those words had been used more to bad purposes." For him, *liberty* was more or less synonymous with tar and feathers.

But the noise grew, and rattled the serenity of Europe's ruling dynasties. Soon, its aftershock could be felt on every continent. If not quite apocalyptic, still, the Revolution changed the world, and endured all attempts to suppress it. In fact, it never seemed to end. Long after Yorktown and the Treaty of Paris, the world order (including the United States) was still working to tamp down the enthusiasms that had been unleashed. First, there were small echoes—around 1784, a British ship touched on the Comoros Islands, near Madagascar, and observed local African slaves asking their Arab masters, "America is free. Could we not be?" Then came the more suitably cataclysmic revolutions in Paris and Saint Domingue, both of which owed something to the American precedent. Finally, in the aftermath of the French and Haitian upheavals, history coughed up an enormous range of rebels, cranks, and iconoclasts who spent much of the last two centuries citing Jefferson to argue that they have the right to do whatever they like.

This provincial rebellion at the edge of the British empire undeniably had and continues to have global consequences. That is one of countless paradoxes stemming from the Big Bang of American history. Just as astronomers measure light emitted by ancient cosmic events, from the beginning of time itself, so we still feel the wind and dust kicked up by the democratic revolution that created the United States. No other nation worships the moment of its creation as we do—in part because no other nation can locate its origin as easily as we can. Our celebration of the founding is in itself something to be celebrated, a bracing look at the hard circumstances that forged a durable form of government. But admittedly, our infatuation has a fatuous quality. Surely the founders did not want us to agree with something merely because they felt it was true in the late eighteenth century. Few generations, in fact, were more skeptical of inherited wisdom. In *The Federalist*, Alexander Hamilton ridiculed ancestor worship and the idea that Americans might be less inclined to corruption than other peoples: "Is it not time to awake from the deceitful dream of a golden age, and to adopt as a practical maxim for the direction of our global conduct that we, as well as the other inhabitants of the globe, are yet remote from the happy empire of perfect wisdom and perfect virtue?"

That is instructive counsel. The unanimity with which latter-day Americans pay homage to the Revolution and Constitution conceals the important fact that Americans were hardly unanimous as they undertook their vast rewriting of history. They bickered; they dithered; and they contradicted themselves endlessly. They built a powerful federal government while celebrating the individual's freedom from government; they proclaimed an earthshaking skepticism about religion while articulating their faith in an overarching Providence; they declared their freedom from the cynical diplomacy of the Old World while pursuing a diplomatic strategy worthy of Talleyrand. And they articulated a bracing new set of ideals that governments should stand for, summed up magnificently in the Declaration and the preamble to the Constitution—while subverting those ideals daily, at least in their application to African-Americans and others denied entrance into the cathedral of American freedom. This conservative revolution—an oxymoron—remains many things to many people. A fuller appreciation of our divisive origins and the muddle of our early foreign policy is newly desirable at another moment when so many people around the world are divided about what it is, precisely, that the United States stands for.

The revolutionary pantheon is crowded with visitors today—books about the founders have never sold as well. New museums need to be built to keep up with the flood of people seeking entrance, literally, into our history. The Revolution is certainly claimed, in a powerful way, by its Sons and Daughters, the genealogical obsessives who feel an intense desire to be related, in as few generations as possible, to the heroic actors of yesteryear. But it also speaks to millions of unrelated Americans, including sixties people (Paul Revere and the Raiders), right-wingers (the Federalist Society), reenactors fleeing the modern world, and world-changers embracing it too tightly. Nor has it has ever ceased to speak to non-Americans, from Lafayette to Ho Chi Minh to the heroes of Tiananmen Square. Perhaps the ultimate measure of the Revolution's ongoing relevance can be found on Madison Avenue. "An American Revolution" recently replaced "Like a Rock" as Chevrolet's slogan, despite the inconvenient fact that the engines are now built in China.*

It could be argued that the American Revolution *was* a world revolution—so Thomas Paine insisted when he wrote, not long after his arrival here, that "the cause of America is in a great measure the cause of all mankind." So Arnold Toynbee once insisted, in a book titled *America and the World Revolution*. And so nearly every president has insisted when explaining the march of democracy abroad.

*GM must have known that "The Chinese Revolution" was unlikely to stimulate buyers (although it cheerfully proclaims "The Indian Revolution" when pitching Chevys in India).

In light of these global aspirations, I'd like to argue a few counterintuitive points about this seminal episode in our past, now so familiar that we can barely see it anew. As the British learned, to their dismay, it is unwise to underestimate the capacity of the revolutionary generation to surprise us. It is a lesson we need to relearn on occasion. We should restore some of that generation's audacity, and its foreignness as well. They lived in a different country than the one we inhabit. And for all of their exemplary attributes, they were hardly united or consistent in their quest for independence. They sought a New World in their way, and nearly all of them commented on their disdain for the past. Yet there is no doubt that earlier history shaped the revolutionaries as profoundly as their history has shaped us. They pursued an intensely local struggle, which claimed the right of self-determination against a distant empire—and yet they wanted the entire world to pay attention and follow their example. They proclaimed liberty throughout their dominion (whatever that was), but their claim on liberty was compromised by an incomplete understanding at home, and a complete inability to export it anywhere else. In other words, their desire to spread freedom vastly exceeded their ability to do so. Resolving all of these contradictions is a fool's errand, but acknowledging their existence seems like a promising way to begin a fuller conversation than a Chevy ad allows.

To historians, the march of eighteenth-century Americans toward their inevitable destiny was perfectly logical, the result of a long sequence of imperial blunders by the British and the rising ability of the colonies to protect their interests. To the Revolution's participants, history's trajectory was far less clear. But it does not take too much subterranean probing to discern that the same old fantasies about America's providential role were alive in the hearts and minds of the founders.

Famously, John Adams wrote of "minds and hearts" in his letter to Hezekiah Niles in 1818, many years after the event, when he asserted that the surface actions of the Revolution were less important than the intellectual springs that lay beneath: "What do we mean by the American Revolution? Do we mean the American war? The Revolution was effected before the war commenced. The Revolution was in the minds and hearts of the people; a change in their religious sentiments, of their duties and obligations."

It's true that a radical change did take place in the way that people thought about government. But it's equally true, though less obvious, that they retained old beliefs, including "religious sentiments," that asserted America's ancient claims on the rest of the world. For all their skepticism about "priestcraft," the founders were still enthralled by the notion that God had ordained a special Providence for the new nation. Furthermore, the Revolution embraced a far wider territory than we, or even they, normally admitted. I would particularly like to look at a problem that has never quite disappeared from American foreign policy, though the circumstances facing Americans in the twenty-first century could hardly be more different from what they were in the revolutionary era. Simply put, the United States had two foreign policies that had little to do with each other. First, a modest set of achievable aims, designed to reject the grandiosity of the world's arrogant monarchies, and to reflect the commonsense outlook of a people who had fought their way to a foothold in the wilderness. And second, an ingrained sense that God was guiding the first steps of the infant republic, and that therefore it could do no wrong. When Franklin proposed that Congress open its meetings with a prayer, Alexander Hamilton snorted that the body had no need of "foreign aid." But even those founders who were disinclined to follow normal forms of religious behavior felt a strong sense of sacred purpose guiding the infant republic.

FROM REVELATION TO REVOLUTION

> Here independent power shall hold her sway,
> And public virtue warm the patriot breast:
> No traces shall remain of tyranny,
> And laws, a pattern to the world beside,
> Be here enacted first
> . . . .
> A new Jerusalem, sent down from heaven,
> Shall grace our happy earth . . .
>
> —Philip Freneau

In September 1775, near the beginning of the Revolution, a most unusual military expedition assembled. Not long after Concord and

Bunker Hill, the Continental Army needed to strike a blow for freedom. Although the war was seemingly a defensive struggle against the occupying British, the Americans reached back to an earlier impulse and decided to do what Anglo-Saxons have always done in a time of crisis: attack the French. Their ultimate destination was Quebec, where they hoped to topple the French citadel, now a part of the British empire but still redolent of the papist menace to God-fearing New Englanders.

But before heading north to Quebec and enduring one of the most brutal campaigns of the entire war, the expedition stopped in Newburyport, Massachusetts. There they found the tomb of the great English evangelist George Whitefield, a catalyst of the Great Awakening, which had swept across the American colonies in the 1730s and 1740s. The official chaplain to the brigade preached over Whitefield's grave. Then he and a few officers climbed into the tomb, removed the lid from Whitefield's coffin, clipped his collar and wristbands, cut them into pieces, and handed them out to the reverent soldiers. In truth, Whitefield was only being asked to do from the grave what he had done when still among the living. And it worked. Whipped to enthusiasm, Americans went to war.

Why would a dead evangelist hold such power over the troops? Why would anyone want to invade Quebec, under any circumstances? And in winter? To answer those questions, it's necessary to retreat further into the past, and to remember how alive religion was to the colonists, fighting against a distant imperial authority as they believed that the earliest Christians had fought the Romans. That is only one of many historical comparisons that occurred to them as they launched their great effort at self-determination, borrowing from ancient time, recent time, and events entirely out of time to find their role models. While it would be unwise to focus exclusively on religion as a motivating factor, it also seems foolish to ignore it completely, as so many historians have, uncomfortable with the old millennial thunder.

One doesn't have to look far in our early national history to hear the thunder. In fact, on Day One, July 4, 1776, the Continental Congress convened a blue-chip committee of Benjamin Franklin, Thomas Jefferson, and John Adams to design a seal for the new nation they had invented. Each was in his own way a skeptic, but as they cast about for suitable imagery, they instinctively reached back to biblical imagery for the Great Seal. Jefferson, the architect of the wall of separation between church and state, proposed the children of Israel in the wilderness. Franklin, another alleged scoffer, suggested "Moses standing on the Shore, and extending his Hand over the Sea, thereby causing the same to overwhelm Pharaoh who is sitting in an open Chariot with a Crown on his Head and Sword in his Hand. Rays from a Pillar of Fire in the Clouds reaching to Moses, to express that he acts by Command of the Deity." Clearly, the wall of separation was more of a picket fence, with eyeholes to peek through.

Perhaps the most famous religious skeptic of the founders was Thomas Paine. And yet his writings are chock-full of evangelical accents, along with the sense of being born again, in a secular bath of liberty. The republic *was* his religion. Ronald Reagan loved to cite Paine's phrase, "We have it in our power to begin the world over again," from *Common Sense*. But consider the lines that follow: "A situation, similar to the present, has not happened since the days of Noah until now. The birthday of a new world is at hand, and a race of men, perhaps as numerous as all Europe contains, are to receive their portion of freedom from the event of a few months." His liberty is not all that distant from the Calvinist Internationale—he criticizes Jews and Muslims as being too willing to accept monarchs, and he disdains kings as "the Popery of government." Was this not a kind of secular millennium?

The pudgy lawyer John Adams may have been the most grounded of all the founders. Who else would refer to God as "the Legislator of the Universe"? Yet even he was capable of extraordinary flights of fancy concerning America's place in the world and a destiny that seemed to be rooted as much in the Bible as in the laws of realpolitik. As a mere nineteen-year-old, then a young teacher, he wrote a letter to a friend that revealed a shocking national ambition:

> Soon after the Reformation, a few people came over into this New World for conscience's sake. Perhaps this apparently trivial incident may transfer the great seat of empire to America. It looks likely to me; for if we can remove the turbulent Gallics, our people, according to the exactest computations, will, in another century, become more numerous than England itself.

> Should this be the case, since we have, I may say, all the naval stores of the nations in our hands, it will be easy to obtain the mastery of the seas; and then the united force of all Europe will not be able to subdue us.

These are startlingly global thoughts for a young provincial. Yet they were widely shared by his countrymen, well in advance of American independence. And they lasted throughout a long lifetime of service to his country. Ten years later, a more settled lawyer, Adams returned to the theme of American exceptionalism in his *Dissertation on the Canon and Feudal Law* (1765): "I always consider the settlement of America with reverence, as the opening of a grand scene and design in Providence for the illumination of the ignorant and the emancipation of the slavish part of mankind all over the earth." By later excising the last sentence before republication, he only rendered it that much more interesting to posterity.

There was little doubt whom Adams meant. The Whore of Babylon! Or, in more moderate language, the Catholic Church. Adams attacked the "wicked confederacy" that had historically linked "the Romish clergy" with the monarchies of Europe—a combination that was "calamitous to human liberty." He detected conspiracies everywhere—among popes and kings, among Stuarts trying to take away New England's charters in the seventeenth century, and among priests everywhere. The discovery and settlement of America, at just the right moment, in close proximity to the advance of the Reformation, had dealt a severe check to "ecclesiastical and civil tyranny." The polarities of "tyranny" and "liberty" would be explored by Adams many times in his career, though never again in the nakedly religious language of this unexpurgated riposte.

Why did so many sober founding fathers go off the deep end when it came time to define America's destiny? It would be too simple to say that they were expecting the Second Coming of Christ, as so many of their ancestors had. But that intense feeling of expectancy—that *something* might be coming—translated effortlessly into the secular hopes of a people with nothing in Europe to return to and a huge amount of real estate to build on. A good deal of history separates the founders from the earliest English settlements in North America—

nearly as much time as has elapsed between the founders and ourselves. But that passage of time should not prevent us from traveling into the deep past to find a fuller sense of where the boldness of the founders' global vision came from.

How do we find the founders' founders? One way to begin is simply to look at the very first histories of the Revolution—the attempts to divine its meaning as it was beginning to unfold. There is no doubt that they were fighting for what they felt to be ancient liberties, both political and religious. In May 1777, the local historian Jeremy Belknap saw the incipient struggle as something very old. More specifically, he identified the new tensions as the latest version of the struggle against Antichrist that had consumed earlier Americans. Proudly, he pointed to the past to insist that no "rotten toe of Nebuchadnezzar's image" or "seven-headed beast" would ever dominate America. To be likened to Nebuchadnezzar's toe was just about the worst thing that could be said about a New England politician, as John Adams would learn to his dismay.

In short, many pasts were in the air as the revolutionaries commenced their struggle to build something new. Behind their meager ranks they imagined entire regiments of ancestors and biblical patriarchs, ready to smite the oppressor—any oppressor. Throughout the colonies, Americans nursed vivid memories of historical episodes in which liberties had narrowly been preserved from usurpers, be they British administrators or French Jesuits or marauding natives.

New England in particular was anything but a normal settlement—nor did it want to be one. Increase Mather wrote that nothing is worse than to be "like the rest of the Nations." From the failure of the English civil war to the onset of the Revolution, colonists had nurtured an abiding sense that their liberties were precious and all too easily removed by royal authorities. A now obscure book detailing an early claim, Jeremiah Dummer's 1721 *Defence of the New-England Charters*, was called by Adams the "handbook of the Revolution." Countless fireplace legends circulated, some more true than others, of regicide judges and other Commonwealth-Men who lived in secrecy in America, deathless, ready to do battle again against kings—the story milked by Nathaniel Hawthorne in "The Gray Champion." At the time of the Revolution, Franklin cited the old judges who had condemned Charles I as a way of inspiring Americans to rediscover their freedom.

Of course, New England, like all the colonies, was growing more cosmopolitan in the eighteenth century, as its trade spanned the Atlantic world and newcomers brought new, less cloistered ideas about culture, politics, and religion. American newspapers paid close attention to the rest of the world, particularly the endless European wars, eager to remain relevant to the worldwide struggle against priestcraft and kingcraft. Colonists devoured English disquisitions on liberty, from Locke to John Wilkes.

But another set of meanings also attached to the word *liberty* in the middle of the eighteenth century, emanating from a very different source. Since the imprecise moment it began, the Great Awakening has never been easy to define, seemingly in a dozen places at the same time, with evangelists and flocks spurring each other to new and more fervent expressions of faith. These religious revivals of the 1730s and 1740s were not the first to strike America, but something about their intensity altered the landscape, and with it, the way Americans talked about themselves. A future Yale president, Ezra Stiles, described the 1740s as a time when "multitudes were seriously, soberly and solemnly out of their wits."

To some extent, that view still prevails among political historians, who find religious frenzy undignified. It's easy to look down upon people writhing on the ground; indeed, it is often the only way to see them. True, the doctrines of the Awakening can be difficult to swallow, or even to understand. But something elemental in the national character was forged in those decades. For one thing, it *was* a national phenomenon. Itinerant preachers traveled up and down the colonies, reaching out to people in cities and backwoods, learning from each other, and forging a new kind of vocabulary. New England, the middle colonies, and the South spoke to one another as never before. Further, the Awakening acted as a centrifuge of sorts, speeding up tendencies that were latent and compressing words to release new meanings.

Liberty was a most important concept to the New Lights, as the Awakened were known. It connoted different things in different settings, especially the freedom of preachers to travel widely, outside of supervision, and of people to leave their home parishes to hear them. Another essential word was *union*, which signified not only the mystical bond between God and believers, but between the faithful themselves, as an earthly community. Jonathan Edwards even used the term *great society* now and then, anticipating Lyndon Johnson by more than two centuries.

As these religious ideas blended with their secular counterparts, and as people from the different regions merged as well, the Great Awakening had a tremendous impact on the emerging political union of the American people. Increasingly, the accents of Southerners, Northerners, and everyone in between commingled. It would be difficult to underestimate the influence of George Whitefield—Franklin, for one, was mesmerized by his oratory—and it's ironic to think that an Englishman stirred a revival that ultimately held so many anti-British undertones.

The Awakening was a profoundly spiritual enterprise, but one of the ways it drew believers together was by depicting the events of the world in a comprehensible narrative. To be sure, there was plenty of fire and brimstone, prophesying the horrific fate awaiting the enemies of the faithful. But at the same time, many of those old sermons contained a social program, and a most egalitarian one at that. Not a few New Lights believed that by building a more just society they could take one step closer to the millennium, and perhaps even—dare they say it?—initiate it themselves. If Americans could start things off, then the world might just follow, and men and women would be free at last. This new version of a millennium built by human beings might not be so apocalyptic after all. Jonathan Edwards often spoke rhapsodically of the better world that was coming, in terms that sounded less like a revival speech than a Law of the Sea conference at the United Nations:

> Then shall all the world be united in one amiable society. All nations, in all parts of the world, on every side of the globe, shall then be knit together in sweet harmony. All parts of God's church shall assist and promote the spiritual good of one another. A communication shall then be upheld between all parts of the world to that end; and the art of navigation, which is now applied so much to favour men's covetousness and pride, and is used so much by wicked debauched men, shall then be consecrated to God, and applied to holy uses.

Of course, no revival worth its salt can be *all* sweetness and light. Since the Great Awakening also coincided with the rise of tensions with the French, in both the Old World and the New, frequent attempts were made to demonize a familiar enemy, or more specifically three: the triple alliance of "the French King, the Pope and the Devil." No insult was strong enough for this early axis of evil, and in war after war, preachers urged their flocks to attack France, Spain, Rome, Babylon, and Hell simultaneously.

One episode has never, to my knowledge, been described before in a book on American foreign policy. In 1745, the War of the Austrian Succession, one of the countless wars that usually pitted France against Britain, broke out in America. A ragtag New England army was preparing for the immense challenge of taking Louisbourg, the formidable French fortress on Cape Breton. Local authorities asked George Whitefield to speak to the troops, and he gave a sermon before they embarked, asking for the blessing of Providence and urging them to fight for Jesus Christ as "soldiers of David." A flag brought by the expedition carried a motto supplied by Whitefield: "*Nil desperandum, Christo Duce*" (If Christ be captain, no fear of a defeat). Whitefield's approval galvanized the faithful, and sparked recruiting efforts. This may well be the first time in American history that an invasion force went into battle fortified with the expectation that God was on its side. The millennium was no longer a vague aspiration for all humankind, it was now a weapon in the American arsenal.

Inspired, colonists joined in great numbers, and to the amazement of everyone—the British, the French, and themselves—they succeeded in taking Louisbourg. Even more striking were the aftereffects of this holy war. New Englanders were beside themselves with pride, only to see Britain trade Louisbourg for Madras in India three years later, as part of the backroom deal that formed the Treaty of Aix-la-Chapelle (1748), ending the war. Many Americans were furious. Further, once all that millennial energy had been deployed against the French king, it was not difficult to transfer it to the House of Hanover, now atop the British throne. Is it a coincidence that Jonathan Mayhew presented his famous *Discourse Concerning Unlimited Submission and Non-Resistance to Higher Powers*, a brave assault on the divine right of kings, in 1750—just after the British had given Louisbourg back to the French, and the centennial of the execution of Charles I? British royalists were deeply offended by Mayhew's dredging up the ghost of Cromwell, "whose spittle he hath lick'd up, and cough'd it out again, with some addition of his own filth and phlegm." We may forget the seventeenth century, but the founders never did. A phrase from Mayhew's sermon, "Resistance to tyranny is obedience to God," was sewn into battle flags during the Revolution and nearly became the motto of the United States. It is often attributed mistakenly to the man who admired it, Thomas Jefferson.*

The 1750s saw one crisis after another neatly placed within the context of the never-ending struggle. When a terrible earthquake struck Europe, Mayhew saw it as the work of "Babylon the great, the Mother of Harlots." Harvard created a lecture series that still exists, dedicated in part to proving "that the Church of Rome is the mystical Babylon." The French and Indian War brought back a more familiar enemy, and New Light preachers were again quick to see the signs of the Last Things on the horizon. In the backwoods of Pennsylvania, a minister worried that the "Triple Alliance" (devil, pope, French king) might "extinguish the Protestant Lamb." The successful invasion of Quebec in 1759, and Britain's defeat of France in the contest for North America, ended more than a century of geographical rivalry; it decided the perpetual contest that had existed between two bitterly opposed religious systems in northern North America. The cry that announced Quebec's capture was "Babylon the great is fallen, is fallen!"

As in 1748, the aftermath of the war was in some ways worse than the war itself. Whitefield warned his American friends that a "deep laid plot" against their "civil and religious liberties" was being hatched at the time of the Stamp Act. Americans interpreted the new tax as an attack on "the ark of God" and likened it to "the Beast," or "the sum total of all his wickedness." From the pulpit came thunderous denunciations of evil kings of the past and summonses to remember the Glorious Revolution and Commonwealth. Clearly, spiritual concerns (the fear that Britain might impose a bishop) were felt as acutely as political ones. In addition to flogging the latter, Sam Adams took care to protest "the utter loss of those religious Rights, the enjoyment of which our good forefathers had more especially in their intention, when they explored and settled this new world."

The many causes of the Revolution make it difficult to choose one,

*The phrase originated in the English Revolution, often attributed to the regicide John Bradshaw.

but it's interesting to note that the British general Thomas Gage did exactly that when he identified the Quebec Act passed by Parliament in 1774 as the great turning point. Not only did it protect Catholicism in Quebec, enraging Protestants, it also prevented westward migration, enraging them further. An expansionist energy always lay at the heart of the Awakening, with its pronouncements on world peace, its interior audiences, and itinerant ministers ready to gallop over the next hillside. Thirty years later that energy was alive and well.

When the Revolution broke out, the old millennial brickbats came flying once more. James Otis called on "the trump of the arch angel" in the famous speech against the writs of assistance that John Adams identified as the beginning of it all. The Boston Massacre was described as the day "when Beelzebub broke loose, and with infernal train, joined with the scarlet throng, with George's livery." King George was denounced as the Antichrist, and there were repeated claims that the Revolution had initiated the Last Days. The people of eastern Massachusetts nearly saw it happen on the so-called Great Dark Day of May 19, 1780, when a weather disturbance caused the sky to go dark.

Of course, nothing here should be construed as denying the powerful role that nonevangelical actors played in the Revolution. Without merchants, pamphleteers, journalists, recent immigrants, and hundreds of other types, the Revolution would have come to naught. Without European thinkers in every nation advancing the new doctrines of the Enlightenment, the idealistic republic-to-be, based on rights and responsibilities, would have been far less likely. All of these disparate seekers were in search of some kind of "liberty." The very word was a selling point in immigrant manuals, and the historian Bernard Bailyn has described a pervasive "fear of a comprehensive conspiracy against liberty throughout the English-speaking world." But the same could easily be said of the evangelicals, who felt a profound "spirit of liberty and union" in 1775 and even identified God with it: "What is Liberty in all its beauties? Is it not the image of JEHOVAH?" Of course, then as now, some were eager to say words merely because others were saying them. As Nathaniel Niles wrote, "Many visibly espouse the cause of liberty purely for the sake of rising into popularity." Whatever else may be said of it, it is a tradition with a notable pedigree.

The American Revolution absorbed all of these energies, reconstituting them into a political millennium that was just vague and optimistic enough to please all the participants. What may be most remarkable about the Revolution is not just that so many of its leaders were claiming that world history was changing at that moment—but that their claims turned out to be true. A new time was indeed beginning.

Thus, well before the first shots were fired at Lexington and Concord, a familiar way of talking about liberty was enmeshed in the American psyche. Lawyers, ministers, merchants, farmers, sailors, all grew used to the millennial accents and the strong dichotomies that were contained inside them—tyranny vs. liberty, the Vatican vs. the Calvinist internationale, Antichrist vs. Christ the King, and government by fiat vs. government by the people. These tight polarities have never entirely disappeared.

In this supercharged context, "liberty" became a battle cry, a panacea, and a placebo for thousands of Americans, from evangelical and secular backgrounds alike, chanting its three syllables incessantly. In the 1770s an observer commented, "The minds of the people are wrought up into as high degree of Enthusiasm by the word liberty, as could have been expected had Religion been the cause." Exactly.

MY COUNTRY IS THE WORLD

> My country is the world, my countrymen are all mankind.
>
> —Thomas Paine

The Revolution was not only an idea, it was very much a military struggle in the real world. And if the desire for independence was chronologically confused and interspersed with reflections on Cromwell, the Great Awakening, and the Last Things, then the actual fighting of the war also suffered from some geographical uncertainty. As with the millennial thinking that contributed to the war, there were few boundaries to the struggle. We dutifully trek to Lexington, Concord, and various Freedom Trails around the country to relive those glorious days. Those trails tend to be well tended, well marked, and well trod. But an argument could be made that a most significant location of the Revolution is just off the coast of Brittany, near the island of Ouessant, where the French navy first engaged the British on behalf of the Americans. How many Americans know that John Paul Jones's greatest naval victories took place just off the coast of England—that in a sense we were attacking *them*? Or that some of the largest naval engagements between the French and British were fought in the Caribbean? Or that the first combat between Germans and Americans was arguably the battles fought between Continentals and Hessians? Or that General Cornwallis, after losing at Yorktown, enjoyed a distinguished career in India, where he died and is buried? Or that the final naval engagement between France and Britain was in the Bay of Bengal, long after Yorktown? From start to finish (and its true finish was at Paris, in the rue Jacob, where the treaty was signed), this was a profoundly international confict—if you prefer the term, a world war.

If the Revolution brought radical new ideas about sovereignty, it also revolutionized the tired world of diplomacy, and not merely because it was an epic power struggle between France and Britain that destabilized both and changed European history forever. Alongside the ideas that inspired the Americans to propose a better system of self-government were a number of dramatic new proposals for changing forever the way that nations interact. This poorly understood component of the Revolution may be one of its most lasting legacies.

The brand-new United States found it awkward to devise a foreign policy when it became a nation in 1776. The Continental Congress had its hands full keeping an army fed, and its thirteen states together, and its people supportive. But there *was* a foreign policy, and it was crucial to independence. In fact, Americans had a foreign policy well before 1776. The Continental Congress created a secret committee for foreign relations on November 29, 1775, well in advance of the Declaration. But even before that, of course, Americans enjoyed extensive mercantile relations, both legal and illegal, with other nations. They had a sophisticated network of intercolonial relations (which were a foreign policy of sorts when large groups of settlers came from different European nations, as with, say, the Dutch of New York).* They had un-

*The English at Plymouth negotiated a trade agreement with the Dutch in 1627; Jamestown signed a treaty with them in 1660.

official and official relations with Native Americans and French and Spanish settlers to the north, west, and south. Even during the war, and long after, these informal relationships continued and were a major concern of the new government. Large areas of the interior remained barely under U.S. control after the Revolution was completed, and imposing nominal control was a major test of the new government's legitimacy. In a sense, you could argue that we became the United States by invading ourselves.

But of course, European diplomacy was an entirely different animal. Ancient traditions dating from medieval times dictated every feature of the way that kings and nations communicated, down to the tiniest rituals of behavior and the articles of clothing worn by emissaries. Treaties were often made complicated by secret codicils. Alliances were tricky because international relationships were often intrafamilial relationships as well, with cousins at war and messy family feuds in the background of what should have been the unemotional science of foreign relations. No European power worth its salt showed any remorse about aggressive acquisition of new land, if it could get away with it; the great diplomatic historian Samuel Flagg Bemis wrote, "They cut and pared states like Dutch cheese."

Against this backdrop, leading thinkers of the Enlightenment proposed a better system of foreign policy: fewer dynastic obligations and medieval courtesies, more openness in treaties and communications, reciprocity in commercial relations, considerate treatment of neutrals, and far more free trade. It would be hard to think of a set of proposals more perfectly suited to Americans. They embraced the new ideas enthusiastically as their new nation came into existence, so much so that the two became synonymous. The 1778 treaty of alliance between France and the United States—which more or less legitimized the new nation—was based on the ideas of the so-called Model Treaty, a streamlined document that John Adams had drafted during the summer of independence. It is not so long a leap from the Model Treaty to the "open treaties, openly arrived at" that Woodrow Wilson would urge at Versailles when he became master of the world, briefly, in 1919.

In other words, the American Revolution was also a foreign policy revolution. In theory, and in practice, this was a nation like no other, and Americans came out of the war with an enhanced sense of the global ramifications of their independence movement. Some of America's historic exceptionalism can be traced to the simple fact that the United States became the only democracy in the world in 1776 and remained so for some time. It's easy to be exceptionalist if you are, in fact, exceptional. One of the main goals of the Declaration of Independence was simply to get Europe's monarchies to admit that such a bizarre new government existed. But the feeling gained force from the sentiment, nurtured by Franklin's brilliant success in Paris, that American frankness was improving the entire world order. The various vogues for America, apparent everywhere from Marie Antoinette's hairdos to new fashions in French clothing, were all part of a naive but charming sense that the world had, in fact, become a little better after the simple Yankees had been granted their freedom.

It could be argued that the great triumph of the Treaty of Paris—in which the new nation outnegotiated both its ally and its adversary—was the most significant achievement of the Revolution, even beyond Washington's military successes and Jefferson's superb language about human rights. Without an actual country legitimized by the treaty, it would have been difficult to advance the ideals that the country stood for. After 1783, the world would never again be able to claim that monarchy was part of the natural order, ordained by God. From that point forward, democracy and liberty were strategic national interests, backed by a state with sovereignty. Ironically, the first royal house to feel the sting of the nettle inside the Treaty of Paris was the Bourbon line. Within a decade of its signing, France's royal household was wiped out.

Thomas Pownall, a former royal governor of Massachusetts, and one of the shrewdest observers of the international scene, saw instantly, with astronomical clarity, that a great new force existed, a counterweight that would change the world order forever: "North America is become a new primary planet in the system of the world, which, while it takes its own course, must have effect on the orbit of every other planet, and shift the common center of gravity of the whole system of the European world." He predicted, accurately, that the United States would develop a great navy, strong relationships with South America, the Pacific, and China, and eventually become "the chief carrier of the commerce of the whole world." While this might in some way benefit Britain, he also saw the ultimate demise of the old privileged mercantile elite and the vast monopolies, such as the Hudson Bay Company, that had carved up so much of the world. Pownall guessed that the United States would become "the arbitress of commerce, and, perhaps, the mediatrix of peace." Yet even this scientific appraisal was not immune to the metaphysical reflection that accompanied so much conversation about America. In a letter to Benjamin Franklin in 1783, he added the thought that the American Revolution "has stranger marks of divine interposition, superseding the ordinary course of human affairs, than any other event which this world has experienced."

But even if most Americans, and not a few Europeans, were tempted to say that the United States had metamorphosed into the perfect nation, the problem remained that the new nation was run by Americans, and Americans, for all their talents, are human beings like anyone else. The founders were not exceptions, and what is perhaps most extraordinary about Franklin's diplomatic triumph in Paris is that he accomplished it with such a bumbling cast of fellow diplomats. Silas Deane, for example, tried to recruit a pyromaniac to burn a British shipyard, considered inciting an Irish rebellion, and hoped to seize an island in the Mediterranean for the United States—not exactly a flourishing example of the new diplomacy. Thomas Jefferson daydreamed throughout his life about ways to expand his Empire for Liberty toward Florida, Cuba, and the Southwest. After the Revolution, John Adams predicted that popular government would "spread over the northern part of that whole quarter of the globe." As if that were not specific enough, he also wrote, "Canada and Nova Scotia must soon be ours; there must be war for it; they know how it will end, but the sooner the better."

If 1783 was a highly idealistic moment, it was also a time for the expression of private skepticism. A secret pact of the 1778 U.S.-French alliance was far less utopian than the public document based on the Model Treaty, and promised piratical benefits to each country that generations of European foreign ministers would have understood (France had the right to seize the British West Indies, and the United States had the right to seize Canada). Then the Americans broke their promise to France not to settle separately with the British, infuriating their ally. Without a doubt they had accomplished something just short of miraculous by winning a war against a superior adversary, securing the support of a historic enemy, and then running roughshod over the interests of both in the treaty that ended the war. But it was a curiously nonidealistic way to advance America's famous idealism.

Still, independence had been achieved, a republic launched, and a millennium of sorts introduced on earth. Best, the thought began to take root that this was a millennium open to all, at least in theory. The Calvinist internationale may have been restricted to a certain kind of believer, but liberty demanded no passport. Thomas Paine was the founder most attuned to the idea of America's essential openness (since he himself was a recent immigrant). But Franklin, writing from Paris as he was willing his country into existence, quickly grasped that the Revolution's availability to the world gave it unworldly importance:

> Tyranny is so generally established in the rest of the world, that the prospect of an asylum in America for those who love liberty, gives general joy, and our cause is esteemed the cause of all mankind . . . Glorious is it for the Americans to be called by Providence to this post of honor.

A PROSPECT INTO FUTURITY

> A great revolution has happened—a revolution made, not by chopping and changing of power in any one of the existing states, but by the appearance of a new state, of a new species, in a new part of the globe. It has made as great a change in all the relations, and balances, and gravitations of power, as the appearance of a new planet would in the system of the solar world. —Edmund Burke

Nothing expresses the strangeness of the infant United States like the fact that so many Europeans resorted to extraterrestrial imagery to describe it. What exactly was this new planet? Was it, as Thomas Pownall presumed, part of the existing system of states? Or was it a comet unto itself? Americans had succeeded brilliantly in breaking free—but would they ever be able to live up to their nearly unachievable ideals?

Without a doubt, the creation of the United States did advance liberty, by almost any index of measure. More people could vote after the

Revolution, the example of republican government led to stirrings abroad, and even the most hidebound governments around the world were forced to examine themselves and wonder if they were doing all that they could to serve their people. A spectacular example had been given to the world of what people were capable of if left to their own devices.

But it is not difficult to find ways in which the United States failed to live up to its own standards. All countries do. Still, what peculiarly characterized the early United States was its occasional failure to support liberty while specifically talking about liberty. That slavery was a shocking counterexample to all of the soaring generalities of the Declaration is obvious. What is even more disturbing is to see how often Americans defended slavery in the name of freedom. How strange it must have been to see a ship named *Liberty*—a literal ark of the liberties—unloading its human cargo (at least one such vessel existed). Slave rebellions often invoked "liberty" in exactly the same language that white Americans were using to secure economic and political rights. In South Carolina's Stono Rebellion (1740), for example, the slaves marched under a banner that said simply, "Liberty." That noble plea, based on their own example, was uncomfortable for white Americans to refuse, though they managed, with great effort, to do so.

Sometimes, as the historian Edmund S. Morgan has shown, the very people who spoke most loudly about liberty in the years leading up to the Revolution were the ones least likely to grant freedom to enslaved African-Americans. It does not surprise that during the war, the Earl of Dunmore was able to recruit slaves successfully for his Ethiopian Regiment in the British army in Virginia by simply promising emancipation. One wonders what the Continentals thought as they came face-to-face on the battlefield with their former slaves, fighting under a banner that read "Liberty to Slaves"—more or less exactly what they claimed to be fighting for, in a different context.

Despite its imperfections, the Revolution easily won the hearts and minds of most Americans, and grew to assume a cosmic significance for future generations, especially as the founders aged into patriarchs. In 1787, as one revolution was winding down and several new ones were beginning, John Adams tried to peer into the mists of the future. Its size was daunting, and he wrote, "A prospect into futurity in America is like contemplating the heavens through the telescopes of Herschel." For the rest of their long lives, he and Jefferson would write each other in amazement at the vastness of what they had wrought. But for all their satisfaction, America was never quite enough, and the world was always in their thoughts. Adams predicted, "Our pure, virtuous, public-spirited, federative republic will last forever, govern the globe, and introduce the perfection of man." Adams wrote in another letter to a friend that the Revolution's effects had already been "awful over a great part of the globe," adding, "When and where are they to cease?" The answer to that is simple: never and nowhere. Jefferson's final letter, clearly written to posterity, left no doubt that he expected the Revolution to go on, forever and everywhere. "May it be to the world, what I believe it will be, (to some parts sooner, to others later, but finally to all), the signal of arousing men to burst the chains," wrote the high priest of democracy from his deathbed.

There can be no denying that independence was an extraordinary achievement. Americans did not precisely invent liberty or democracy, and neither word perfectly described the imperfect system put into place. But now, at last, the people of the United States had given the world the first working model of what the future might look like. *Liberty* was no longer a philosopher's word, an electrical filament to be plucked from the ether. Hereafter, it was real. The French thinker Condorcet put it well: "It is not enough that the rights of man be written in the books of philosophers and the hearts of virtuous men; the ignorant and weak man must be able to read them in the examples of a great people. America has given us this example." "The Declaration of Independence makes a difference," Melville wrote a friend decades later. Its claims would not always be honored by other nations—more often they were not. But by writing out a realistic catalogue of human liberties, and signing their names to it, the founders had put those liberties on the map. Once again, a new world had been sighted.

Despite the optimism of its founders, the young republic faced severe challenges as it raced to confront the nineteenth century and beyond. No nation on earth held more potential, yet no nation was more inconsistent. At times modest and conciliatory, at other times blustery and dismissive, the new nation's rhetoric expanded and contracted like a wheezy accordion. Americans enjoyed precise, lawyerly statements of their rights as citizens; but they listened ecstatically to vaporous statements about the immense future. They sought a new system of relations between nations, based on the Enlightenment; but they violated the rules like every other nation, angled for advantage wherever possible, and looked covetously on land that was not theirs. They blithely ignored the Old World as they developed the New; but they suffered from the particular version of attention deficit disorder that all younger siblings know, wondering why the older powers were not paying it more heed. Like the Liberty Bell itself, this compound of many elements had a few cracks from the moment it was cast.

It would be difficult for any nation, so conceived and dedicated, to live up to all of these expectations. Now Americans had to confront the double strangeness of inhabiting a country like no other—the world's avatar of freedom—and a normal country as well, with treaties, and boundaries, and all the problems that afflict societies, especially those growing quickly. All in all, it would be fair to say that the United States of America was utterly unprepared for the vast global responsibilities it claimed to possess. The new government, finally stable after several misstarts, barely knew where its powers began and ended, or where its territory was demarcated. But perhaps the future would offer sufficient time and space to work out some of these inconsistencies. *Liberty* has always been a large word, able to contain multitudes. In the next century, its coordinates would become slightly more precise.

CHAPTER FOUR

EMPIRE OF LIBERTY

WHERE LIBERTY DWELLS

The United States appears to be destined by Providence to plague America with misery in the name of liberty. —Simón Bolivár

The glorious nineteenth century, predicted by all patriotic Americans to be an era of transcendent greatness, opened with a voyage so humbling that it is easy to understand why it quickly faded into grateful obscurity. The USS *George Washington*, the pride of the Navy, had been dispatched to the Mediterranean to sort things out with the stubborn pirates, emirs, and deys of North Africa. Since independence, American ships were unprotected by the British Navy and vulnerable to all manner of assaults on their dignity by the handful of small states that dotted the Barbary coast, including a constant demand for bribery and tribute that was eating up a large share of the foreign-policy budget. The *George Washington* set off with the noblest intentions, but quickly learned how little power the world's only republic wielded. Not only did the dey of Algiers commandeer the ship; he then sent her and her crew to Constantinople, loaded with the additional bribes that he was expected to pay the sultan.

The ignominious result was that the *George Washington*'s hold was crammed to the gills with ill-gotten gains, the gift of one undemocratic regime to another. In addition to cash and jewelry, the tribute included hundreds of African slaves, cows, horses, sheep, antelope, lions, tigers, ostriches, and parrots. Despite the echo of Noah, this was no ark of the liberties. In addition to the stench and the insults of the Algerians, the Americans were chagrined by the knowledge that their country was more or less a laughingstock in the Mediterranean.

There was one bright spot, however. The sultan thought that the American flag was pretty—its stars reminded him of Islam's crescent moon, and he felt a "celestial affinity" with another people who worshiped toward the sky. The United States of America had little power to project, and God knows its democratic ideals impressed no one at the sultan's court, but at least its founders had an attractive design sense.

The odoriferous realities of that voyage could not have contrasted more starkly with the glittering generalities being spoken at home. In the heady days following independence, no prediction of America's future greatness was too outlandish. From all corners of the union, especially the corners that kept moving westward, Americans longed for the day when the United States would be at the center of global events rather than their periphery. Despite the feebleness of a government that was laughably small compared to Europe's monarchies, a telltale heart beat expansively at the center of this new political entity—even then called an empire of the future.

Our Declaration of Independence may invoke the right of self-determination against distant tyranny and claim that all nations ought to make their own way in the world, free from imperial dominion. But even on the shakiest days of the early republic—and there were many—we never effectively concealed our longing for the spread of our democratic revolution to other nations, and by extension our influence upon them. These thoughts were not always expressed in the pronouncements of high officials—especially while the country was led by a great champion of moderation, George Washington. But still, a restless longing for more—more land, more sway, more respect—can be detected well before the United States achieved the power necessary to wrest it.

Some of this imperial drive stemmed from the natural gregariousness of a people with a relentless energy for making friends and business partners. Their staggering ambition can be measured quite precisely by the numbers of miles they were willing to travel to find new markets in Asia, South America, and Africa. But American expansiveness was also tied to the unique circumstances of the new nation's political position in the world. As freedom's petri dish, the United States had a great deal to prove.

If *liberty* was the knell of the Revolution, it was equally audible in its aftermath, as a wobbly United States tried to join a community of nations that was not especially disposed to welcome it. Seeking to explain their new situation to themselves, their dwindling number of friends, and their rising list of adversaries, the founders fell back effortlessly on the vocabulary of American destiny. Often in private, occasionally in public, the first generation of American leaders articulated their deep yearning for the day that liberty would reign from sea to shining sea. The poet-diplomat Joel Barlow compared the birth of the nation to the birth of the Savior (it was proven by the fact that the three kings had walked from the east to the west, toward America). Like the Puritan millennialists, these prophets of American grandeur felt a particular fascination with the Near East. Barlow predicted that "freedom's cause" would

> Brave the dread powers, that eastern monarchs boast
> Explore all climes, enlighten every coast;
> Till arts and laws, in one great system bind,
> By leagues of peace, the labors of mankind.

Just after the peace treaty that codified American independence was signed, Ezra Stiles, the president of Yale, gave a remarkable sermon that celebrated the arrival of "God's American Israel" and predicted its new place in the world, citing that old millennial favorite, the book of Daniel:

> This great American revolution, this recent political phænomenon of a new sovereignty arising among the sovereign powers of the earth, will be attended to and contemplated by all nations. Navigation will carry the American flag around the globe itself; and display the Thirteen Stripes and New Constellation at Bengal and Canton, on the Indus and Ganges, on the Whang-Ho and the Yang-Tse-Kiang; and with commerce will import the wisdom and literature of the east. That prophecy of Daniel is

> now literally fulfilled—ishotatu rabbim vetrabbeh hahaugnt—there shall be a universal travelling to and fro, and knowledge shall be increased. This knowledge will be brought home and treasured to America; and being here digested and carried to the highest perfection, may reblaze back from America to Europe, Asia and Africa, and illumine the world with TRUTH and LIBERTY.

Nor was this poetic license. A hundred years earlier, a Puritan divine's meditation on Babylon would simply have been the result of too much time cloistered in a library. But these were no longer place names from biblical antiquity—they were real ports in real contact with the American traders now crisscrossing the map like so many lines of longitude. The first American vessel to reach Canton, *The Empress of China*, departed New York in 1783, the very year the war ended. A year later, the *United States* left for India, launching that commerce. Soon the Stars and Stripes were fluttering over Indonesia, Indochina, Hawaii, and the Philippines. Between 1786 and 1810, 578 American vessels stopped at Mauritius! Between 1795 and 1805, American trade with India exceeded that of all European nations (then conveniently at war with each other) combined. Tiny islands in the South Pacific were suddenly named after George Washington and New England townships. An 1828 Navy report claimed that Americans had discovered 233 islands, reefs, and rock clusters in the Pacific alone. These were commercial ventures, of course, but they brought intellectual commerce as well, and the new vocabulary of republicanism flavored the bartering. Far from North America, the word *liberty* spread, almost as a synonym for the strange new people swarming around the world.

After the Revolution, Condorcet wrote, "The rights of men were nobly upheld and expounded without restriction or reserve, in writings that circulated freely from the shores of the Neva to those of the Guadalquivír." In 1790, the Flemish declared independence from the Austrian Hapsburgs in very American language. Greece, the birthplace of democracy, began to stir with aspirations for statehood, inspired by the nation that it had inspired. Ireland was roiled, not for the last time, by rumors of revolution—and would-be revolutionaries found it immensely significant to look to the sunset and see that the western skies bore "the resemblance of an immense pile of fuel, the flame breaking out," coming from the fabled "Land of Liberty." Had not the northern lights first appeared to the Irish people at exactly the time of the American Revolution?

In 1786, a Boston merchant described a strange scene unfolding before him in the ancient Portuguese-Chinese port of Macao, a shrine to imperialism if ever there was one. It would be hard to find a den of thieves less likely to pay attention to the pieties of the new republic coming into existence on the far side of the world. And yet Samuel Shaw saw tables that "were ornamented with representations, in paper painted and gilt, of castles, pagodas, and other Chinese edifices, in each of which were confined small birds. The first toast was Liberty! and in an instant, the doors of the paper prisons being set open, the little captives were released, and, flying about us in every direction, seemed to enjoy the blessing which had just been conferred upon them."

But in spite of these expectations, all was not perfect at home. In some ways, the first generation of U.S. citizens lived in a paper construction of their own. Our hushed reverence for the founders has obscured our grasp of how awkward a predicament they were in immediately after creating the new nation they freighted with the hopes of all humanity. It is not simply that their position was relatively weak as their experiment began. They also created such high expectations for American greatness among their own people that it was difficult to live up to them, or even to define them precisely.

These inconsistencies were suppressed at first, albeit barely, as the new government struggled for its footing. But from the earliest hours of the federal experiment, America's place in the world was a lightning rod of controversy, and the feral arguments that foreign policy produced among the first generation exposed all too many weaknesses in the new system. These tensions, added to the difficulty of starting a new country, gave our early foreign policy a chaotic, lurching quality we do not remember as clearly as we should. A glimpse at the bitter debates of the 1790s suggests that the anxieties we fight over today are deeply rooted. All of it, the swagger and the doubt, was present at the creation. American policy-makers wandered in a diplomatic wilderness of their own making, alternating between grandiose claims of God's providence and violent hostility toward foreigners. It is as if the designers of our nearly perfect federal machine allowed one of the essential cogs to be cast with an inferior metal.

Consider how odd it must have been to be a government official in the early republic, trying to balance unwieldy aspirations of greatness with the practical necessities of governing a new nation with little idea of where it began and ended. Americans had declared a new world order—yet it was starkly clear that no one else had joined this new order. Americans had declared no limits to their expansiveness as a people, but in fact, there were precise limits, from treaties to rivers and oceans, that served as a check on expansion. Americans believed a more idealistic foreign policy was possible, but they issued a series of fraudulent treaties with Native Americans—nations in their own way—that they refused to honor; between the natives and the various frontier insurgencies, one could argue that as many people were trying to flee the new government as support it. Americans had declared that freedom was the inevitable, irresistible wave of the future. But that future was very much in doubt during the first decade of the republic, especially after the carnage of the French and Haitian revolutions, keenly felt in the United States, where thousands of refugees fled from liberty's excesses. Furthermore, the world's monarchies felt a strong interest in ensuring that democracy would be stillborn, confined to the mutant civilization of the North American forest, where it could be dismissed as an anthropological oddity, like a dancing bear or a two-headed dog.

The United States would ultimately achieve the greatness its boosters longed for. But it would do so only after overcoming the opposition of the established powers, and quite a bit of self-inflicted damage. In one of those stirring quotations that the founders always seemed ready to provide future speechwriters, Benjamin Franklin said, "Where liberty dwells, there is my country." His disciple Thomas Paine responded, "Where liberty is not, there is mine." Although similar on the surface, there is a world of difference between these two remarks. The story of the first century of the United States is more or less the passage from the first to the second.

THE AMERICAN ÆRA

> I will agree to be stoned as a false prophet if all does not end well in this country [France]. Here is the first chapter in the history of European liberty.
>
> —Thomas Jefferson (1789)

On the tiny island of Minorca, near Spain, there is a small, forlorn cemetery that contains thirty-seven graves, nearly all young Americans who died far from home in the service of the U.S. Navy. Local tourists, spilling out of discos, can be forgiven if they are oblivious of the cemetery and its significance. For this site also marks the graveyard of America's first aspirations to put some teeth into its optimistic foreign policy. Long before the Naval Academy was created, in the earliest years of the new century, this remote harbor served as the training ground for Americans seeking to defend their country's honor from the depredations of Christian Europe and Islamic Africa. It was abandoned in 1848, the year that so many hopes for Europe failed. Adjusting American ideals to fit the world's reality would be an eternal work in progress.

Why was early foreign policy so difficult? Part of the reason is simply that hopes ran so high, and ideology was confused with genuine national interest. Hamilton generally kept his emotions in check, but Paine and Jefferson claimed an "American Æra" was beginning that would complete the Revolution by extending its soaring principles to peoples on every continent. It did not matter that our victory had been completely dependent on France, or that our definition of liberty did not extend to all Americans. What was essential was that a new history had begun.

But there were a few questions the founders had not thought through very well while designing their utopia. Since the American Æra would eschew war, there was no need to maintain a large army and navy, and Congress obliged by disbanding the latter and nearly eliminating the former as well. Since the American Æra would eschew unfair trade barriers between nations, which ought to respect each other as equals, there was little need for customs agents. Since the American Æra would eschew the arthritic protocols of the old diplomacy, there was little need for a foreign ministry. In 1790, the State Department had a grand total of twenty-eight employees, twenty of whom were stationed overseas.

In unguarded moments, the founders sometimes voiced the hope that a day might come when no foreign policy apparatus would be needed at all. Hamilton hated the thought that we might be "a ball in the hands of European powers, bandied against each other at their pleasure." Adams thought that we should "recall every minister from Europe and send embassies only on special occasions." Most extreme of all, Jefferson wanted to imitate China and avoid all commerce and interaction with Europe—a wish he nearly fulfilled with his disastrous embargo of 1807. In a perfect world, foreign countries would not even exist, and Americans would be left with their contemplative reveries about human perfection.

These pleasant fantasies had an unfortunate tendency to reduce the influence of the world's only democracy, and for that reason the American Æra had some difficulty finding its footing. To begin with, it was hard to tell that the Americans had achieved any kind of victory in the war for independence. While the Treaty of Paris confirmed independence, it did not provide much in the way of security for a lonely nation at the periphery of civilization. The British had promised to remove their forts in the interior of North America, a promise they flagrantly failed to fulfill. Years after the treaty, the forts were still there, in such places as Detroit and Niagara, taunting the Americans. When Spain threatened to close access to the Mississippi River, the United States was powerless to stop it.

To add insult to injury, the infant United States was not very successful at policing its own borders. Large sections of the interior were under the most tenuous control of the federal government, thanks to frequent attacks by natives and their various allies, British, Spanish, and French. Of course, the most rebellious insurgents may have been the Americans themselves. One of the earliest examples of a people inspired by the Declaration of Independence were the residents of Vermont, who in 1777 imitated its language and seceded from New York and Great Britain—before it was clear that they would join the United States!

When Pennsylvanians launched an armed uprising over a tax on whiskey in 1794, forming "Friends of Liberty" as they had during the Revolution, George Washington considered it a grave threat to his administration and personally led the American army into battle one more time, against his own people. This was essential, he explained, because "we had given no testimony to the world of being able or willing to support our government and laws." Even a skirmish with farmers needed to be explained in terms of the global significance of the American experiment.

This was only one of countless challenges faced by George Washington as he sought to give an identity to a foreign policy whose substance invariably lagged behind its aspirations. One especially difficult test case for liberty unfolded almost exactly as Washington's administration began. The storming of the Bastille in Paris occurred about ten weeks after the new U.S. president was sworn in on April 30, 1789. And if it came as a surprise, it was not entirely a coincidence. By its example, and even more by its expense, the American Revolution had quickened the revolutionary tendencies that began to seize the French monarchy by the throat in that year.

To many Americans eager to grasp at anything that would validate their bold experiment, the news from Paris seemed the culmination of something very large indeed. Many Americans felt desperate enthusiasm for this new manifestation of liberty, and none felt it more keenly than Thomas Jefferson, then minister to France. Jefferson was deeply involved with the early stages of the French Revolution. It was fitting that the author of the Declaration of Independence should help to compose the great French charter of liberty, the Declaration of the Rights of Man and the Citizen, and Jefferson hosted revolutionaries in his apartments when the Revolution still seemed like an Enlightenment parlor game, an innocent reshuffling of the royal deck, and not yet a bloodbath.

But Jefferson's enthusiasm was countered by the coolness felt by other officials toward anything that might embroil the new American government in circumstances beyond its control. And so, near the beginning of U.S. history, a deep gulf over foreign policy divided the government, and this gulf was itself the crucible of the earliest political parties in our history. In 1790, Jefferson became secretary of state, and from this position he began to build the nation's first opposition, originating in exactly the question that we still labor to answer: Where does the American Revolution begin and end? Many of Jefferson's friends—including large numbers of people fleeing the old regimes of Europe—felt that America was implicitly interested in any effort to topple foreign monarchies. Their opponents, the Federalists, behind Washington and Hamilton, felt that the world worked better with clear boundaries and clear definitions of the national interest. Jefferson tried to explain away some of the French Revolution's excesses with an offhand remark to Lafayette, suggesting that one does not travel "from despotism to liberty in a feather-bed." After a few more years of savagery, the French writer Camille Desmoulins would offer an even more cynical observation about beds, nearly unprintable: "Liberty is a bitch who likes to be bedded on a mattress of cadavers." By that point, many Americans would have agreed with him.

As might be expected, the earliest attempts of the U.S. government to support or even to affect foreign revolutions were inconsistent and weak. It was simply impossible, with limited military strength and an ocean of separation, to influence Europe directly. But at the same time, idealists among the founders wanted desperately to believe that the Declaration of Independence would live up to its global message. How, precisely, this would happen was a matter of deep division. It was a diplomatic challenge for Americans to arrange treaties with foreign governments, few of whom reposed much confidence in the new regime; it was perhaps even harder for them to come to terms with each other. A series of irritants in the 1790s brought out, time and again, how little agreement there was over American foreign policy. When a French diplomat, Edmond Genêt, tried to excite Americans to send military aid to France, he nearly caused riots. Decades later, in a letter to Jefferson, John Adams used a strikingly modern word—*terrorism*—to describe his horror at the huge crowds that had assembled in the name of liberty to argue for a new war against Britain, to defend France and the cause of international liberty:

> You certainly never felt the Terrorism excited by Genêt, in 1793, when ten thousand People in the Streets of Philadelphia, day after day, threatened to drag Washington out of his House, and effect a Revolution in the Government, or compel it to declare War in favour of the French Revolution, and against England.

John Jay was nearly hanged in person and repeatedly in effigy merely for negotiating a commercial treaty with Britain. Intense emotions were unleashed by the XYZ Affair, in which the French tried to exact bribes from Americans; by the assaults of both British and French navies upon American commerce; and by the vitriolic arguments at home over all of these events. The notorious Alien and Sedition Acts, promulgated by John Adams, were designed precisely to get his critics to shut up—an impulse that many modern presidents can surely relate to.

Why was the arid world of foreign policy so fraught with emotion? A quick answer is that the entire American experiment seemed to be riding on it. Europe's great powers, despite their distance, could inflict crippling harm on the young republic's economy if they chose, and the threat of another invasion was never far away. With Britain and France nearly always at war, it was all the United States could do to stay out of harm's way. But another answer is that the experiment felt so experimental. How else to explain the bitter mood swings between the warring camps inside the first cabinet? Also, Americans themselves were changing rapidly due to the large numbers of immigrants arriving and the destabilizing movement of huge populations toward the west. These immigrants, fleeing authoritarian regimes in Europe, subscribed naturally to the antimonarchical rhetoric Jefferson favored—and irritated the wealthier Americans who had little interest in disrupting the standing order. But an older explanation for the excitement lay just below the surface. If the French Revolution pleased secular thinkers, eager to see the separation of church and state, it also thrilled American evangelicals for the special hostility it reserved for members of the Catholic clergy.

It is intriguing to go back into their writings to see how enthusiastically Americans followed events in Paris. France may have been a recent ally, but, no matter, the news that kings and cardinals were suffering terribly came as thrilling news to Americans who had long been familiar with the older accents of millennialism. Some dared, once again, to think that it was the beginning of The End. Trumpets were sounding, vials were opening, and the destruction of Babylon was imminent. The first postmaster general, Samuel Osgood, even wrote books on the subject, and judged that humankind had entered the period of "the feet and toes," a preliminary phase. More patient than most, Osgood expected the final phase to come around 1970—a judgment many conservatives might have agreed with during the 1960s.

The convulsion of a major ally would have been plenty for most presidents to handle, but Washington also had to deal with a second revolution, closer to home. If the French Revolution seemed apocalyptic at times, it paled in comparison with the horrors of the Haitian Revolution, inspired by it to a degree. It would be satisfying to argue that America's love of liberty, so vocally expressed in the French context, extended to the closer reaches of the Caribbean. Unfortunately, the case is not that simple. Some early Americans compared the American Revolution to a sunrise, with rays of light bathing humanity for the first time, but judging from the Haitian perspective, this solar event had more in common with an eclipse, where the amount of light available depended very much on what part of the earth you were viewing it from.

The obscurity of the Haitian Revolution, far bloodier and closer than the French Revolution, is itself an indication of a fact that remains as true now as it was in 1791, when it began. Haitian ideas about liberty fit uncomfortably alongside American ones. When *liberty* justified African-Americans freeing themselves, and killing white masters to do it, the word began to take on a quality that many Americans found disquieting.

This was all the more awkward because many leaders of the Haitian Revolution had gained their first notions of war and liberty while fighting alongside the Americans in their War for Independence. To be sure, the contending Haitian factions were imperfect in their quest for a democratic ideal, spilling rivers of blood in a brutal factional struggle that sickened observers. But Toussaint-Louverture did at least voice the aspiration toward freedom, and he spoke the magic word *liberty*. "I wanted to make the cause of liberty legitimate and sacred even to its ardent enemies," he explained to those who would listen. Employing a logic that few Americans could have disagreed with, Haiti's new leaders proclaimed that liberty was preferable to slavery: "Swear then to live free and independent, and to prefer death to every thing that would lead to replace you under the yoke."

The U.S. government was equally imperfect in its support of this fledgling freedom movement. But to its credit, it did not stand by in complete idleness. Under Washington, and then Adams, a policy of quiet indifference gradually turned into commercial and even military support—support without which it would have been impossible for the experiment in black democracy to survive. Several founders were impressive in their active sympathy for Haiti—particularly Alexander Hamilton and Timothy Pickering, secretary of state under Adams. Hamilton, whose childhood best friend, Edward Stevens, was the U.S. consul to Haiti and close to Toussaint, even drafted a constitution for the Haitian republic. An exasperated British official, already sympathetic to Toussaint, complained that the Americans were even more sympathetic: "Our Policy is to protect, theirs to destroy the present Colonial System. Our views only go to a partial, theirs to a complete opening of the Saint Domingo market. We are willing to submit to a temporary evil to avoid a greater; they see no evil and some of them much good in the present situation of Saint Domingo."

It is counterintuitive to learn that the Federalists, normally dismissive of idealism and revolution, went to these lengths to sustain Toussaint, while the Republicans, normally so enthusiastic, went to great lengths to cut him off. But racial politics have never been easy to interpret in American history, and Thomas Jefferson's are especially impenetrable. The murk of early American Haiti policy only deepens when it is recalled that large numbers of Haitian refugees, from all backgrounds, were flooding into American cities in this decade, all clamoring for an elusive justice that the United States was in no position to provide. Still, the overwhelming sensation left by any reading of these distant and poorly assembled materials is that the world's avatar of freedom did little to support the cause of freedom in the first major opportunity that presented itself.

As if two revolutions and a bitter partisan divide at home were not enough to deal with, George Washington also had to confront a surprising range of problems in the Islamic world. North African ships had been pursuing American traders since at least 1783, and thanks to some help from an unlikely source (Spain), one of the first treaties signed by the United States with a foreign power was concluded with Morocco in 1787. It was ratified by the old Congress while the Philadelphia Convention was preparing to replace it. But the occasional seizures of American ships by North Africans continued, all the more annoying because American merchants were bottled up by British strictures and had to find new trade routes. This was one of the earliest lessons that independence would be more complicated than the founders had originally bargained for.

In fact, the Middle East had never been as far from American foreign policy as we might imagine, or as the phrase *Middle East* would suggest. The United States has been in the Middle East nearly as long as it has been in North America. It was a perfect place, then as now, to learn a basic truth: the world as it should be is a long way from the world as it is. Surprisingly, Islam was often mentioned by the founders as they sought to demonstrate their tolerance of different faiths. It was a rather easy thing to tolerate, given the relative absence of Muslims in America at the time, but still, the important thing is that they said it at all. "Even if the Mufti of Constantinople were to send such a missionary to preach Mohammedanism to us," Benjamin Franklin declared, "he would find a pulpit at his service." In what might be the finest thing he ever wrote, Washington's letter to the Jewish community at Newport, Rhode Island, described a world of mutual toleration with Middle Eastern landscapes, where "every one shall sit in safety under his own vine and figtree."

In sum, the presidency in its first years had no shortage of foreign-policy predicaments, many with ramifications that modern audiences will instantly recognize. Americans fought among themselves, offered imperfect responses to crises abroad, encountered difficulties with Islam, and experienced a persistent gap between the reality of what they could do in the world and the idealism of a self-appointed destiny.

Fortunately, there was a potent cure for these familiar ailments. If we have too often indulged in grandiloquent schemes about our place in the universe, we have also, at just the right moment, been brought back down to earth by unusually sane leaders. As usual, George Washington was there to provide his excitable countrymen with a perfectly modulated response. He steadily advocated neutrality throughout his presidency, including an important proclamation in April 1793 that stated clearly his idea that the United States would not be drawn into European wars—setting an important precedent in international law. The Farewell Address he delivered to the American people in September 1796 codified his thoughts even further. It remains the finest departure statement in our history and left Americans with a brilliant template for U.S. foreign policy in the century to come.

Washington's genius lay not only in what he said, but how he said it.

Before compiling the finished document, he asked for drafts from both James Madison and Alexander Hamilton, former friends who had written most of the *Federalist Papers*, but were now implacably divided into rival factions. The address is still lively to read, with modern resonance throughout. The former commander in chief warned against "overgrown Military establishments, which under any form of Government are inauspicious to liberty, and which are to be regarded as particularly hostile to Republican Liberty." He castigated politicians who exaggerate the faults of their opponents to gain power. And he argued throughout for the simple power of a union dedicated to the good of the whole and not to any constituency.

Some passages in this seminal document appear to be almost un-Washingtonian. Drawing on ideas from deep within American history, including the Great Awakening and the Enlightenment, the great realist wove an idealistic vision of a nation capable of a higher virtue, which might "give to mankind the magnanimous and too novel example of a People always guided by an exalted justice and benevolence." But he also argued forcefully against irrational emotions in the cold business of foreign relations and especially against long-term alliances with single nations for sentimental reasons: "The Nation, which indulges towards another an habitual hatred, or an habitual fondness, is in some degree a slave." He then urged that Americans refuse to "entangle" their peace in European power struggles when they can choose a higher "Destiny of Nations," unlike any that has gone before. He ended with a request, still so moving that later generations of Americans pause on occasion to reflect on his words:

> But if I may even flatter myself, that they may be productive of some partial benefit, some occasional good; that they may now and then recur to moderate the fury of party spirit, to warn against the mischiefs of foreign Intrigue, to guard against the Impostures of pretended patriotism; this hope will be a full recompence for the solicitude for your welfare, by which they have been dictated.

Of course, a pure disentanglement from foreign nations was impossible. No people can ever exist entirely separate from others, and especially not a people lusting for foreign trade, with ships crossing the

Atlantic and Pacific oceans at all times. Or a people populated, in perpetuity, by immigrants fleeing foreign governments that they tend to despise. Or a people eagerly awaiting the union and regeneration of all humanity according to God's blueprint.

But those caveats reveal exactly why Washington's soothing balm was necessary in 1796. For all its limitations, his Farewell Address set in stone a moderate foreign policy that was desperately needed at the time, and that served the United States well for more than a century.

ENTANGLED

> Most of what is now the American continental homeland was once foreign territory, and became U.S. territory as a result of diplomacy and war.
>
> —Walter Lippmann

At first glance, Thomas Jefferson appeared to be continuing in Washington's tradition when he became president in 1801. His celebrated inaugural address echoed Washington's Farewell Address by modestly promising to avoid "entangling alliances." But near the end of the speech, Jefferson also reached back into the vocabulary of exceptionalism to call the United States the "world's best hope." In his second inaugural, in 1805, he went further still, likening America to Israel and the Promised Land.

Of course, he was entitled—the author of the Declaration could say more or less whatever he wanted to about our national destiny. But it surprises a little that the man who wrote Virginia's statute of religious freedom felt so comfortable in the evangelical idiom. And yet nothing about Jefferson was ever predictable, except that he was an adroit politician who knew how to speak to Americans in a language they enjoyed.

A closer look at the 1800 presidential campaign reveals that it surged with the energy of a camp meeting. Jefferson's running mate, Aaron Burr, was the grandson of the great revivalist Jonathan Edwards—which may have gained him one hundred thousand born-again votes, according to one handicapper. He was extremely popular in the evangelical regions where the flames of the Great Awakening still flickered. The more evangelical of Jefferson's supporters made no bones about linking their kind of religion with Jefferson's election—which they called "the Republican Millennium." One of them looked closely at the evidence and decided that the third candidate for the presidency in 1800, rotund and balding John Adams, resembled nothing so much as Nebuchadnezzar's toe—a well-known evil symbol from the book of Revelation. That is the kind of political attack it can be hard to recover from.

Jefferson's soothing inaugural words also appealed to Americans who were frankly exhausted by all the arguments over foreign policy that had characterized the first three presidential terms. The failure of John Adams to win reelection was in many ways a repudiation of his foreign policy, which had embroiled the United States in a quasi-war with France, continual difficulties with Britain, and harsh repression of his critics, increasingly vocal within his own party. Jefferson's call for unity came at a moment when Americans needed to hear it.

But an important reorientation was under way in Jefferson's thinking and would soon manifest itself in his policy. America's earliest millennialists had normally looked to Europe and the Holy Land for signs of premillennial activities—wars, religious purges, and the like. Jefferson was clearly past that and absorbed by the opportunities that lay immediately before him. Specifically, he was fascinated by the continent that spread toward the Pacific from his Virginia estate, Monticello—and anyone who has ever stood in his front hall, with its rickety animal skeletons and rotting hides, knows how close to the frontier our third president truly was. The West begins in that foyer.

As a younger man, Jefferson had observed the proprieties and understood that American expansion was clearly prohibited by a number of binding treaties. To the extent that he thought the West would develop—which he certainly did—it was as a foreign country, or a series of allied republics, sticking to each other like Velcro, with the help of the United States. He often expressed disdain for foreign adventures—especially when they involved the Haitian Revolution. In 1791, as secretary of state, he expressly denied that the United States had any designs on the Caribbean: "Whatever jealousies are expressed as to any supposed views of ours on the dominion of the West Indies, you cannot go farther than the truth in asserting that we have none. If there be one principle more deeply rooted than any other in the mind of every American, it is—that we should have nothing to do with conquest."

But eventually, for reasons of his own as well as the opportunities that Providence presented him with, Jefferson emerged as one of the greatest continental thinkers in American history. His "empire for liberty" became a crucial concept as the model republic broke away from one way of thinking (modest liberties, based on good government in a limited space) and embraced another (immodest liberties, based on universal rights in a limitless space). The Louisiana Purchase did not truly square with Jefferson's earlier ideas about strict construction and a limited executive. But Jefferson had reversed himself before, and only a shrill idealist could object to his decision to relax his principles before the greatest real estate offer in history.

That the West belonged to the United States was of course not a new thought—it was just that no government official had ever uttered it with quite the frankness that Jefferson now employed. But it was one thing to expand into the western region of an existing state or territory. It was quite another to enter a foreign country—which is exactly what the land across the Mississippi was before 1803. We have so many inaccurate notions about our westward expansion that it is difficult to list them all, but to suggest that our pioneers simply walked into land that was unoccupied, or occupied only by Native Americans, is blatantly wrong. Since the great European explorations of the sixteenth century, and the various land swaps thereafter, much of the North American interior was mapped and apportioned by Spain, France, and Britain. The simple act of crossing a river toward Texas might conceivably bring international consequences—as, in fact, it does today, for Mexicans traveling north. Before 1803, each settler's decision to cross that line—and there were many—was a violation of another nation's sovereignty. We built this country on thousands of tiny invasions.

Despite his punctilious observation of international law, Jefferson had cocked his eye toward the West many times before. In the 1780s, when he heard that the Spanish governor at New Orleans might allow American immigrants to come into Louisiana on the condition that they become Spanish citizens, he wrote, "I wish a hundred thousand of our inhabitants would accept the invitation. It will be the means of delivering to us peaceably what might otherwise cost us a war."

Jefferson also felt a lifelong pull south of the border, and toward the Caribbean in particular. He even floated the dubious theory that the U.S. might claim it someday, on the basis that the Mississippi flows into the Gulf of Mexico. But his normal sympathy for rebellion foundered upon the island of Hispaniola, where Haitians were trying to complete the revolution they had started in 1791. His new administration quickly reversed the tolerant policy toward Toussaint-Louverture that had been pursued by his predecessors. One historian, Roger Kennedy, seeking to explain Jefferson's curious aversion to revolution in this one instance, could find no explanation better than a stark statement of his racial beliefs, uttered in an unguarded moment. To the British ambassador, he wrote, blacks were "as far inferior to the rest of mankind as the mule is to the horse, and as made to carry burthens." Another explanation lies in the terror that the Haitian Revolution was unleashing every day, as Americans learned from the survivors themselves in the United States. Several frightening racial rebellions took place in the immediate aftermath of the Haitian Revolution, including the rebellion led by a Virginia blacksmith named Gabriel in 1800, the year of Jefferson's election. After this bloody incident, a slave informer remembered the haunting motto of the flag that the slaves had carried into battle: "Death or Liberty." Somehow, one doubts that this was the precedent the designers of New Hampshire's license plate had in mind.

Given Jefferson's loathing of Haiti, it is highly ironic that it was Toussaint who finally forced Napoleon to wash his hands of America and sell Louisiana. Beleaguered on all sides, tired of fighting the slaves and the diseases that were ravaging his army, Bonaparte finally agreed to the historic sale in 1803. In other words, Jefferson gained his Empire of Liberty through the exertions of an African people who were fighting for their liberty with no help from his administration. Henry Adams, our finest historian of the early republic, explained, "The prejudice of race alone [has] blinded the American people to the debt they owed to the desperate courage of five hundred thousand Haytian negroes who would not be enslaved."

The Louisiana Purchase transformed everything, of course, including the presidency, and the East as much as the West. The entire economy tilted toward the interior, as European as well as East Coast investors purchased land, and transportation systems quickly evolved to get people across the Appalachians as rapidly as possible, with goods flowing in the opposite direction. Territorial expansion now seemed so essential and permanent that it was difficult to understand that an intellectual revolution had just taken place. Around the time of the founding, the loose idea in popular currency was that American influence would expand around the world intangibly, as a result of the new nation's moral excellence. Now the United States would expand its influence simply by expanding itself.

It would be pleasant to agree with Jefferson that this enormous new acquisition of space did, in fact, create an Empire of Liberty. To be fair, in many ways it did. Europeans fleeing difficult situations were able to build homesteads and new careers that had been denied to them; immigrants were able to worship as they pleased; the land was generous to those willing to work it. But to see this new terrestrial reality as an expansion of pure American liberty is to ignore several important qualifications. Several recent historians have argued that the Louisiana Purchase benefited no one so much as the planters of the Deep South, who needed to expand the plantation economy for it to survive. They, too, spoke often of "liberty," but in a different sense than a Northerner might have used the word. A punctilious wordsmith might have noted that when they said "liberty," they meant "slavery." In fact, the laws punishing slaves in Louisiana grew substantially stricter after the United States purchased the territory.

But to give Jefferson credit, he did work on expanding some forms of liberty, and he did so far from American shores. Despite our early misadventures in the Mediterranean, the situation began to improve with a modest show of force. From 1801 to 1805, Jefferson sent vessels from the fledgling U.S. Navy to the coast of North Africa to prevent pirates from capturing American merchant vessels and demanding bribes from them. He did so from a sense of outrage that Americans were being denied the essential rights of free trade—a cardinal point of American foreign policy since its origins. But he also did so because it was a popular cause back home. The effective way in which the navy achieved its objectives and secured lasting treaty benefits for American traders taught Europeans as well as North Africans that the United States was willing to put firepower behind its idealism when the terms of the conflict were advantageous.

Of course, Americans were going other places as well, all the time. The geographer Jedidiah Morse built a great business in distributing maps of the world, subtly coloring them to strengthen American claims. It turned out he was a closet millennialist as well—a speech he delivered in 1810 predicted that what he called the Eastern and Western Antichrists (the Ottoman empire and the papacy) would end in 1866, at which point Jews and Muslims would be converted and the millennium would begin. The year 1810 also saw the founding of the American Board of Commissioners for Foreign Missions, which would lead to the creation of a network of American missionaries teaching and preaching around the world, with particular success in the Middle East. At its peak, their numbers dwarfed those of the State Department; their reports, dutifully compiled year after year, tell a remarkable story of Americans fanning out across Asia and Africa, in the most remote places possible.

The natural expansiveness of Americans took them south in great numbers as well, to Florida and Texas at first, where they settled with the permission of Spanish authorities, and then far beyond. Soon Latin America and the Caribbean were flooded with Yankees seeking opportunities for charity, investment, or just plain trouble. In the early years of the nineteenth century, the Declaration and Constitution were translated and distributed up and down the hemisphere, laying the groundwork for the wave of revolutions that would free the South American republics from Spain.

The pull of the south had other consequences. The War of 1812 has often been portrayed as a war for freedom, and so it was, in a remote sense. A chief irritant between the United States and Britain was the British practice of impressing (seizing) American sailors—a flagrant violation of human rights. One of the war's slogans was "Free Trade and Sailors' Rights." But a closer look at the congressional wellsprings of this conflict reveal how much of it was due to the hunger for land that consumed Southern and Western politicians. Liberty had precious little to do with it.

Support for the war was especially strong in a crescent that ran along the interior of the United States, from the hinterland of New England through upstate New York and the Great Lakes, the old Northwest, Kentucky, Tennessee, and the Southwest. This was the heartland of Jeffersonian Republicanism, and also of revivalist religion. Two overwhelming urges moved these supporters—in the Northwest, to annex Canada once and for all; in the South, to wrest Florida from Spain. These two urges were understood to be compatible, on the somewhat flimsy pretext that Great Britain (which controlled Canada) and Spain (Florida) were then allies. But a more credible explanation is that even at this early juncture, politicians were worried about the balance between free and slave states and thought that the country could quietly soothe those tensions if both regions could be acquired at the same time. There is fairly good evidence that a deal was struck to pursue exactly this plan. Evidence also suggests that the Southern plan favored by the slave states was pursued far more aggressively than the Northern counterbalance.

The longing for adjacent British territories had a venerable pedigree. New Englanders and New Yorkers had always dreaded the raids they suffered from the French and Indians to the north. As early as September 1776, Benjamin Franklin had sketched out a fairly outrageous set of terms that he hoped the British would agree to, including the cession of Quebec, Newfoundland, Nova Scotia, Bermuda, Florida, and the Bahamas. Even Gouverneur Morris, opposed to expansion, had written in 1803 that "all North America must at length be annexed to us—happy, indeed, if the lust of dominion stop there." Some of this was the hunger for land—but it also proceeded from the conviction that the British were arming Native Americans for the border raids that never stopped along the frontier.

In 1810, a group of "war hawks" in Congress began to agitate for a war to pursue these aims. They were young, talented, and intensely ambitious. Henry Clay, representing Kentucky, one of the centers of expansionist feeling, rose in Congress to declare his "hope to see, ere long, the new United States (if you will allow me the expression) embracing not only the old thirteen States, but the entire country east of the Mississippi, including East Florida, and some of the territories to the north of us also." John Calhoun of South Carolina was deeply involved, and the entire war party was supported by the administration of James Madison, Jefferson's successor and former secretary of state.

Of course, these sentiments, while true, were not as persuasive in the court of public opinion as the flowery language that Americans loved to hear about freedom, and so speeches turned to injured rights. Madison's annual message of November 5, 1811, attacked Britain for "trampling on rights which no independent nation can relinquish" and announced that Congress will soon put the country "into an armor and an attitude demanded by the crisis, and corresponding with the national spirit and expectations." Supporters predicted a quick and easy victory, followed by wealth. Critics complained about the new rhetoric, including a hilarious diatribe by John Randolph of Virginia against the monotony of these speeches ("We have heard but one word—like the whippoor-will, but one eternal monotonous tone—Canada! Canada! Canada!") and a curt dismissal of their real motive: "Agrarian cupidity, not maritime right, urges the war."

The early accents of Manifest Destiny were heard as another Kentucky congressman began to recompose the national boundaries in his mind: "The waters of the St. Lawrence and the Mississippi interlock in a number of places, and the great Disposer of Human Events intended those two rivers should belong to the same people." A New Hampshire counterpart added, "The Author of Nature has marked our limits in the south, by the Gulf of Mexico; and on the north, by the regions of eternal frost."

Understandably, the regions of eternal sunscreen beckoned more enticingly than the tundra to the north. Since the earliest days of the republic, Americans had been migrating with varying degrees of legality into Spanish regions, and the notorious Aaron Burr conspiracy of 1805–6 was built on the idea that restless men of the Southwest would flock to form a new empire that included Mexico and its vaunted silver mines. As far back as 1792, Jefferson fused the language of freedom with that of something more acquisitive when he ingeniously devised a claim to the Floridas and Louisiana based on the principle that the rivers flowing southward to the Gulf of Mexico were critical to the "natural rights" of settlers to send their commerce to the world.

The language of rights was conspicuously missing, however, as the Madison administration and its Southern allies set about acquiring Florida even before the war had officially begun. In March 1812 we might recognize, without too much difficulty, a predecessor for better-known events in the twentieth century. The White House agreed to turn the other way while secretly giving support to an underground militia group of self-styled "patriots" (mostly from Georgia) who planned to invade a Spanish fort in Florida (at Saint Augustine), then offer it to the United States on behalf of "local authorities." The Spanish caught wind of the plan and denounced it in no uncertain terms as an "invasion" that revealed "the depraved intentions" of the U.S. government.

The story is tawdry enough to begin with, but unfortunately it was colored further by an ugly racial component. To justify the attacks on Spanish Florida, George Matthews, the chief plotter of this "Revolution," spread the rumor that the British had ordered a detachment of black troops into the region to protect it. This was to justify Matthews's decision to order the "preoccupancy" of the region by American forces. The flag of the "patriots" showed a soldier charging with a bayonet, under the motto "Vox Populi Lex Suprema." The bayonet was a curious image to support a flag claiming to represent the voice of the people—but that was only one of several miscues in the operation. The entire charade fell apart when a local officer of the genuine U.S. military refused to offer support to what seemed to him an illegal enterprise. After a long period of silence, the White House maintained its plausible deniability and distanced itself from the effort.

War fever was hardly unanimous—the declaration on June 18, 1812, passed by only 79–49 in the House and 19–13 in the Senate. But once hostilities had commenced, the dreams of Florida and Canada became more legitimate, and proper expeditions were fitted out. Jefferson, watching a Virginian militia train, wrote that "the only inquiry they make is whether they are to go to Canada or Florida." In a letter to his friend Thaddeus Kosciuszko, the Polish hero of the American Revolution, Jefferson wrote, "Upon the whole, I have known no war entered into under more favorable auspices." He predicted that all British possessions in North America would soon be a thing of the past and added to another friend, "The acquisition of Canada this year, as far as the neighborhood of Quebec, will be a mere matter of marching."

That was only one of a number of things Jefferson was startlingly wrong about. He also thought New York might be burned, but that sympathetic dockworkers in London would retaliate against the British authorities. Curiously, almost nothing about the War of 1812 went as planned. The vaunted Royal Navy lost important battles, and the American army that had been so effective in the Revolution proved to be nearly invisible.

By the time the war finally ended, it had become unpopular in nearly every region of the country, especially those that depended on foreign trade. Despite Jefferson's confidence, Canada was never taken—the fourth invasion by Americans in a century (1745, 1759, 1775, 1812) resulted in no change whatsoever. An Ohio senator wrote, "War is a very pretty thing in theory, how it may terminate in practice is altogether a different consideration." Andrew Jackson's smashing victory over the British at New Orleans in January 1815 afforded a measure of respectability, but in truth the war had accomplished none of its objectives, and the White House had been burned in every sense. When the peace treaty was signed at Ghent on Christmas Eve 1814—two weeks before Jackson's victory—no language about the sacred rights of Americans was included. Nevertheless, Jackson and many others were quick to see the hand of God in their good fortune: "If ever there was an occasion on which providence interfered, immediately, with the affairs of men it seems to have been on this. What but such an interposition could have saved this Country?"

That question remains difficult to answer. Surely, Americans were endowed by their Creator with a remarkable love of liberty and a formidable ability to fight for it. But in the generation following the Declaration of Independence, they had shown an inconsistent talent for defining what, precisely, that liberty was.

THE MONROE DOCTRINE

John Quincy Adams is dimly remembered as the junior half of the first pair of father-son presidents. Yet he deserves to be honored by new generations not only for the single-minded virtue he brought to a career in public service that spanned half a century, but for his role as the chief architect of American foreign policy. Others have dramatically modified the structure since then—William Seward and Dean Acheson spring to mind—but for breadth and depth of service, no secretary of state has ever left a legacy comparable to that of John Quincy Adams. He took the feeble infrastructure bequeathed to him by the founders, gave it new strength of purpose, and left it intact for many generations to come.

More than most, he was bred to the job. As a child, one of his earliest memories was witnessing the plumes of smoke rising over Boston during the Battle of Bunker Hill in 1775. He lived so long that he was able to witness, as the Mexican War was ending, the beginnings of the argument that would culminate in the Civil War. His 1848 funeral, in turn, was one of the earliest memories of Oliver Wendell Holmes, Jr., the great jurist who lived into the FDR administration. The entire history of the United States can be traced in just a few lifetimes.

Adams occupied the White House for four years (1825–29), but his fame rests more enduringly on his contributions before and after his stint as president. In his long after-presidency, he spoke on behalf of the rising body of Northern antislavery opinion, earning the sobriquet Old Man Eloquent. Before his presidency, he did more to shape the way we interact with other nations than any other secretary of state before or since.

Adams was fortunate in his inheritance, and not only because he had two brilliant parents. He also inherited many of the finest qualities in both strains of American foreign policy—enough idealism to know what was precious and distinct about the United States, and enough realism to advance its cause effectively before the doubting councils of Europe. While he had some of his father's prickliness, he had also learned to improve upon it during a long and varied diplomatic career that took him from Russia to Holland and many places in between. Versed in many languages and protocols, he was extraordinarily effective in pressing for the needs of a growing country. In 1819, he distinguished himself in negotiating for Florida from Spain and securing the nation's eventual right to expand someday to the Pacific—a right that had not been recognized after independence. Adams was unlike most New Englanders in the continental breadth of his vision; he insisted that all of North America was "our proper dominion." He avoided unnecessary entanglements, but he advocated aggressively for the United States and was cowed by no one. It is rather typical that the act for which he is best remembered, the Monroe Doctrine, bears another's name.

But James Monroe, heir to Madison and Jefferson, also deserves credit for the extraordinary impact of his annual message of December 1823. Like his two Virginia predecessors, Jefferson and Madison,

Monroe was an ardent champion of American expansiveness. Since 1815, when the Napoleonic wars and the War of 1812 had finally ended, a welcome stasis had characterized both European and American politics. In the United States, the disappearance of the Federalists led to one-party rule, which was at the time considered healthy and normal. But America's growing wealth and population, combined with events in the hemisphere, led to renewed tension with Europe.

In a way, Napoleon was to blame, as was so often the case. After his invasion of the Iberian peninsula had profoundly destabilized Spain, the Spanish peoples of Central and South America had begun to agitate for their independence. In 1810, independent juntas formed in Buenos Aires, Bogotá, Caracas, and Santiago, and for the next two decades the republics of South America tried to come into existence, over the opposition of the European monarchies, and with the tacit and sometimes the active support of the United States. In 1811, James Madison expressed "a friendly solicitude in the welfare of these communities." For a time, it appeared that Spain would succeed in reasserting itself, but after 1817 the Latin American republicans began to turn the tide, and enthusiasm in the United States grew exponentially. The most ardent advocate in Congress of Pan-American independence was Henry Clay, the former war hawk, who lavished praise on South America in orations on the House floor.

This type of speech, now quite familiar, called on the United States to support the spread of freedom in the world and resist the dark forces that would oppose it. In this case, that meant the Holy Alliance that had sprung up in the wake of Napoleon—the European coalition dominated by the reactionary monarchies of Russia, Austria, and Prussia. In 1820, they came out and formally agreed to a position that Americans had long suspected, promising that they would suppress any internal political movements and republican tendencies they could find. Soon they proved their willingness to do so, as republican efforts in various sections of Italy were mercilessly extinguished. American indignation rose, and in 1822, the United States formally recognized the emerging new republics of Latin America—the only nation on earth to do so. In other words, the world picture was roughly the opposite of the way it is now: Americans were considered naively liberal and Europeans mindlessly conservative.

In these years of growing discord, Adams had done his part to fan the flames. A strong speech he gave on July 4, 1821, called for nothing less than the dismantling of the entire colonial apparatus. As he wrote to the British minister, in language that sounds like something Frantz Fanon would have used a century later, "The whole system of modern colonization was an abuse of government, and it was time that it should come to an end."

That Fourth of July speech is still quoted at length, for it eloquently captured an important point. Despite a few misadventures, the United States was still firmly on the side of the human rights articulated in the Declaration of Independence, and against the diplomacy of force that defined Europe. "She goes not abroad, in search of monsters to destroy," Adams said, because "she is the well-wisher to the freedom and independence of all. She is the champion and vindicator only of her own." Tellingly, Adams warned that if American policy were to change "from liberty to force . . . she might become the dictatress of the world," but "would no longer be the ruler of her own spirit."

The Monroe Doctrine drew on all of these thoughts, and took shape over 1823 as czarist Russia pressed to define its American possessions while Europe murmured about retaking South America. Although less than a decade had passed since their last war, the British and Americans began to see eye to eye, and neither liked the way the wind was blowing. For the British, any military incursions into the Americas would be bad business and disrupt the greater profits that they had been enjoying since the Spanish were booted out. For the Americans, Europeans were simply unwelcome. The so-called special relationship may have begun that August, when the British foreign secretary, George Canning, dispatched a note proposing that Great Britain and the United States sign a joint communiqué discouraging the European colonial powers from trying to recolonize South America. That was a flattering offer from the world's greatest military power. But it was not enough for Adams and Monroe, who wanted to issue a ringing proclamation of American ideas about liberty in the hemisphere, with no help from the British or anyone else. Adams wrote, "It would be more candid as well as more dignified to avow our principles explicitly to Russia and France, than to come in as a cock-boat in the wake of the British man-of-war."

Not only did the United States reject the right of a European nation—presumably France, then invading Spain—to intervene in the former Spanish colonies; it rejected the right of any European nation, including Russia, to intervene in the Americas at all. Monroe explained himself to Jefferson in terms the latter would have liked, still remembering the incomplete revolutions of the eighteenth century:

> Our relation to Europe is pretty much the same as it was in the commencement of the French revolution. Can we, in any form, take a bolder attitude to it, in favor of liberty, than we did? Can we afford greater aid to that cause, by assuming any such attitude, than we do now, by the force of our example?

Underlying the strong stance taken by Adams and Monroe was the conviction that democracy and monarchy were simply incompatible. Just as seventeenth-century Americans had imagined a global contest against papists, their nineteenth-century counterparts feared an international coalition of monarchies forming cabals against them. In 1822, Brazil had become a monarchy (its vibrant green and yellow flag takes its colors from two royal houses, the Braganças and Hapsburgs), and no one knew if other kings would follow. The domino theory may be a distant descendant of the idea that incompatible political systems cannot share a border without trying to subvert each other.

Europe was dismayed by the new doctrine, to put it mildly. The French responded by saying that "it ought to be resisted by all the powers possessing either territories or commercial interests in that hemisphere." Even the British were appalled, and Canning wrote, "We cannot acknowledge the right of any country to proclaim such a principle, much less to bind other countries to the observance of it." One could hardly have asked for a more satisfying response than that given by the spokesman of reaction (or perhaps I should say overreaction), Metternich. His anger revealed how wide the gulf truly was separating the New World from the Old World in 1823, and hinted at the religious differences that lay at the core of the two systems:

> These United States of America, which we have seen arise and grow, and which during their too short youth already meditated

> projects which they dared not then avow, have suddenly left a sphere too narrow for their ambition, and have astonished Europe by a new act of revolt, more unprovoked, fully as audacious, and no less dangerous than the former. They have distinctly and clearly announced their intention to set not only power against power, but to express it more exactly, altar against altar. In their indecent declarations they have cast blame and scorn on the institutions of Europe most worthy of respect, on the principles of the greatest sovereigns, on the whole of those measures which a sacred duty no less than an evident necessity has forced our governments to adopt to frustrate plans most criminal. In permitting themselves these unprovoked attacks, in fostering revolutions wherever they show themselves, in regretting those which have failed, in extending a helping hand to those which seem not to prosper, they lend new strength to the apostles of sedition, and reanimate the courage of every conspirator. If this flood of evil doctrines and pernicious examples should extend over the whole of America, what would become of our religious and political institutions, of the moral force of our governments, and of that conservative system which has saved Europe from complete dissolution?

Some European thinkers saw more in the Monroe Doctrine than audacity. Canning, for example, worried that he had unleashed a monster, and that "the great danger of the time" was "a division of the World into European and American, Republican and Monarchical; a league of worn-out Govts. on the one hand, and of youthful and strong nations, with the U. States at their head, on the other." The Russian ambassador to France wrote, "The Christian World tends to divide into two parts, distinct from, and I fear, hostile to, one another; we must work to prevent or defer this terrible revolution, and above all to save and fortify the portion which may escape the contagion and the invasion of vicious principles." That was language the Puritans would have understood, amid the global turmoil of the Reformation and Counter-Reformation. It is language that we still hear today, in a very different context.

The beauty of the strong language of the Monroe Doctrine has given rise to the belief that it was a vital bulwark of American liberty at the time and helped to avert a crisis. In fact, the United States had little authority to say any of the things it did, and no ability to do much if anyone disagreed. It did not own South America, and many European nations had legitimate possessions scattered throughout the hemisphere. The danger was almost certainly imaginary, for a close examination of the European powers at this moment suggests strongly that none of them had the capacity or the desire to undertake a military expedition to the Americas. Even if they had, the United States had almost no way to stop them, unless it acted in concert with the British. The U.S. Navy was less than an eighth the size of Russia's; it was about a quarter the size of France's.

In other words, the Monroe Doctrine was a tissue of highly exaggerated claims about what the United States would do, if it could, in response to a European invasion that was not going to happen, in places the United States had no jurisdiction over. Once again, our desire to influence the world outran our capacity.

But it was wonderful political theater, and as such, held currency. As a fact, the Monroe Doctrine may have been a failure. As an idea, it was a smashing success. The message was spectacularly popular at home. Old man Jefferson, to whom Monroe had sent an early version of the message, used the highest praise in his register: "The question presented by the letters you have sent me, is the most momentous which has ever been offered to my contemplation since that of Independence. That made us a nation, this sets our compass and points the course which we are to steer through the ocean of time opening on us." In Paris, Lafayette called it "the best little bit of paper that God had ever permitted any man to give to the World."

For all its limitations, it was truly a watershed moment in the history of our foreign policy, and it gave that much more ballast to the ark of the liberties, still sailing into strong headwinds. It not only proclaimed the United States worthy of making a major statement to Europe, but also held out the hope that the other Americas in the hemisphere might someday take comfort in the broad shade of the Declaration. Its echoes would reverberate far into the future—with Theodore and Franklin Roosevelt, with the Cuban Missile Crisis, and with the still powerful idea that this hemisphere must set a democratic example to the old. It will never stop reverberating.

GREEK FEVER

One of the strongest ideas in the Monroe Doctrine was the notion that the two hemispheres would agree not to interfere with each other; in other words, that the United States would leave Europe alone if it returned the favor. That notion, rooted in centuries of seeing the hemispheres as two different halves of the world (as countless maps depicted it), gave a philosophical and historical justification to the broad principles outlined. Amusingly, it was the relatively powerless Americans and not the Europeans who found it hard to live up to the new arrangement. At nearly the exact time that Monroe delivered his message, an enormous wave of sympathy crested in the United States for the Greek people, fighting for independence from the Ottoman Empire. For many reasons—democracy's origins in Greece, innate dislike of empires, and particular discomfort with empires of foreign faith—the American people underwent a brief but intense mania for the latest champions of liberty. Greek fashions in clothing and architecture swept the United States. Leading magazines took up the cause, including a definitive piece in the *North American Review* by Edward Everett that insisted that Americans had a strong role to play: "Liberty is the lesson, which we are appointed to teach . . . It is taught in our settlement, taught in our revolution, taught in our government; and the nations of the world are resolved to learn."

To a surprising degree, the debate over this foreign crisis reached to the highest circles of power. The situation was seriously debated on the floor of Congress, and resolutions were passed expressing sympathy with Greek insurgents. Daniel Webster gave a stirring speech that proclaimed eternal American sympathy with the fighters of revolutions against tyranny. The United States did not intervene—again, it could not have, even had it wanted to—but private sympathizers went to extraordinary lengths to send aid to the rebels, including ships fitted out from New York City, paid for by prominent citizens. Not much came of American involvement, and in fact the United States concluded an important military treaty with the Ottoman sultan in 1830, not long after the Greek uprising, proving that our tradition of realism in the Middle East is nearly as old as our tendency to fantasy. But the moment was interesting for showing, yet again, how badly Americans wanted to play a more important role than they were able to.

Part of the reason for the intensity of this infatuation was that it occurred at a moment of profound self-awareness for Americans, as they approached the fiftieth anniversary of their own independence and found countless anniversary occasions for the rhetorical excess that they craved. The rise of oratory was itself, in its way, a tribute to the Greek precedent, and Americans indulged in it as often as they could, from college campuses to county courthouses and everywhere in between. These speeches, rarely consulted by historians, offer an illuminating window into the way that Americans felt about themselves at the half-century mark.

Liberty, of course, was the word on the lips of these orators more than any other. But to read their speeches closely is to see how unresolved the word still was for most Americans. Audiences loved to hear grand promises of foreign liberation and thrilled to the belief that the American model was spreading, inevitably, to remote continents. But they were inconsistent—to put it charitably—about liberty at home. Nor were they all that consistent abroad, renouncing empire and grasping at it simultaneously. John Quincy Adams knew our inconsistency better than anyone else. A year after the Monroe Doctrine, he was elected president, and soon after his inauguration he determined to send a U.S. delegation to a Pan-American congress convening in Panama to discuss issues of hemispheric concern, including all the ideas expressed in the Monroe Doctrine, and other topics of great interest to the United States, from free trade to the rights of neutrals and the freedom of the seas. But the U.S. Congress refused to send the delegation, largely to spite Adams, but also because Southern leaders could not accept the idea that American diplomats might meet Haitian diplomats on equal terms. Missouri senator Thomas Hart Benton noted the delicacy of the relationship with Haiti, so near and yet so far from our model republic: "We purchase coffee from her, and pay her for it; but interchange no consuls or ministers . . . And why? Because the peace of eleven states will not permit the fruits of a successful negro insurrection to be exhibited among them."

In other words, the United States had a golden opportunity to enlarge upon the broad hemispheric principles it had just outlined in the Monroe Doctrine, and to assume a real position of leadership with its neighbors—and flubbed it. It was a curiously selective liberty that Americans were advancing.

Nevertheless, it was impossible not to be impressed by the United States fifty years after the founding. The claims of providential destiny could be tiresome, but truth be told, divine favor *did* appear to smile upon the young republic, and not merely because Thomas Jefferson and John Adams had the self-discipline to expire on July 4, 1826. Enormous wealth was being generated by new industries. Millions of people were flocking to these shores in search of a second chance. Some twenty Declarations of Independence modeled on our own had been signed in other nations by 1826. By almost any standard, the "great experiment," as George Washington termed it, was a success.

As the ark continued to sail on what Jefferson called "the ocean of time," it even began to grow comfortable with the way this quirky collection of federated states related to the world at large. The shocks of the 1790s had shown how much Americans still had to learn about international affairs. But Americans tend to fail upward, and after Jefferson "put the ship on her republican track" and doubled the size of the republic, a calm seemed to settle on the United States that allowed her to focus on internal development. With each decade, as America's strength grew, the distance narrowed between her aspirations and her power to achieve them.

But a question would always remain—the question that drove so much of this expansiveness. Would all this progress, enough for almost any nation, satisfy America? Having defined forward momentum as a permanent condition, could our peripatetic people ever rest content with anything less? And would liberty's contradictions here at home ever be resolved? In a way, that is what Henry Adams, the grandson of John Quincy Adams, meant when he ended his massive history of the early republic with a deceptively simple query: "What object, besides physical content, must a democratic continent aspire to attain?" With our first successful war of invasion, and the acquisition of an enormous amount of new land from Mexico, those questions would acquire far more urgency.

CHAPTER FIVE

LIBERTY ENSLAVED

> I do not hesitate to say that it is especially in the conduct of their foreign relations that democracies appear to me decidedly inferior to other governments . . . Foreign politics demand scarcely any of those qualities which are peculiar to a democracy; they require, on the contrary, the perfect use of almost all those in which it is deficient.
>
> —Alexis de Tocqueville

A GRAND BEDLAM

In the center of sprawling Mexico City, at the heart of the famous Halls of Montezuma—in fact, on the very site of Montezuma's house—is the Palacio Nacional. Its staircases are lined with enormous murals by the great painter Diego Rivera that depict a very different version of American history than the one we sing in the Marines' Hymn. Rivera shows the gawking tourists a scene of utter carnage—of hirsute *norteamericanos* pillaging his ancient civilization and "invaders from the North" desecrating all they touch. Describing the same scenes from the Mexican War, the Marines' Hymn almost sounds like a travel brochure, promising to defend freedom from "the snow of far-off northern lands" to "sunny tropic scenes." The hymn's final verse promises to defend an even more exotic location—heaven itself—although it does not explain how a land-based service branch will deploy there.

Reconciling these two creative interpretations of American history is a challenge indeed. But a glimpse at the stormy years before the Civil War supports both arguments. Surely liberty was advanced in a profound sense by the persistent efforts of generations of American statesmen to argue its cause before a cynical world. On those fitful occasions when other peoples seized the right to self-government, the example of the United States was always before them. More than that, Americans actively supported liberty in the world, sending money and even arms to those who would free themselves from oppressive governments. On the rare occasions when these liberation movements succeeded—as in Greece in the 1820s, or in France, briefly, in 1848—Americans had a right to feel self-congratulatory. The small aid of armaments meant something; the enormous example of democracy meant everything.

But any serious effort to tell the story of America's place in the world must also reckon with our many failures to live up to our own standards. On more than a few occasions we not only failed to advance freedom, we positively reversed it. Even worse, we did this in the name of something we called "liberty" but that was clearly something darker—liberty with a bar sinister. To undermine our highest ideal in the very name of that ideal is as close to a national sin as we are capable of—and our penance was the greatest tragedy in American history. Ulysses Grant stated the case with his usual military efficiency: "The Southern rebellion was largely the outgrowth of the Mexican war. Nations, like individuals, are punished for their transgressions. We got our punishment in the most sanguinary and expensive war of modern times."

If American foreign policy had an unreal quality in the beginning, dominated by excessively luminous projections of Liberty Ascendant and excessively dark visions of Nebuchadnezzar's toe, that unreality was doomed to fade away as the United States entered more fully into the global community in the hustle-bustle nineteenth century. Mexico was only one of a number of serious problems Americans encountered as the nation grew at an unbridled pace and our ability to export liberty began to catch up to our desire.

By the century's middle decades, the U.S. economy was intimately connected with the great markets of Europe. The American military, historically puny in comparison with the imperial armies that were always summoned to fight each other, was earning grudging respect from Europe. America's astonishing population growth impressed all observers. What was not to like? Europeans found all the raw materials they could need here, inexpensively, and large populations to sell their finished products to. Better yet, the United States offered a natural safety valve for their restless populations. America, it seemed, had truly been invented for the happiness of all.

A cursory glance at the writings of the Jacksonian period and its aftermath confirm that Americans had lost none of their exuberant notions about their special Providence. From Emerson to Whitman to a thousand inferior poetasters and politicians, there were simply no limits to the nation's imagined future. Of course, a few inconsistencies remained to be ironed out. A slave nation heralding freedom to all mankind; a modest nation, eager to avoid European-style war and pretension, yet gobbling up territory and issuing threats to interlopers; an exquisitely balanced constitutional democracy, yet always in peril of upsetting that balance. That was the beauty of the phrase *manifest destiny*—it could mean absolutely anything to anyone.

It is difficult to blame Americans for feeling confident. Has any nation ever grown into its potential as quickly? By any standard of measurement—population, wealth, extent—the United States was the most successful new nation in history. In fact, *becoming* may be too modest a word to describe the complete transformation of a people doubling in size every generation, expanding madcap in all directions, and beginning to feel its strength on the world stage. This strength was not yet military; it was a power that emanated as much from American ideals as from the growing economic might of a surging people, naturally inventive, blessed with abundant resources.

Even if American force remained relatively puny, the United States was quickly emerging as a regional power and something more. The radius of its influence never ceased expanding, and in every direction Americans were pressing at the margins, insisting on rights both real and imagined. This was a national phenomenon, shared equally by all the American regions. To this day New England closets and museums overflow with the bric-a-brac that enterprising merchants brought back in these decades from China, Indonesia, and the farthest reaches of the Pacific. Southerners traded throughout the Americas and the Caribbean, to say nothing of an African slave trade that did not entirely cease despite its official end in 1808. Westerners were in constant motion across the continent, filling in the many empty places that could still be found on the map of North America.

One might have expected that this exposure to the peoples of the world would have led to a deeper sense of human differences and a restrained notion of America's potential to revolutionize humanity. Yet to a surprising degree, the old ideas about special providence persisted well into this more modern time. They can be found in all of the places where a nation's innermost thoughts express themselves—in the essays of popular magazines, in the ruminations of writers, and in the speeches of politicians, who knew instinctively that no one was ever voted out of office for being too optimistic about the American future. Anyone who peruses the thousands of orations about America's place in the world in the 1840s and 1850s—a blast of air that could power a fleet of clipper ships—can see that a bottomless confidence in our right to reshape the world was the dominant idea of the era, all the more striking for our knowledge that the country was on the brink of catastrophe. The one politician who failed to express this irrational exuberance—and who at times suffered terribly for his inappropriate modesty—was the greatest leader in our history, Abraham Lincoln. Thank God he showed up when he did—a special providence indeed.

As Europe wrestled with its own complex destiny, and people began to long for representative forms of government, this republic served as a natural model for the new systems coming into existence, or trying to. The American Revolution found new life as royal houses teetered on their thrones, impatient populations clamored for self-government, and impatient immigrants poured across the Atlantic to seize liberty for themselves.

How wonderful it is to see the contempt with which the corrupt old dynasties of Europe greeted this upstart from the New World! Perhaps the clearest index of America's revolutionary potential is the extent to which the privileged orders belittled her. In the wake of the Age of Revolution, the dynastic houses were deeply irritated that a democracy such as the United States even dared to exist. Frederich von Schlegel, lecturing in Vienna in 1828, called the United States "the real school and nursery of all these revolutionary principles" upsetting the world since 1776. Amazingly, the Spanish royal censor prohibited Washington Irving's beloved story "Rip Van Winkle" because it could be interpreted as an attack on King Ferdinand! An Italian professor was jailed for claiming to admire George Washington. In the Hapsburg empire, gentlemen regarded the United States as "a grand bedlam, a rendezvous of European scamps and vagabonds." As late as 1866, Cambridge University haughtily rejected an endowed lectureship to treat American history and institutions.

That revolutionary fire was cherished by Americans eager to seize their destiny and prove themselves before a skeptical world. Each president seemed to claim a little more: Jefferson had promised no entanglements, then purchased Lousiana; Monroe and Adams drew an invisible fence around the hemisphere; Andrew Jackson did not stop at the hemisphere, concluding his farewell address with the thought that "Providence has showered on this favored land blessings without number, and has chosen you as the guardians of freedom, to preserve it for the benefit of the human race."

But a troubling flaw lay close to the surface of the seemingly benign idea that this was a chosen people. If the size of the nation was one way its greatness was measured, and if additional greatness was desired, then there was no way to achieve it except at the expense of America's neighbors. That would ultimately mean conflict, and conflict was a strange way to advance liberty. These tensions grew even more acute when the neighbor in question—Mexico—was a republic that had successfully fought for its independence from Spain and had eliminated slavery to boot, while the United States seemed to be invading for the express purpose of restoring it.

No sane American commentator would exactly regret the conflict with Mexico that ensued—without it we would have no Los Angeles and no Las Vegas, and without Las Vegas, the United States might cease to exist. But it's healthy to understand what the historical record tells us, if we are willing to listen: that our devotion to the stirring ideals of liberty did not always match our commitment to those ideals on the ground. At the end of the day, Americans were still human beings, and as the Puritans knew, that meant a crowded boatload—an ark's worth—of inconsistencies.

LIBERTY AND UNION

Beyond a doubt, the wise statecraft of John Quincy Adams and James Monroe had placed the United States on a sounder footing in the world. The continental vision that Adams nurtured served America well in both theory and practice, giving the United States its first toehold on the Pacific, and linking the ideas of morality and expansiveness in a way that would create a template for many leaders to follow—including leaders with far fewer scruples than Adams. But as America's physical coordinates changed, so did its words. At the center of the debate over how far the United States should expand lay a profound disagreement over what, exactly, was expanding and how to describe it. One of the paradoxes of our geography is that the crevice between North and South deepened for every mile that we moved westward.

The phrase *Liberty and Union* seems almost as if it were designed to mask this problem. By insisting to any who would listen that they were part and parcel of the same idea, Americans cloaked some of the incongruity that lay at the heart of a federal system based on the idea of freedom from authority. "Liberty and Union" was the motto of a well-known flag of the Revolution, the Taunton Flag of 1774. But the phrase enjoyed its greatest popularity at exactly the moment when the union began to feel imperiled, in 1830, when Daniel Webster of Massachusetts issued his stirring appeal to national pride in reply to a states' rights argument advanced by South Carolina's Senator Robert Hayne. Generations of schoolchildren were forced to commit its peroration to memory:

> When my eyes shall be turned to behold for the last time the sun in heaven, may I not see him shining on the broken and dishonored fragments of a once glorious Union; on States dissevered, discordant, belligerent; on a land rent with civil feuds, or drenched, it may be, in fraternal blood! Let their last feeble and lingering glance rather behold the gorgeous ensign of the republic, now known and honored throughout the earth, still full high advanced, its arms and trophies streaming in their original lustre, not a stripe erased or polluted, not a single star obscured, bearing for its motto, no such miserable interrogatory as "What is all this worth?" nor those other words of delusion and folly, "Liberty first

> and Union afterwards"; but everywhere, spread all over in characters of living light, blazing on all its ample folds, as they float over the sea and over the land, and in every wind under the whole heavens, that other sentiment, dear to every true American heart,—Liberty *and* Union, now and for ever, one and inseparable!

Those words were indeed inseparable at the time of the founding, when the fight against British tyranny demanded that Americans maintain a united front. But the pressures of relentless growth and westward expansion in the nineteenth century conspired to undermine their relationship. In fact, it was becoming hard to know what exactly *liberty* meant. More and more, the definition depended on *where* it was defined.

To the North, an evolving sense of human rights began to include all people, including African-Americans, within its rubric. *Liberty* was the word of Faneuil Hall, of the Liberty Bell, and of New York City, then as now home to a certain freedom from restraint. Year after year, the Declaration of Independence was reread by Americans eager to rediscover the fountainhead of their ideals. And when slavery seemed a violation of those ideals, *liberty* served quite well as a weapon. William Lloyd Garrison called the antislavery newspaper he launched in 1831 *The Liberator*; the antislavery party that began to run serious candidates in 1840 was called the Liberty Party; and the nation founded by African-Americans returning to Africa was naturally named Liberia.

But Southerners also took shade under *liberty*'s umbrella. For them, the word embodied the freedom to live one's life free of interference. Clearly, this was a different kind of liberty—for whites only. John Calhoun argued that Northern tariffs would "destroy the liberty of the country." When the argument became serious, at the time of the Nullification crisis, he called it a battle between "liberty and despotism." In an interesting formulation, South Carolinians argued that antislavery advocates were "hereditary drudges of imperious taskmasters," while pro-slavery exponents were "the free and undisputed heirs of the liberty and land which our fathers bequeathed." As a new generation of aggressive Southwestern politicians rose to power, they claimed a "liberty" to absorb new territories far more ambitiously than the founders would have dreamed. Yet these acquisitions came not from Americans defying a distant king, or purchasing real estate from a beleaguered emperor, but through the force of arms, against a sister republic.

On the surface, of course, all Americans were in favor of liberty—anything less was heresy. But the pressures on the country inevitably became pressures on the word itself. Liberty was one of the main reasons cited for the need to expand—because to expand America was in effect to expand liberty. But as tensions rose with the neighboring nations expected to surrender before this expansion—usually Mexico—many Americans began to take a second look at *liberty* and to wonder if the word had a dark underside. By the time of the Civil War, liberty was one of the reasons cited by the seceding states to justify the destruction of the union.

These contradictory interpretations of one of our most basic words did not augur well for the future. Strangely, at exactly the moment when Northerners and Southerners were failing to communicate, a new movement came along that proclaimed America's single-minded destiny in sharper language than it had ever before been expressed. Failing to find common ground, Americans simply sought more ground.

MANIFEST DESTINY

One of the most popular catchphrases in American history, *Manifest Destiny* is vaguely known to most of us. How many high school students have lived in dread of the moment when they would be asked to define it on an exam? The term is still bandied about to this day; a casual Google search produces everything from neo-Nazi rants to heavy-metal bands. Yet its familiarity conceals a great deal of mystery behind a term that sprang up almost overnight in the 1840s to articulate a vivid new sense of purpose for the United States.

Oddly, the storied phrase entered existence so seamlessly that its author was apparently unaware that he had invented it. The statement of a desire that was not achievable, it was expressed by someone who was not in a position to be speaking for the government, and it was soon spun by other people to mean something quite different from what the author intended. In other words, it was a spectacular triumph, the sound bite of the century. In 1845, the author of the phrase, John O'Sullivan, predicted that America's stunning population growth would bring it to global dominance in exactly 1945. What a guess!

The phrase became so universal so quickly that it is difficult to locate its first use, but archival digging has unearthed two uses in 1845, both by the same editor. Who was John L. O'Sullivan? Like everything connected with Manifest Destiny, that is no simple question to answer. Although Manifest Destiny grew linked to a kind of Anglo-Saxon racism, O'Sullivan was the son of an Irish Catholic immigrant and deeply committed to social justice. Yet this ultra-American was barely American at all. He was born off the coast of Gibraltar and educated in France and England before graduating from Columbia and beginning a journalism career. He loved Latin America throughout his life. His prize creation, the most exciting magazine of its day, was the *United States Magazine and Democratic Review*, founded in 1837. In its early years, the *Review* adopted one noble cause after another. It opposed the death penalty, and war, and any form of snobbery; it supported young writers, labor rights, world peace, and worldwide liberalism. Although plenty of writers had sung hymns to the greatness of America's future, the incantatory quality of O'Sullivan's writing caught the spirit of the age. He knew history, too; more than most of his contemporaries, he had read the Puritans and could speak their language of intense expectation. Only twenty-four at the time he founded the *Review*, he brought a new energy to the task of defining the America Yet to Come.

Here are a few sample sentences from his essay "The Great Nation of Futurity," which appeared in November 1839:

> Our national birth was the beginning of a new history, the formation and progress of an untried political system, which separates us from the past and connects us with the future only; and so far as regards the entire development of the natural rights of man, in moral, political and national life, we may confidently assume that our country is destined to be the great nation of futurity . . . The far-reaching, the boundless future will be the era of American greatness. In its magnificent domain of space and time, the nation of many nations is destined to manifest to mankind the excellence of divine principles; to establish on

> earth the noblest temple ever dedicated to the worship of the Most High—the Sacred and the True. Its floor shall be a hemisphere—its roof the firmament of the star-studded heavens, and its congregation an Union of many Republics, comprising hundreds of happy millions, calling, owning no man master, but governed by God's natural and moral law of equality, the law of brotherhood—of "peace and good will amongst men."

Why were these clichés so effective? O'Sullivan's charm lay in his inclusiveness. This was no simple jingoist ranting against inferior nations. O'Sullivan loved America's pan-ethnic quality, and the ebullience of his worldview endeared him to a variety of audiences. The millennium he promised was most inviting, full of human rights, egalitarianism, and respect for all of Europe's peoples (he was less inviting to African-Americans). He cultivated the most interesting new writers (Hawthorne was a close friend); he moved in exciting circles; he advanced the most progressive causes. The geographical vagueness of his dream only increased its appeal. A country that borders on heaven—why not?

But for all of O'Sullivan's optimism and geniality, a troubling thought lay buried deep beneath the fine language about democracy and destiny. Like so many writers who would follow in his path, he believed that any means justified the end of advancing freedom. In figurative language, but real language nonetheless, he argued that America's example "shall smite unto death the tyranny of kings, hierarchs, and oligarchs" to fulfill "its blessed mission to the nations of the world." To hear a well-known advocate of nonviolence argue that war was necessary to make peace was surprising, especially when no nations were threatening the United States. But if the nation of futurity required it, then so be it. After all, America had "been chosen."

In July 1845, O'Sullivan used the magic words for the first time ("our manifest destiny to overspread the continent allotted by Providence"), and then five months later he used them again, in the *New York Morning News*, a newspaper he had created ("our manifest destiny to overspread and to possess the whole of the continent which Providence has given us for the great experiment of liberty").

Immediately afterward, a congressman used *manifest destiny* derisively, to criticize its assumptions. Ironically, the House member who did not like the phrase was Robert Winthrop of Massachusetts, the descendant of John Winthrop, whose "city upon a hill" was Manifest Destiny's ancestor. As he listened to the primitive drumbeat of nineteenth-century expansionism, Winthrop felt nothing but ridicule: "The right of our manifest destiny! There is a right for a new chapter in the law of nations; or rather, in the special laws of our own country; for I suppose the right of a manifest destiny to spread will not be admitted to exist in any nation except the universal Yankee nation."

If it is possible to pile up one irony upon another, it was Winthrop's caustic repetition of the phrase *manifest destiny*, dripping with sarcasm, that finally gave wide currency to the term. The more that people (especially New Englanders) attacked its arrogance, the more the rest of America liked it.

It is extraordinary to watch the nearly invisible way in which the vaguest of phrases can turn into national policy. Throughout the early life of Manifest Destiny, Americans had only the fuzziest awareness that any of its assumptions might actually affect other countries. O'Sullivan blissfully celebrated America's right to expand while assuming that there would always be space to expand into. In fact, his original essays were directed toward the British (blocking access to Oregon) as much as Texas and Mexico. Like George Kennan's theory of containment a century later, the essays expressed an aspiration toward a new global posture, resisting European monarchies and other kinds of "tyranny," but notably imprecise when it came to actual confrontation. In general, expansionism tends to rise when it is uncontested, and to diminish when peoples and armies are blocking the way. Mexico would end up bearing the brunt of the enthusiasms unleashed in 1845; but in its original incarnation, Manifest Destiny was not intended as a declaration of war against a single country.

Nor was it alone in the pantheon of sound bites. A number of other vaporous slogans entered the atmosphere at the same moment. The bellicose slogan "Fifty-four Forty or Fight!" was coined to justify America's claim to a chunk of northwestern territory well north of what the British regarded as the correct position (few scholars feel that the United States had a strong legal position in Oregon). John Quincy Adams, ever the continentalist, argued that "the finger of nature" pointed that way, and that the book of Genesis had urged the American people (but not, seemingly, anyone else) to go forth and multiply there. Bloviating congressmen claimed that America's right to Oregon came from "High Heaven," from "destiny," and from America's commitment to liberty—"the spirit of republicanism, that permits not the contaminating spirit of monarchies upon the soil that we have consecrated to the rights of man." Some politicians went further still; Stephen Douglas wanted the United States to absorb all of Canada. This was more than just hot air; in December 1845 a navy gunboat was sent to the Pacific to reconnoiter and establish contact with American settlers.

Texas was a very different kind of foreign policy problem. After American settlers had poured into what was then a Mexican province (and confirmed as such by John Quincy Adams in the treaty that acquired Florida), Texans had rebelled against Mexico and created their own republic in 1836. Nearly at once they clamored to join the United States, but powerful resistance came from Americans who feared violating a legal treaty between the United States and Spain, offending world opinion, and, perhaps worst of all, opening up a new can of worms over slavery. The enormous size of Texas, Northerners worried, would lead to the creation of numerous slave states.

To make matters worse, Texans showed little inclination to observe what had been the southern border of Texas—the Nueces River—and instead claimed the Rio Grande, farther south. In other words, the United States was not only under pressure to expand—it was being pressed to expand by a group of people who desired a lot of additional expansion. In fact, Texans were making noise about seizing New Mexico even before they were admitted to the United States, and they sent out a failed expedition in 1841. At times it was unclear whether the United States would absorb Texas or vice versa.

In such an overheated environment—several presidential campaigns foundered upon the question—it was a useful distraction, as always, to talk of freedom. The Texans—who were both former and future Americans—were skilled in the art. Sam Houston even promised that they would extend "liberty" to Nicaragua: "With these principles we will march across the Rio Grande, and . . . ere the banner of Mexico shall triumphantly float upon the banks of the Sabine, the Texian standard of the single star, borne by the Anglo-Saxon race, shall display its bright folds in Liberty's triumph, on the isthmus of Darien."

The problem, of course, was that "liberty" was only available for Anglo-Saxons. In fact, the creation of the Texas Republic had set liberty back considerably for large numbers of Mexicans who refused to be absorbed into the breakaway province, and African-Texans who found that slavery was reintroduced, after having been banished by Mexico. John Quincy Adams, who had done more to secure new territory than any other living American, and who never lost his appetite for Oregon, strongly rejected Texas's petition to join the United States and even signed a statement with twelve congressmen arguing that its acquisition was illegal, unconstitutional, and would ultimately lead to the dissolution of the union. To counter these doubts, pro-Texas voices in the federal government, including President John Tyler and Secretary of State John Calhoun, resorted to the old trickery of alleging that Great Britain was trying to seize Texas—a threat that roused all the old patriotic fears of foreign influence. When that failed to persuade, there was always the pull of a magical "destiny," the belief, as one senator said, that "destiny had established intimate political connexion between the United States and Texas."

Perhaps no one was more persuasive on that theme than Andrew Jackson, still enormously popular, still alive, though barely, in 1845, and respected for having opposed slavery's advocates on many previous occasions. Jackson wrote a famous letter in 1843 that urged "extending the area of freedom," a phrase that quickly joined *manifest destiny* and *fifty-four forty* as a catchword of the era. Jackson died in the summer of 1845, as Manifest Destiny was springing to life, but not before having the satisfaction of seeing Texas approach the altar. His disciple James Polk promised in his first annual message that this enormous acquisition of slave territory would support "the expansion of free principles." On top of that, he warned all European nations away from America's sphere, telling them bluntly that the Monroe Doctrine would now apply "with greatly increased force," and taunting Britain in particular over Oregon.

In this charged atmosphere, O'Sullivan coined his mystical phrase, an assertion that seemed to sum up all the excitement of the moment without getting into any of the ugly particulars. As the breezes of Manifest Destiny wafted over North America and a thousand speeches bloomed, Americans began to feel that they had a right—more than a right, really, an *obligation*—to expand wherever they wanted to, in the name of freedom. It was not only for the good of the United States, it was for the good of the world. But more than a few noticed that what was expanding was not so much "liberty" but slavery. Nor would this accusation have troubled Southern expansionists—that was precisely what they were trying to achieve. A prominent Southern apologist, George Fitzhugh, wrote, "The Anglo-Saxon race is manifestly destined to eat out all other races, as the wire-grass destroys and takes the places of the other grasses."

Manifest Destiny not only shaped American history; it showed how shapable it was, and not always for the better. It seems obvious to say that a democratic nation ought to set policies that conform to the will of the people. But that pleasing thought becomes complicated when one sees that by the mid-nineteenth century, shaping public opinion had become an important subcategory of political science. With the advent of O'Sullivan and other talented professionals in the business of words and slogans, something had changed in the simple republican formula designed by the founders. The phenomenal success of these two words showed how important it had become in American politics to electrify and entertain the public, especially given rapid advances in communications. Politicians and media barons alike quickly learned that it was far more popular to issue blustery threats and demand new land than to preach moderation, and so a new kind of speech was born. In late 1845, the virus of hypernationalism, always latent, suddenly developed a powerful new immunity.

Of course, Manifest Destiny was not entirely bad. Nothing that popular could be. I have tried to show that it emanated from a natural expansiveness that was already well developed in the American character. In science, in commerce, in technology, Americans were simply everywhere. In exactly the same years as the Texas fever, the first serious government-funded science expedition, the United States Exploring Expedition, was traveling around the Pacific Ocean gathering important data (and incidentally establishing numerous American claims in uncharted waters). John Frémont was taking suspiciously well-armed scientific parties into the Utah territory. A new treaty in 1844 opened five Chinese ports to American commerce. American missionaries were fanning out around the world, in truly impressive numbers, doing great things in many regions, particularly in the Middle East. A government expedition sent an explorer from the U.S. Navy nearly to the Euphrates River in 1847, the closest an American had yet approached to Babylon. He was recalled just before reaching the fabled city, but had the satisfaction of finding what he believed to be Sodom and Gomorrah.

But this expansiveness was accompanied by an aimlessness that troubled observers. Many Americans were disturbed by Manifest Destiny—by its vagueness, its high volume, and its insistence on easy gratification over long-term stability. Its loudest adherents cited the founders while ignoring them, bullied critics while proclaiming their openness; and ignored basic scriptural teachings while claiming divine inspiration. Liberty was not supposed to be a club for the right people.

Alexis de Tocqueville, so often quoted on America's strengths, was no less verbose on the subject of our flaws, although he is rarely quoted that way. Something in his bones told him that running a foreign policy based on popularity was sure to be disastrous, and he knew that it was dangerous to base a political culture on vapid speeches. Tocqueville admired the ability of Americans to sit through them and not pay too much attention ("the inhabitants of the United States . . . show their long experience of parliamentary life, not by abstaining from making bad speeches, but by courageously submitting to hear them made. They are resigned to it as an evil that they know to be inevitable"). But he knew that a business as serious as foreign policy needed more subtlety than whipped-up emotions. As a student of the French Revolution, he knew how quickly a fiery oration could lead to bloodletting.

From the moment John O'Sullivan coined *manifest destiny*, the clock was ticking, and five months later, war with Mexico was at hand. It was the fulfillment of one vision of American history and the abandonment of another. In one of his idealistic pronouncements, O'Sullivan had said, "There are some things this nation will never do. It will never be the forcible subjugator of other countries; it will never despoil surrounding territories; it will never march through the blood of their surrounding inhabitants; it will never admit within its own Union those who do not freely desire the boon." They were beautiful words. But now, for the first time in its history, the United States was conducting a large-scale invasion of a sovereign nation. It claimed to be fighting a defensive war when it was clearly the aggressor. It claimed to be "extending the area of freedom" when it was extending slavery. It claimed all this as destiny when it was clearly a war of choice. It is dangerous to cite Providence under such circumstances.

MONTEZUMA'S REVENGE

American presidents have often claimed that the United States has never attacked another country. Ronald Reagan insisted that "we will never be an aggressor" in his 1983 Star Wars speech; many Democrats have said similar things. If only history were that uncomplicated.

The Mexican War began as a small skirmish in April 1846 and quickly grew into something much larger. It was immensely significant to the history of the United States, yet it is rarely treated that way. It nearly doubled our territory, adding 1.2 million square miles to a country that had 1.788 million. It educated an entire generation of young American officers—soon to be fighting against one another—in the art of war. And it marked a course change of the highest significance in the history of American foreign policy. From the American Revolution onward, the prevailing assumption had been that the United States, for all its ambition, would advance democracy peacefully, inspiring others by the force of example rather than the example of force. In May 1846, that changed forever. If the Mexican War marked an advance for the United States in many senses of the word, it signaled a retreat in just as many.

The war's facts are available in many books, tucked away in the military-history section of most libraries, but the full story of the conflict remains obscure to Americans, overshadowed by the more melodramatic Civil War to follow. It began in the spring of 1846 under circumstances that it would be charitable to call muddled. It would be more honest to admit that the United States put so much military pressure on Mexico that it was inevitable a spark would set it off. After Polk sent General Zachary Taylor into disputed territory and Taylor put his cannon into position to fire into the Mexican city of Matamoros, the spark was provided. Mexican troops shot at a small detachment of American troops near the Rio Grande, which Americans were trying to claim as the new boundary, in defiance of all known precedent. Three Americans were killed; about thirteen thousand more would die before the war ended.

Upon receiving news of the border incident, President Polk delivered a highly charged war message to Congress—the first time that a president informed Congress that a war had begun rather than asking its permission to wage one. He emphasized that Mexico had started the war and "shed American blood upon American soil." But given that no other parties accepted American claims to the Rio Grande, that was a creative rewriting of history. Still, it was persuasive in that electric moment, as the news flashed around the country, accelerated by that new invention, the telegraph. After little debate, the United States declared war on May 13, 1846. For the next two years, American and Mexican armies fought each other in a number of locations, and the U.S. military displayed remarkable prowess, often defeating much larger forces. The Treaty of Guadalupe Hidalgo, signed on February 2, 1848, made the United States a truly continental nation.

How were Americans persuaded to share Polk's war fever, and to seek vengeance against a neighboring republic that had done little to provoke them? Ulysses Grant offered the unvarnished truth. Reviewing the entire story, which he saw from a near perspective, he concluded that the movement to populate and then annex Texas was nothing more than "a conspiracy to acquire territory out of which slave states might be formed for the American Union." When Texas was finally admitted, and war resulted shortly afterward, Grant vented, "For myself, I was bitterly opposed to the measure, and to this day regard the war, which resulted, as one of the most unjust ever waged by a stronger against a weaker nation. It was an instance of a republic following the bad example of European monarchies, in not considering justice in their desire to acquire additional territory."

When Americans poured into territory that was either currently or formerly Mexican and then ignored Mexican sovereignty, it was similar to the strategy that the Americans had tried in Florida during the War of 1812. But with Mexico, it was much harder to make the case that the United States was in a global contest against tyranny or imperialism or monarchy or anything. Mexico had secured its independence in 1821 and adopted republican principles two years later. Its government was relatively weak and not always able to administer its vast territory, but in the court of world opinion, Mexico was a sovereign and independent republic. That was highly inconvenient for the Americans who coveted its vast reaches.

Still, those facts did not interrupt the rhetoric about freedom that seemed to get kicked up, like a sandstorm, whenever something dramatic was about to happen involving the United States and another country. Throughout the war, *liberty* was the watchword draped over American aggression. A Mississippi senator bragged that liberty was "a banner of moral regeneration" that would be extended to all Mexicans. Southerners, particularly from the expansive Southwest, argued for "the increase of our territory, and consequently the extension of the area of human liberty and happiness." The *New Orleans Picayune* bragged, in apocalyptic language, that "the principle of liberty" was so strong that it would survive "an epidemic conquest embracing in its ravages all Christendom."

As that quotation would suggest, liberty is never more persuasive than when accompanied by its old, reliable partner, religion. The evangelical trumpets pealed across the Americas as speakers justified the conflict, recalling the older millennial language that had preceded the American Revolution, and its seventeenth-century antecedents. Sam Houston compared American success in the war to God's support of the Israelites, saying it was an example that "the Divine Being has been evidently carrying out the destiny of the American race." An ugly anti-Catholicism surfaced as well, with some blaming the Catholic "monster" for Mexico's woes and urging a full-scale evangelical effort. Americans speculated that the full force of Protestantism, so long excluded from Mexico, would transform the place as efficiently as democracy, its adjunct. A frenzied literature of speculation sprang into existence in the newspapers, describing the Americanized Mexico about to come into existence—or so Americans thought.

The war was supposed to be brief and cathartic, as wars are always supposed to be. Predictably, it was neither. As it dragged on, irritation increased in Congress and elsewhere, but so did the appetite of the public for more retaliation against the Mexicans and for more of their land. And so the great prize, California, came into the conversation, which was easily expanded to include New Mexico, and ultimately all of Mexico itself. A series of stunning victories by American forces suddenly gave these claims credence.

These victories increased the excitement of the American audiences devouring news of the battles in the penny papers and dispelled many doubts of those who, like Walt Whitman, had wondered about the dubious moral argument for the war. Whitman was converted and began to write that any gain for American forces would see "the increase of human happiness and liberty."

But the lust for land unleashed by the war often found its way into channels that had precious little to do with religion or liberty. A startling number of speakers described Mexico's new availability in sexual language. The *New York Herald* promised that Mexico would learn to "love her ravisher." Sam Houston, speaking in New York, said that all the "beautiful señoritas" would make America's march across the continent that much more pleasant. A poem published in June 1846 in Boston, "They Wait for Us," described the ladies of Mexico waiting for their liberators:

> The Spanish maid, with eye of fire.
> At balmy evening turns her lyre
> And, looking to the Eastern sky,
> Awaits our Yankee chivalry
> Whose purer blood and valiant arms,
> Are fit to clasp her budding charms.
>
> The man, her mate, is sunk in sloth—
> To love, his senseless heart is loth:
> The pipe and glass and tinkling lute,
> A sofa, and a dish of fruit;
> A nap, some dozen times a day;
> Sombre and sad, and never gay.

Such was the glory of Manifest Destiny. But as the war continued, month after month, and finally into a second year, a striking wave of dissent countered these uglier claims of ethnic and racial superiority and began to weigh heavily upon the White House. Like most dissent movements, it was not organized, but it represented a deep feeling that something important in the American mission—something more important than land—had been violated in the way that the war had been sold to the American people.

Manifest Destiny had always been more attractive when it applied to what were believed to be relatively vacant sections of the continent, or to distant places that might someday join the confederation. It was quite a different matter to read reports of Mexicans and Americans dying in battle to pursue a war with no clear aim. Even if American armies were winning, a growing chorus of voices called for a reasonable end to the conflict.

As Americans reflected more soberly on the war's origins, after the fact, they felt a growing conviction that something harmful had occurred in the rush to battle orchestrated by a president working behind the scenes with no congressional oversight. The founders had designed a system to prevent exactly this situation, and to give a deliberative Congress the right to approve or reject war. Polk had expertly sidestepped all the restraints built into the system, whipping up popular opinion—which the founders could not have been more explicit about mistrusting—into a war frenzy against a sister republic. Advancing liberty through force—an oxymoron—was a complete rejection of the idea of the founders that America would exert influence through her example.

These sentiments were especially pronounced in New England, distant from these Southwestern adventures and fearful of a slave empire. Emerson wrote in his journal, "The United States will conquer Mexico, but it will be as the man who swallows the arsenic which brings him down in turn. Mexico will poison us." But the growing doubts were not confined to the Northeast. Many leaders of the Old South also grew alarmed at the war's progress. Calhoun began to make noises against it as he worried about the power of an executive branch that seemed out of control. His fears deepened as an "All Mexico" movement grew that urged the absorption of the entire country. Calhoun, who had been so outspoken for Texas, was now horrified at the new prospect of an entire nation of "impure races" (his term) who would presumably be given political rights and reduce the South's influence by that much more. It was one thing to acquire a little room; it was quite another to enfranchise a nation of 8 million, and Roman Catholics to boot.

Suddenly, Calhoun began to speak in a very different language from that of Manifest Destiny. Specifically, he rejected the idea that the United States had a mission to spread liberty—because in his opinion, other peoples were simply not up to the challenge of self-government. Daniel Webster, so rarely aligned with Calhoun in these years, agreed, admitting that while he loved free institutions, he was "by no means sure that all people are fit for them." But they were both losing ground rapidly to a new generation of younger politicians, hungry for power and attention, who would do anything to advance America's boundaries.

Polk's problems increased when the fall election of 1846 handed control of Congress to the opposition Whigs. An extraordinary debate began that called into question all of his motives for leading the nation to war, and for the first time in American history, Americans began to speak openly of a president's distortions and how they had tricked the nation into going to war. A Tennessee congressman, one of Polk's neighbors, called his war message "an artful perversion of the truth—a disingenuous statement of facts—to make the people 'believe a lie.' " Alexander Stephens of Georgia, the future vice president of the Confederacy, said that he could find no better example of duplicity in all of history than the sitting president, "Polk the mendacious." Congress was further infuriated when it learned that Polk had been promoting top generals for political reasons—because they were Democrats—and threatening Whig critics of the war with treason.

All of these pressures, along with the cost of the war, increased the desire to end the conflict, settle with Mexico, and move forward. But infuriatingly, Mexico would not surrender, despite one loss after another. Even after Winfield Scott occupied Mexico City, Americans learned, not for the last time, that it is one thing to occupy a country and quite another to force it to accept defeat. At long last, a peace treaty was cobbled together that smoothed over the many differences remaining (the handiwork of a creative American envoy who ignored many of his instructions from Washington) and allowed both sides to extricate themselves from a conflict that had become embarrassing. For the sum of $15 million, the United States received Mexican acceptance of the Rio Grande boundary, giving it an immense territory reaching all the way to the Pacific, including California, Nevada, Utah, and large sections of Arizona, Colorado, and New Mexico. In some ways, it was galling to Polk to accept what were the minimum gains he had instructed his envoy to demand. The United States paid dearly in other ways, both in the cost of the war (reckoned at $100 million) and in the large number of men who had been sacrificed. Negative reactions came from both boosters (who thought the treaty took too little) and critics of the war (who thought it took too much). But in the end, Polk and Congress had little choice but to accept the treaty, with considerable relief that the conflict was finally finished. California was a great prize—but purchased at a great price.

That may sound like the judgment of a modern writer, looking back at the past with all-too-convenient hindsight. In fact, that feeling was shared by many contemporaries, especially those with a keen sense of the idealistic country that the United States had been when it was founded. One of them, an important participant in the founding of the United States, still alive during the Mexican War, did not hesitate to venture his opinion of it.

Albert Gallatin is sadly unknown now, but he was still famous in 1847, when he wrote a pamphlet entitled *Peace with Mexico*. It would have been impossible to have better credentials with the expansionist crowd, unless Andrew Jackson himself had risen from the dead. Gallatin was one of the great Jeffersonians (he was his secretary of the treasury) and a leading continentalist (he negotiated the Treaty of Ghent, ending the War of 1812, and arbitrated many border claims with Britain). He represented ultrademocratic western Pennsylvania during the earliest days of the republic, when keeping western Pennsylvania in the union was no simple matter. Striking out on his own as a young man, he emigrated from Switzerland to America in 1780, in the midst of the Revolution, and never looked back. In 1847, he was eighty-six years old and still had a great deal to say.

Gallatin was worried about the fate of the republic he had helped to found and would brook no disobedience from the young whelps who were distorting America's purpose in the name of founding ideals they cited without understanding them. He recalled the earliest days of the republic in moving terms:

> Here, for the first time, was the experiment attempted with any prospect of success, and on a large scale, of a representative dem-

> ocratic republic. If it failed, the last hope of the friends of mankind was lost or indefinitely postponed; and the eyes of the world were turned toward you.

More than his younger contemporaries, Gallatin seemed to understand the importance of the shift in tone of American diplomacy. Americans had never "voluntarily injured any nation," every acquisition was "honestly made," every military act "in self-defense." But then this paragraph:

> At present all these principles would seem to have been abandoned. The most just, a purely defensive war, and no other is justifiable, is necessarily attended with a train of great and unavoidable evils. What shall we say of one, iniquitous in its origin, and provoked by ourselves, of a war of aggression, which is now publicly avowed to be one of intended conquest?

Abandoning man's best hopes, recent American foreign policy had instead catered to "your worst passions; to cupidity; to the thirst of unjust aggrandizement by brutal force; to the love of military fame and of false glory; and it has even been tried to pervert the noblest feelings of your nature." Gallatin then uttered a radical thought, which only an elderly founder could get away with:

> Devotedness to country, or patriotism, is a most essential virtue, since the national existence of any society depends on it. Unfortunately, our most virtuous dispositions are perverted not only by our vices and selfishness, but also by their own excess. Even the most holy of our attributes, the religious feeling, may be perverted from that cause, as was but too lamentably exhibited in the persecutions, even unto death, of those who were deemed heretics. It is not, therefore, astonishing that patriotism carried to excess should also be perverted.

Gallatin praised the soldiers and felt no anger toward "those who, led by their patriotic feelings, though erroneous, flock around the national standard." But he could not "extend the same charity to those civilians who coolly and deliberately plunge the country into any unjust or unnecessary war." This Swiss immigrant reserved special anger for the obscene racism of Anglo-Saxon jingoists who argued "that the people of the United States have an hereditary superiority of race over the Mexicans, which gives them the right to subjugate and keep in bondage the inferior nation. This, it is alleged, will be the means of enlightening the degraded Mexicans, of improving their social state, and of ultimately increasing the happiness of the masses."

Gallatin was not the only American with memories of the founding to speak out at this highly charged moment. But their numbers were thinning, and thinned further in February 1848, when John Quincy Adams died on the floor of Congress, immediately after voting against a measure in support of the war. If America's most distinguished early advocates of expansion opposed the Polk administration's strategy of conquest, it suggested that the American present was profoundly out of sorts with American history. It has never been a simple thing to reconcile the idea of America with the fact, but some episodes bring out the tension more clearly than others. In a philosophical moment, Emerson wrote, "The people are no worse since than they invaded Mexico, than they were before, only they have given their will a deed."

That deed would continue to have enormous consequences.

LIBERTY AND GUANO

> The word *liberty* in the mouth of Webster sounds like the word *love* in the mouth of a courtezan. —Ralph Waldo Emerson

If Manifest Destiny had worked the way it was supposed to, the Mexican War would have ushered in a new era of peace, prosperity, and angelic choirs. So it seemed it had, for a brief shining moment in the spring of 1848. Almost exactly as news reached Washington that the Mexicans had agreed to terms, an equally exhilarating blast of fresh air came from Europe, announcing the revolutionary excitement under way in Paris. In France and around the continent, the young and democratically inclined tried to reform or even to seize their governments. Every ship brought more remarkable news than the one previous; it seemed as if all of Europe was casting off its chains. Once again, international democracy was in the ascendant, and otherwise cautious thinkers were unmoored by their enthusiasms. Nearly all Americans wished success to the young radicals storming the barricades, although that would change in the South after it was learned that their idea of freedom did not include slavery. Some Americans even sent guns and ammunition. Many found themselves once again daring to think the unthinkable. Could this be, at long last, the millennium of liberty? The millennium itself?

But once again, the millennium was short-lived. The revolutions in Europe were snuffed out, and things at home began to go south—literally. It rapidly became clear that Mexico's cession contained a Pandora's box of unforeseen problems. Is it a coincidence that Nathaniel Hawthorne wrote *The House of the Seven Gables*—about the curse of ill-gotten real estate—at exactly this time? Immediately after the peace terms were announced, a Pennsylvania Democrat named David Wilmot offered an amendment requiring that the new land be free of slavery—a rather fitting request, since "freedom" had been a principal goal of the conflict. The ensuing firestorm nearly ripped the union apart, and it took all the baling wire that Henry Clay could find to hold things together. The national mania for Californian gold, at exactly this moment, did not calm the waters.

The force of these aftershocks terrified observers both North and South, who began to glimpse the abyss dividing them. But their fears did not seem to lessen the American appetite for expansion. If anything, they heightened it. Despite the disruptions of the Mexican War, despite the bitter acrimony unleashed by the debates that followed the war, Americans raced headlong into the new decade, eager to spread Americanism as far and wide as an obliging planet would let them. A new noun, *spread-eagleism*, sprang into existence to characterize the high-flown rhetoric echoing through the halls of Congress and in assemblies around the country. Some of this new expansiveness was noble in intent—attempts to furnish aid to beleaguered democrats around the world (especially after the revolutions of 1848 were suppressed). But much of it was not, and the advocates of slavery were particularly obnoxious in the final decade before secession, stirring up foreign adventures wherever they could find them and seeking to extend their system of chattel labor as far across the hemisphere as possible. To them, Manifest Destiny was simply a euphemism for More Slavery. To the rest of America, it became a slogan that lingered well after its expiration date.

History classes usually concentrate on the domestic crises that led to the Civil War: the Kansas-Nebraska Act, the Dred Scott case, John Brown's raid. What is missing from that balance sheet is the deep impact of foreign adventures on the situation at home, worsening a situation that was bad to begin with. In the Caribbean, up and down the isthmus of Central America, and far across the wastes of the Pacific, legitimate and illegitimate agents of the United States were everywhere, seeking to open new markets, overthrow foreign governments, and enlarge "the area of freedom." It is possible that the 1850s witnessed the worst foreign policy in the history of the United States. Nor was it confined to the South, or to the Democratic Party. A kind of madness seized the country, culminating in the suggestion of Secretary of State William Seward, on April 1, 1861, that Americans avert the secession crisis by declaring war on Spain and France rather than on each other.

The failure of the 1848 revolutions in Europe was only the first of a series of disappointments that would plague the defenders of democracy and teach them that Manifest Destiny did not always live up to its rhetoric—or even worse, actively caused disaster. In short succession, a series of erratic episodes brought out just how poorly thought out America's policy of perpetual revolution was. In the final analysis, the only government the Americans succeeded in subverting was their own.

First, in 1851, Lajos Kossuth, the charismatic leader of Hungary's failed revolution against Austria, came to America to collect his thoughts and collect supporters. The ecstatic response of Americans to this living, breathing antiroyalist in their midst showed how hungry they were to reclaim their revolutionary birthright, even with a foreign cause that had nothing to do with any perceivable American interest. For seven months, the champion of Hungary was lionized everywhere he went, drawing enormous crowds. He gave them the raw meat they craved, promising to return to Europe and overthrow an evil empire that was thwarting liberty—a promise he was in no position to fulfill. As Americans were careening toward the greatest crisis in their history, Northerners and Southerners alike were utterly consumed by the distractions provided by a Hungarian dissident.

Audiences thrilled to the idea that American forces might actually return Kossuth to his homeland—the first time that U.S. intervention in Europe was seriously considered. They lapped up his promises to advance liberty against one of the most conservative regimes on earth, the Hapsburg empire. They loved it when the secretary of state, Daniel Webster, responding to an Austrian complaint about American "ignorance" concerning their internal affairs, asserted the eternal right of the United States to promote liberty around the world, since "the broadest principles of civil liberty" are "the only principles of government which meet the demands of the present enlightened age."

Still, even this blip on the screen shows how delicate the conversation about liberty was becoming. As it became apparent over Kossuth's seven months in America that he disapproved of slavery, half of America turned against him and his cause, while the other half disapproved that he did not denounce slavery more quickly.

Closer to home than Hungary, and far more enticing to those who wanted to sustain slavery, was the island of Cuba, which had beckoned to Americans—particularly Southern Americans—for decades. The twentieth-century tradition of the Cuban exile, plotting in the United States for the overthrow of a government in Havana, has deep roots in the nineteenth century as well.* As early as 1823, John Quincy Adams had called Cuba "an object of transcendent importance" to the United States. James Monroe, and Jefferson before him, had floated the dubious argument that Cuba helped to form, with Florida, the "mouth" of the Mississippi River and might therefore someday belong to the United States. Our incestuous love of Cuba goes back nearly as far as our earliest promises never to infringe on another land's freedom.

The most extreme of the Cuban plotters was surely Narciso López, a fiery Venezuelan who tried repeatedly to seize power in Cuba between 1849 and 1851, armed and endowed by an influential group of American supporters, connected to sympathetic Cuban planters who were tired of Spanish control. Working from New Orleans, where expansionist sentiments were strong, and veterans from the recent Mexican War were not hard to find, López curried favor with some of the most elite soldiers and statesmen in the United States. The word *fili-*

*In fact, Americans have been invading Cuba since at least the eighteenth century, when they formed sizable contingents within British expeditions.

buster—an old French word for "pirate"—sprang into use to describe a new kind of person in the United States, the adventurer trying assiduously to sabotage and overthrow a neighboring government. The press loved it and wrote of Cuba in heated terms, charged with sexuality: "She is of age—take her, Uncle Sam!"

This was no random group of freebooters, however. López's supporters included all manner of surprising celebrities, including prominent generals of the Mexican War (Robert E. Lee and Jefferson Davis were deeply interested, before withdrawing) and the familiar author of Manifest Destiny, John O'Sullivan. This came as a surprise to many of his old friends, who remembered his earnest editorials for peace, but as the winds of temptation blew across Florida and the Caribbean, they did strange things to people. The poet John Greenleaf Whittier, an old friend of O'Sullivan's, wrote a poem called "The Haschish," which likened the Cuban obsession to a dangerous narcotic:

> The man of peace, about whose dreams
> The sweet millennial angels cluster
> Tastes the mad weed, and plots and schemes,
> A raving Cuban filibuster!

There was something to Whittier's point. O'Sullivan had been one of the most eloquent exponents of America's mission, reading deeply in early American history and finding beautiful words to advance the population's understanding of how special its place in the world was. He supported peaceful change, opposed violence, and expected Manifest Destiny to ensue effortlessly. But now, a few years later, he was helping to round up soldiers and supporters for a violent invasion of another country. Moreover, he and his new friends were using the language of liberation to describe a plot that had precious little to do with liberty. Of course, no international law recognized an American right to intervene in Cuba, but many Americans were beginning to claim the right to act in local regions simply because they were nearby and theoretically touched upon the safety of the United States (a Spanish historian ridiculed this theory, saying, "It might lead, little by little, to the conquest of a world").

On three occasions, López tried to bring his army of supporters to

Cuba, convinced that the people would greet him with acclamation. His first attempt was foiled by Zachary Taylor's administration, which blockaded his ships and argued (quite correctly) that López and his supporters were violating the U.S. Neutrality Act of 1818. López paid little attention and tried again the next year. He landed at Cuba successfully, but the populace failed to embrace him, and he was forced to flee back to Florida, landing minutes ahead of the Spaniards chasing him. In 1851, he made his third and most serious attempt. On July 4, one of his friends, hiding in the mountains of Cuba, issued a proclamation that Cuba was placing itself under the protection of the United States. López landed soon afterward with four hundred men. But once again, the people showed no particular interest in being liberated. Spanish forces caught up with López, captured his ragtag army, and put an emphatic end to this early chapter of U.S. aggression by garroting him in a public square. When they heard the news, mobs in New Orleans nearly destroyed the Spanish consulate.

It would be easy to dismiss the López expeditions as an obscure episode, unworthy of the great American tradition of generally benign foreign policy. But it is hard to deny the extent to which major government figures were involved. James Polk had tried to purchase Cuba while he was president, and now three serious armed attempts had been made on Cuba by ships sailing from the United States, with American soldiers who had recently been fighting in Mexico, and paid for by Americans. Future officers of the Confederacy were especially involved, and this bit of subterfuge, with so many echoes in the twentieth century, was never entirely forgotten by the people of Cuba. Perhaps the final irony is that the Cuban flag, with its echoes of the American flag, was designed by Narciso López while plotting his invasion in Manhattan.

Even after Lopez's nasty end, the pot continued to simmer and occasionally even boiled over. In the otherwise undistinguished administration of Franklin Pierce (1853–57), the call for American intervention abroad reached a new crescendo. His attorney general bragged about the United States as "that colossus of liberty." Everyone in his administration seemed dedicated to the idea that the United States had the right to do anything it wanted, anywhere on earth. One of the loudest diplomatic delegations in history was sent out to exactly those countries it was likely to offend. The signature achievement of this "conclave of cuteness," as the European press labeled it, was the Ostend Manifesto of 1854. Gathering at Ostend in Belgium, the three American envoys to Britain, France, and Spain signed a document proclaiming America's right to invade Cuba if Spain refused to sell her for a reasonable price. The diplomats argued, in language that fell quite short of the Declaration of Independence, that Cuba was "necessary" to the United States and belonged naturally to "that great family of states of which the Union is the Providential Nursery." If Cuba threatened the United States in any way—a rather large opening—then the United States could invade.

The extreme opinions of Ostend were renounced—just barely—by the Pierce administration, but their stench lingered in the air afterward. Americans made Europeans nervous with all their talk of revolution and republics. A former senator, Robert Walker of Mississippi, wrote a pamphlet in 1852 that looked forward to the time "foretold in Holy Writ—When the world shall be United States, with one commerce, one language, and one confederacy." Admirers called his vision "the one true millennium." In 1852, a congress of German immigrants founded the American Revolutionary League, calling on all peoples to throw off tyrants, apply to join the union, and form "the World's Republic." The *New York Herald* called the spread of liberty a glorious, manifest, "throbbing dream by night."

Not long afterward, an enterprising Tennessean, William Walker, took it upon himself to "liberate" vast stretches of Central America and became the leader of Nicaragua from 1856 to 1857, reinstating slavery while in office. The "grey-eyed man of destiny" was fairly honest about his motives and no longer felt any need to talk of spreading democracy. What he was interested in was power, and race-based power specifically:

> They are but drivellers who speak of establishing fixed relations between the pure white American race, as it exists in the United States, and the mixed Hispano-Indian race, as it exists in Mexico and Central America, without the employment of force. The history of the world presents no such Utopian vision as that of an inferior race yielding meekly and peacefully to the controlling influence of a superior people.

Of course, there were legitimate forms of expansion as well. Few people today regret the opening of U.S.-Japanese relations, an act made possible by the forcible entry of U.S. warships into Tokyo Bay, under the command of Matthew Perry in 1853. Like so many other Americans of his generation, Perry had honed his skills in Mexico, where he had spent the war trying to advance American claims for a canal across the isthmus to speed passage to the Far East. In the early 1850s, the United States also made its first inquiries about annexing Hawaii.

Throughout the decade, the American flag flew farther and farther from home, as American sea captains and politicians pushed to extend the dominion of the United States as far as possible. One of the stranger rationales for expansion came about because of a unique economic concern that briefly united North and South. Because Southern farmers had discovered that guano—bird excrement—was useful in rehabilitating worn-out soil, and because New England captains kept finding abandoned islands in the Pacific with enormous guano deposits, a guano movement of sorts was launched in the late 1850s, in the hopes of claiming some of these rich mineral sources. After Peru declined to grant Americans a stake in the islands off its coast, the United States passed the Guano Islands Act in 1856, which allowed any American happening upon a large pile of guano to lay claim to it, in the name of the United States, if it was unclaimed by another nation (a law that remains in effect). A claim was soon made.

In 1857, an American sea captain landed upon the island of Navassa, a small spit of land, shaped like a teardrop, thirty miles west of Haiti. Sighted by Columbus's crew at the dawn of American history, it was claimed in 1504, then neglected for centuries, though it was understood to belong to Haiti. After its rediscovery in 1857, the United States claimed it under the Guano Act, and a company quickly formed in Baltimore to harvest its guano and phosphate. Haiti disputed that action then and still does today. In fact, this island, now maintained irregularly by the U.S. Department of the Interior, is still claimed by both the United States and Haiti, though inhabited only by rats, goats, and feral dogs. Its annexation by the United States marks the first outright seizure of another country's land in our history. Navassa also became America's first noncontiguous territory, far in advance of Hawaii, Alaska, or any of the larger Caribbean islands.

But these scattered islands were not the only places where guano could be found. As the Civil War drew closer, and speeches grew angrier, a dangerous form of high-flying rhetoric could be heard on the floor of Congress, asserting the right to do more or less anything in the name of liberty. By the end of the decade, it seemed that being American offered a license to either enslave or liberate whomever one felt like, in whatever order felt appropriate. In sum, American foreign policy was completely out of control.

BETTER ANGELS

That it came back under control was due in no small measure to the rise of an American figure so famous that we don't always think through his origins clearly enough. Like George Washington, his idol, Abraham Lincoln was profoundly troubled by the tendency of his nation toward extreme foreign policy. In his own way, he, too, brought the ark back to its true course. Lincoln's greatness lies as much in his restraint as in his capacity for action. In retrospect, he seems almost to have been called into service for the express purpose of calming these baser instincts and summoning our better angels.

Lincoln is not especially thought of as a foreign policy president. But America's untrammeled expansion into foreign lands activated his conscience and brought him into national politics. His only federal experience before the presidency was the single term he served in Congress from 1847 to 1849, during the height of the Mexican War. In January 1848, he rose in the House to give an extraordinarily harsh speech about Polk and the war. That a freshman member of Congress called the president of the United States to task for exceeding his war powers is remarkable enough; it is even more so knowing that Lincoln would wield war powers far beyond those dreamed of by Polk.

Lincoln's speech still has the power to shock today. Not only did he refuse to show deference toward Polk, he could barely contain his fury in respectable language. Lincoln was irate that a war had been started with no clear purpose, and the more Polk tried to defend it, the more his evasions infuriated him. Lincoln's rage was nearly theological. Fittingly, he resorted to the language of the Bible—which he did not quote often as a young man. The young congressman predicted that the president "feels the blood of this war, like the blood of Abel, is crying to Heaven against him." He attacked that "exceeding brightness of military glory" as an "attractive rainbow, that rises in showers of blood," and as if that were not vivid enough, as "a serpent's eye, that charms to destroy." Shockingly, he likened this ambitious president to a mere insect, "vacillating like a tortured creature on a hot surface." Throughout the speech, he asked hard lawyers' questions about the war's origins—including the exact spot where it began. His speech was so angry that he failed to win reelection, and for a time he was known back home as Spotty Lincoln.

Lincoln's forced retirement kept him out of politics for a time, but the rapidly disintegrating situation in the 1850s, including the ongoing disaster of American foreign policy, drew him out again. When the Republican Party emerged in the middle of the decade, one of its original platform planks was the rejection of the Ostend Manifesto, which claimed a right to invade Cuba. In other words, the Republican Party owes its origins to a preference for a modest foreign policy.

Lincoln never abandoned this way of thinking, and as he rose to prominence, his calm and reasoned approach to foreign policy began to draw voters. It was present at every stage of his thinking, and particularly characterized his rivalry with Stephen Douglas, who had been connected to Manifest Destiny since its origin. That Lincoln disapproved of Manifest Destiny and its borderless ambitions is quite clear. Sometimes one can sense that *disapproval* is too weak a word. This passage is from a letter he wrote in 1855:

> Our progress in degeneracy appears to me to be pretty rapid. As a nation, we began by declaring that, "all men are created equal." We now practically read it "all men are created equal, except Negroes." When the Know-Nothings get control, it will read "all men are created equal, except negroes, and foreigners, and catholics." When it comes to this I should prefer emigrating to some country where they make no pretence of loving liberty—to Russia, for instance, where despotism can be taken pure, and without the base alloy of hypocracy [hypocrisy].

This is not the language of someone expressing mere irritation. It is the language of someone deeply in love with liberty and democracy, aggrieved at the persistent misinterpretation of those exalted concepts by people claiming to be patriots but sabotaging their country's true destiny. When composing his first inaugural address, Lincoln muted the millennial tone of a phrase suggested by Seward ("guardian angel of the nation") and turned it instead into the breathtaking "better angels of our nature." Arguments over words may seem semantic, especially a century and a half later, but it would be no exaggeration to say that the Civil War stemmed from exactly these issues. Americans simply could not agree over what liberty was, who should claim it, and how far around the world that claim should extend.

One of the uglier features of the Southern drive for nationhood was its final conclusion that "liberty" was not what the founders had in mind when they created the United States. Leading statesmen of the South renounced the idealism that had inspired the world in 1776, rewriting history to suit their needs. Jefferson Davis forced a hat change on the statue of Freedom planned for the roof of the Capitol, because the so-called Liberty Cap implied a dislike of slavery. The Declaration of Independence, with its inconvenient emphasis on equality, came in for special hostility. In his famous "Corner-Stone Speech," Alexander Stephens, the Confederacy's vice president, said that "our government is founded upon exactly the opposite idea; its foundations are laid, its corner-stone rests upon the great truth, that the negro is not equal to the white man." George Fitzhugh—the author of *Cannibals All!*—wrote that the Declaration "had nothing more to do with philosophy than the weaning of a calf. It was the act of a people seeking national independence, not the Utopian scheme of speculative philosophers, seeking to establish human equality and social perfection." It is highly doubtful that his fellow Southerner Thomas Jefferson would have agreed with that assessment. When it came time to write the charter documents of the Confederate States of America, soaring paeans to liberty were conspicuously lacking.

Until the last minute that he was a citizen of the United States, Jefferson Davis was trying to acquire more foreign territory to expand slavery into. In 1860, he renewed the demand that Cuba join the Union and even had it written into that year's Democratic platform—although he must have known that he was on his way out of the Union. He also urged that states be given the right to renew the African slave trade if they chose. In short, he argued that there be no restraint on the South whatsoever.

In the confusing days between the South's secession and Lincoln's inauguration, a number of desperate compromises were attempted to hold the Union together. But a key sticking point for Lincoln was that they refused to restrict Southern filibustering. On January 11, 1861, he wrote, "A year will not pass, before we shall have to take Cuba, as a condition upon which they will stay in the Union." And that would only be the beginning of a policy of permanent acquisition, and "the end of us, and of the government." A few weeks later, on February 1, he repeated his implacable opposition to his incoming secretary of state, William H. Seward: "Any trick by which the nation is to acquire territory, and then allow some local authority to spread slavery over it, is as obnoxious as any other."

On the eve of Lincoln's inauguration, Jefferson Davis bade farewell to the Senate, arguing that the United States had already in effect become two different nations. Extending that point to its ultimate conclusion were the South Carolinians guarding Charleston harbor in the spring of 1861, eyeing the U.S. troops at Fort Sumter as an occupying foreign power. Thus, when they shelled the fort on April 12, igniting the Civil War, it was not only the beginning of the worst domestic tragedy in our history. It was also, in a sense quite unexpected, the latest foreign policy disaster for a people—now two foreign countries—still struggling to find their place in the world.

CHAPTER SIX

THE NEW COLOSSUS

Here first the duties of today, the lessons of the concrete,
Wealth, order, travel, shelter, products, plenty;
As of the building of some varied, vast, perpetual edifice,
Whence to arise inevitable in time, the towering roofs, the lamps,
The solid-planted spires tall shooting to the stars.
—Walt Whitman, "The United States to Old World Critics"

LIBERTY ISLAND

Franz Kafka is not normally considered the most expert observer of the United States, and for good reason. His novel *Amerika* opens with a glaring, unforgettable mistake: the Statue of Liberty guards the approaches to New York City with a gigantic sword instead of a torch. Kafka paints the surreal scene with complete nonchalance, describing the arrival of his sixteen-year-old hero: "A sudden burst of sunshine seemed to illuminate the Statue of Liberty, so that he saw it in a new light, although he had sighted it long before. The arm with the sword rose up as if newly stretched aloft, and round the figure blew the free winds of heaven."

But perhaps that error contains more truth than we recognize. Most statues of Liberty (and there are many) include subtle suggestions that she is quite capable of defending herself. The statue atop the U.S. Capitol was originally named *Armed Freedom*, though we are now supposed to call her *Lady Freedom*, a name the founders would surely have rejected for its aristocratic pretensions. (Can anyone imagine a male statue titled *Sir Democracy*?) Although the Statue of Liberty holds no sword, or weapon of any kind, the huge metal spikes protruding from her brow suggest a capacity to inflict a serious hurt on any adversaries foolish enough to come near her hair. Yet she is also beloved as a symbol of refuge.

These are only a few of the contradictions lying beneath Liberty's deceptively calm countenance. She embodies America, but faces toward Europe. She counsels moderation, yet suggests, none too subtly, that the days of Europe's kings are numbered. She is rooted firmly to her little island, now named after her, but her full title is *Liberty Enlightening the World*, as if this hemisphere were too small for her global aspirations (it should be noted that she was indeed a lighthouse until 1902—the light from her torch could be seen twenty-four miles out at sea). She is feminine, as Liberty must be, and yet there is a masculine heft to this statue that is hard to ignore. She is universal, but her features allegedly came from a single woman, the mother of the sculptor, Frédéric-Auguste Bartholdi. Unfortunately, history tells us that Madame Bartholdi was "something of a religious bigot," a rather severe Alsatian Protestant who drove one of her children to madness when she prevented him from marrying a Jewish woman. (Perhaps *Liberty Nagging the World* would be a more fitting title?)

For all of these reasons, the great statue perfectly captures America's inconsistent aspirations during the decades that elapsed between the end of the Civil War and the beginning of the Spanish-American War. In fact, it took much of that period to erect the great statue, which was conceived in the early 1870s by a group of Frenchmen, but not completed until 1886, ten years after the anniversary it was designed to celebrate.

We may think of these as relatively uneventful years, to the degree that we think of them at all. But incontestably, America was expanding by leaps and bounds, whether measured by exports, population, or cultivated land. Like the Statue of Liberty, the United States showed a capacity for both restraint and conflict during these pivotal years of maturation. Having barely survived the Civil War, Americans did not relish confrontation with anyone, and American foreign policy was notably calmer in the three decades after the Civil War than it had been during the fifteen years previous. Still, every year brought a new consciousness of strength. Huge numbers of immigrants entered the nation, at Ellis Island and elsewhere, inspired by the same ideals that were expressed by the Statue of Liberty. The American economy grew at breakneck speed, and with economic strength came many of the preconditions that lead to international tension—new markets, raw materials, and a strong navy to protect trade. Slowly, all of these pressures, and the cyclical nature of history, conspired to pull the United States back toward Manifest Destiny, reasserted with a new intensity in the 1890s, and to its inevitable by-product: war.

In fact, war was never far from the Statue of Liberty, even when she was just a gleam in the eye of her creator. The gift was conceived in the wake of the disastrous Franco-Prussian War of 1870, when a group of Frenchmen sought to cement America's affection for our original ally. That was not a bad idea, considering that U.S.-Prussian relations were warming. In his memoir of the project, Bartholdi recorded his private fear that the United States might begin to supply arms to Prussia. There were also local reasons—the construction of a giantess named Liberty in Paris was itself a political event and an inspiration to French republicans; more than three hundred thousand people came to visit Bartholdi in his workshop as she grew. Bartholdi shared these republican sympathies; he had worked on several other huge projects already, including a similar plan for building a lighthouse in the shape of a woman at the entrance to the Suez Canal in Egypt. Had that project been built, the Statue of Liberty would have had an elder sibling in the Middle East.

Progress was slow for years, due to financial constraints and the inevitable delays. Many European leaders were not thrilled to see a shrine to democracy built at all. But slowly, the great lady began to arrive in bits and pieces—a disembodied hand and torch on display at the Philadelphia Centennial, a head at the Paris Exposition of 1878, and then the full-blown statue, erected in her enormous entirety in Paris before being taken down and shipped in 210 cases to New York for reassembly. The idea that liberty can be exported has always been central to American thinking—but here, for once, Liberty was an import.

Ultimately, the scale of the project drew in many others, including the Hungarian immigrant Joseph Pulitzer, a refugee himself, who helped raise the final funds through a heroic campaign led by his newspaper, *The New York World*.

At long last, she was unveiled and dedicated by President Grover Cleveland on October 28, 1886. A short speech concluded with an image of a light designed to "pierce the darkness of ignorance and man's oppression, until Liberty enlightens the world." The universality of the sentiment would have been easier to prove if the U.S. Congress had not severely restricted Chinese immigration in 1882. But in spite of that, the statue was a magnificent achievement. In 1886, the structure's 305 feet from base to summit made it the tallest structure in New York. To Latin Americans who were already calling the United States *el colosso*, she must have seemed the perfect embodiment of our huge nation. In the heyday of 1850s expansionism, Caleb Cushing, a diplomat and attorney general, had called the United States "the colossus of liberty." Now the world could see that idea made flesh, or rather, metal. In keeping with her designer's universal hopes, she has been imitated around the world, from her birthplace in Paris, to Germany, and to Tiananmen Square. Only a year after the dedication, one version of the statue was sent by the proud French government to Hanoi, Vietnam, where she became known as *Tu'ọng Bà đầm xòe*, or the Statue of the Open-Dress Dame. By a painful irony, she was taken down by the Vietnamese in 1945, for the simple reason that they were eager to avoid any relics of empire in the new era beginning that year. Evidently statues of liberty, like the word *liberty* itself, can be lost in translation. That lesson was relearned, for the millionth time, when Ronald Reagan celebrated "Miss Liberty" on her hundredth birthday in 1986, and praised the "Quakers" for their city on a hill. That was a moving thought, but it would have been more moving still if he had not ascribed it to the exact group whom the Puritans had tried so hard to keep off their hilly utopia.

LAST BEST HOPE

That a huge statue to liberty would be donated by the French would have struck most Americans during the Civil War as a preposterous attempt at Gallic humor. Among the serious threats that a beleaguered

Lincoln administration had to confront throughout the war was that France and Britain, with their deep ties to the Southern cotton industry, might recognize the Confederacy—a disaster that was avoided by the barest of margins. The *Times* of London called the expected end of "the American Colossus" a good "riddance of a nightmare." And Napoleon III took full advantage of the crisis to reassert France's right to meddle in the fortunes of the New World, leading a united effort of French, Spanish, and British troops to topple the Mexican government, assume control of Mexico's silver mines, and prop up a Hapsburg as emperor. The famous Cinco de Mayo national holiday of Mexico commemorates a victory over the French invaders in 1862.

The French adventure was short-lived, but it still constituted the most serious European violation of the Monroe Doctrine before the Cuban Missile Crisis. American opposition was intense. Northern and Southern commanders seethed equally at French opportunism—Grant called it "an act of hostility against the United States"—and Francis P. Blair nearly achieved a joint Union-Confederate force in December 1864, while the Civil War was still being fought! Indeed, it was the rising threat of U.S. invasion that convinced Napoleon III to end his military support for Emperor Maximilian, in effect condemning him. Edouard Manet's memorable depiction of Maximilian's execution, in 1867, might be said to capture the Civil War's final casualty.

The apocalypse of the Civil War could have been expected to disabuse Americans once and for all of the notion that they had a Manifest Destiny to do, well, whatever they wanted to. That dawning realization lay at the heart of Lincoln's second inaugural address, which acknowledged, as no speech before or since, that there may be more to the divine plan than we mortals understand. "The Almighty has his own purposes," Lincoln said, with unanswerable logic. It remains the most eloquent response to the virus of religious self-importance ever written. It was also in its way a speech about foreign policy, and ended with a promise to seek peace "among ourselves, and with all nations."* Although Lincoln's assassination brought Americans back to the idea that

*The French were relieved by these words, for they had worried that the end of the war would be followed by "the appearance of an American fleet of ironsides in the port of Havre, or a fleet of gunboats sailing up the Seine to take Paris!" (*Chicago Tribune*). The United States would indeed invade Normandy, but under very different circumstances.

a special Providence was guiding the United States (he was killed on Good Friday, as hundreds of ministers reminded their flocks), our greatest president had done extraordinary work to recalibrate America's moral compass, and to reassert the modesty of the founders at their best.

In 1862, during some of the war's darkest days, Nathaniel Hawthorne worried that America's destiny had been tainted no matter which way the war went. If the South won, the idea of America would be damaged forever. But if the North won, there might be a new vogue for military leaders, or as he put it acidly, "one bullet-headed general will succeed another in the presidential chair." He wondered, "Will the time ever come again, when we may live half a score of years without once seeing the likeness of a soldier, except it be in the festal march of a company on its summer tour? Not in this generation, I fear, nor in the next, nor till the millennium; and even that blessed epoch, as the prophecies seem to intimate, will advance to the sound of drum and trumpet."

Still, many Americans maintained faith in a mission that had been tarnished, but not beyond recognition. Ministers in both Northern and Southern pulpits thundered forth promises of divine favor throughout the war, and many of them reached back effortlessly to the militant music of the Old Testament. When Julia Ward Howe penned her lyrics to "The Battle Hymn of the Republic," first published in February 1862, she borrowed heavily from the language of Apocalypse, depicting a surprisingly Puritanical millennium of wrathful vengeance rather than the sweetness and light one might have expected from a Victorian poetess. To this day, we hum its pleasant melody, and perhaps sing a bar or two, only dimly aware that we are calling on the avenging angel to visit our enemies with death and destruction. All her imagery, from the trampling of vintages to the sounding of trumpets, came from the book of Revelation, specifically Revelation 14, which describes the scenes following the fall of Babylon.

Even Lincoln, for all of his humility, never relinquished the better parts of that vision. Beneath every public utterance of his presidency lay the assumption—sometimes explicit, sometimes less so—that the progress of democracy in the United States was urgently important to the world. He expressed the thought repeatedly, beginning with the series of moving autobiographical remarks he made as he migrated from

Springfield to Washington to assume the presidency. Before the New Jersey Senate, he remembered his great excitement, as a child, reading about the exploits of the American Revolution and expressed his hope—with perfect modulation—that he might be "an humble instrument in the hands of the Almighty, and of this, his almost chosen people." Almost! The next day, he gave those thoughts even more power, in capsule, when he stopped at Independence Hall in Philadelphia: "It was not the mere matter of the separation of the colonies from the mother land; but something in that Declaration giving liberty, not only to the people of this country, but hope to the world for all future time." A newspaper recorded "great applause" at precisely this moment. His Special Message to Congress on July 4, 1861, presented to "the whole family of man, the question of whether a constitutional republic, or a democracy—a government of the people, by the same people—can, or cannot maintain its territorial integrity." A year later, in his 1862 Annual Message, he promised to save "the last best hope of earth"—a phrase nearly identical to one that Albert Gallatin had used in his pamphlet on peace with Mexico. Of course, the most gemlike crystallization of this line of thinking came at Gettysburg and has not been improved upon since.

If Lincoln was trying to involve the world in the struggle, the impulse came from an idealist's sense that Americans liked to feel that their national epic was relevant to humanity. But surely it also came from a realist's sense that the world *was* involved with the outcome. If Britain and France were slow to support the Union, then other countries were surprisingly solicitous. The Ottoman sultan, for example, was an early supporter of Lincoln's government, a result of the good American-Islamic relations that had stemmed from the treaty of 1830. Czar Alexander of Russia was another surprising ally, and the arrival of a squadron of Russian warships in both New York and San Francisco sent a strong message to Europe's crowned heads not to recognize the Confederacy. It is a fitting tribute to the vagaries of history that the earliest and most important support for the world's last best hope came from two of the most autocratic rulers on earth. Still, it mattered.

Of course, American foreign policy did not cease simply because the United States had split in two. Normal policy was constrained, but international relations continued, and in some cases the United States showed extraordinary international ambition, even under a president who had made no secret of his disdain for Manifest Destiny. On July 16, 1863, only two weeks after the Battle of Gettysburg, the USS *Wyoming* engaged in a series of offensive actions in Japanese waters against warlords who were attacking foreigners—actions that were surprising not only for their distance from American shores, but because the United States joined France, Britain, and the Netherlands in a brief alliance against the warlords.

In fact, the Civil War, like the Revolution, was a far more global struggle than most Americans recognize. Confederate vessels were fitted out in English yards—an object of acute diplomatic sensitivity that was not resolved until 1872, when an international tribunal awarded the United States $15.5 million in damages. One of the war's most famous naval battles, between the CSS *Alabama* and the USS *Kearsarge*, took place off the northern coast of France, not far from the site of the D-day landings. The Confederates planned several raids from Canada on an unsuspecting North; and in the immediate aftermath of the war, Union veterans of Irish extraction invaded Canada in several locations, including a genuine military conflict near Buffalo in 1866 after an army of "liberation" invaded in the name of the Irish Republican Army, the first time that term was used. As is so often the case, the most lasting legacy of this aggression may be the opposite of that intended, for the so-called Fenian Raids helped to form modern Canada; the fragmented provinces of British Canada were so offended by the raids that they voted for confederation in 1867. There were also naval engagements in the Caribbean and off South America, and Confederates scattered to Brazil and other countries in the aftermath of defeat. Throughout the war, Spain, like France, was trying to recapture some of her lost empire, in this case by invading the Dominican Republic and threatening war with Peru. Russia's decision to sell Alaska to the United States was hastened by the Confederate cruiser *Shenandoah*, which destroyed Russian whalers in the Bering and Okhotsk seas in 1865. Indeed, our most northern state could be the Confederacy's biggest legacy to the United States.

That successful purchase, brilliantly engineered by Secretary of State William Seward, brought more than half a million square miles into the United States for the meager sum of $7.2 million. In the chastened aftermath of the war, it was a surprisingly difficult sell to the American public, with some editors (notably Horace Greeley) ridiculing the purchase, and many lampooning the new wilderness as "Seward's icebox" or "Andrew Johnson's polar bear garden." That in itself is a measure of how far the United States had retreated from the excesses of Manifest Destiny. In fact, the chief reason that Americans were persuaded to accept the purchase is that it was presented as a favor to Russia—which needed to sell the land since it could not defend it—and Americans felt deep gratitude to the czar for his gestures on behalf of the Union. When his brother Grand Duke Alexis came to the United States in 1871, the poet Oliver Wendell Holmes greeted him with these verses: "Bleak are our coasts with the blasts of December / Thrilling and warm are the hearts that remember / Who was our friend when the world was our foe."

William Seward deserves attention here as one of the great links in the chain of American foreign policy. To an extent, he is known as a politician in his own right—the man Lincoln outmaneuvered to secure the 1860 nomination—but that understates his essential role as secretary of state, during the war, when he superbly managed the foreign crises that never ceased to plague him, and then, just as important, as a rock of stability during the presidency of Andrew Johnson that followed.

Like his hero John Quincy Adams, Seward acted out of a deep sense of American history. In fact, he wrote a biography of Adams, dedicated to "the friends of equal liberty and human rights throughout the world." That book enthusiastically praised America's previous efforts to support international liberty, from Latin America to Greece, as part of "the ever-advancing American Revolution." Without indulging in the extremes of Manifest Destiny, he still felt a profound sense of American continental grandeur, peppering his early speeches with references to "liberty and empire," and expressing a vision of the world that in some ways exceeded the ambitions of the pro-slavery annexationists. Like them, he talked about extending "the area of freedom," and he occasionally lapsed into the hemispheric language that Americans thrilled to. In 1853, in Ohio, he predicted that America's borders "shall be extended so that it shall greet the sun when he touches the tropics, and when he sends his gleaming rays towards the polar circle, and shall include even distant islands in either ocean."

But this staunch antislavery advocate meant something quite different from those who counseled seizure and war. "I abhor war, as I detest slavery," he said at the time of the conflict with Mexico. Seward argued, more temperately, that "the sword is not the most winning messenger that can be sent abroad." In his view, commerce was the natural vehicle for American energies. "The nation that draws the most materials and provisions from the earth," he explained, "fabricates the most, and sells the most productions and fabrics to foreign nations, must be, and will be, the great power of the earth." Inevitably, according to his scheme, the U.S. population would swell, to 200 million or so by 1950, and Americans would peacefully displace all obstacles to their expansion by simply trading and repopulating themselves in perpetuity. They would eventually spill over into Mexico and Central America. He even predicted that the capital of the United States would ultimately be located there.

Seward was also deeply intrigued by the possibilities of Asia, and *continental* is too small a word to describe the global commercial system he hoped to build, with New York and San Francisco as its headquarters. A bit of poetry he wrote conveyed his theory efficiently: "The Eastern Nations sink, their glory ends / And empire rises where the sun descends." His relationship with Russia was profound, and he advanced an extraordinary attempt to build an intercontinental telegraph between St. Petersburg and St. Louis, via Siberia. American trade was growing in China and Japan (and in Korea, where an American gunboat nearly attacked Pyongyang in 1866—an incident that North Korea continues to rehash, claiming that Kim Il Sung's ancestor defeated the Yankee invaders). Seward could even adopt missionary language when the moment was right, arguing that American commercial influence would lead to inevitable political change and democratic redemption. Or, in his words, the "political alembic" of the United States "would disclose the secret of the ultimate regeneration and reunion of human society throughout the world."

Like the founders, he felt a strong instinctive sympathy for the freedom of the seas and the absence of trade barriers between nations. He negotiated important treaties toward this end (the Burlingame Treaty with China in 1868 placed the relationship on a more modern footing), acquired Midway Island in 1867, and laid some of the groundwork for the enormous interoceanic presence of the United States in the twentieth century by expressing strong interest in Hawaii and a canal across Central America.

Alaska would prove to be his most lasting legacy—that, and the brilliant way he kept Britain and France just off-balance enough during the Civil War that neither ever quite recognized the Confederacy. He also pursued more tropical acquisitions, but with less luck. After the plot against Lincoln nearly removed him as well, Seward recuperated in the West Indies, and before long he was hatching schemes for the purchase of additional territory in the Caribbean.

Throughout the 1860s, Seward worked toward annexing Santo Domingo, by its own volition, into the United States—but postbellum feelings against Manifest Destiny lingered and Congress steadfastly resisted. Seward also spent a great deal of energy persuading Denmark to sell its insular possessions in the West Indies, another near possibility that went bust. Americans, exhausted by war and reconstruction, craved nothing so much as stability. Grant's secretary of state, Hamilton Fish, said that Americans were simply against all expansion. The journalist Whitelaw Reid put it crudely when he wrote that the nation's "gastric juices" were so busy trying to incorporate 3 million former slaves into the body politic that it was impossible to consider the addition of "the inferior mixed races of outlying tropical and semi tropical dependencies."

Seward left office in 1869, but never stopped working to extend America's influence around the world. In 1870 and 1871, he circumnavigated the globe in a most unusual trip that lasted fourteen months. His widely publicized voyage demonstrated a deep appreciation of what we would now call cultural diplomacy. He and his daughter Olive traveled to some of the most out-of-the-way locations ever visited by an American statesman—Japan, China, India, and the Middle East, where he spent month upon month. Olive wrote a best-selling book about the journey, describing her father's thoughts and adventures as they traveled, and it brought home to thousands of Americans how large the world was, and how prominent a role Americans might play in it in the years ahead.

The culmination of the trip came on July 4, 1871, in Constantinople, the capital of the Ottoman empire, with a most unusual celebration of the United States. The occasion was the completion of the first American college campus to be built outside the United States. In

1863, in defiance of the odds, Robert College had opened its doors to the youth of Turkey, Armenia, and the Balkans. Seward had been an important ally in the unlikely endeavor.

Most of us have no idea that a university built by Americans has stood at the heart of the Islamic world for a century and a half: it is older than MIT, the University of California, or the University of Texas. An American missionary, Cyrus Hamlin, had grown frustrated with the constraints of simplistic missionary policy and had begun to nurture hopes of a more ambitious educational venture when he met a wealthy New York merchant, Christopher Robert. The college they decided to build placed a strong emphasis on English-language instruction, science, and a liberal arts education. It immediately offered something unprecedented to the Ottoman capital.

Although the idea of a Protestant college raised some hackles, Hamlin's relatively secular approach impressed local authorities, and in the long run he was allowed to build Robert College in one of the most prominent places in Istanbul—high atop a ridge overlooking the Bosporus. Further, the sultan granted his blessing and offered a guarantee of extraterritoriality, meaning that the infant college could fly the U.S. flag as if it were an embassy, where all the vessels traveling through that busy waterway could see it. It was the only foreign flag ever allowed above the Bosporus until 1971, when the college became a Turkish institution.*

The creation of a single college may seem like a minor detail in the global scheme, but I mention it to stress the many ways the United States influenced foreign policy in an era when it had little military might. One reason the Ottoman sultan allowed Americans to build Turkey's first institution of higher learning is because Americans were then regarded, in that simpler time, as more benign and disinterested than other peoples—certainly more so than the Europeans who were chipping away at the frontiers of the sultan's domains. To most Turks, America seemed a virtuous land that was geographically and ideologically removed from the tawdry machinations of the Old World. Robert College was also important beyond its size because it inspired other creations on the same model—the American University of Beirut

*A high school called Robert College is still administered by a U.S.-based board.

(1866) and the American University of Cairo (1919), to name two of the most important examples. Each of those irreplaceable institutions set an example of the highest magnitude for its city and region. With a minimum of bluster and a maximum of efficiency, they offered a decent secular education and brought people from different groups together. Their influence extended across generations, shaping nations and families, including this author's.

For the next century, the American universities of the Middle East did the essential work of cultural diplomacy long before that term was coined. Distinguished graduates acted as natural mediators in disputes, and one reason that the United States and Turkey never declared war on each other in the First World War was because of the intercession of friends of Robert College on both sides. Particularly when international peace conferences were in session, as in the aftermath of the First and Second World Wars, the alumni of these institutions proved their worth, for in a way the colleges had themselves been international peace conferences, drawing students from a wide range of ethnicities and religions. In ways dramatic and humble, they helped to make the United States more cosmopolitan as well. Not entirely coincidentally, *National Geographic* was built into a great magazine by two young editors, Gilbert and Edwin Grosvenor, who had grown up on the Robert College campus, where their father taught. That simple magazine, with its enormous subscription lists, may have done more than any other instrument to persuade Americans that the world was literally at their doorstep.

THE DISTANT BROUGHT NEAR

The same year that Seward went to Constantinople, Walt Whitman published "Passage to India," his meditation on Columbus. Like the admiral, Whitman embarked on a poetic journey of great globe-trotting ambition, arguing that the dream of Columbus had never died and that the United States was now accomplishing it, bringing Asia closer with new technology (railroads, underwater telegraph cables) and trade. Envisioning what he called "rondure," Whitman saw something close to globalization:

Passage to India!
Lo, soul, seest thou not God's purpose from the first?
The earth to be spann'd, connected by network,
The races, neighbors, to marry and be given in marriage,
The oceans to be cross'd, the distant brought near
The lands to be welded together.

It was a vision of great power, but events took some time to catch up to it. A first glance at the developments of American foreign policy between Seward and the Spanish-American War does not indicate a record of much achievement. The infrastructure of American diplomacy remained feeble, a testament to how little Americans felt threatened by the rest of the world. The foreign service was still tiny, its appointments contingent upon the whims of party patronage. The secretary of state barely had enough staff "to fill the seats at a small conference table." In 1881, when some thought was given to a show of military strength against Chile, the idea was called off when Chile's navy was discovered to be more powerful than that of the United States. The entire U.S. Army numbered around twenty-five thousand, roughly the size of a single division today. Its activities were largely confined to the West and the nasty business of clearing the land of its original inhabitants.

But still, despite the reluctance of the Civil War generation to deal with additional crises of any kind, the United States was deepening its foreign relationships around the world. To an extent, this was simply the result of the huge influx of immigrants from 1863 into the early decades of the twentieth century. For all their naivete about the brass tacks of foreign policy, Americans were an exuberant people, eager to take on the world. The successful laying of the Atlantic cable in 1866 made communication with the Old World instantaneous. Foreign coverage improved in American magazines, and well-to-do Americans flocked to Europe to take the grand tour for themselves. To be sure, this new wanderlust was easily parodied, and no one succeeded more viciously than Mark Twain in *The Innocents Abroad*, but still, the New World seemed closer to the Old than ever before.

Another important tour by an American in these years was Ulysses Grant's epic journey undertaken between 1877 and 1879. In a way, it was a voyage of liberation; the trip originated because he "felt the need of relaxation and complete freedom from all care." If nothing else, it showed that the rest of the world was as interested in America as America was in it. A hundred thousand Britons came out to see the former president in Newcastle. In Germany, Bismarck dropped everything to meet him. Indefatigable, Grant trudged on to places that American ex-presidents would not return to for more than half a century. In Egypt, he "felt that he was entering an entirely new world," and so he was, until he encountered American army officers advising a local dignitary. In Constantinople, the sultan gave him two Arabian stallions. In China, he was announced as "the King of America." He visited Burma, Vietnam, and Japan, where he was the first American to shake the emperor's hand. His tumultuous return to San Francisco, where many thousands greeted him, proved that the world was indeed round.

Global ties were also tightening because of the might of American capital, with its insatiable appetite for natural resources from around the earth and its efficiency at sending wares back in the opposite direction. The full extent of this traffic became evident at the Centennial Exposition of 1876, held in Philadelphia to celebrate the Declaration of Independence. Instead, it was a Declaration of Industry, displaying American technical wizardry before an awestruck world. Thirty-seven nations sent delegations and displays, and the exposition became what one newspaper called "a vast world-school," teaching Americans about foreigners and vice versa. By a stroke of good fortune, 1876 was also the first year that the United States achieved a positive balance of trade.

Still, America's self-confidence lagged behind its wealth, as Henry James confirmed with his cycles of stories about gauche social climbers. Nothing revealed this maturity problem more clearly than the adulation showered upon the highest-ranking foreign dignitary who could be enticed to the Centennial, Emperor Dom Pedro II of Brazil, the first reigning monarch to visit the United States. Bowing and scraping before a crowned head was an odd way to commemorate the Declaration, but the fact that any head of state attended could be counted as a minor success.

Like the American people, Congress expressed a fitful interest in the world. Charles Sumner tried hard to annex Canada, but failed to persuade his fellow senators. Americans continued to ignore the blandishments of empire, rejecting possibilities in both Samoa (which proposed annexation) and Haiti (which occasionally offered its harbors). The United States did possess a large number of guano islands in the Pacific—some fifty by the 1880s—but these random deposits of bird droppings hardly constituted an empire.

Still, the wheels of American foreign policy were beginning to turn. As the American economy grew by leaps and bounds, entangling Europe's economies with it, the need for raw materials and safe systems of transport grew apace. This meant, of course, a stronger navy and a better developed set of bases and coaling stations around the world. In the aftermath of the Civil War, the navy had been reduced to a fraction of its former size, but that trend was reversed in the early 1880s with a series of new vessels ordered by Congress and a Naval War College created in Newport, Rhode Island. Between 1883 and 1889, thirty-four steel vessels were built, and in 1890, Congress authorized three first-class battleships.

To a remarkable degree, the enormous changes that would take place over the next decade were the result of a single clique of friends. The story of Alfred T. Mahan, Theodore Roosevelt, John Hay, and Henry Cabot Lodge has been told many times, both individually and collectively. Each felt a rising consciousness of America's potential role in the world; each felt that military power was extremely useful in advancing that role; and each felt no aversion to foreign entanglements or, indeed, to war itself. Their influence was pervasive. Henry Adams wrote that war was "the last and most crucial test of a nation's energy," and before long, the words, thoughts, and deeds of these activists would lead America to exactly this test.

Mahan's career was perhaps the most unlikely; it would be hard to think of another intellectual who influenced American policy more directly, with the possible exception of George Kennan. An obscure naval historian, Mahan studied the rise of the British overseas empire in the seventeenth and eighteenth centuries and concluded that maritime power underlay all of it. Applying those lessons to the late nineteenth century, he argued persuasively, in a series of widely distributed essays, that American commerce needed the navy, and the navy needed new and more distant bases. More precisely, "having therefore no military establishments, either colonial or military, the ships of war of the United States, in war, will be like land birds, unable to fly far from their own shores. To provide resting-places for them, where they can coal and repair, would be one of the first duties of a government proposing to itself the development of the power of the nation at sea."

Mahan was first and foremost a military thinker (he taught at the new Naval War College), but he was also a master persuader, and his thinking was infused with a deep appreciation for the kinds of things that Americans liked to hear about themselves. In fact, he found rhetoric and public relations to be crucial tools of military preparation and argued that "the sentiment of a people is the most energetic element in national action." How else could a strong foreign policy flow from a democracy? Like so many of the new nationalists, he grounded his theory of American preparedness in strangely airy theology. Britain's maritime supremacy had emanated in some way from God's "Personal Will"; why could the same not happen to the United States?

The original Special Relationship appealed to other thinkers as well, including some enormously popular writers who combined old religious doctrine with new science, particularly with Darwin's theory of natural selection. Americans loved Darwin, not least because he loved America and found "the wonderful progress of the United States" to be evidence of natural selection. The historian John Fiske wrote a highly influential article in *Harper's* in 1885 with the inflammatory title "Manifest Destiny." In Fiske's theory, nothing proved Darwinian science so clearly as the fact that Darwin's people—the international Anglo-Saxon race—were displacing so many others. With serene satisfaction, he predicted, "The work which the English race began when it colonized North America is destined to go on until every land on the earth's surface that is not already the seat of an old civilization shall become English in its language, in its religion, in its political habits and traditions, and to a predominant extent in the blood of its people."

Another closet Darwinian, in those distant days when religion and science walked hand in hand, was the minister Josiah Strong. His book *Our Country*, published that same year, was hugely influential. At times, it almost seemed written by Cotton Mather, a comparison that would not have displeased him. Strong worshiped the Puritans, denounced the peril of "Romanism," and heralded the new time rapidly approaching when vital Anglo-Saxons ("unless devitalized by alcohol and tobacco") would "Anglo-Saxonize" mankind through the spread of liberty. There was a great deal to object to in *Our Country*, including its distrust of immigrants and its hatred of America's teeming metropolises. Strong's city on a hill was not much of a city at all. But he sang his hymn to progress with confidence, and his book sold like hotcakes. Millions read, and perhaps even believed, his prediction of the great things to come:

> I believe it is fully in the hands of the Christians of the United States, during the next ten or fifteen years, to hasten or retard the coming of Christ's kingdom in the world by hundreds, and perhaps thousands, of years. We of this generation and nation occupy the Gibraltar of the ages which commands the world's future.

To their credit, Fiske and Strong were learned men who knew their early American history well. But a distasteful smugness undeniably pervaded their thinking. Manifest Destiny, for all its air of benevolent inevitability, was never so distant from the theories of racial superiority we deplore in rival nations. Theodore Roosevelt, for example, dismissed criticism of America's previous land seizures with the simple explanation that "we were the people who could use it best, and we ought to have taken it all."

These early aspirations toward a new school of Manifest Destiny began to come together into something recognizable around 1892. That year the Republican platform publicly embraced Manifest Destiny in a way that would have been unthinkable a few years earlier, and one of the GOP's rising stars, Henry Cabot Lodge, publicly called on America to absorb the world's "waste places."

Also in 1892, the four hundredth anniversary of 1492, Frederick Jackson Turner famously announced the disappearance of the frontier at the World's Columbian Exposition in Chicago. Even more important may have been Mahan's discovery that Americans were beginning to pay more attention to the world outside their frontiers—"the turning of the eyes outward, instead of inward only, to seek the welfare of the country." That Chicago World's Fair proved it, offering a sparkling backdrop for the wishful projection of American might. A highly idealized canvas was presented for exuberant imaginations to play upon; not quite a city upon a hill, but a "White City," complete with an imaginary world government, including not only a "Parliament of Religions" but a "World Congress of Beauty." Most of these ideas were merely fanciful, but the architecture of the White City inspired the twentieth-century look of Washington, D.C., and the Hawaiian exhibit at the fair was the scene of annexationist activity that was very real.

Almost overnight, the sleepy kingdom of Hawaii suddenly shifted from the periphery of attention to center stage. A series of treaties in the 1870s and '80s had given the United States the exclusive right to build a naval repair station at Pearl Harbor, and a growing community of American planters, working in the sugar trade, had gained substantial political influence, making their desire for annexation felt.

One particularly aggressive diplomat provided the catalyst for action. John L. Stevens, the U.S. consul, wrote to his secretary of state in November 1892 urging annexation, arguing that "destiny and the vast future interests of the United States in the Pacific clearly indicate who at no distant day must be responsible for the government of those islands." In his final months in office, President Benjamin Harrison began to follow the precedent of James Polk, urging annexation because of the vague threat that other powers would intervene if Americans did not.

Things came to a head in January 1893. After the Hawaiian queen, Liliuokalani, attempted to proclaim an illegal new constitution by royal fiat, she set loose all of the kingdom's dormant tensions. A U.S. naval vessel, the *Boston*, arrived exactly as these events were under way. Stevens asked that troops come ashore to provide security for Americans. The next day, he recognized a provisional government that had quickly formed, in effect asking the queen to abdicate, which she did under duress. Two weeks later, on February 1, he had the U.S. flag raised over the government buildings for the first time.

The situation calmed down when Grover Cleveland returned to office in March. He ordered a review of the situation, which found considerable fault with the actions of the United States, and he tried to restore the queen to power. But the provisional government was by this point unwilling to be removed, and the question remained unresolved. Into this vacuum a torrent of hot air inevitably entered, fanned by newspaper editors and politicians. Alfred T. Mahan leapt into the fray with an 1893 essay, "Hawaii and Our Future Sea Power," which argued that the islands were essential to America's future. Simply put, the "Gibraltar of the Pacific" was key to control of that ocean, "in which the United States, geographically, has the strongest right to assert herself." Senator Orville Platt said those opposed were fighting against "fate, the stars in their courses, and the inevitable westward march of empire."

Not all Americans were so easily cowed. Progressive magazines such as *The Nation* saw economic interests at work behind the patriotism and fretted that this was a revolution "of sugar by sugar and for sugar." Carl Schurz wrote a penetrating piece for *Harper's* (like John Fiske's, also titled "Manifest Destiny"), arguing that Hawaii's annexation would be unethical, and unwise from a military point of view because the islands could not be defended.

The situation soon became chaotic, with anger rising on both sides, ugly racial comments about Hawaii's queen, and disorganization on the ground. The provisional government proclaimed a republic on July 4, 1894, but this republic prevented nearly all people from voting. Grover Cleveland never budged from his principles. Shortly after leaving office for the second time, he stated his views categorically: "I regarded, and still regard the proposed annexation of these islands as not only opposed to our national policy, but as a perversion of our national mission. The mission of our nation is to build up and make a greater country out of what we have, instead of annexing islands."

Cleveland had in fact been a strong defender of U.S. international interests, and helped to resolve a difficult border dispute in Venezuela between that country and Great Britain. He wanted to develop the navy further and expressed interest in the Central American canal project. By resisting the stampede to annex Hawaii, he was acting out of principle and tradition, and many Americans approved.

But destiny usually favors the people who claim, most loudly, to have destiny on their side. And slowly, over this decade, American foreign policy underwent a fundamental shift of profound importance. The advocates of muscular intervention eventually just outshouted their opponents. The 1896 Republican platform went further than its predecessor, calling for U.S. control of Hawaii, an American canal in Nicaragua, strong defense of the Monroe Doctrine, and as if that were not enough, Canada as well: "We hopefully look forward to the eventual withdrawal of the European powers from this hemisphere, and to the ultimate union of all English-speaking parts of the continent by the free consent of its inhabitants."

The old language of the 1840s was heard everywhere, and politicians spoke reverently of America's "cosmic tendency," duty, and inevitable fate, as well as the "white man's burden," "benevolent assimilation," and a thousand other euphemisms that would eventually lead to war in 1898.

The Republican tide surged in 1896 with the election of William McKinley, who promised Carl Schurz that there would be "no jingo nonsense under my administration." But like so many expressions of fine sentiment in this era, that prediction turned out to be just that—sentiment.

For one thing, it turned out to be impossible for McKinley to control the most fervent advocates of expansion inside his party, or even inside his administration. His assistant secretary of the navy, Theodore Roosevelt, was particularly active, writing inflammatory letters to Alfred Mahan and other sympathizers, overdramatizing Japanese encroachments on Hawaii, and doing everything in his jurisdiction (and a few things that were not) to bring America to the edge of war.

The near approach of the new century only deepened the millennial expectation that something momentous was about to happen. As usual, the only questions were where and when. Mahan again nudged the debate forward with his 1897 *Harper's* piece, "A Twentieth-Century Outlook," which foresaw an enormous struggle between Western civilization and Asia, requiring a large U.S. naval presence in the Pacific.

DRIFT

> Ah, who shall soothe these feverish children?
> Who justify these restless explorations?
> —Walt Whitman, "Passage to India"

Theodore Roosevelt used a mariner's word—*drift*—to describe the course his nation was on. He warned the secretary of the navy that there would be trouble "if we drift into war butt end forward, and go at it in higgledy-piggledy fashion." It was not an entirely fair term to use, because Roosevelt's hand was more firmly on the tiller than he implied. But it accurately characterized the aimless way in which the United States entered its first war against a foreign power in six decades, ending the longest such stretch in our history.

Near the end of the American Revolution, the Spanish ambassador to France had written a secret memo to his king, predicting that as the Americans grew stronger they would inevitably come after Spain's possessions in the Caribbean. It took longer than he thought, but his prophecy was more than fulfilled by an explosion of activity—including actual explosions—in the summer of 1898. A feeling of déjà vu accompanied the Spanish-American War, for this was not the first time Americans had coveted the Spanish islands. Yet this was a serious war, unlike the filibuster expeditions, and it pitted the muscular young republic against a venerable royal house of Europe. Spain was an optimal adversary—monarchical, Catholic, and conservative, and all three points were mentioned as tensions rose. Further, she was weaker than the other great colonial powers, and overextended.

The tornado of vaporous speeches, hot-blooded headlines, and millennial expectations created a war fever that would have been difficult for any politician to resist. President McKinley was clearly not up to the task. Early in his term, he had appointed a supporter to a consular post in the Philippines, explaining that it was "somewhere away around on the other side of the world," but he did not know "exactly where." Before becoming vice president, Roosevelt complained, "McKinley has no more backbone than a chocolate éclair."

When war finally came, it came at sea, as all had expected. After a slew of poorly understood but widely publicized problems in the relationship between the United States and Spain, culminating in the famous explosion on the USS *Maine* in Havana harbor, hostilities commenced in April 1898 in two theaters. In the Pacific, Roosevelt dispatched Commodore George Dewey, who sailed from Hong Kong and stunned the Spanish fleet at Manila with a smashing triumph that cost only a single American life (and that from a heart attack). Closer to home were a series of naval and land battles on the old battlegrounds of the Caribbean. It was all over quickly, and by the end of summer, Spain had capitulated, leaving American forces in control of Cuba, Puerto Rico, Guam, and the Philippines.

The surprising mismatch left Americans nearly speechless with excitement—except for the flood of orations and newspaper essays lionizing the victors. Laxatives, sailor hats and chewing gum (Dewey Chewies) were named after the Hero of Manila. Evangelical magazines compared his guns to "God's own trumpet tones." Even those who had not been clearly for Manifest Destiny, such as William Jennings Bryan, joined the celebration.

But victory was not quite unconditional. As usual, America's most difficult enemies proved to be those of her own creation, and a welter of contradictory emotions about the nation's place in the world were expressed in the wake of the triumph, cautiously at first, but then more openly. The biggest problem was that this "splendid little war" was not so little. In fact, it showed no sign of ending.

The problem lay in the Philippines, where guerrillas who had fought alongside Americans against the Spanish now wanted their independence, in keeping with American promises that this was a war to liberate them. In fact, they were quite well informed about American history; their leader, Emilio Aguinaldo, considered the United States "the cradle of genuine liberty" and a bulwark against foreign tyranny. His hero was George Washington.

But again the United States drifted, contemplating whether it should retain a coaling station in the islands, or turn them into a protectorate with Filipino cooperation, or annex them outright. An unusually pompous senator, Albert Beveridge of Indiana, urged the latter course, in fulfillment of America's mission, and with "gratitude for a task worthy of our strength, and thanksgiving to Almighty God that He has marked us as His chosen people, henceforth to lead in the regeneration of the world." McKinley waffled, then turned to the Special Relationship. As he told a visiting delegation of Methodist missionaries, he paced the White House in darkness, unsure of his course. Then he kneeled to beg "Almighty God for light and guidance," and experienced a revelation of sorts. He could not let European rivals take the Philippines, nor could he give power to the Filipinos ("unfit for self-government"). Instead, the United States would take over, and nobly "educate the Filipinos, and uplift and Christianize them, and by God's grace do the very best we could by them, as our fellow men for whom Christ died." Instantly, the former anti-imperialist had become America's leading imperialist. With remarkable ease, an empire had been acquired—not Madison's "empire of reason" or Jefferson's "empire of liberty," but something very much like the real thing.

As it turned out, "the very best we could" do turned out to be an improvement over the Spanish administration in many ways. But progress came at a heavy cost. The splendid little war became a nasty little insurgency, as Filipino guerrilla fighters struggled to retain their independence. American military tactics were every bit as muddled as the thinking that had led to the decision to annex the islands. U.S. commanders could win battles in the open, but had great difficulty finding the enemy, or separating combatants from civilians. The United States claimed to be fighting "a harsh and philanthropic war at the same time," a clear indication of drift, and to insist blandly that its soldiers had come "not as invaders or conquerors, but as friends to protect the natives in their homes."

Before long, the "friends" were inflicting extraordinary cruelties on each other. Americans found their troops decapitated, or killed in horrific ways, and they began to retaliate in kind. Entire villages of Filipino men, women, and children were wiped out, and those who survived often were tortured. A disturbed Senate held hearings on the torture allegations, including a "water cure" that dated back to the Spanish Inquisition—precisely the kind of practice the Americans had claimed to be ending with enlightened rule. As the war continued, it seemed to be favoring the Filipinos, whose relative casualty rates declined from 1899 to 1900. But then, unexpectedly, Aguinaldo was captured in March 1901, and his independence movement withered. A strong Muslim resistance continued on the island of Mindanao (John J. Pershing would gain distinction fighting there before achieving glory in Europe), but, in effect, the war had ended.

Relieved Americans quickly put the episode behind them, and surrendered to uplifting publicity about progress and the spread of civilization. But even after both victories, the easy one in the Caribbean and the hard one in Asia, it was unclear what exactly the United States had won. More than four thousand Americans had died to hold a distant archipelago, and they had killed a huge number of Filipinos in order to do so (between 250,000 and 1 million out of a population of 7.5 million). That possession brought an obligation to defend the Philippines, which, as Spain had shown, was harder than it looked. Writing years later, after the Japanese attack on Pearl Harbor—and the Philippines—had brought the United States into the Second World War, Walter Lippmann looked back at the Philippine occupation as the height of stupidity, not because it violated a few moralistic maxims, but because it was literally indefensible. To his credit, Teddy Roosevelt worried about this, too, and predicted that continuous rule there would make the islands "our heel of Achilles if we are attacked by a foreign power." Those words would resonate on December 7, 1941.

Further, the uncomfortable new role of liberator/occupier unleashed a debate about the role of the United States in the world that essentially has never ended. A rising chorus of voices expressed disgust at the severity and length of the conflict. One of the angriest voices belonged to the great humorist Mark Twain, who railed against the occupation in essays dripping with venom. No one lamented the passing of American innocence with more anguish—perhaps a natural response from an author perpetually searching for his childhood.

When the Spanish-American War started, Twain, like most Americans, expressed enthusiasm for its goal of liberation. But as he followed events in the Philippines, first with regret and then with revulsion, his volcanic anger could not be contained, and he began to question everything he once held sacred. He sketched a brutal new version of "The Battle Hymn of the Republic" that began, "Mine eyes have seen the orgy of the launching of the Sword / He is searching out the hoardings where the stranger's wealth is stored." His essay "To the Person Sitting in Darkness" proposed that the Stars and Stripes be replaced by the Skull and Crossbones. He listed the words that he was beginning to find objectionable (including *liberty*), since they invariably clouded murkier motives, and wondered if there might be "two Americas, . . . one that sets the captive free, and one that takes a once-captive's freedom away from him, and picks a quarrel with him with nothing to found it on; then kills him to get his land."

More calmly, William James wrote with sound advice to a friend going to lead the American administration in the Philippines:

> Nurse no extravagant ideals or hopes. Be contented with small gains, respect the Filipino soul whatever it prove to be, and try to

> educe and play upon its possibilities for advance rather than stamp too sudden an Americanism upon it. There are abysses of crudity in some of our popular notions in that direction that must make the Almighty shudder.

In sum, the promising new century did not begin so promisingly; rather, it promised to be difficult as the United States worked its way, island to island, toward a destiny more complex than the inane pieties of William McKinley. A most important new fact had been established, that American military might was on a par with the world's leading powers, and that fact would never stop being relevant. The United States was now incontestably a great nation by any standard, with vast trade encircling the globe, and distant dependencies. Its prodigious output dwarfed the competition, and the total value of American manufactures equaled that of any two other nations. American wheat fed the world; American steel was building it.

But the equally important *idea* of America—an island of freedom, separate from the foibles of the Old World—had been tarnished in the jungles of the Philippines. The ark had briefly gone adrift in a distant Pacific archipelago, a navigational error that Herman Melville had specifically warned against. Indeed, Theodore Roosevelt's advice about drift had been more prescient than he knew. Once again, Americans had failed to calibrate their remarkable abilities with their even more limitless ambitions. But a new administration—his own—was soon under way, and with it, the eternal promise of a new time beginning.

CHAPTER SEVEN

LIBERTY CABBAGE

It is a wonder that historians who take their business seriously can sleep at night. —Woodrow Wilson

MYOPIA

Anthropologists tell us that societies tend to weave elaborate creation myths about themselves, frequently involving supernatural actors and ancestors of unusual prowess, endowed with prodigious physical attributes. Inside the Beltway, one of these creation myths concerns the origins of the American Century, involving two forceful presidents who lived at nearly the same time but now occupy very different places in the national Valhalla.

Theodore Roosevelt and Woodrow Wilson, so different in so many ways, always seem to be linked by pundits seeking to explain the two sides of our national character. Henry Kissinger began his book *Diplomacy* with a meditation on their differences, and similar views have bounced around the Washington echo chamber for decades. At its most primitive, this argument parades the two leaders like a pair of turn-of-the-century Kewpie dolls, each standing for a simple principle. Teddy Roosevelt, the man of action, is a "realist," because he vigorously asserted U.S. military might, clearly understood our strategic interests, and brought the United States to new eminence in the world; Woodrow Wilson is an "idealist," tortured by naive aspirations for democracy, and reluctant to project the full force of American power. Worse, he is seen as someone who quixotically tried to reshape an unwilling world in America's image, as if that were somehow out of step with our history—when in fact it is the essence of our history.

The realist-idealist template, struck at the beginning of the twentieth century, has survived for more than a hundred years, leaving the false impression that Republicans have always been committed to an interventionist foreign policy, while Democrats fret about ways to improve human behavior. Understandably, no one has done more to nurture this way of thinking than Republicans themselves. In his resignation speech, Richard Nixon spoke to "TR" almost as if he were in a trance, mumbling incantations as heartfelt as any South Pacific islander's prayer to his ancestors.

Of course, Roosevelt and Wilson *were* very different, useful counterweights even in their own day. In fact, their differences may be keeping them together, like a dysfunctional couple who enjoy bickering. But like most creation myths, this one has little to do with reality. To force these men into realist and idealist camps distorts each of them, with the result that both famously bespectacled presidents remain out of focus. Neither would be happy with our myopia. To think of Roosevelt as a man who did not think about ideas or the spread of democracy or improving human behavior is simply to ignore history. In fact, he promoted the idea of a League of Nations before Wilson did. To think of Wilson as a man reluctant to use force, stuck in a cloud cuckoo land of his own making, is equally wrong. There was steel to his democracy. He was the first president to intervene in a European war, and his deployment of nearly 2 million U.S. troops vastly exceeded what Roosevelt ever did or even threatened to do. It was decisive; it was revolutionary; and it changed the world forever.

In many ways, we still live in Wilson's world—the presidential rituals he created (the State of the Union speech, for one), the forceful projection of American power he unleashed, and the diplomatic machinery he also tried to launch, including the United Nations, the spiritual heir to the doomed League of Nations. Yes, we are grateful to Teddy Roosevelt for a few national parks. But we forage in the environment that Wilson left to us.

Perhaps more than anything else, the way that Woodrow Wilson talked continues to shape us. I don't mean his voice, though that, too, is interesting—Edison's cylinders capture a surprising basso that contrasts markedly with Roosevelt's rapid-fire treble (to say nothing of his curiously English accent). We may express distaste for Wilson's simplistic idea that the world will eventually resemble the United States—but every president since then has voiced a similar aspiration.

Wilson's speeches had something new: a refreshing candor and a desire to move beyond the nineteenth century and build something better—to build "new frontiers," as he put it, not the last time that phrase would see the light of day. But there was something very old as well—a vein of subterranean American thinking more nakedly exposed than usual. Wilson's hope for a kind of global regeneration was clearly rooted in his heartfelt Christianity, and beyond that, in the religion of American history, the close study he had made of Lincoln and the founders. Who would dare to dismiss Lincoln or Jefferson as "idealists"? Yet surely that is what they were, just as surely as they were utter realists. Immersed in this history, Wilson felt the ancient urge to return to the work of redemption, and to drag the rest of the world—kicking and screaming if necessary—along for the ride. Like all of his distinguished predecessors, he failed to build his private millennium, and his failure was more public than most. But it would be cynical in the extreme to say that his efforts were for naught.

Roosevelt watched his successor's failure, or most of it, and contributed his mite toward it as well. But it is naive to think that he would have avoided the same problems. Our oversimplification of their reputations has trained us to see Wilson as messianic and Roosevelt as pragmatic. But when they both ran for president in 1912, it was not Wilson who gave the astonishing speech that concluded, "We stand at Armageddon, and we battle for the Lord." Henry Kissinger wrote, "Nothing annoyed Roosevelt so much as high-sounding principles backed by neither the power nor the will to implement them." I would argue that Roosevelt had neither the power nor the will to commence a battle at Armageddon, nor even the faintest knowledge of where, exactly, Armageddon was.*

*Although it should be pointed out that there is a site called Megiddo, currently in Israel, that may be the original Armageddon. In fact, there was an important battle there in 1918, between the British and Arabs on one side, and the Turks of the Ottoman Empire on the other. This battle—believed by the Baha'i faith to be the literal Battle of Armageddon—had far-reaching consequences in reshaping the Middle East after the First World War.

Instead of looking for evidence of the differences separating our twenty-sixth and twenty-eighth presidents—evidence that will never be hard to find—we should concentrate our efforts on something larger. It feels more useful to see them both as part of a historical continuum, each connected in fascinating ways to the past, but grappling his way forward in a bewildering new century. In fact, what surprises, after a close examination of Roosevelt and Wilson, is how alike they were. Their strengths were not so different—eloquence, stubbornness, and a righteous confidence in their ability to force change upon the world. Their weaknesses were more or less exactly the same.

Roosevelt lived from 1858 to 1919, Wilson from 1856 to 1924. Each was a superb historian in addition to a historical actor in his own right. Roosevelt wrote so many books that it is exhausting to even list them, let alone read them. One title gives an idea of his endless power to observe events and then dilate upon them: *President Roosevelt's List of Birds: Seen in the White House Grounds and About Washington During his Administration* (1908). Wilson had far more professional training as a historian than Roosevelt, and extensive teaching experience as well. He remains our only president with a Ph.D.—another reason, perhaps, that Republicans love to hate him.

Yet for all that these two men did to rewrite American history, they never debated each other. They were never even photographed together. It is almost as if these two vectors, straight and unbending, could never intersect, at least not until Franklin Roosevelt arrived on the scene, ready to absorb the best of both legacies.

TR

There has been no shortage of popular biographies of Theodore Roosevelt—he is as popular among Democrats as Republicans, for his environmental and reform measures were as much of his legacy as his swagger and stick. Even as a child, he gave signs of the remarkable career to come. In April 1865, he witnessed Abraham Lincoln's funeral cortège snaking through New York—and astonishingly was photographed doing so. As a mere stripling, he listened with fascination to the stories of his maternal uncles, both American naval officers, though not in the conventional sense—they had fought for the Confederacy. One, in fact, fired the last gun discharged by the *Alabama* in her famous battle against the *Kearsarge*, off France. After the war, they retired to England, which probably did not diminish the Anglophilia that Roosevelt nourished throughout his life.

From these stories he carried away a lifelong devotion to the navy, and to a new idea undergirding it: the global projection of American power. While only twenty-three, he converted his senior thesis at Harvard into an eminently readable book, *The Naval War of 1812*, which owed much to his uncles, whom he thanked, archly, in his preface, as "formerly of the United States Navy."

Roosevelt's meteoric career seemed to bring him, even as a young man, into remarkable situations at the fulcrum of world events. At the age of thirty-eight, he was appointed assistant secretary of the navy, a position he used to kickstart the Spanish-American War. It becomes dizzying to follow the sequence of posts that followed—Rough Rider, governor of New York, vice president, and then president after the assassination of McKinley in September 1901. He never stopped talking or writing in these years—often doing both at the same time (he dictated many of his books while shaving). Curiously, the book that he wrote at precisely the moment of his consideration for the national platform was an admiring biography of Oliver Cromwell, which appeared in *Scribner's* between January and June 1900. Roosevelt piled on the praise for "the greatest Englishman of the seventeenth century," so much so that a friend joked that Roosevelt had written a fine study of Cromwell's qualifications to be governor of New York. But he also showed a deep familiarity with the specific forms of political and religious liberty that Cromwell and his American admirers had pursued in the seventeenth century, showing that Puritanism was not entirely dead in American political circles. Intriguingly, Roosevelt paid particular attention to a speech Cromwell gave near the end of his rule, in which he claimed divine inspiration for his actions—a mistake that Roosevelt pounced on, arguing that an effective leader "must be most cautious about mistaking his own views for those of the Lord." He would have trouble following his own advice.

If McKinley had occasionally shown ambivalence toward the new empire he acquired, no such feelings ever seemed to constrain

Theodore Roosevelt, and once he became president, the office seemed to swell to new size. From September 1901 to March 1909—a defining decade for the as-yet-unnamed American Century—Roosevelt's bravado and skill put the United States on the map in a way that it had never been, even after the smashing victories of 1898. It was not merely his bluster, though there was plenty of that (an amazing amount, really, for someone who bragged about his ability to speak softly). It was also his diplomacy, a diplomacy that rested on his shrewd reading of men, his close friendships with well-informed peers, and his firm knowledge of what he wanted to do.

His plan was to expand America's role in the world, and by extension his own. So he did, exploiting a strategic opportunity that he was keenly aware of. To an unprecedented degree, the European powers now needed the United States as much as the United States needed them, and probably more. The precarious balance of power in Europe, and rising concerns about war, not only diminished fears about America's new strength, but made essential the rise of a neutral partner that could mediate between the bickering dynasties. They sent their best young ambassadors to Washington, and Roosevelt cultivated them perfectly, riding horses, entertaining constantly, and bringing his enormous physical capacities to the work of diplomacy. Not until the Kennedy administration was there again a sense that it was as exciting—and fun—to forge foreign policy. For Roosevelt, the intermingling of friendship and the national interest were seamless—and he often did it all himself, ignoring his hardworking minions in the State Department.

Roosevelt also expanded America's importance the old-fashioned way—by piling up territories. Cuba, recently liberated from Spain, soon became the first American protectorate, although that precise term was not used. Even before Roosevelt became president, he had worked to attach the Platt Amendment to the Army Appropriation Act of 1901, which set up the conditions for Cuban independence, but in a way that guaranteed U.S. domination of the island, including the right to intervene whenever it deemed necessary. The Platt Amendment also required a long-term naval base to enforce these demands, the promise that eventuated in Guantánamo Bay, America's oldest overseas military base (and the site of Cuba's only McDonald's). Every time its name has been mentioned in the intervening century, from the Cuban Missile

Crisis to the torture of suspected terrorists, Theodore Roosevelt's ghost has silently been present.

A second protectorate was soon added in Panama, which essentially became a nation because Roosevelt willed it into existence. For decades, Americans and Europeans had been dreaming of a canal across the isthmus, and attention had eventually focused on Nicaragua and Panama, still a part of Colombia. Feeling empowered by the new dominance of the United States in the Gulf of Mexico, Roosevelt forged ahead, ignoring some regional sensitivities, and also the treaty with Britain signed fifty years earlier that prevented either nation from controlling a canal. Roosevelt's masterful command of history could become quite imperfect when necessary, and in 1902 he signed the Isthmian Canal Act and sought to arrange a long-term lease from Colombia.

Unfortunately, that lease proved elusive, and quickly negotiations bogged down over money, control, and other irritants. Exasperated by Colombia—he called its negotiators "contemptible little creatures"—Roosevelt allowed a revolt in Panama to proceed unmolested in 1903. In fact, U.S. naval vessels were essential in preventing Colombia from asserting control over its breakaway province. Fifteen days later, Panama signed a treaty with the United States giving Roosevelt everything he wanted. Colombia had committed many blunders in the negotiations, but still, the United States had not acted much like an honest broker. Even so, the completion of a canal was an enormous step forward, and when Roosevelt inspected it in person in 1906, he became the first sitting president to venture outside the United States—rather an important first in a nation that always insisted the eyes of the world were upon it.

Having finally acquired the canal, Roosevelt also tightened American control over its approaches. During his seven years in office, the Gulf of Mexico began to resemble the American lake that Jefferson had envisioned a century earlier. Roosevelt had once expressed a willingness to look the other way while European governments threatened Caribbean nations defaulting on their debts, but he changed his mind after an ugly German-British effort to strong-arm Venezuela in 1902 awakened all the old fears of foreign penetration of the Americas. To prevent the sight of German battleships in the Caribbean, deeply threatening to the United States as well as Latin America, Roosevelt articulated a new theory, the Roosevelt Corollary, in December 1904. The Corollary went well beyond the Monroe Doctrine to claim that the United States had a right to intervene in disputes between European powers and their creditors in this hemisphere—that, in effect, the United States would use force to collect Europe's debts to prevent Europe from doing so itself.

Whether that came as a relief to Latin America was and remains debatable. Certainly the Corollary had imperialistic elements. It would be hard to find a more naked statement of America's newfound power, and as critics suggested, it more or less claimed the right to intervene wherever a fiscal mess could be found—in short, anywhere. But Roosevelt also guaranteed that any country acting "with reasonable efficiency and decency in social and political matters," and paying its bills on time, "need fear no interference from the United States." There was an altruistic element to Roosevelt's thinking—he never did anything without consulting his sense of honor. But as he listed the respectable Protestant virtues he admired ("stable, orderly and prosperous"), then contemplated the list of Roman Catholic nations he thought likely to need intervention, one can almost hear the old rivalry between England and Spain that defined the sixteenth-century contest for the New World.

The Corollary did not take long to go into effect. In 1905, the United States took over some of the Dominican Republic's responsibilities, such as customs collection, and it, too, became something of a protectorate. Objections were raised over these actions—Congress resented Roosevelt's independent style, and Latino intellectuals criticized *el colosso*—but praise was also offered, including from Latin Americans, who felt this fate to be preferable to the specter of European intervention. It should be added, also, that when Cuba was on the verge of anarchy in 1905, Roosevelt resisted calls from Congress to annex it permanently to the United States.

Diplomacy helped, too. Roosevelt's capable secretary of state Elihu Root traveled more widely in the region than any predecessor, cultivating additional goodwill. A hemispheric conference in Rio de Janeiro in 1906 was particularly helpful, and Root stopped at countless regional capitals on his way back to Washington. Root also worked on a number of initiatives that sound positively radical by today's standards, including an international court of justice for the American nations and several measures to outlaw war between them.

In fact, the president, sometimes seen as an archimperialist, was acutely aware of the advantages of skillful diplomacy. It's true that Roosevelt ignored the occasional treaty when it constrained him, but in general he worked effectively through existing channels and opened up a few new ones of his own, including far more personal consultation with fellow heads of state than any of his predecessors had thought possible or desirable. If 1898 had shown America's unexpected military might, Roosevelt's tenure revealed an equally surprising diplomatic prowess. State Department cables that had once limited themselves to Venezuelan credit, Cuban sugar tariffs, and other hemispheric matters now probed deeply into the maelstrom of European intrigues. Roosevelt worked hard to maintain the balance of power at a moment when the balance seemed to change with every gust of wind, and in his way, this most martial president was also a champion of peace. He skillfully kept France and Germany from hostilities over their rivalry in Morocco by calling an international conference at Algeciras in Spain in 1906. Among other effects, his efforts to promote stability in Morocco reinforced the prevailing idea in the Middle East that the United States was a far more trustworthy friend than any of the European colonial powers. In effect, he was going past the Monroe Doctrine, and even the Roosevelt Corollary, into a new way of thinking that argued that the United States had a responsibility to solve the world's problems in addition to its own.

This the United States tried to do in ways that seem minor, but that marked progress of a sort. Roosevelt and Elihu Root worked out a large number of so-called arbitration treaties, designed to lessen tensions between nations—Root negotiated twenty-five in his last years alone. Roosevelt also lent support to efforts to restrict armaments, and to lessen the likelihood of war by adjudicating disagreements in a new World Court at The Hague—a cause for which Americans then felt the keenest sympathy. Roosevelt deliberately advanced a test case to strengthen that court—interestingly, a case that stretched back far into early American history, concerning a complex claim that linked the Jesuits who came to California in the sixteenth century, the Spanish government that sent them, the Mexican government that succeeded Spanish authority, and the American government that succeeded Mexico. History never sleeps.

The crowning achievement of Roosevelt's diplomacy was his masterful arbitration of the Russo-Japanese War in the summer of 1905. In the unlikely site of Portsmouth, New Hampshire—chosen to avoid Washington's insufferable heat—representatives of two venerable autocracies came to experience a little democracy and to work out what seemed to be an intractable conflict on the other side of the world. Roosevelt was involved every step of the way, beginning a long tradition of direct presidential intervention for peace in places far from American shores. Henry Adams congratulated him on becoming "the best herder of Emperors since Napoleon." For these actions, Roosevelt was awarded a Nobel Peace Prize—the only Nobel ever to go to a sitting president.

Of course, like all of his successors, Roosevelt had his imperfections. His favorite word, *bully*, could be an accurate description of the way he treated the peoples of lesser nations. He felt that different policies ought to apply to different regions. He disliked "uncivilized Asia and Africa" and had no objections—unlike his cousin Franklin—to Europe's desire to rule those regions with an iron hand. He even applauded it: he told Congress in 1902 that it was "incumbent on all civilized and orderly powers to insist on the proper policing of the world."

To some extent, the United States participated in that policing. Throughout his presidency, Roosevelt tried to manage tensions in China, including anti-American riots over unfair U.S. immigration laws, boycotts of American goods, and other difficulties. In 1906, Roosevelt even sent naval vessels to the Chinese coast, and plans to land fifteen thousand men to protect American business interests ended only when Chinese authorities reasserted control.

Periodic flare-ups also marred the American relationship with Japan, despite Roosevelt's admiration for the Japanese. Like the United States, Japan had a vocal press given to extremes of jingoism, and when it learned that students of Japanese descent suffered segregation in the schools of San Francisco, the papers quickly turned it into an international incident and even threatened war. Amazingly, Kaiser Wilhelm revealed to Roosevelt that Japanese reservists had landed in Mexico, and he offered German military help if the United States were attacked. Such an attack, and a joint German-American response, might dramatically have changed the history of the twentieth century.

Perhaps the culmination of Roosevelt's expansiveness was his encouragement of a giant display of American naval power, cloaked under a mantle of friendliness to all nations. In December 1907, sixteen spanking new battleships, painted white, set out from Hampton Roads, Virginia, with fourteen thousand sailors for a circumnavigation of the globe. Over the next fourteen months, the Great White Fleet (as it was named after the fact) traveled forty-three thousand miles, and touched at twenty ports of call on six continents. Its itinerary included a journey along the Arabian peninsula and through the Suez Canal, and several diplomatic stops in Ottoman Turkey. It returned on February 22, 1909, ten days before the end of Roosevelt's presidency. An enormous crowd greeted the fleet at Hampton Roads, including, of course, the president. Every ship fired a twenty-one-gun salute to him in passing. *The New York Times* called it "the apotheosis of Roosevelt, the one supreme, magnificent moment."

To the end, the work of diplomacy continued. On the last day of the administration, Elihu Root signed a treaty that finally fixed an argument over fishing rights off Newfoundland that had dogged relations between the United States and Britain since the former was acknowledged to exist, in 1783. Diplomacy is not always rapid; but still, the wheels turn. Having confronted so many new problems in American foreign policy, Root and Roosevelt had now fixed the country's oldest disagreement as well.

This was hardly the end of the story; Theodore Roosevelt would continue his globe-trotting with expeditions to South America and Africa, nearly as punishing to him as they were to the animals he was constantly bagging. And he never stopped talking, even when he seemed out of earshot—a fact that Woodrow Wilson would learn, to his distress. But Roosevelt's moment in the sun ended the day he left the White House, which he had expanded nearly as dramatically as the presidency itself (he added the West Wing in 1902). Through his skill and his bluster, he had shown that Americans could do far more than occupy the world stage—they could command it.

WILSON

Like Theodore Roosevelt, Woodrow Wilson was a child during the Civil War, but with a key difference—he grew up in the South. His earliest memory was hearing the news that Lincoln had been elected, and that war was therefore coming. The experience of total war may have been nearer to Armageddon than Roosevelt ever got in his life. For a time, Wilson's father's church served as a Confederate hospital, and the churchyard held Union prisoners. While the Wilsons were never in danger, the trauma must have left a deep impression on a sensitive child, and it goes a long way toward explaining the revulsion he felt toward conflict throughout his life.

That Woodrow Wilson ever became president is rather extraordinary, for the rigorous study of American history has never been considered much of a training ground for those who seek to enact it. He was not the only university president to have been called to the White House—Dwight Eisenhower was likewise in 1952. But Ike had several other qualifications on his résumé.

It is probably fair to say that no chief magistrate, including Theodore Roosevelt, knew more about the story of America at the time of his election. Wilson was a deeply learned student of the past and had been teaching and writing U.S. history for decades by the time he was called to his new profession. Ironically, his specialty was domestic politics, and his early scholarly work paid almost no attention to any other nation. His first book, *Congressional Government* (1885), made only a fleeting reference to foreign affairs. Not long after taking office, Wilson said, "It would be the irony of fate if my administration had to deal chiefly with foreign affairs."

But Wilson was not naive about the world, or America's place in it. He knew that the age of isolation had ended, and that the United States would have a large role to play in shaping the new century. And he knew that the president would have the largest role of all: "Our President must always, henceforth, be one of the great powers of the world, whether he act greatly and wisely or not." Interestingly, he shared many of the assumptions we might ascribe to more conventional imperialists—that America was expanding inexorably, by an irresistible fate, which Wilson called "plain destiny." He said, in words that might have come from any of his Republican opponents, "This great pressure of a people moving always to new frontiers, in search of new lands, new power, and the full freedom of a virgin world, has ruled our course and formed our policies like a Fate."

Many commentators have explored the Presbyterian legacy that Wilson inherited as the son, grandson, and nephew of distinguished parsons. It would not quite be true to say, as some have, that Wilson was therefore a seventeenth-century person living in a twentieth-century world. Writing of Wilson's parents, Richard Hofstadter noted that "the Calvinist spirit burned in them with a bright and imperishable flame" and suggested that the apple had not fallen far from the tree. Clearly religion meant a great deal to him, as it did to Roosevelt, and his vivid sense of right and wrong informed everything that he said and wrote. "The stern Covenanter tradition that is behind me sends many an echo down the years," he offered once, stating the obvious.

One of his earliest essays was a newspaper piece titled "Christ's Army" that appeared in the *North Carolina Presbyterian* in 1876, a month after the centennial, under the byline "Twiwood." It seemed to come from an earlier time, or from outside of time entirely. He began, "One of the favorite figures with sacred writers in their references to the inhabitants of this world is that of representing mankind as divided into two great armies." One was led by the "Captain of Salvation," and the other by the "Prince of Lies," and soon he was describing the final struggles of Revelation in vivid detail. "The field of battle is the world," Wilson wrote ominously, and added, "There is no middle course, no neutrality." That inflexibility would not help him in 1919, when the field of battle truly *was* the world.

Messianic language would fortify Wilson's oratory forever, even when it became clear that he was not going to be a preacher himself. He spoke often of the new time coming: in 1900, "there is no masking or concealing the new order of the world"; in 1901, "a new era has come upon us like a sudden vision of the things unprophesied, and for which no polity has been prepared." Then, of course, "the war to end all wars" and the era of peace and harmony that was to follow it. His access to the sound of angelic trumpets was a great strength, and it marshaled millions to join his armies of righteousness.

Wilson's political hero was Grover Cleveland, and like Cleveland, he tried to fight back against some of the imperialist excesses of the age. Roosevelt often ridiculed Wilson's altruistic sound bites as "milk and water" and attacked him as an isolationist. But as Henry Kissinger points out, Wilson did not want the United States to separate from the world—he wanted the entire world to be remade in the image of the United States. If anything, his vision was more ambitious than Roosevelt's. Not since Lincoln had a president revealed a more mystical communion with the founders. To Wilson, the Declaration marked a turning point in human history. Providence called upon him to testify, and he responded, offering an ecstatic vision of America's origins and destiny.

Here he is in 1912, introducing himself to the American people:

> If I did not believe in Providence I would feel like a man going blindfolded through a haphazard world. I do believe in Providence. I believe that God presided over the inception of this nation; I believe that God planted in us the vision of liberty; I believe that men are emancipated in proportion as they lift themselves to the conception of Providence and of divine destiny, and therefore, I cannot be deprived of the hope that is in me—in the hope not only that concerns myself, but the confident hope that concerns the nation—that we are chosen, and prominently chosen, to show the way to the nations of the world how they shall walk in the paths of liberty.

In speech after speech, he returned to these themes, hitting the comforting notes of Providence, destiny, and liberty but altering the mood and tempo like Jelly Roll Morton. The pace picked up after 1914, but well before the outbreak of the Great War, Wilson was speaking of his expectation that America had an immense role to play. For Wilson, past and future were conjoined, and the previous chapters of American history were building up to a greatness yet to come. His language of yearning—of glimpsing the barest outline of a new world—was there from the beginning.

Wilson's message carried a deep resonance within the United States—as it does to this day. He is often given credit for inventing a new way of thinking about U.S. foreign policy; it is probably more accurate to say that he tapped into old feelings that had never entirely disappeared.

Despite the obvious increase in U.S. military activity in 1898 and its aftermath, American public opinion still held strongly that peace was not only desirable but achievable, and that Americans had a special responsibility. Even a half century after the Civil War, memories of the carnage were vivid. In the summer of 1913, as storm clouds were gathering over Europe, more than fifty thousand veterans assembled at Gettysburg on the fiftieth anniversary of the battle for an orgy of speeches, reenactments, and festivities. Nine who had survived the original battle died during the reunion! That same year, Andrew Carnegie donated $1.5 million toward an enormous Peace Palace in The Hague, where it still serves as the home of the International Court of Justice; the principal symbol of the World Court, derided by so many Americans as un-American, was built by an American.

As he stepped into his presidency, Wilson gave full voice to these peaceful aspirations and carefully undid some of the more arrogant actions of his three predecessors. He retreated from the "dollar diplomacy" that Taft had inflicted upon China, he paid back Colombia and expressed regret for the way in which Panama had been wrested from it, and he took steps to advance self-government in Puerto Rico and the Philippines. Grover Cleveland would have been proud. In a speech given at Mobile, Alabama, in 1913, Wilson promised, "The United States will never again seek one additional foot of territory by conquest." As he pursued these virtuous ends, Wilson found an able second in his evangelical secretary of state, the former Democratic standard-bearer William Jennings Bryan (known as Grape Juice Billy for his refusal to serve wine at diplomatic dinners).

But Wilson, like so many of his predecessors, discovered that the noblest intentions do not always square with reality. In one part of the world after another, he encountered resistance to the perfect liberty he described with such power in his speeches. As usual, imperfection began close to home, in the Caribbean and Mexico. In some places, the United States expanded its influence peacefully—in 1916, the long-desired purchase of the Danish Virgin Islands was consummated, fulfilling Seward's vision and tightening American control of the lake. But in other places, the extension of U.S. influence was more heavy-handed, imposing authority from above as much as it encouraged democracy from below. The United States more or less told Nicaraguans whom to elect, placed Haiti under control of U.S. advisers, and the Dominican Republic under a U.S. military government. The marines landed in the latter two places. Wilson and his advisers were obviously seeking some sort of stability, and stability was in fact the result. Furthermore, U.S. troops left after a decent interval. But the use of military power to achieve these ends undoubtedly fell short of the ideals of liberty that Wilson was endlessly talking about.

There were also perpetual tensions in Mexico, where a civil war had erupted, and the country was divided into warring camps. Ultimately, Wilson grew so exasperated over a minor disagreement—Mexico had failed to properly salute the U.S. flag—that he sent the Atlantic fleet into Mexican waters. In April 1914, American sailors and marines occupied the city of Veracruz, where they stayed for six months. Relations between Mexico and the United States remained troubled for years, and reached a new nadir when Pancho Villa, one of several revolutionaries competing for attention, crossed the border into Columbus, New Mexico, set fire to the town, and killed nineteen Americans. It was the first armed invasion of the United States from foreign soil since the Battle of New Orleans—unless you count Confederate incursions. In response, Wilson sent a "Punitive Expedition" of nearly seven thousand men into Mexico, which chased after Villa and fought several skirmishes with his followers but failed to capture him. They remained there until the beginning of 1917, increasing friction everywhere they went. Only after their removal did relations begin to improve.

Around the world, American values seemed even more difficult to inculcate. In 1912, a most promising development seemed imminent when two thousand years of imperial rule came to a crashing end in China with the inauguration of a republic. Connected to China by their missionary traditions and business ties, Americans had reasons to feel a special interest in this sort of antimonarchical event—especially when it was led by a charismatic young republican, Sun Yat-sen, called the George Washington of the Far East. Sun's doctrine of Three Principles of the People was inspired by Lincoln's flourish concerning "government of the people, for the people, and by the people" at the end of the Gettysburg Address. Those principles are still in effect, nearly a century later, in Taiwan—still the Republic of China.

But for all this idealism, the Republic of China encountered deep difficulty as it tried to introduce American ideas about government into everyday use. Sun's presidency of the republic lasted from January 1 to March 10, 1912. Terrible infighting then resulted, which never really ended until 1949. Predictably, China's stronger neighbors, including Russia and Japan, did all they could to capitalize on China's distress. The United States tried to stand by its newly republican ally, and particularly its educational institutions, many of which Americans had founded. But the United States generally overlooked Japan's incursions, accepting the principle that Japan's nearness to China gave it a special right to do as it pleased—a rather unfortunate interpretation of the Monroe Doctrine.

In all these regional crises, Wilson tried to use American influence for modest good, hoping to improve on the heavy-handed tactics of his Republican predecessors. But there was nothing modest about the enormous conflagration about to engulf the world—a conflagration nearly worthy of the apocalypse Americans had been expecting for some time.

By following Wilson's speeches in 1914, we can see him bracing for the conflict, trying, with mixed results, to translate his love of the Declaration into a meaningful planning document for the coming catastrophe. Just as Lincoln did, he went to Independence Hall (the "holy ground" of liberty) to make peace with the fact that he would soon have to make war. "Have you ever read the Declaration of Independence or attended with close comprehension to the real character of it when you have heard it read? If you have, you will know that it is not a Fourth of July oration. The Declaration of Independence was a document preliminary to war." The word *war* is jarring, except for the fact that the speech was given six days after the assassination of the Archduke Ferdinand. Then Wilson moved to the central premise of his lay sermon, that liberty does not consist of "mere general declarations of the rights of men," but in translating those resolves into action. And that action can itself be faulty, as when cruel things are done to other nations, even in the name of liberty. "It may upon occasions mean that we shall use it to make the peoples of other nations suffer in the way in which we said it was intolerable to suffer when we uttered our Declaration of Independence."

But from that curiously honest moment, he rose to give a spirited defense of America's best intentions, intentions without limits or boundaries of any kind. "We set this nation up, at least we professed to set it up, to vindicate the rights of men. We did not name any differences between one race and another. We did not set up any barriers against any particular people. We opened our gates to all the world and said: 'Let all men who wish to be free come to us and they will be welcome.' "

Four weeks later, these ideals would be tested severely when Europe fell apart and World War One began.

OVER THERE

> Once lead this people into war, and they'll forget there ever was such a thing as tolerance. To fight you must be brutal and ruthless, and the spirit of ruthless brutality will enter into the very fiber of our national life, infecting Congress, the courts, the policeman on the beat, the man in the street.
>
> —Woodrow Wilson

Of course no speech could entirely predict what was about to happen when the war to end all wars broke out in August 1914. It is doubtful that any president would have been entirely prepared for the carnage that ensued. Understandably, Wilson sought to keep America out of the war, both for his own reasons and for the weight of two centuries of general neutrality in European conflicts. His reelection slogan in 1916 was memorably blunt: "He Kept Us out of War."

Historians have often attributed this reluctance to the ongoing power of American isolationism, enjoying renewed life under the Wilson-Bryan ascendancy. There is some truth to that. But the word *isolationism* simplifies a complex situation and does not fully convey what an international nation the United States had already become. By 1914, no nation on earth was not represented in some sense inside the United States. Thomas Paine's vision of a nation of immigrants—perhaps the most modern vision entertained by any founder—had finally come true. Obviously, this was a deeply Anglo-Saxon nation, in many ways the second English nation of the world. But it was also the second German nation of the world. Huge sections of the country—particularly in the Midwest—felt ties to their German homeland. Large populations with no German sympathy whatsoever—the Irish, for example—expressed a deep interest in their cause merely because they were fighting the British, and the Irish were not without political power in Washington. And so Europe's revolutions and animosities festered inside the United States well before there was any declaration of war.

Despite Wilson's moving exhortations for peace ("We are too proud to fight"), the United States was inexorably drawn into the conflict. The reasons were everywhere: a rising clamor came from Americans calling for intervention, including, at a shrill decibel level, from Theodore Roosevelt. There was the age-old feeling that Americans ought to fight for "democracy" against oligarchy—though that was complicated by the fact that Great Britain was as monarchical as Germany, and far more imperialistic. Russia was even more autocratic, though that problem began to dissipate with the onset of the Russian Revolution, at which point it was unclear if anyone at all led Russia's government.

But the real reason that the United States could not stay out of the conflict was another old one—its rights as a neutral were being trampled, just as they had been during the Napoleonic wars more than a century earlier. Once again, these rights were contested in the great waterways between Old World and New—particularly the North Atlantic. Over and over, with rising tolls, the Germans sank merchant vessels and passenger liners carrying Americans. The worst single incident, the sinking of the *Lusitania* on May 7, 1915, took 1,198 lives, including those of 128 Americans.

There were irritants on the other side, as well. In 1916, Britain's brutal suppression of the Easter Rebellion in Ireland antagonized a huge section of American society. Further, the British did not make any friends by interfering with the mails and publishing a blacklist of American corporations doing business with Germany and its allies.

In this context, hemmed in by hostility, Americans had little choice but to prepare for the inevitable. A rapid military buildup by the U.S. Congress in the years 1915 and 1916 ensued. And as history has shown, time and time again, once a formidable arsenal is paid for and assembled, it is extremely difficult not to use it.

To the end, Wilson labored for peace. His speech to the Senate on January 22, 1917, outlined the Pax Americana he sought. It reached back deeply into American history, recalling many of the ideals of the revolutionary generation: freedom of the seas, reduction of arms, equality of nations, and broad acceptance of the fundamental idea—hardly celebrated in Europe—that "governments derive their just powers from the consent of the governed."

A terrible German blunder at precisely this moment destroyed the cautious diplomacy Wilson was trying to pursue and awakened several old American nightmares simultaneously. A telegram was sent by Germany's foreign secretary Arthur Zimmermann to the German minister in Mexico, asking Mexico to become Germany's ally if the United States entered the war and offering to restore to Mexico all of "the lost territory in Texas, New Mexico, and Arizona" that had come to the United States after the Mexican-American War. It would have been hard to write a message more calculated to inflame American opinion. It violated the idea that American soil was sacrosanct; the fact that America was still at peace; and the serene but slightly inaccurate sense that American history was a progression of extensions of democracy to new places, none of which could be undone by Germany or Mexico. The Zimmermann telegram challenged the Monroe Doctrine, the U.S. neutrality policy, and all of American history.

Wilson's famous war speech of April 1917 contained a number of ideas that we now take for granted. The United States had war thrust upon it—it did not create the war. It was fighting not against a single enemy, but for ideals, the very ideals woven into its existence at the moment of creation: "for democracy, for the right of those who submit to authority to have a voice in their own governments, for the rights and liberties of small nations, for a universal dominion of right by such a concert of free peoples as shall bring peace and safety to all nations and make the world itself at last free." It was a war against the past itself. A new time was coming. The "old, unhappy days" were numbered: "It was a war determined upon as wars used to be determined upon in the old, unhappy days when peoples were nowhere consulted by their rulers and wars were provoked and waged in the interest of dynasties."

And so, after centuries of threatening to take their case to the world, Americans were finally doing so. At last the United States was engaged in the enormous battle predicted in one generation after another, and it was global enough to be called all-encompassing. In one of the war's earliest naval battles, Germany defeated Britain in the South Pacific, off Chile; Britain won its revenge not long afterward in the South Atlantic, by the Falklands. Germans fought Australians in Papua New Guinea, and British and Indians in East Africa. Between May and October 1918, five German U-boats harassed American shipping off the eastern seaboard of the United States—and one U.S. naval vessel, the *San Diego*, was sunk, ten miles south of Fire Island, not far from where planes take off from JFK Airport today.

The United States had a decisive impact on the war, both psychological and real. This was not a foregone conclusion. Despite Wilson's talk of righteous fury, the American army was only the seventeenth largest in the world and had not seen any large-scale operations since the Civil War. It was unclear how American troops would fit into the allied command structure. But all of these problems were sorted out, and the arrival of the Americans came at a decisive moment, as Germany was moving soldiers freed up by Russia's collapse to the western front. For starters, the Americans came in prodigious numbers. By the middle of 1918, hundreds of thousands of fresh recruits a month were crossing the Atlantic, and their cumulative effect began to overwhelm the desperate Central Powers.

During the nineteen months that the United States was at war, Wilson's speeches showed an interesting shift. He never lost the exalted sense of the World Yet to Come, the cosmic optimism for which we remember him. But he also conveyed, often in frightening tones, a vivid sense of the evil that Germany now symbolized to him—evil for its central authority, its disdain for the rights of sovereign peoples, and its brutal military efficiency. Wilson's ability to channel the American past opened up old rhetorical avenues, and in his rage against the German military machine, Wilson began to discover the monstrous apparitions that had tortured the revivalists of the Great Awakening. One war speech dipped into the vocabulary of a fear so deep and shapeless that it almost resembled science fiction: "This intolerable Thing of which the masters of Germany have shown us the ugly face, this menace of combined intrigue and force which we now see so clearly as the German power, a Thing without conscience or honor or capacity for covenanted peace, must be crushed and, if it be not utterly brought to an end, at least shut out from the friendly intercourse of the nations."

Wilson did not treat all of his new enemies as Antichrist. He tried to be conciliatory to Austria-Hungary, which he acknowledged to be a satellite of Berlin's, and he was impressively restrained toward the Ottoman empire. Though both Turkey and Bulgaria (which had recently liberated itself from that empire) were in theory allied to Germany, Wilson avoided declaring war on them out of respect for the American missionary tradition in those countries and America's long-standing tradition of avoiding power struggles in the Middle East. That restraint, greatly appreciated by the peoples of the region, would help the United States maintain its reputation as a friend during the confused aftermath of the war, when a resurgent Turkey reasserted itself, in defiance of all the European powers that had tried to carve her up. Atatürk would say, "The United States is more acceptable than the rest."

If Wilson handled his adversaries well, he often encountered difficulty with his allies—who were not, technically, his allies at all. In deference to Washington's Farewell Address and the long tradition of American nonentanglement, Wilson insisted that the United States was an "associate," and not an ally, of the allied powers. Nor was that the only awkwardness that Americans encountered as they joined a European conflict for the first time. Wilson felt an intense dislike for secret treaties, like many of his predecessors, and there were plenty to dislike. As American involvement deepened, he discovered the plan that Britain and France had made to carve up Germany's empire and attach it to their own. That did not square with Wilson's idea of peoples fighting for their right to determine their own destinies, and he occasionally voiced his dislike of these "imperialistic" policies. Sometimes, the United States did not attend top-level allied planning meetings at all. This business of becoming a great power would take time for a nation that still did not quite understand how to interact with its peers on the main stage.

Inconsistency was readily apparent on the home front as well. Despite the theme of liberty promoted in Wilson's speeches and millions of posters, war-bond advertisements, and other forms of communication, Americans who were troubled by their country's new belligerency—and there were many—were not always accorded the respect they were entitled to. America's huge German-American population bore the brunt of this intimidation campaign. Germans were called Huns, and concert halls refused to host Beethoven and Bach concerts. Dachshunds, never much of a threat to anyone, were renamed *liberty hounds*, sauerkraut became *liberty cabbage*, and curiously, German measles was renamed *liberty measles*, as if measles was something that liberty needed to take credit for.

Nor was this intimidation entirely confined to the German-American population. The artist Joseph Pennell designed a terrifying print, intended to sell bonds, that depicted New York City after a devastating aerial attack, with the city in flames and the Statue of Liberty decapitated. It was titled "That Liberty Shall Not Perish from the Earth." Ordinary dissenters to the war—which, after all, constituted a gigantic shift in American policy—were routinely bullied for articulating their beliefs. A series of eloquent debates, now mostly forgotten, took place in Congress, trying to find the right balance between personal liberties at home and the fight for liberty abroad.

The steady progress of American arms soothed tensions, and euphoria increased as the end of the war drew near in November 1918. Perhaps too much euphoria. On November 7, an overeager UPI correspondent reported that it was all over, and wild celebrations erupted across the country. *The New York Times* called it "the most colossal fake news story ever perpetrated upon the American people," but four days later, the news was real and the war was over. Now the challenge would be to make the peace real as well.

VERSAILLES

> The final judgment on everything that happens in the world will be made up long years after the happening—that is, the student always has the last say.
>
> —Woodrow Wilson

It was fitting that Versailles, where so much of the American Revolution was negotiated, became the place where the latest new world was invented. *Invented* is perhaps the right word to use, because building a new and improved version of civilization would be an act of faith as much as an act of will. Much of that faith came from the American who was increasingly able to inflict his faith *and* his will on a prostrate world.

Wilson's two journeys to the Paris peace conference in 1918–19 remain the longest trips any president has made outside the United States, by far. They revolutionized both the office he filled and the nation he served, which would never occupy any position but center stage from this moment forward. With Europe reeling, the conference may have signaled the best chance to remake the world since Christ himself walked the earth. It seems probable that the parallel crossed Wilson's mind. Certainly it crossed others'. After he articulated his famous Fourteen Points, the French premier, Georges Clemenceau, jested that God had needed only ten commandments.

Throughout 1918, far in advance of the end of hostilities, Wilson had sketched his idea of what the postwar world would look like. In fact, he had been exploring the concept for years, since well before his presidency. (What academic doesn't dream of how the world might look if it were perfect?) In January 1918, he gave formal utterance to the Fourteen Points before Congress. With exquisite timing, he presented an ideal to the world so tempting that the world could not resist.

Nations would be equal, democratic, and at peace. They would trade freely. They would protect the freedom of the seas. They would act in concert. It was a modern plan, with special relevance to 1918, but its origins went back to 1776 and the Model Treaty. All in all, it presented a most beguiling vision, and the world poured out feelings to Wilson as to few leaders before or since. After he came to France in December 1918, huge crowds lined the streets wherever he went. He was lionized as the "God of Peace," the "Savior of Humanity," the "Moses from Across the Atlantic." For the first time in history, it seemed that America's hopes for the world were equaled by her power to see them through. In fact, there was so much excitement in the air that it briefly seemed like the millennium itself. H. G. Wells described the utter pandemonium that followed Wilson during his moment: "So eager was the situation that humanity leapt to accept and glorify Wilson—for a phrase, for a gesture. It seized upon him as its symbol. He was transfigured in the eyes of men. He ceased to be a common statesman; he became a Messiah. Millions believed him as the bringer of untold blessings; thousands would gladly have died for him."

That enthusiasm was, in fact, a key to Wilson's strategy; enthusiasm and revivals have always gone hand in hand, and there was a bit of the preacher in his call for a "union of hearts" to support the plan. Wilson considered the people more than innocent bystanders in the work of diplomacy. In good democratic form, he saw them as essential agents of change—the authors of their own destiny. That radical thought, occasionally voiced during the eighteenth-century Enlightenment, had not been much expressed since then in Europe, and certainly not in the highest circles of government. As he prepared for the deliberations, the people's excitement gave him power, and whenever he encountered resistance to his arguments, in Europe and the United States, his first instinct was usually to take to the hustings and whip up support. This galvanic power was a force in its own right, and nothing to be trifled with.

Wilson also believed in *self-determination*, a term that meant several different things (democratic government, but also the right of ethnic peoples to form their own nations), because he believed, as the founders had, that a democratic people voting freely was far less likely to go to war than a people under the iron grip of a despot. That theory has been discredited, thanks to Hitler, the rise of militant Islam, and dozens of other examples. But Wilson believed that he was carrying out the same errand that the founders had performed, only on a global scale.

His popularity with the people lining the streets did not, of course, naturally translate into popularity inside the conference. One of the most sensitive points was the disposal of Germany's former colonies, since Britain and France were still keenly interested in their own, and Japan was building a rival empire in northern China and Korea. But Wilson, true to his reading of American history, felt colonial empires to be unjust and stated so publicly and privately. The fifth of his Fourteen Points promised that the "interests of populations" would have significant weight in determining sovereignty, a revolutionary idea at the time, and he adamantly insisted that Germany's stripped possessions could not end up in the hands of rival European powers.

But once again, the United States was inconsistent, defining *self-determination* differently in different settings, and even resorting to military means in order to enforce the right kind of self-determination—an oxymoron, of course. One of the strangest episodes of a strange period came about in the summer of 1918, when Wilson allowed several thousand American soldiers to land in Russia to participate in an allied effort to revive the eastern front, if possible, and to create a more pliant Russian government than the emerging Bolshevik state.

Americans were genuinely excited by the Russian Revolution when it broke out in March 1917—as they had always been excited about popular uprisings that overthrew kings. The United States was one of the first nations to recognize the new provisional government. The sixth of Wilson's Fourteen Points clearly called for Russia's "unhampered" and "independent determination of her own political development." At the time, hundreds of American engineers were in Russia trying to rehabilitate its railroad system, at the request of Leon Trotsky.

But slowly Wilson began to accede to French and British pressure to send troops into the strange new world of Bolshevik Russia, principally to avoid the possibility that its vast materials would sustain the German army, freshly freed from the obligation of fighting on the eastern front. And so American soldiers joined in two unlikely campaigns. To the far north, they were placed under British command and entered Russia at Archangel. And to the far east, they joined the Japanese in entering Vladivostok, ostensibly to help a group of besieged Czechs trying to flee Russia and rejoin the fight against Germany. This was the only hot war that Russia and America ever fought.

The number of casualties was small, but the legacy of this misadventure loomed large for decades. Indisputably, the United States had sent troops into sovereign Russian territory, providing limitless fodder for anti-American Russian rhetoric throughout the twentieth century. And plenty of inferences are still possible, for the intervention was conceived in confusion, executed in confusion, and remembered in confusion. The troops stayed too long, until the middle of 1919, long after the war had ended. George Kennan called the "maze of influences" that led to these bizarre incidents a "fantastic brew." A lurid article in *Pravda* in September 1957, at the height of the Cold War, suggested that Russians believed that the Cold War had in fact originated with these actions. As late as the Gorbachev era, the Soviet Union was asking for damages from the United States for its role in the allied expeditions. But a careful look at the evidence reveals that Wilson was trying to relax the more genuinely imperial aspirations of his Japanese and British allies, and to preserve the Russian right to self-determination.

If the Russian misadventures degraded liberty abroad, it was degraded at home by the way in which left-wing sympathizers were treated in the United States between 1918 and 1920. Led by Attorney General A. Mitchell Palmer, Wilson's government allowed a more vigorous persecution of American dissidents than at any time since the Civil War. They were rounded up, questioned, charged, and even deported for activities that would barely have raised an eyebrow a decade earlier. In December 1919, a ship, the *Buford*, that removed a group of activists was nicknamed the Russian Ark. These persecutions had enduring ramifications. One of the government employees tasked to research America's potential enemies was J. Edgar Hoover, who rose rapidly in the climate of fear that ironically accompanied Wilson's great push for international justice abroad. By October 1919, he had collected 150,000 names for his list of possible subversives.

Wilson's struggles hardly ended with the war, or even the Versailles treaty. Possibly the greatest fight he ever fought was his battle to enlist the United States in the newly proposed League of Nations. He had spoken on the subject for years. It had a deep resonance for any student of American history, for it pitted America's traditional distrust of alliances against the traditional American desire to rewrite the rules of diplomacy. And ultimately, it pitted two good historians against each other: Woodrow Wilson and Henry Cabot Lodge, the Republican senator who led the charge against the League. In many ways, their struggle resembled the ways in which the founders—say, Jefferson and Hamilton—argued about the destinies of the republic and where, ultimately, the United States fit into the world. Though Wilson lost the battle, it remains unclear who will finally win the argument.

It is undeniably true that Wilson believed too strongly in perfectibility and had a penchant for starting utopian organizations. When he married his first wife in 1885, he proposed to her that they start "an Interstate Love League (of two members only that it may be of manageable size)," including a constitution. But his idea of an international organization built around collective security was an important step forward, even if imperfect, and certainly better than doing nothing at all. History proved him tragically correct when he promised a second world war within a generation if his proposals were shouted down with no better alternative in place.

As the founders had done, Wilson expressed a near total contempt for the way the states of Europe conducted their foreign policy. In his mind, the entire system was broken and needed to be rewritten. Secrecy and elitism were the cause of the betrayals and aggressions that had nearly wrecked the Continent. The allies were as guilty as the Central Powers. In the future, the world needed "a new and more wholesome diplomacy," without protocols, without secret agreements and with a decent respect for the opinions of mankind. His Fourteen Points began with a ringing declaration for "open covenants, openly arrived at."

Much good common sense was in Wilson's proposals, but also some ideas that seem naive with hindsight. For example, he proposed "the destruction of every arbitrary power anywhere that can separately, secretly and of its single choice disturb the peace of the world." What nation might not ultimately fall into that category? Indeed, the age of terrorism has shown us that every individual has the power to disturb the peace of the world.

The Middle East came up in several ways during the negotiations over the new world beginning. The territory of the Hejaz—a region of the Arabian peninsula that includes Mecca—became a focal point in the argument in the U.S. Senate over the League of Nations. Henry Cabot Lodge objected to many points, but none more strenuously than Article Ten of the League Covenant, which obligated the United States to come to the common defense of another League member if attacked. In his Senate speeches, Lodge was withering in his sarcasm about the Hejaz, arguing that the United States should never commit itself, in a military sense, to such a distant place. That absurd idea—that the United States might someday have a military interest in the Middle East—helped to doom Wilson's project. The League would soldier on without the United States, and throughout the 1920s the United States would fitfully talk about joining it, but never with the enthusiasm that Wilson had brought to the cause.

But surely that enthusiasm was part of the problem. At a moment when Americans were returning to bread-and-butter issues and trying hard to extricate themselves from Europe, Wilson did not alter his messianic oratory a whit. Arguing before the Senate in 1919, he claimed that the League was not his idea, but the Almighty's. America had been given the leadership of the world "by no plan of our own conceiving, but by the hand of God who led us into this way. We cannot turn back. We can only go forward, with lifted eyes and freshened spirit, to follow the vision. It was this we dreamed at our birth. America shall in truth show the way. The light streams upon the path ahead, and nowhere else."

No one is less likely to compromise than someone who believes that God has appointed him to a task. That refusal to retreat even an inch from his demands, even though many of the senators were making principled objections to his plan, spelled the end of his Covenant.

The rest of the story is well known. Wilson tried to appeal to the American people, over the heads of the Senate, and undertook a grueling tour—essentially a full-blown political campaign—to speak on behalf of the League. Beginning in September 1919, he made thirty-six speeches in seventeen states, an itinerant preacher spreading his gospel in the heartland. On September 25, in Pueblo, Colorado, he suffered a cerebral thrombosis that damaged his body and his presidency, and doomed his side to defeat in the battle over the League. Some parts of the speech he gave that day are still worth quoting, for the memorable combination of inspiration and desperation that will always be part of the Wilson legacy.

His final lines, just before the stroke, seem to anticipate the calm coming to him, if not to the world:

> There is one thing that the American people always rise to and extend their hand to, and that is the truth of justice and of liberty and of peace. We have accepted that truth and we are going to be led by it, and it is going to lead us, and through us the world, out into pastures of quietness and peace such as the world has never dreamed of before.

It later became convenient to blame the onset of the Second World War on Wilson, for his millennial faith did seem woefully simple by the time that his canny assistant secretary of the navy, Franklin Roosevelt, became president. But such an evaluation is too easy. It's true that Wilson might have created a better architecture for foreign relations, by compromising more with senators (and keeping the United States in the League) and less with America's allies (who imposed unduly harsh conditions on Germany at Versailles and tended to emphasize Wilson's arguments only when they helped their interests). But in fact, he had already taken several remarkable steps. He had articulated an ethical and openly stated foreign policy—still a concept that guides nations around the world, and nowhere more than in Europe. He had done more for the idea of a concert of nations than any other leader in history, even if his own nation had rejected the idea. He had spoken up for all nations, small and large, and more important, for the people who constituted them, rejecting the idea that kings and councillors determine policies, with no consequences. He had inspired the people of every continent with a message of hope and liberty that still held a surprising power to inspire a tired and cynical world. And finally, despite his defeats, he had placed America at the heart of the world's deliberations. His audacious way of talking about America's past and future had come close to fulfilling its own lofty expectations.

That was only one of several ways in which America's position in the world was greatly enhanced in the aftermath of World War One. The war effort had also galvanized the industries behind it and had left the United States in a vastly superior military and economic position. Even in the early years of the war, the United States had reckoned as a comparatively minor power alongside the great armies and navies of France and Britain. By its end, they were shattered and the United States had no rivals.

Still, the bitter debates over the League had shown that Americans felt reluctance to use their power. The mood of triumph that followed the war obscured the harsh realities that were to afflict the rising generation who had fought it. In the complex world of postwar America, patriotic words had new connotations. Liberty remained an inspiring concept to most, but some of its luster had worn off as a result of battle fatigue, and the Palmer Raids, and the ugly fight between Wilson and Lodge over what, exactly, America's destiny in the world was to be. Ernest Hemingway spoke for many of these Americans, veterans in particular, in his conclusion to *A Farewell to Arms*:

> I was always embarrassed by the words sacred, glorious, and sacrifice . . . We had heard them, sometimes standing in the rain almost out of earshot, so that only the shouted words came

> through, and had read them, on proclamations that were slapped up by billposters over other proclamations, now for a long time, and I had seen nothing sacred, and the things that were glorious had no glory and the sacrifices were like the stockyards at Chicago if nothing was done with the meat except to bury it. There were many words that you could not stand to hear and finally only the names of places had dignity. Certain numbers were the same way and certain dates and these with the names of the places were all you could say and have them mean anything. Abstract words such as glory, honor, courage, or hallow were obscene beside the concrete names of villages, the numbers of roads, the names of rivers, the numbers of regiments and the dates.

But that feels like too dark a note to end on in a chapter devoted to a great emissary of light—two, in fact. Wilson was no Theodore Roosevelt, as they both would have happily agreed. But to dismiss him as a sentimental idealist oversimplifies the profound importance of this central protagonist of American history. "I have tried to be a historian at the same time I was an actor," he said, and few were better trained to translate America's oldest yearnings into realities that are still unfolding.

It takes little effort to find examples of things said by Wilson that seemed too hopeful, or naive. In a speech on Memorial Day in 1919, in Suresnes, France, he predicted that "a new order of things" was beginning "in which the only questions will be, 'Is it right?' 'Is it just?' 'Is it in the interest of mankind?' " Near the end of the speech, he wondered why America had been "born," and decided that "she was born . . . to show mankind the way to liberty."

Listening to that, one can almost hear the old tales that were once spun about the hazy islands of the Atlantic, where people lived more freely; places like the Isles of the Blest and the Sunken Land of Buss and a hundred other rocks and reefs and half-seen apparitions. Many of those islands never existed at all, they were simply rumors of better places, just over the horizon. But some did, and their discovery led to others just beyond the next horizon. It was only by searching for them that they were found. That's the extraordinary thing about idealism—it ceases to be idealistic the second that human beings decide to make it real. By giving voice to what had been airy aspirations, and mobilizing the world's peoples, Wilson proved to be a realist indeed.

Wilson died in 1924, a delayed casualty of the Great War. Soon after his demise, it became fashionable to run him down; it still is. But was he less realistic than the Republicans who tried to "outlaw" war in the Kellogg-Briand Pact of 1928? Three of the signatories—Germany, Italy, and Japan—would be at war with the United States within fifteen years. When people began to will his ideas into reality, later in the century, he was always in the room. Franklin D. Roosevelt said as much in 1932, when he accepted his party's nomination, in the speech that named the New Deal: "Our indomitable leader in that interrupted march is no longer with us, but there still survives his spirit . . . Let us feel that in everything we do there still lives with us, if not the body, the great indomitable, progressive soul of our Commander-in-Chief, Woodrow Wilson."

At the moment the U.S. Senate ratified the United Nations Charter, Congressman Claude Pepper said that Wilson was in the chamber. As nations achieved self-determination in the Middle East, Asia, and Africa, Wilson's spirit was certainly felt. Algeria, Egypt, South Korea, and India all fought for independence along lines marked out by Wilson. NATO was Wilsonian in its dependence on collective security. The Helsinki Accords that helped to define human rights and bring down the Soviet Union were influenced by Wilson. So was the speech to evangelical ministers given by Ronald Reagan in 1983, when he argued, "If America ever ceases to be good, America will cease to be great." Mikhail Gorbachev's speech to the UN in December 1988, effectively ending the Cold War, was utterly Wilsonian in its promise to build a "new world" based on consensus and the renunciation of violence. All told, that is not such a bad legacy for an idealist. Perhaps it is best to just admit that idealism *is* realism if the willpower exists to make it so—especially in a nation whose interests and ideals are nearly one and the same.

Enormous challenges would come in the next generation, as Wilson predicted they would. In fact, history unfolded exactly as he expected, a rare achievement for a historian. That is only one of many reasons to reassess this tragic figure, a visionary who saw things not only as they were, but as they needed to be.

CHAPTER EIGHT

THE NEW WORLD IN ALL TONGUES

America has been the New World in all tongues, to all peoples, not because this continent was a new-found land, but because all those who came here believed they could create upon this continent a new life—a life that should be new in freedom.

—Franklin D. Roosevelt, Third Inaugural Address, 1941

NEW-FOUND-LAND

Some of the most fateful events in North American history have happened in the choppy, frigid waters off Newfoundland, England's oldest colony in the New World. It was there that John Cabot sailed in 1497 (only five years after Columbus had made landfall to the south), laying claim to the well-named island in the name of His Brittanic Majesty Henry VII. From that remote outpost, which created a legal foothold that in a sense included all of North America, a primitive notion of English rights would ultimately emanate across the entire continent, embracing the more famous colonies to the south, in what would become the United States. Maryland, in fact, was founded only after its investors had failed in a previous attempt to create a colony in Newfoundland, whimsically named Avalon, after the place where King Arthur is said to rest. For John Donne, Newfoundland and America were more or less one and the same, a virgin territory that he brazenly likened to his naked mistress ("O my America, my new-found-land"), adding the quite un-Puritanical thought that "to enter in these bonds is to be free."

These English rights were only territorial at first, a simple claim that England had a stake in the enormous property that had just been discovered. But they would evolve into far more than real estate, following a broad arc of religious and political sentiments that would themselves be translated, through the constant act of becoming, into human rights. Arguably, the starting point of that arc was Newfoundland, a rocky island that had often served as a way station between American and Europe (Charles Lindbergh flew directly overhead in 1927). It was an auspicious place for new beginnings. Just before disappearing at sea, Newfoundland's founder, Sir Humphrey Gilbert, had consoled sailors on a nearby ship who could hear him shouting into the wind, "We are as near to heaven by sea as by land."

One suspects that those words were familiar to Winston Churchill and Franklin Roosevelt as they met in these historic waters in August 1941. Churchill, after all, wrote a history, *The New World*, that probed deeply into the emergence of the British empire, and he was always drawn to the great English explorers of the sixteenth century. FDR was an impressive naval historian in his own right—the rooms at Hyde Park are lined with his collection of naval prints, and he, too, was drawn to the age of discovery. It was not quite their first meeting—Churchill had brushed off FDR when they were both serving their nations in high administrative capacities during the First World War. But it was their first meeting as heads of state, and it came at a moment when the eyes of the world were truly upon them (or at least searching for them).

Precisely for that reason, they had gone to great lengths to avert attention. "Utmost secrecy" was kept—FDR had merely told his wife he was going fishing, though his mysterious smile told her "he was not telling me all that he was going to do." His presidential yacht, the *Potomac*, then took him toward Martha's Vineyard, where he transferred to a heavy cruiser, the USS *Augusta*, in the middle of the night and began his voyage toward Newfoundland and history.

On August 9, the great meeting was finally brought off. The HMS *Prince of Wales*, playing "The Stars and Stripes Forever," pulled alongside the *Augusta*, and Winston Churchill came aboard. The next day, the president attended a Sunday-morning service aboard the *Prince of*

Wales that included richly symbolic readings and hymns. It struck Churchill's secretary as more than an ordinary service—rather "a sort of marriage service." Even if the meeting had only sealed the formal bond between the United States and the United Kingdom, it would have been important. But it did far more than that. Churchill said that night, "I have a feeling that something big may be happening—something really big." After centuries of aspiring to make its founding principles available to all humanity, the United States was finally in a position to do so.

In a way, Argentia Bay was the last place on earth to expect the president of the United States and British prime minister to be. But in addition to the historical echoes already cited, it was the site of a U.S. base that was quickly being outfitted, in preparation for America's likely entry into the Second World War. That a base could be built for the United States in British territory stemmed from a 1940 deal in which Britain had agreed to exchange rights to bases for urgently needed destroyers. The waters off Argentia were, in a sense, midway between America and England, just as John Winthrop may have been when he delivered his "city upon a hill" address aboard the *Arbella*. With a bit of exaggeration, Roosevelt and Churchill described themselves as "somewhere in the Atlantic."

If all of these predecessors—Cabot, Gilbert, and Winthrop—had advanced a sense of English rights in the New World, FDR and Churchill took the idea quite a bit further during their meeting. From this remote, terraqueous location, they issued a telegram that proclaimed a decisive new path in world affairs. At the end of the summit, on August 14, Churchill and Roosevelt sent a statement to the press, listing eight points of agreement, which added up to fewer than four hundred words. Instantly dubbed the Atlantic Charter, the announcement had a sensational effect on a world starved for good news. It continues to affect people's lives to this day.

The charter's appearance may have been meager—unlike, say, the Declaration, the great document had no signatures, and there wasn't much of a document, either. How does one immortalize a telegram? But its ideas electrified the world. For centuries, in the Declaration, the Emancipation Proclamation, and the speeches of Woodrow Wilson, American leaders had been striving to articulate a theory of human rights for non-Americans as well as Americans. Now, a U.S. president had affixed his name to a promissory note specifying those principles, and applying military might toward those ends. Better yet, his note was endorsed by the British prime minister—the heir to Lord North and all of the other imperialists who had tried to subdue America—as the official policy of the realm. It vowed to fight "tyranny," the bugbear of centuries. It advocated freedom of the seas, another classic American desideratum. And it more or less promised freedom, or something like it, to every person on earth.

The striking bond forged by Roosevelt and Churchill lay in their common experience as high-ranking naval officials early in their careers, and by extension, as theorists of empire. Churchill famously referred to himself as a "former naval person" and had been first lord of the admiralty during the First World War. Roosevelt, like his fifth cousin before him, occupied the crucial position of assistant secretary of the navy during the same conflict. They had even met at a dinner in London on July 29, 1918, though Churchill could not remember it after the fact—an indication that neither FDR nor the United States had quite risen to the level of importance they would later assume for him.

But for all their parallels, it would in time become clear that their theories of empire and human rights diverged in essential ways. That stress would persistently manifest itself, despite attempts to hide it, during the planning of the postwar world that began the day the Atlantic Charter was issued from Newfoundland. Simply put, Roosevelt believed that the soaring idealism of the charter applied to all of humanity. Churchill, despite his authorship of key passages, felt that the British empire would be compromised by too literal an emphasis on the charter's Wilsonian promise of self-determination. Through these swirling convergences and divergences, great historical forces were at play, acting through human instruments who understood their roles clearly and played them to the hilt.

FDR

Roosevelt's importance to the twentieth century has never been in dispute—he was voted *Time*'s "person of the century" near its conclusion.

Winston Churchill went even further, calling the life of Franklin D. Roosevelt "one of the commanding events of human history." But it is worth restating how indebted FDR himself was to history. To a degree unappreciated, he felt himself to be in a continuum, and throughout his life he peppered his speeches with knowing and insightful references to his predecessors. That included Theodore Roosevelt and Woodrow Wilson, of course, for he was profoundly shaped by both men. It's odd to reflect that two presidents, so different from each other, each found the perfect heir in Franklin D. Roosevelt.

Roosevelt has not always been thought of as one of the great bookish presidents—surely he was no Jefferson, and he spent far less time writing down his thoughts than most of the others. Given how long he was president, there is a notable dearth of his writings, except for collections of speeches, which are not really writings at all. But FDR's sense of history was pervasive, embracing not only his predecessors, but also Lincoln and the Civil War, and the American Revolution, and the founding period in particular. It is striking to realize that his father, James Roosevelt, was born in 1828, within Madison's lifetime, and nearly within Jefferson's. Surprisingly, given his background, FDR became a lifelong partisan of Thomas Jefferson, at a time when Alexander Hamilton was the presiding deity of American history in general, and the New York gentry more particularly, and Theodore Roosevelt most particularly of all. A long book review FDR wrote in the *New York Evening World* in 1925 was unrestrained in its enthusiasm for the third president and ended with the suggestive question "Is a Jefferson on the horizon?"

Clearly, he felt that the answer was yes—and it was evident who he thought filled the bill. FDR effectively probed the differences between Jefferson and Hamilton when he ran for president in 1932, and when he died in 1945, the speech left undelivered on his desk was a reflection on Jefferson's legacy—like his, eternally unfinished.

Throughout Roosevelt's childhood, there are tantalizing glimpses of a young and restless intellect, not entirely satisfied with the conventional opinions he was expected to inherit along with the family china (which, in this case, literally came from China). One eternal stimulus was travel, and Roosevelt may have seen more of the world than any president since John Quincy Adams. He first visited Europe at the age of three, and throughout his childhood spent a few months every year in England, France, Holland, and Germany. In 1889, the centennial of the French Revolution, the Roosevelts visited Paris, where seven-year-old Franklin climbed to the top of the brand-new Eiffel Tower to look at "the great city, spread out like a map below." That same year, he spent the winter in Pau, the small city in southern France where Mary Todd Lincoln had gone to recover her sanity. Governesses taught him French and German. Surely he was the only president who grew up with a vacation home in another country—in this case, on Campobello Island, just off the coast of Maine. It may not have felt foreign, but it was as much a part of the British realm as Newfoundland and may have contributed to FDR's lifelong ability to look at stormy American events with a kind of serene detachment—an island contemplating the main.

When Alfred T. Mahan's theories of American expansion became popular in the late nineteenth century, few read them more passionately than the young Franklin Roosevelt. Clearly, this was a globalist in training. Nothing proved it more completely than the stamp collection he began to amass as a boy, gathering tiny bits of paper and ink from every duchy, principality, and emirate on the planet. One wonders what they said to this only child, and how he answered back. Throughout his life, even on the epic journeys to Casablanca, Tehran, and Yalta, when he controlled the destinies of entire nations, he brought trunks carrying his collection, with its thousands of miniature sovereignties. But FDR never simply aped the teachings of his elders. Unlike many young men in his class, he was somewhat dubious about the imperialist urges that began to course through the body politic in the early 1890s. In 1898, while at Groton School, he proudly wrote his parents that he was taking the "con" side in a debate on the question "resolved, that Hawaii be promptly annexed."

That ambivalence also made itself evident in his loyalty to both an ardent exponent of empire, Theodore Roosevelt, and a critic of America's ceaseless ambition for more territory, Woodrow Wilson. Of course, he was not identical to either, and that is perhaps the main point—by combining their strengths while avoiding their most glaring weaknesses, he acted as a missing link between their two traditions and fused them into something far more powerful. He had Theodore Roosevelt's ebullience, personal charm, and magical last name. And in wartime he had Wilson's faith that the personal freedoms rooted in American history, now known by various phrases—*human rights, civil rights, the four freedoms*—were inseparable from the great military effort he was leading, and critical to the new world he hoped to build in its aftermath. More than either of them, he understood in his bones that no pretty words about America's destiny would move people unless there was a tangible connection between the spread of U.S. influence and improvement in the material conditions of their lives. That was true in the New Deal, the first great war he waged, and it was true in all of his foreign policy as well.

It would be hard to judge which mentor he knew better. His fifth cousin Theodore was the great role model of his early life and presided over his wedding to Theodore's niece Eleanor. It would have been difficult for FDR to show a devotion more nearly filial, except for the mild heresy he committed of joining the Democratic Party—though he made an important exception by voting for TR in 1904. By 1907 he was telling his fellow law clerks "that he wanted to be and thought he had a very real chance to be president." He was hardly the first American to voice that aspiration, but unlike most of the others, he had a specific plan. Like his cousin, he expected to become a state representative, assistant secretary of the navy, governor of New York, and finally president.

But Woodrow Wilson was the president FDR worked for, and he occupied the same job in the Wilson administration that Theodore Roosevelt had held under McKinley, at the saber's edge of the growing American empire. FDR had campaigned hard for exactly this job, after being offered others, and insisted that "the assistant secretaryship is the one place, above all others, I would love to hold." As a result, he had deep experience with military administration when he ran for office on his own—deeper than any other twentieth-century president except Dwight Eisenhower. He was alongside Woodrow Wilson as he made the momentous decision to enter the First World War, and he was there for the laborious peace that followed. That experience shaped all of the decisions he would make when his turn came, and he profited as handsomely by his knowledge of what not to do as he did from his certainty of what needed to be done.

From the moment he became assistant secretary in 1913, he had a rare vantage point to witness the innermost workings of the United

States as it completely reinvented its relationship to the outside world. And he was nearly as interventionist as his cousin had been, disdaining the idealism of his superior, Navy Secretary Josephus Daniels, and the secretary of state, William Jennings Bryan.

The story of his reaction to the outbreak of war in Europe is interesting. He wrote to Eleanor on August 3, 1914:

> To my astonishment on reaching the Dept., nobody seemed the least excited about the European crisis—Mr. Daniels feeling chiefly very sad that his faith in human nature and civilization and similar idealistic nonsense was receiving such a rude shock. So I started in alone to get things ready and prepare plans for what ought to be done by the Navy end of things.

That is hardly the sound of a stereotypical Wilsonian idealist, if such a thing even existed. True to his mixed lineage, he met with his cousin Theodore in the months leading up to America's entry into the war. And he gave speech after speech arguing that the United States needed to be on a war footing, before many of Wilson's supporters had reached that view. Specifically, he felt that the navy had to be strong enough to defend the Panama Canal, Alaska, and the "ideals of liberty" that had spread throughout the hemisphere. History was never far in the background—a major speech on preparedness that he delivered in 1915 began with an acknowledgment of all the Civil War veterans in the audience.

Just as he witnessed America's entry into war, so he saw our exit, nearly as complicated. He arranged to attend some of the proceedings of the great peace conference in Paris in 1919 and spoke about the League of Nations with Wilson on the return voyage to the United States. A year later, as the vice presidential candidate of the Democratic Party, he had even more occasion to discuss the League. In speech after speech—a dozen a day—Roosevelt warned against our becoming "a hermit nation, dreaming of the past." He gave more speeches than any other vice presidential candidate in history ever had. And in all of them he flogged the Republican Party for their growing isolationism. Clearly, Roosevelt not only believed in an international stance, he felt it to be good politics as well. Wilson's huge crowds in 1919 proved it.

Despite a convincing loss in 1920, Roosevelt continued his activities on behalf of Wilson's vision, helping to launch the Woodrow Wilson Foundation in 1921, then the graduate school in foreign relations at Johns Hopkins in 1927—the same school that Joseph McCarthy would attack with bitter vitriol at the height of the Cold War. Roosevelt supported the disarmament efforts launched under the Republicans of the 1920s, and his comments at the time reveal an anticolonial sentiment that was already fully mature. "The whole trend of the times is against wars for colonial expansion. The thought of the world leans the other way. Populations themselves have a say. Subjects of dispute are being worked out more and more by amicable means. No, the millennium has not arrived, but the nations are using greater and greater efforts to prevent war."

Roosevelt's first real chance to synthesize his thoughts about the rest of the world came in a piece he wrote for the July 1928 issue of *Foreign Affairs*, "Our Foreign Policy: A Democratic View." This sophisticated, revealing essay displayed some of the ideas, in germ, that would become hallmarks of the New Deal. He blamed the Republicans for their entrenched isolationism, citing the League of Nations and World Court cases in particular. He expressed the thought that the United States ought no longer to intervene at will in the hemisphere, but ought to work with her sister "American Republics" toward a deeper policy of cooperation. And he pointed out that American foreign policy had a long history of oscillating between rather extreme examples of "good will" and "dislike or fear or ridicule"—one of the central tenets of this book. That inconsistency was in itself a source of instability, and Roosevelt tried to paint a more advanced idea of a measured U.S. foreign policy that would uphold Wilson's policies, extricate American troops from their unpopular interventions around the Caribbean, and reduce profiteering on international loans. This eminently decent vision was still somewhat narrow in its geographic scope. In many ways, this hemisphere still framed American foreign relations, as it had for centuries. That would change soon.

A DISTANT MILLENNIUM

> There is in this global war literally no question, either military or political, in which the United States is not interested. —FDR

Despite all of these early signs of interest, foreign policy was far from the top of the agenda when FDR was elected in 1932. Not only was his platform overwhelmingly domestic, his election coincided with a dark moment in international relations that few Americans were prepared to address. Adolf Hitler became chancellor of Germany on January 30, 1933, and he and Roosevelt would serve until their deaths, only a few weeks apart in 1945. But this convergence was hardly evident in 1933, and the two leaders moved in very different directions after assuming office. Hitler began to revive the German war machine almost immediately and withdrew from the League of Nations in October, casting a pall over Europe. Roosevelt wanted to reduce the size of the U.S. Army, though it was already small with only 140,000 soldiers. Like Wilson, he picked an evangelical secretary of state, Cordell Hull, to conduct his foreign policy, and he uttered pleasing but rather ineffectual bromides about international disarmament, which did nothing to arrest the rise of Germany, Italy, and Japan.

Still, there were encouraging signs. Roosevelt not only articulated a fresh approach to hemispheric problems (his first inaugural proclaimed that the United States would be a "Good Neighbor"), he actually carried it out. He had an instinctive understanding—perhaps based on seeing Wilson's ecstatic audiences after Versailles—of the power of presidential presence in the cause of U.S. foreign policy and would eventually travel an unprecedented amount, all the more amazing for his physical disability. His predecessor, Herbert Hoover, made zero international presidential visits. FDR made fifty-two. The earliest of these travels took him on tours through the Americas, where he was received with jubilation and something more—a sense that here was a true champion of international democracy. In 1934, he became the first president to visit South America when he went to Colombia during a Good Neighbor trip around the Gulf of Mexico; two years later, he went on a more extensive trip through the continent. In Rio de Janeiro, Buenos Aires, and Montevideo, huge throngs sang out, "Viva la democracia! Viva Roosevelt!" His surging popularity was based not only on his clear respect for the other nations of the hemisphere, but on their growing sense that Pan-American unity was urgently needed to fight the escalating menace of fascism. "Democracy is still the hope of the world," he assured South America in 1936, a thought that was becoming quite focused with the outbreak of war in Spain and rising German interest in South America. In Argentina, historically the least pro-U.S. nation on the continent, 2 million citizens came out to shower FDR with "wild acclaim."

A number of impressive breakthroughs showed that FDR's commitment to the Good Neighbor policy went beyond mere rhetoric. This was clearly a new kind of Roosevelt. In 1934, the United States repealed the Platt Amendment, which had claimed the right to intervene willy-nilly in Cuba. That same year, FDR withdrew American forces from Haiti earlier than expected, ending a long presence dating back to his last tenure in federal government—and the president of the United States went to Haiti in person to celebrate. He agreed to a principle of nonintervention throughout the hemisphere, and to broad trade agreements. And so he was able to say, with a fair amount of accuracy, that his policy was to "banish wars forever from this vast portion of the earth"—an impressive improvement on the Monroe Doctrine.

In countless other areas, he took strides both large and small to improve the standing of the United States in the world. He met personally with the emissaries of other nations, an informal practice that helped immensely when he needed to explain his thinking and manage tensions—as, for example, he did when he sent a small number of ships to Cuba during a government crisis in 1933. That same year, he took the long-overdue but still bold step of recognizing the Soviet Union (unrecognized since 1917), despite strong opposition from numerous Americans, including the Daughters of the American Revolution, for whom one revolution was evidently enough. He empowered fresh thinkers inside the foreign policy apparatus, including Sumner Welles, a Latin America expert who would become his unofficial chief adviser on foreign policy. Like FDR, Welles had foreign policy in his bloodlines—his great-uncle Senator Charles Summer had tried to purchase Canada and the Dominican Republic in the nineteenth century.

These steps slowly coalesced into a recognizable policy, borrowing

THESE ISLANDS

The "new and strange world," as one writer described it, emerged slowly before a European population inclined to exaggerate both its terrors and its possibilities.

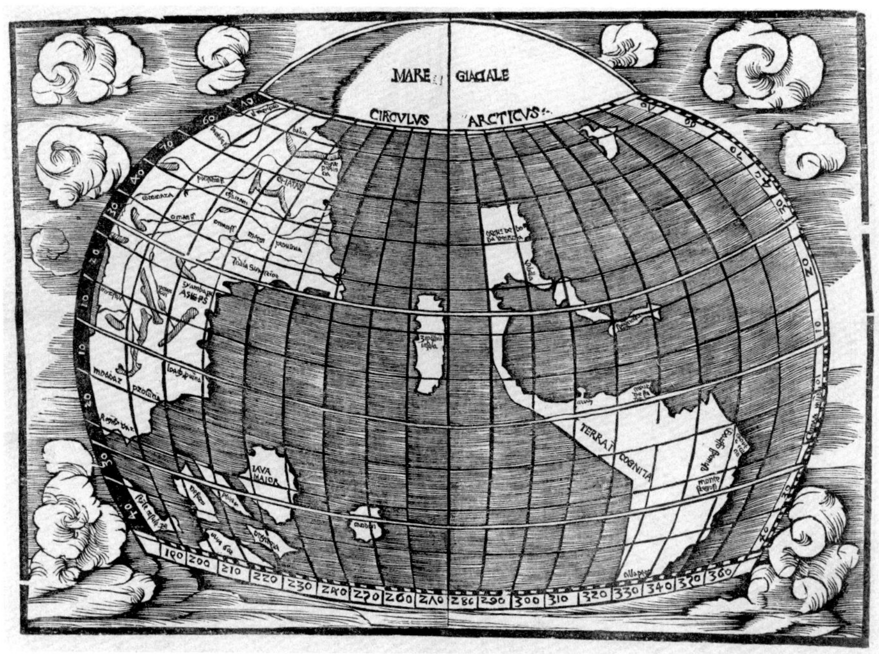

In the beginning, America was more water than land

Fantastic depictions of New World natives

APOCALYPSE THEN

Anglo-Americans perceived themselves to be locked in a global struggle against France, Spain, the pope, the devil, and Antichrist. To fight back against "Babylon," the word that conjured this axis of evil, was to hasten the Millennium, as predicted by the book of Revelation.

The Fall of Babylon.
A Short and Plain
CATECHISM,
Which
Detects & *Confutes* the Principles
OF
Popery:

Cotton Mather attacks Babylon (1707)

George Whitefield preaches on the eve of battle (1745)

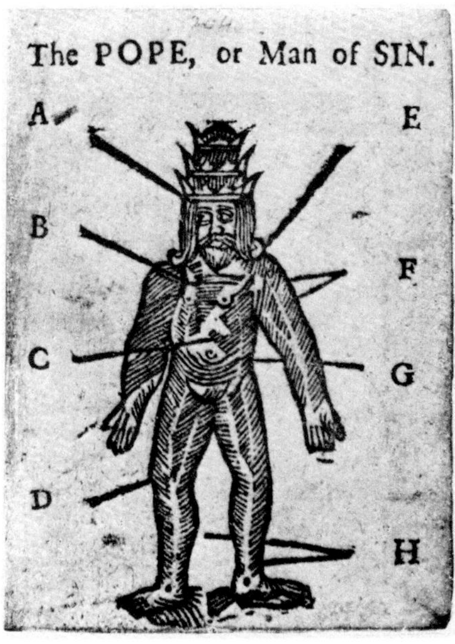

A Puritan caricature of the pope

LIBERTY OR DEATH

An emergent sense of rights and liberties replaced the Millennium but did not eliminate America's desire to shape history. When the Revolution ignited, the world felt its heat as well as its light.

Franklin as a god (1778)

The French enter the American Revolution, off Brittany (1778)

FROM THE HALLS OF MONTEZUMA

Expansion through purchase, conquest, and commerce strengthened the notion that the United States had a calling to spread liberty to the world. But dissent at home suggested that this destiny was anything but manifest.

Abraham Lincoln and Albert Gallatin, at the time of their dissent against the Mexican War

D-Day, 1847

PASSAGE TO INDIA

Few places on earth were immune from U.S. influence by the dawn of the twentieth century; but despite America's reach, new obligations sat uneasily with a people unaccustomed to shouldering the burdens of empire.

Robert College in Turkey

Theodore Roosevelt, globalist (c. 1908)

William Howard Taft in the Philippines (c. 1902)

LIBERTY AND HER SUITORS

The example of American liberty held extraordinary allure in a world not especially inclined to deepen the rights of its citizens; but as America's power grew, so did her sense of vulnerability.

Replicas of the Statue of Liberty in Paris, Tokyo, and Beijing (Tiananmen Square)

A 1917 print showing wartime fears of New York under aerial attack

THE AMERICAN CENTURY

The twentieth century proved that America's power had finally caught up to her aspirations. But even amid the glorious cacophony of the American Age, the ghosts of the past were audible.

Paris greets Wilson as the messiah (1919)

FDR and Churchill off Newfoundland (1941)

Eleanor Roosevelt takes the Universal Declaration of Human Rights to the world (1948)

SLOUCHING TOWARD BABYLON

The modern era has witnessed the utter supremacy of American power, but has not entirely resolved the ambivalence about empire that runs like a mighty stream through our history.

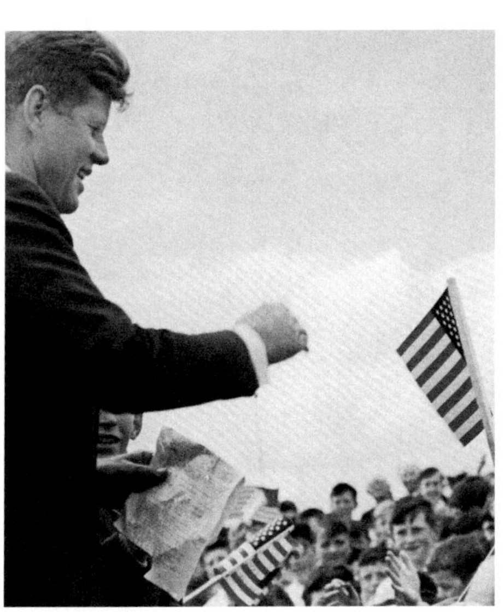

Kennedy in the arena (Ireland, 1963)

Johnson in torment (1968)

Reagan at Pointe du Hoc (1984)

Bush at sea, aboard the USS Abraham Lincoln *(2003)*

from Wilson's idealism to encourage democracy and recognize the rights of small nations to self-determination, but generally avoiding his utopian way of speaking. As Hitler and Mussolini consolidated their power in Europe, and Japan began to threaten the peace in Asia, FDR's pronouncements on liberty and democracy began to acquire more importance. That people have rights and expectations was a basic assumption of his political career, which he had acted upon impressively, first as governor of New York and then as president. In the early years of the New Deal, when his overwhelming priority was easing the economic crises of the Great Depression, he postulated a number of rights that citizens could expect their government to protect, including not only the old right of self-expression, but new and more economic rights to jobs, training, education, health care, homes, safety, and a host of other now standard assumptions of decent living. As he turned to face the growing threat of rampant militarism, FDR instinctively adopted this language of freedom to articulate his response. And so the domestic New Deal slowly became a New Deal for the World.

The result was a profound rethinking of America's obligation to the rest of humanity. It began with assertions of noninterference in the Americas and support for international peace efforts, then graduated to support for worldwide democracy and the sovereignty of small nations (imperiled by German, Italian, and Japanese militarism), and finally resulted in FDR's impassioned warnings to Americans that they needed to arm themselves and others to fight off the fascist menace.

Roosevelt's speeches during this transformation offer a fascinating window into history, in every sense. He was obviously making history as he argued that the United States needed to stand in the vanguard against tyranny; but he was also drawing from it, finding eloquent examples to suggest that Americans had always been interested in a freedom that was broadly defined, encompassing new ideas as they became available, and available beyond the borders of the United States. As he said in a press conference, "When you come down to the definition of American principles, you want to go the whole hog; you want to go all the way, instead of stopping short." Clearly, he saw the Declaration of Independence as only a beginning—that life, liberty, and the pursuit of happiness were fine, but jobs, education, housing, and health were essential to their achievement.

He began to sound the note of warning in the middle 1930s, and he did so in the familiar language of America representing the world's disenfranchised peoples against tyrants. In his State of the Union from January 3, 1936, he noted the growing possibility of war and blamed it on autocrats in Europe and Asia who had "impatiently reverted to the old belief in the law of the sword, or to the fantastic belief that they, and they alone, are chosen to fulfill a mission and that all others among the billion and a half of human beings in the world must and shall learn from and be subject to them." His second inaugural called on Americans to fight for "the survival of democracy," at home and "in other lands."

Roosevelt's rhetoric grew more strident as the number of invasions increased around the world, in what seemed to be a losing battle for democracy. Japan had invaded Manchuria, Mussolini was in Ethiopia; Hitler was bombing Spain, and global war was clearly imminent. Americans were already vulnerable, well before the conflict began. The American gunboat *Panay* was destroyed by Japanese planes on December 12, 1937, four years before Pearl Harbor (Japanese apologies provided small consolation).

During this dark time, Roosevelt faced two difficult and opposing challenges. First, he had to convey the seriousness of the menace facing Americans—a menace that Americans overwhelmingly did not want to face. Second, he had to offer a glimpse of the better world that might be available, after a war, if Americans put all of their resources into building it. Long before Pearl Harbor, FDR began to limn the world as he wished it to be, in a language reminiscent of Wilson's, but leaner and more muscular.

In speech after speech, from 1938 until 1941, Roosevelt stressed that the Old World and the New were no longer as separated as they had once been. The rise of airpower, and German airpower in particular, was altering the old equations, bringing back a sense of vulnerability that the United States had not felt since the early nineteenth century. By 1938, Germany had two thousand planes with a range of thirty-three hundred miles, capable of reaching the Americas from west Africa. Nor was this merely a feeling in the air. German and Italian influence had penetrated deeply into South America, organizing fascist parties, arms sales, and trade agreements. In May of that year, a fascist-inspired party tried to topple the Brazilian government, without success. Rumors of coups were circulating at high levels in Uruguay and Chile, and Roosevelt thought it likely that the Nazis would soon move on Dutch and French possessions in the New World. The map was quickly changing, and one of the more difficult predicaments facing Roosevelt as the war approached was whether the Monroe Doctrine would apply to Greenland if Denmark fell to Germany. In fact, the Nazis did occupy North America, though no one knew it at the time—a remote German weather station was discovered in Labrador in 1981!

Clearly, Roosevelt had to fight back against these threats, and he did, artfully bending the rules to allow military production to increase, despite fierce domestic opposition to any entanglements abroad. But he was constrained by the same Wilsonian legacy that he was trying to honor, and specifically by the series of disarmament and neutrality treaties that war-weary Americans had signed in the 1920s, convinced that this would further the cause of peace, but which actually diminished U.S. military strength vis-à-vis possible rivals.

Other nations, understanding the allure of liberty to Americans, invoked its power. On the eve of France's capitulation to the Nazis, the French premier, Paul Reynaud, wrote to Churchill, "If you cannot give to France in the hours to come the certainty that the United States will come into the war within a very short time, the fate of the world will change. Then you will see France go under like a drowning man and disappear, after having cast a last long look towards the land of liberty from which she awaited salvation." King George VI wrote to FDR personally, asking for destroyers "to carry on our solitary fight for freedom." It is worth lingering on that request. To George Washington, receiving a request for military aid from a British sovereign, in the name of freedom, would have been difficult to imagine.

As the year 1941 dawned, Roosevelt made progress toward both of his goals. American preparedness became more concrete with the passage of H.R. 1776, the Lend-Lease Act, formally known as "An Act to Further Promote the Defense of the United States, and for Other Purposes." And Roosevelt took a large step toward defining his vision of the world with his annual address to Congress, on January 6, 1941, in which he identified "Four Freedoms" he meant to see extended around the world: freedom of speech, freedom of worship, freedom from want, and freedom from fear. Those four phrases were comforting in their way, embracing beliefs dating back to the American Revolution. But the speech made radical assumptions: the obligation of governments to provide benefits to their citizens, and the desirability of spreading American ideas of personal freedom to foreign cultures that had little experience with them. Whatever difficulty lay behind those assumptions did not deter Roosevelt in the least. Note the use of *millennium*, now reduced in size.

> That is no vision of a distant millennium. It is a definite basis for a kind of world attainable in our time and generation. That kind of world is the very antithesis of the so-called new order of tyranny which the dictators seek to create with the crash of a bomb. To that new order we oppose the greater conception—the moral order. A good society is able to face schemes of world domination and foreign revolutions alike without fear. Since the beginning of our American history, we have been engaged in change—in a perpetual peaceful revolution—a revolution which goes on steadily, quietly adjusting itself to changing conditions—without the concentration camp or the quick-lime in the ditch. The world order which we seek is the cooperation of free countries, working together in a friendly, civilized society. This nation has placed its destiny in the hands and heads and hearts of its millions of free men and women; and its faith in freedom under the guidance of God. Freedom means the supremacy of human rights everywhere.

For all his serenity, Roosevelt knew the stakes, and that he was almost certainly committing the United States to war against an implacable foe. He had nightmares about an aerial bombing of New York City. In the spring of 1941, Adolf Berle, a White House aide, recorded in his diary, "The President was telling last night of a dream . . . that there had been a light bombing of New York; that the Secret Service had provided him with a bombproof cave two hundred feet under the cliff near a little cottage he has up on the hill there; that he and several of his people had gone down into it to stay until a squadron of German planes had passed over Hyde Park."

In his speeches that spring, Roosevelt stressed how near the "island outposts of the New World—the Azores and the Cape Verde islands"—were to Germany as well as to the United States, and how they might easily be seized as part of an invasion strategy, repeating the same path across the Atlantic that the original Europeans had taken. In that context, it made perfect sense to hold the summit meeting that led to the Atlantic Charter in an insular location. And so, in August 1941, Churchill and Roosevelt met at Newfoundland and signed the telegram heard round the world.

The Atlantic Charter inscribed the lofty principles of the Four Freedoms upon an ironclad military alliance—symbolized quite literally by the naval vessels off Newfoundland. It embraced all of humanity, and by asserting that the rights of individuals affected the course of nations, offered what one historian has called "a defining, inaugural moment for what we now know as the modern doctrine of human rights"—the same human rights FDR had alluded to in his Four Freedoms speech. And these were not just any rights, but the rights of economic entitlement that FDR had promulgated through the New Deal.

The Charter was such an optimistic document that it may well have been ahead of even FDR's politics. Ironically, Churchill seems to have supplied some of its more anthemic phrases. Certainly, anyone could have pointed out the ways that the United States itself failed to live up to its promises, through racial segregation and immigration quotas and other failures of democracy. The internment of Japanese-Americans, less than a year away, would strike a resounding false note through all subsequent American history. But, as Roosevelt's speechwriter Robert Sherwood wrote, sometimes "when you state a moral principle, you are stuck with it, no matter how many fingers you have kept crossed at the moment."

The global response to the Atlantic Charter fully justified its global ambition. Around the world, hearts were lifted, and stakes were raised. Roosevelt had fused domestic and foreign policy, joining the New Deal to the fight against fascism, and linking America inexorably to foreign liberation and perpetual revolution. Those promises would linger in the air long after the war against Hitler was won. In India, Mahatma Gandhi wrote FDR to clarify how important these ideas were to his people. Even as Western nations claim "they are fighting to make the world safe for freedom of the individual and for democracy," their claim "sounds hollow, so long as India, and for that matter, Africa are exploited by Great Britain, and America has the Negro problem in her own home." In South Africa, Nelson Mandela heard every word.

Those were perceptive observations, and they would not easily go away. As he sailed back toward the United States, Roosevelt must have felt that he had glimpsed a vision worth fighting for.

STRANGE GODS

Roosevelt's success was so complete that we are complacent about it now. We see his head on the dime, where he replaced the figure of Liberty, and to many people around the world those two figures were interchangeable. Americans still live under a government that is indebted to the New Deal, and we hear his words in our head all the time, even when it is unclear where they come from. True, FDR is not recognized at Mount Rushmore—in part, because he came along too late, and also because Calvin Coolidge decreed there could be only one Democrat, who turned out to be Thomas Jefferson. But most Americans recognize that he was one of the greatest presidents in our history, and the greatest of the twentieth century. Ronald Reagan was an unabashed partisan.

Still, there are periodic assaults on his legacy—efforts to roll back the protections of the New Deal, or to paint the UN as an alien presence on American soil, perhaps even the instrument by which Antichrist will finally crush the United States. Throughout his lifetime, FDR acted as a magnet for cranks of all descriptions, as ultraconservatives, isolationists, racists, and the superrich coalesced into a movement of sorts that outlasted his presidency. There were many grounds for their hatred. The extremely wealthy always despised FDR for asking them to contribute more toward the national coffers. Many others were swayed by the demagogues—Huey Long and Charles Coughlin—who trailed FDR like seagulls following a tugboat. Some were legitimately afraid of his strong executive powers and persistent experimentation with the government.

Another unifying cause for the FDR haters, and a more attractive one than those mentioned above, was the fear that he was embroiling

America in foreign entanglements. That was a legitimate fear, for in truth, FDR *was* placing the United States on a new footing in the world. He did it by leading America into the largest war it had ever fought, and he did it all over again by building a set of global organizations to keep the peace afterward. Few historians today would argue that he was wrong to do either, but large numbers of Americans still detest the United Nations as an anti-American plot to subvert liberty, when in truth it was conceived, named, and put into motion by the president of the United States himself, in service to ancient American ideals.

That FDR faced formidable opposition to his policies in the 1930s is hardly a secret. Frankly, it is a wonder that he accomplished a tenth of what he did. As he grew concerned about the deteriorating world situation and took steps to prepare America for the conflict to follow, he was hounded by critics from all sides of the political spectrum who objected in the most vitriolic language to his preparedness.

Some of the objections were based in the simple and obvious fact that the United States had fought a serious war in Europe within living memory. In 1936, the Nye Committee issued a congressional report blaming American entry into the Great War on arms manufacturers and international financial cartels—the same sorts of shadowy, menacing threats from abroad that had fueled the populist crusades of the late nineteenth century. Alarmed by the report, Congress passed a series of stringent laws that prevented the United States from giving loans to belligerents—effectively starving Britain and France for money as Hitler's war machine was reaching peak capacity.

To some extent, this opposition was political. Many in the Republican Party, and their wealthy supporters, found paying higher taxes a greater threat to their "liberty" than the rise of Hitler and funded a variety of organizations designed to counter FDR's warnings. The same senator who had led the committee investigating arms manufacturers, Gerald Nye of North Dakota, was deeply involved in the America First Committee, a loose organization of anti-FDR activists that drew as many as eight hundred thousand people at its peak, largely from the Midwest. Its most prominent spokesman was Charles Lindbergh, who publicly attacked FDR from 1939 to 1941, right up to the eve of American entry into World War Two.

Like weeds in a sidewalk, other critics sprang up over what seemed relatively innocent actions. For example, FDR had tried to sustain Theodore Roosevelt's great interest in the World Court and was persistently opposed by a band of Republican senators—progressive Republicans at that. In 1935, opposition to the World Court reached a fever pitch in the United States, uniting opponents from the conservative Hearst newspaper syndicate to the radio demagogue Charles Coughlin, who insisted that the World Court was yet another instrument of unchecked power, organized by international financial cabals. Rejecting it outright was the best way to "keep America safe for Americans." After that failure, FDR wrote of the senators who had voted against him, "I am inclined to think that if they ever get to Heaven they will be doing a great deal of apologizing for a very long time—that is if God is against war—and I think He is." Roosevelt also used religion on a different occasion to explain his critics. Discussing the rise of hate radio, and the success that his most virulent critics were enjoying with it, he said, "In normal times the radio and other appeals by them would not have been effective. However, these are not normal times; people are jumpy and very ready to run after strange gods."

"Strange gods" hit the bullseye, for religion was certainly fueling Coughlin, and many of the Roosevelt haters spoke in a language of exalted self-righteousness. If faith had historically fueled the millennial aspirations that underlay American ambitions to reshape the world, it also had fueled the sense—not entirely unrelated—that the rest of the world was a dark and sinful place. As usual, much of the most extreme language was cloaked in the language of patriotism, and of liberty in particular. Just as the defenders of slavery had found *liberty* a most capacious word to defend their right to expand, so those who hated FDR's economic policies and his hostility to Hitler found that same banner useful when organizing to oppose him.

The most obvious offender was the American Liberty League, founded in 1934 by Republicans and conservative Democrats and funded by large corporations, including Du Pont, Standard Oil, U.S. Steel, Goodyear, General Motors, and many others. The league was more concerned about domestic issues than international ones (for good measure, it labeled FDR both a socialist and a fascist). But its hateful energy spread in many directions, and it spent huge amounts of money on media operations and publications designed to discredit FDR. Another group, the Crusaders for Economic Liberty, or "White Shirts," brought a similar venom, though on a smaller scale.

But of course, FDR was gifted at making patriotic arguments of his own and skillfully dismantled most of his opposition with his ready arsenal of wit, common sense, and confidence. Although he was, in fact, steering America toward a completely new global orientation, he did it with such a placid conviction of America's place in the world that few recognized it for the revolution it was. FDR's "rendez-vous with destiny" was less shrill than Manifest Destiny and changed the world more profoundly as a result.

Nothing undermined FDR's critics more effectively than the growing recognition that he was right. During the 1930s, it became increasingly clear that Adolf Hitler was no ordinary foreign threat. It would take time before the full extent of his monstrosity was known, but each act of Nazi treachery weakened the isolationist argument in the United States, and the combination of Pearl Harbor and Hitler's declaration of war on the United States in December 1941 finally brought clarity to the global situation FDR had been preparing for.

The result was not only the great triumph of arms we all know from the history books (or at least the History Channel). It was also FDR's extraordinary performance as teacher in chief. Over the course of the Second World War, he stated American ideals in language that was unusually moving to the rest of the world. With Wilson's commitment to the spoken word, and his sense that the peoples of the world were listening even when their governments were not—but without Wilson's delusionary notion that God had appointed him to the task—FDR rewrote history. It was as if a new writer had been hired to take over a faulty script. The result was a far better product, and the story of America's involvement with the world had a far better ending in 1945 than anyone might have imagined in 1941. Few would doubt any more that the cause of America was the cause of all mankind.

To read through FDR's many orations during the Second World War is to see and hear a master craftsman at work. Through fireside chats and open-air addresses and casual remarks before reporters, he conveyed his thoughts about America's global responsibilities with eloquence and seeming effortlessness. But beneath his jaunty air lay a most sophisticated sense of what moved people—the legacy of Wilson—and what was in fact possible—the legacy of Theodore Roosevelt.

From the moment of America's entry into the war, FDR made it clear that he was not merely fighting against a specific enemy, Japan, but against a "form of treachery" that "shall never again endanger us." Many considered the most shocking part of the story of Pearl Harbor to be that Japanese envoys were pretending to negotiate peacefully while their planes were in the air—a shocking example of the Old World's diplomatic perfidy. Not only had the United States been attacked—we had been lied to as well!

The best way to oppose such perfidy was to declare principles openly, in the American way, and so, on January 1, 1942, the "Declaration by United Nations" was signed by twenty-six allied governments. They pledged not only their mutual military assistance, but, even before that, to uphold the principles of the Atlantic Charter, to "defend life, liberty, independence and religious freedom," to "preserve human rights and justice in their own lands as well as in other lands," and to do all that they could to fight against "the savage and brutal forces seeking to subjugate the world."

To celebrate Washington's birthday in February 1942, Roosevelt gave a fireside chat that not only upended Washington's warning against foreign entanglements, but insisted that the freedom of any person "anywhere" in the world was dependent upon the rights of liberty and justice "everywhere" in the world. This great address, which took the unprecedented step of asking Americans to "take out and spread before you a map of the whole earth," explained in careful detail how Roosevelt intended to take the fight to the Axis.

But there was of course far more to it than that. Roosevelt's genius was that he actually lived up to his promises. And he did commit in a profound way to an idea of liberation that took hold around the world. As the war went on, he deepened his definition of the rights that Americans were fighting for, beginning with the rights of those doing the fighting. He outlined the GI Bill of Rights in a radio address on July 28, 1943, including guarantees of income, education, credit, and health care to all veterans. Toward the end of the war, he began to articulate a "Second Bill of Rights," which promised a wide range of personal freedoms and went a considerable distance toward fusing the aims of the

New Deal with those of the war. In his annual address to Congress, in January 1944, he enumerated these rights in detail, including the right to a decent job, the right to do business without unfair competition, the right to a decent home, the right to decent medical care, the right to an education, and the right to feel unafraid of old age, accidents, and unemployment. Furthermore, he committed to the extraordinary promise that "after this war is won, we must be prepared to move forward, in the implementation of these rights, to new goals of human happiness and well-being. America's own rightful place in the world depends in large part upon how fully these and similar rights have been carried into practice for our citizens." In other words, he seemed to be saying that we would not win the war unless we extended economic benefits to all U.S. citizens. It's no wonder that conservatives hated him.

This was only one of the ways in which the Second World War deepened the idea of freedom. Another was simply in its inherent expansiveness. There was not a continent on earth that did not see some sort of conflict between those who were clearly fighting for freedom and those who were clearly fighting against it. In these same years, the full reach of the American economy and military became clearer than ever. In the few places where Americans were not fighting, their supplies were being used by their allies. In every latitude and longitude, from pole to pole, the world discovered "the American people in their might," in Roosevelt's famous phrasing. It was as if the United States, without intending to, had finally found a way to fulfill the outrageous global ambitions that had been voiced by windbags of the 1890s and the prophets of Manifest Destiny before them. Americans were simply ubiquitous.

They also expanded in another sense—by learning about people other than themselves. In addition to every other change it wrought, World War Two was a time of great geographical learning for Americans. Roosevelt's advice to "look at your map" was only one of dozens of ways the people of the United States were able to follow the war. The U.S. government issued weekly maps and news bulletins to public libraries, and atlases and geographical publications struggled to keep up with enormous public demand for information. Thinking globally came naturally to a generation acting globally. Roosevelt's 1940 opponent, Wendell Willkie, wrote a charming travelogue in 1943, *One*

World, that introduced millions of readers to North Africa, Iran, and Russia, while meditating thoughtfully on America's role in the world.

One of the finest statements of American purpose to emanate from the war was the short and moving prayer that Dwight Eisenhower distributed to the troops massed before the D-day invasion. Issued near the English Channel, where John Winthrop's fleet had set sail in 1630, it repeated his world-changing language, but with the serene confidence that an enormous army can provide:

> You are about to embark upon the Great Crusade, toward which we have striven these many months. The eyes of the world are upon you. The hopes and prayers of liberty-loving people everywhere march with you. In company with our brave Allies and brothers-in-arms on other Fronts, you will bring about the destruction of the German war machine, the elimination of Nazi tyranny over the oppressed peoples of Europe, and security for ourselves in a free world.

As the American armies and those of their allies slowly fought their way to victory in 1945, liberation clearly meant something profound to peoples who had been under the yoke of the Axis powers. It also grew clear, as Russian and American armies slogged their way to Berlin, that liberation meant different things to different liberators.

But those disturbing details would remain secondary while the great fight to defeat Germany and Japan was under way, and while Franklin Roosevelt was alive. He was not a perfect crusader for freedom. His most obvious lapse was the internment of roughly 120,000 American citizens of Japanese descent during the Second World War. But there were other mistakes—the slowness with which the United States allowed refugees, particularly Jewish refugees, to flee Europe in the 1930s, and the occasional disdain he showed for protecting any freedoms that might interfere with the war effort. Sometimes, for example, he asked his attorney general, Francis Biddle, to take action against critics or journalists whom he suspected of providing too much aid to the enemy.

Like Lincoln, FDR needed to win the war before he could attach the idea of freedom to it. But clearly, he had wrought a transformation of sublime importance in the histories of America and the world, now more or less the same. That was exactly the point. Americans now accepted what they had questioned under Wilson, that their safety at home depended on their willingness to stand up for their beliefs on beaches and bridgeheads around the world. To everyone who heard him—in other words, to nearly everyone on earth—FDR was far more than a head of state, or even the commander in chief of a powerful army of liberation. He was nothing less than the philosopher-king of the new world coming into existence.

The stamp collector who once hoarded every foreign object he could find now had the entire world under his magnifying glass. Even before the United States entered the war, he articulated the freedoms that would follow in the wake of American armies. Those freedoms went beyond anything expressed before—in fact, we have not yet caught up to all that he was saying. At the same time, they were firmly rooted in the three centuries that had brought America to apotheosis. They were the product of a single nation's struggle with its demons and its better angels—but they were now offered to "all" people, a crucial word used eight times in the Atlantic Charter. At long last, America's capacity to change the world had caught up to her desire. The ark was sailing at full speed. The only question remaining was an old one: What would this new world look like when it was finally glimpsed?

CITIZENS OF THE WORLD

> We have learned that we cannot live alone, at peace; that our own well-being is dependent on the well-being of other nations far away. We have learned that we must live as men, not as ostriches, nor as dogs in the manger. We have learned to be citizens of the world, members of the human community. We have learned the simple truth, as Emerson said, that "the only way to have a friend is to be one."
>
> —FDR, Fourth Inaugural Address, 1945

We usually give FDR credit for two great triumphs—victory over the Depression, and victory over fascism. In fact, he deserves credit for a third, though he was not there to witness it—victory over the colonial system that had governed much of the world since the dawn of the American project.

That he was planning something new and better is clear from reading his statements during the war. For how long he had been harboring a dislike of the British and French empires is hard to say. Certainly, he was as guilty of the petty snobberies toward people of different races and religions as most people from his background. Yet he harbored a disdain for empires that bordered on the radical.

Perhaps it was simply that, as any student of American history knew, a strong emphasis on personal rights, based on the theory that each person has an equal vote, was inimical to the imperial system. Perhaps it was simply a distaste for the way that the war had started—with powerful countries invading weaker ones. Arguably, the war had started not with Hitler's aggression, but with Japan's invasion of Manchuria in 1931 and Mussolini's invasion of Ethiopia in 1935. Each invasion was a step toward an empire: Japan's "Greater East Asia Co-Prosperity Sphere" and Mussolini's "New Roman Empire." Each, to Roosevelt, was anathema.

As long as the United States was fighting, in theory, for the freedom to vote, it was fighting for a world that had not previously existed. Furthermore, FDR's growing emphasis on economic rights and freedoms—as spelled out in his Economic Bill of Rights—must have sent a clear warning to all those who hoped forlornly to return to the labor practices of the antebellum years. As the idea of the United Nations germinated, with exactly these rights in mind, it became clear how deeply Roosevelt wanted to change the world.

The first test case was relatively easy to think through, because it involved a part of the world that no ally had any jurisidiction over. French Indochina had fallen to the Japanese after France had fallen to Germany and suffered an oppressive wartime occupation. Roosevelt had no interest in defeating the Japanese only to turn the region back over to the French colonial forces. He made this clear in a memo to the secretary of state on January 24, 1944, which argued that Indochina should be administered "by an international trusteeship" after the war. After all, he noted, little had changed in a century, and "the people are worse off than they were at the beginning." He understood that this would make things uncomfortable for the British, because it was ultimately aimed at the "future independence" of their colonies as well, but he felt no remorse on that account. "Each case must, of course, stand on its own feet, but the case of Indo-China is perfectly clear. The French have milked it for one hundred years. The people of Indo-China are entitled to something better than that."

The issue of colonial policy after the war was a particularly jagged rock sticking up out of the waters off Newfoundland. The subject of empires inevitably came up in the long discussions FDR held with Churchill, and it became clear that their disagreement was not only real, but profound. Around the time of Churchill's visit to the White House in January 1942, FDR alluded to some of these differences.

"You know, my friend over there doesn't understand how most of our people feel about Britain and her role in the life of other peoples. Our popular idea of that role may not be entirely objective—may not be one hundred per cent true from the British point of view, but there it is; and I've been trying to tell him that he ought to consider it. It's in the American tradition, this distrust, this dislike and even hatred of Britain—the Revolution, you know, and 1812, and India and the Boer War and all that. There are many kinds of Americans of course, but as a people, as a country, we're opposed to imperialism—we can't stomach it." Eleanor Roosevelt added, "The President has been having considerable trouble in getting the Prime Minister to grasp what kind of a country we are."

Daringly, FDR even tried to give advice to Churchill on India and how to allow it greater self-determination after the war. He wrote him with "a new thought" in 1942 that borrowed a few ideas from early American history (specifically the Confederation period, 1781 to 1789) to set up a body to work on a permanent form of government. Churchill did not even venture a reply, though he privately grumbled over "the difficulties of comparing situations in various centuries and scenes where almost every material fact is totally different." He wrote Harry Hopkins to complain, "The President's mind was back in the American War of Independence, and he thought of the Indian problem in terms of the thirteen colonies fighting George III."

Some casual remarks of Roosevelt's, recorded at a press conference on February 5, 1944, show how alive the issue was to him. He called Gambia "the most horrible thing I have ever seen in my life" and blamed the British for allowing it to remain underdeveloped, because "for every dollar that the British have put into Gambia, they have taken out ten. It's just plain exploitation of those people." A press conference records FDR saying, "I am taking up with Churchill at the present time—he doesn't see the point yet—I think he will (laughter)."

What is fascinating about the exchange is that it took place before a group of African-American journalists. Obviously, Roosevelt felt the connection between his own policies at home and the larger goals the United States was fighting for overseas. He went right to the heart of the matter, saying that Churchill had tried to get him to keep his nose out of British Africa by threatening to expose conditions in the South. "He thought he had me," Roosevelt added, continuing, "Go ahead and do it. Tell the world . . . We have got some things to be ashamed of, and other things that are not as bad as they are painted. It wouldn't hurt at all—bring it out." That was FDR at his finest.

What is also interesting about the exchange is its acknowledgment of the power the United Nations would have, even before the organization existed, to bring about reform. Roosevelt and Churchill were specifically talking about UN commissions that would investigate conditions after the war. And Roosevelt's confidence in the idea stemmed from his sense that the United States had less to apologize for than most nations.

Near the end of his life, he became even more adamant. In March 1945, he told an aide that he was concerned about the world's "brown people," because "they are ruled by a handful of whites and they resent it." Looking far into the future, he ventured the thought, "1,100,000,000 potential enemies are dangerous," then added, "Churchill doesn't understand this." Roosevelt's new world would be genuinely new, and genuinely global.

The term *United Nations* had originated with Roosevelt, as a simple way of describing the nations allied against Germany, Italy, and Japan. But during the war, a series of conferences gave deeper definition to the term, and the idea of an international organization, far more powerful than the League of Nations, and with the full backing of the United States, began to take shape. The Atlantic Charter, even before the United States entered the war, signaled the first of these founding moments. It called for the elimination of force as a diplomatic tool between nations, and a stable peace that would allow all people to live "in freedom from fear and want," under "a wider and permanent system of general security."

Then the other conferences came in quick succession. The Declaration by United Nations, made at Washington on the first day of 1942, did more than cement the military alliance. It advanced rights of independence and religious freedom, and united its members in a feeling of solidarity toward something better. Its six-month anniversary was celebrated around the world on the U.S. Flag Day, as marchers reveled in China, India, and London.

In January 1943, Churchill and Roosevelt met at Casablanca to discuss war aims, and there Roosevelt came up with the term *unconditional surrender* (he remembered that Ulysses Grant had used the same words to Robert E. Lee). Hot Springs, Virginia, was the site of a UN conference on food issues in May 1943—and while that may not sound like a controversial topic, this conference identified world poverty as a major source of hunger, identified "freedom from want of food" as a major goal of the postwar era, and called for conferences on international financial issues to follow. In November 1943, forty-four nations signed a document pledging resources toward the relief of those disrupted by the war and met in Atlantic City to advance those ends. A month later, summits were held in Cairo and Tehran to specify war aims. In the latter city, the "Declaration of the Three Powers" proposed "the elimination of tyranny and slavery, oppression and intolerance," proposed "a world family of Democratic Nations," and looked forward to the day when "all peoples of the world may live free lives, untouched by tyranny, and according to their varying desires and their own consciences."

Finally, the Bretton Woods conference, held in New Hampshire in July 1944, created the financial machinery essential to the smooth functioning of a single world economy and set the stage for the emergence of the United Nations itself, in San Francisco in April 1945. What FDR called the "Great Design" was finally coming together. The new time was beginning at last, and a genuine international order coming into view, built on a foundation of Wilsonian promise and Lincolnesque clarity. The word *millennium* was never spoken at all. Piety was kept to a minimum, promises of success were muted, and great attention was paid to the needs of both small and large nations. As the founders had discovered when they built the federal machine, things sometimes work better the second time around. What allowed the UN to function when it finally appeared was the fact that it was based less on the perfectibility than the imperfectibility of the species it was designed to serve.

Each of these conferences advanced the idea of human rights by deepening the precision of the language used and oiling the gears of the complex global mechanism coming into existence for the first time. Each conference taught peoples from very different parts of the world how to speak and eat and live together in the same place for a few weeks and come away with something tangible gained. And each allowed the world's representatives to become a little more comfortable with the American idea of freedom—hardly a universal concept at the time. Each, in other words, was a small island on the route to the new world.

The more one studies all of the possible areas of disagreement that might have separated the allies, the more one feels amazement that the United Nations came into existence at all. That it did was a tribute to Franklin Roosevelt. Nothing manifested his extraordinary personal devotion to this end more than his willingness to travel enormous distances to make it happen. It is astonishing that he flew, given his physical condition, but more so that he did it at a time when few world leaders ever stepped onto an airplane, and when it was impossible to guarantee his safety in the parts of the world he flew to.

One trip in particular boggles the mind—the arduous journey that took him to Cairo and Tehran at the end of 1943. Such was his desire to meet Stalin that he flew nearly to his doorstep. (Stalin, too, made an effort—his flight to Tehran was the first he had ever taken, and the first time Stalin had left Russia since the Revolution.) So dangerous was the trip that Roosevelt barely escaped a terrorist attack, planned by German and Japanese spies, with the help of 170 local Iranians. Here, in a city that would later be seen as the graveyard of American idealism, FDR sketched out his most complete ideas yet concerning the UN. Stalin agreed in principle, and Wilson's dream had come a great distance closer to reality.

That trip brings out another surprising fact, the degree to which the president of the United States felt free to travel throughout the Islamic world during the most volatile period in the history of the world. That was not only a tribute to his courage, but to his confidence that the United States had no reason to fear the repercussions of its policies. On the contrary, FDR felt a serene confidence that the freedom he and his country represented were available to all peoples, and that the United States was popular throughout the region for its long history of benign initiatives. That confidence was reciprocated in the warm response of the Islamic world toward him in Casablanca, in Cairo, in Tehran, and everywhere else he went on the way home. Before Stalin insisted on Tehran as the site of their meeting, the summit very nearly took place in Basra, Iraq—and it is worth noting, also, that Iraqi representatives were among the first to sign all of the major conference documents leading to the creation of the United Nations.

FDR's radio address to the American people upon his return from that conference, on Christmas Eve 1943, was one of his most brilliant. It combined a detailed description of war aims with the powerful sentiment that he had flown over the little town of Bethlehem on his way back and hoped all people would think of the "star of faith" that once shone above it. Noting that America's 10 million troops were extended so far around the world that they were in different time zones and even different days, he observed that he could literally say that "today is tomorrow." That message, so welcome to children on Christmas Eve, was no less heartening to a world desperate to try anew.

Near the end of the war, the planning became more specific. The triumphal moment was designed for April 25, 1945, in San Francisco, when Roosevelt intended to personally inaugurate the conference that would bring the UN organization into existence, before five thousand people from around the world. He planned to take his wife, Eleanor, to the conference; he even told her to buy nice clothes.

On April 12, three days before the first special trains were scheduled to leave the East Coast to bring delegates to San Francisco, Roosevelt was resting at Warm Springs, Georgia, summoning strength for the conference. In the morning, he approved the design for a stamp ("Toward United Nations") and spent a contented hour with his collection. After lunch, he said, "I have a terrible headache," slumped over, and died. The international response to his death was immediate, universal, and profound.

But his death also proved to be a kind of apotheosis—literally, the word the Romans gave to describe the decree that made a secular leader into a god. Throughout the conference that gave birth to the UN, FDR's name was invoked to give order and inspiration to the proceedings. It worked. Out of the chaos of the meeting, with 2,636 press representatives (one named John F. Kennedy) eager to report on the creation of the new world, a new world was actually born.

Remarkably, FDR had planned another trip, for just after San Francisco. In late May or early June, he was going to visit Europe in what would probably have been the greatest presidential journey of all time. He was going to take a steamer to Southampton, then spend several days in Buckingham Palace. Churchill predicted that FDR "is going to get from the British people the greatest reception ever accorded to any human being since Lord Nelson made his triumphant return to London." From there, he would visit American soldiers, then go to The Hague—a symbol of old hopes for a better world—and then finally descend upon Paris. It would be hard to find a more perfect symbolism. For it was in Paris that Woodrow Wilson had first tried to sketch his plan for a more durable global architecture. And it was in Paris that his successor could have announced that the plan had at last been carried out.

Then, amazingly, there was more. As if all of this travel were not enough, FDR hoped to spend "a couple years in the Middle East to help bring parts of the desert to life with reforestation, irrigation, proper farming, and conservation." Perhaps, after all those centuries of Americans lusting for Babylon's downfall, Roosevelt was right to think that real change might come through a calmer agency, such as crop rotation or improved topsoil. A great deal of the world's problems can be solved by distributing the fertilizer a little more evenly.

None of those voyages happened, of course. But to the best of his ability, Harry Truman embraced his predecessor's busy agenda. So did most Americans, willing for the first time in their history to devote significant resources toward the fulfillment of an expensive plan to bring sanity to the world. Healthy majorities endorsed the United Nations, proud that it was coming to life in the United States. And why not? It was an American plan, conceived and dedicated on these shores. No nation would benefit from it more than the one most obviously linked to its creation.

In the chaos of the postwar years, the UN took shape day by day.

Even before a permanent home was created for it, its bricks and mortar were the same ideals of rights and freedoms that FDR had been grasping toward for the better part of twenty years. And it seemed fitting that when the ultimate global definition of those rights was created, the Universal Declaration of Human Rights, his wife, Eleanor, sat at the head of the drafting committee. It borrowed from the Declaration of Independence; it borrowed from the American educational tradition in the Middle East (one of the principal drafters, Charles Malik, was an alumnus of the American University of Beirut); and it borrowed from Eleanor Roosevelt herself. Her pride, when speaking of it in 1948, seems justified:

> This Universal Declaration of Human Rights may well become the international Magna Carta of all men everywhere. We hope its proclamation by the General Assembly will be an event comparable to the proclamation of the Declaration of the Rights of Man by the French people in 1789, the adoption of the Bill of Rights by the people of the United States, and the adoption of comparable declarations at different times in other countries.

It's true that the document has not always lived up to its promise. Like Wilson's Fourteen Points, it is not so much a terminus as a way station. But few statements have ever defended human rights more deeply. Long after the fact, it continues to have a life of its own, and to give life. It was in the air when the black citizens of Montgomery launched a bus boycott; when Nelson Mandela walked out of his prison cell; and when the Berlin Wall fell. Like the Declaration of Independence, it has a moral force that cannot easily be contained.

The United Nations remains a deeply imperfect institution, and its human rights commissions especially so. There is something sickening about seeing representatives from nations that systematically oppress their people using the human rights commissions as vehicles to criticize the United States. But that is the price that a great nation must occasionally pay for the privilege—not quite a freedom—to host this great international organization on its soil.

In 1944, at the height of the global war that created the United Nations, Reinhold Niebuhr wrote *The Children of Light and the Children of Darkness*—subtitled *A Vindication of Democracy*, despite having plenty to say about democracy's pitfalls. One of his sentences summarized the endless frustration of an international order composed of human beings: "The world community, standing thus as the final possibility and impossibility of human life, will be in actuality the perpetual problem as well as the constant fulfillment of human hopes." In other words, we are likely to fail, but we must try anyway. Franklin D. Roosevelt said the same thing as he prepared for the end of the war, and his own demise: "No one can say exactly how long any plan will last. Peace can endure only so long as humanity really insists upon it, and is willing to work for and sacrifice for it."

FDR never knew the ultimate location of the United Nations, which was still undecided at the time of his death. At one point he thought that the Azores might be appropriate—so he said in a press conference, sailing between yet another Islamic nation (Algeria) and the United States. Far from shore, he had a vision that one of the islands—a small one, without any media allowed on it—would be the perfect setting for international diplomacy. That was one of the few ideas he did not put into effect. But when the UN did finally find its permanent home, on the east side of Manhattan, it was highly appropriate that it was built on yet another Atlantic island. For centuries, the islands, both fictitious and real, had pointed the way toward America, from Atlantis to the Azores to Newfoundland. Now, at last, the ancient longing to build a better world, somewhere across the Sea of Darkness, had found its terra firma.

CHAPTER NINE

THE COLD WAR: DAWN

Sal Mineo: Do you think the end of the world will come at night?
James Dean: No, at dawn.

—*Rebel Without a Cause*

BRAVE NEW WORLD

As Americans surveyed the map of the world in 1945, they could be forgiven for blinking their eyes in astonishment. For centuries, the most pie-eyed aspirations had been emanating from the United States about how to overturn the crooked old order and build a new world of millennial redemption, republicanism, free trade, free love, or whatever. One could even argue that American idealism had drawn its force from the fact that it was so unlikely to be enacted. A longing to change Europe, without any clue how to do so, was a nearly permanent condition of American intellectuals from the Puritans to their progeny and beyond.

Now, amazingly, American hopes for a better-run world seemed achievable, even imminent. For the first time in history, our power was proportional to our imagination. The United States possessed a military might that had not been seen since the height of the Roman empire. The arc of liberty was at perihelion. Surely, the American Way would now become the way of the world. Or so it seemed to most.

To wield imperial sway was a surprising result for a republic that had fought against empire since time immemorial. Certainly, the United States had never aspired to become the British empire and had spent considerable energy deflating its assumptions. One could argue that these immense responsibilities were thrust upon Americans, rather than the other way around. But at the same time, there were glimmers that Americans had always expected a kind of global preeminence. Year Zero, as one writer called it, had been predicted with an eerie specificity by John O'Sullivan, the philosopher of Manifest Destiny, who wrote in 1845 that the United States would be the world's leader in exactly a century. Other ancestors would likewise have recognized the situation. George Washington, for all of his warnings against entanglement, would have approved the way Americans rose as one to meet a dire military threat—and he would especially have appreciated that Congress was paying its soldiers on time. While it is deeply ahistorical to say so, some Puritan predictions had come true as well. An evil concentration of foreign power had been defeated, a set of beliefs about individual responsibility was spreading around the world, and a new time of sorts was indeed beginning. Franklin D. Roosevelt did not diminish expectations by predicting, in his final State of the Union, "The year 1945 can be the greatest year of achievement in human history."*

At this seminal moment of new-world building, it was remarkable to contemplate the economic sway of the United States. Europe's farms and industries were in total disarray, while America's GDP had doubled in less than four years. In the first year of peace, the United States accounted for 50 percent of the world's economic output. But America's attraction was also based on its resonant cultural appeal to the millions of people whose lives had been shattered by the destruction of the war. At a moment when the Old World had no models left to cling to, the United States offered it all: food, money, optimism, and a potent model of democracy that seemed to include everything from the Bill of Rights to fishnet stockings. Americans seemed to be everywhere—starting new businesses, helping new governments, punishing the wicked, and protecting the vulnerable. Their ideas, ranging from freedom of assembly to air-conditioning, spread effortlessly in their wake. From Latin Amer-

*In private, Churchill expressed skepticism: "The Americans are new on the world stage, and they always take generalities too literally."

ica to the Middle East to Indochina, millions of people wanted to enter this new time. They sought liberty, democracy, and independence, even when the precise meaning of those words was not altogether clear, either to them or to the Americans who loved to repeat them.

Yet it would not quite be right to say that all was sweetness and light in 1945. Or at least not the kind of light usually associated with that phrase. If foreign governments were quick to answer American requests, it had as much to do with the radioactive flashes over Hiroshima and Nagasaki as it did with the shining light of freedom. As the unique possessor of the atomic bomb, Americans had indeed seized the apocalypse, as they had been threatening to do for centuries.

Awestruck observers naturally borrowed theological language to respond to this new and irreversible fact of life. Appropriately, the nuclear era began at dawn. Brigadier General Thomas Farrell witnessed the first atomic blast at 5:29:45 a.m. on July 16, 1945, the so-called Trinity Test. He described what he beheld in reverential phrases that would have pleased John Cotton. It seemed to come straight from the Old Testament:

> The effects could well be called unprecedented, magnificent, beautiful, stupendous and terrifying. No man-made phenomenon of such tremendous power had ever occurred before. The lighting effects beggared description. The whole country was lighted by a searing light with the intensity many times that of the midday sun. It was golden, purple, violet, gray and blue. It lighted every peak, crevasse and ridge of the nearby mountain range with a clarity and beauty that cannot be described but must be seen to be imagined. Seconds after the explosion came, the air blast pressed hard against the people watching, to be followed almost immediately by the strong, sustained awesome roar which warned of doomsday and made us feel that we puny things were blasphemous to dare tamper with the forces heretofore reserved to the Almighty.

Just as the earliest American forays into foreign policy had been incursions into a continent that did not entirely belong to the United States, so we entered the atomic age by first bombing ourselves. The

Trinity site was in New Mexico, on land won in 1848; for centuries before that it had formed a part of the great Camino Real, or King's Road, that linked Mexico City and Sante Fe under the Spanish empire. The old name for the site was the Jornada del Muerto, almost literally the Valley of the Shadow of Death. Eight possible targets had been considered, ranging from San Nicolas Island, off California, to Padre Island, in the Gulf of Mexico; all were once part of the Spanish empire. Of the several theories about the name *Trinity*, the most poetical is that J. Robert Oppenheimer had read the fourteenth Holy Sonnet of John Donne, which begins,

> Batter my heart, three person'd God; for you
> As yet but knocke, breathe, shine, and seeke to mend;
> That I may rise, and stand, o'erthrow mee, and bend
> Your force, to breake, blowe, burn and make me new.

Like radiation, the seventeenth century has a way of persisting in the atmosphere.

The blast marked a quantum leap forward—literally—for American force. But it is difficult to frighten people and inspire them at the same time, and the disjuncture between these two different kinds of light might have warned Americans that the liberation of the world that so many expected in 1945 was not going to come as easily as expected. E. B. White captured some of the strangeness of the moment, noting that the Hiroshima blast came nine days after the Senate had ratified the UN Charter: "The preparations made at San Francisco for a security league of sovereign nations to prevent aggression now seem like the preparations some little girls make for a lawn party as a thunderhead gathers just beyond the garden gates. The lemonade will be spiked by lightning."

The cause of America was also weakened immeasurably by the disappearance of its chief spokesman, Franklin Roosevelt. His demise, like that of Lincoln at another supreme moment of American triumph, augured something that the Puritans knew all too well. Any plan designed to be implemented by human beings is bound to have mistakes wired into it, for the simple reason that humans are ultimately both fallible and mortal.

The fortress of freedom built by FDR seemed impregnable in 1945; yet it was soon under attack, from enemies, friends, and false prophets of liberty here at home. Three challenges above all presented themselves. First, the United States began a new and terrifying struggle against the Soviet Union, its former ally, nearly as soon as World War Two ended. Second, Americans found themselves in a difficult situation around the world as their newfound power made them seem the embodiment of a kind of imperial muscle, despite the rhetoric of freedom, a situation that became all the more uncomfortable as the United States interfered with and even suppressed the aspirations of some peoples struggling to be free in the 1950s. Third, these new responsibilities and threats unleashed a torrent of contradictory emotions at home, from the fears of liberals on the left that the Truman and Eisenhower administrations were needlessly provoking war to delusions on the right that the American government itself had been taken over by communists and quislings.

Reading these diatribes long after the fact, it would seem that the American people were unready for the huge global responsibilities that history had placed on their shoulders in the aftermath of the Second World War. Certainly they were being asked to do a great deal as the United States effectively reinvented itself, rejecting the model of a nonaligned refuge from the rest of humanity and adopting a new role as the chief broker of the world's disputes. In effect, the United States was beginning a completely new history in 1945, as Harry Truman explained in his first State of the Union: "The evolution of centuries has brought us to a new era in world history in which manifold relationships between nations must be formalized and developed in new and intricate ways."

This was worrisome to a people who wanted nothing so much as to welcome their sons and daughters home from the war; to make matters worse, it was frightfully expensive. Ordinary Americans would foot most of the bill for the UN, the Marshall Plan, and other instruments of the postwar peace, and it was inevitable that discontent would surface, fueled by political opportunists. But fortunately, calmer voices generally prevailed over the paranoia that accompanied this huge shift in America's outlook. Still, it would take many decades to resolve these tensions, if indeed they have been entirely resolved.

In effect, America's story had taken a dramatic new turn. The nation that had begun as an island of sorts, isolated from the rest of the world, had never completely surrendered its insular status. True, it was a large island, ultimately encompassing much of a continent, and even, in its occasional daydreams, the world itself. But still, the ability to raise the drawbridge and proclaim separation when convenient was comforting. With the advent of a peace that was in some ways more difficult than the war, and new technologies of communication and travel that further shrank the oceans, it was necessary to dismantle the drawbridge and build something more permanent. And so the United States built a series of permanent connections to the rest of the world, ensuring that it would forever be tied to Europe in the most profound sense. *Entanglement* does not begin to cover the range of responsibilities that the United States assumed at the dawn of the Cold War, obligations that were political, economic, and most definitely military. John Donne, who had written about America when it was little more than an erotic daydream to him, had famously asserted that "no man is an island." After 1945, the American island would forever be a part of the main.

These new responsibilities placed generations of American leaders in a rhetorical bind. How best to express a sense of revolutionary possibility when the United States could be perceived as a colossal weight upon the world's desire for change? How to wield nearly limitless power when the United States had always opposed the idea of power without check? How to draw inspiration from our oldest ideas about liberty, human rights, and new beginnings when we did not extend full rights to significant numbers of our own citizens? How to express our historical hatred of large-power interventions in small countries when we could be guilty of the same tendency? These questions seemed especially uncomfortable at a time when American power had become global, affecting all people on earth, but American thinking could still be deeply local. For many Americans, tired of war and calamity, the world was simply exhausting, and it was tempting to retreat into older pockets of thinking, as far removed from Europe's problems as possible. But comforting platitudes about the New World's separation would no longer hold. The New World was now part of a brave new world, and all people lived there, whether they liked it or not.

The new order was just coming into focus when Harry Truman gave a remarkable address on foreign policy, in late October 1945. The speech outlined twelve fundamental goals of the United States, and it is compelling to realize how malleable the postwar order still felt at that waxy moment, before Cold War realities set in and a new mold of thinking was cast. Those twelve goals conveyed not only a considerable debt to Franklin Roosevelt, but to Woodrow Wilson as well, repeating America's commitment to self-determination, freedom from invasion, freedom of the seas, free trade, freedom of expression, and a right to safe, clearly marked borders that would not be trampled. As if that were not enough, Truman added that Americans subscribed to the Ten Commandments, and for good measure, he threw in the Golden Rule, which he officially stated as U.S. policy. With a new captain steering the ark, it would help to have a Bible nearby.

RED NIGHTMARE

But these lofty aspirations were darkened by the growing awareness of shadows creeping across the postwar landscape. One fact in particular made it clear that the new world would be less idyllic than expected, and that fact was very large. The Soviet Union, our ally during the war, quickly became something less than a friend, if not quite a full-blown adversary. Every week that followed the historic meeting of Russian and American troops at the Elbe in late April 1945, crushing Germany from opposite directions, made it seem more likely that these two mighty armies might someday face each other. Shrewd observers had predicted this problem well before it came into the open. Even during the Quebec conference of 1943, FDR anticipated Russian ambitions for Europe. Churchill had expressed his pessimism with the usual grandiosity: "There might be a more bloody war. I shall not be there. I shall be asleep. I want to sleep for billions of years."

But of course he *was* there, and he was centrally involved in the strange new conflict that emerged between East and West; or more specifically, between two versions of the West. It was he who named the "Iron Curtain" that separated these two global entities, in a speech he gave in 1946, in Fulton, Missouri, about as far from the Iron Curtain as could be imagined. But what better place than a small Presbyterian college in the heartland to paint a dark picture of the heartless force Americans needed to unite against? Only a few years later, in the same town, a young Ronald Reagan would give an early speech expressing his certainty that God was firmly allied with the United States.*

For quite some time, prognosticators had been predicting that these two enormous lands on either side of Europe would eventually come into conflict. Famously, Tocqueville had ended thc first volume of *Democracy in America* with a meditation on the two systems, so different, one devoted to freedom and the other to servitude, and each "marked out by the will of heaven to sway the destinies of half the globe." A gloomy precedent had been set by Wilson's halfhearted decision to send American troops into Russia at the end of the First World War, though that could hardly be called a calculated thrust at domination. In its way, Wilson's Fourteen Points had also been a reaction to the strange leveling force of Bolshevism. Point six in particular tried to do the impossible, by rolling back the Russian Revolution to a moment where it might be possible to start again and build an American-style democracy on the ruins of the czarist state. That fantasy was unrealistic. But history could also point to unexpected moments of cooperation between the two enormous nations, as with the czar's support for Lincoln in the Civil War, and the amicable purchase of Alaska.

That was ancient history, however, in 1945. For that matter, 1944 was ancient history in 1945. With the defeat of the Nazis, a huge number of suppressed aspirations rose to the surface, and the map of the Old World became as porous as that of the New World had once been. Countries changed their borders, cities changed their names, and a new Europe began to emerge from what Leon Trotsky called the ash heap of history. It is difficult to pinpoint the precise origin of the Cold War, just as it is difficult to call it a war in the conventional sense. U.S.-Russian tensions had grown more apparent in the waning months of World War Two, as it became clear that Stalin was trying to occupy as much neighboring territory as possible with the Red Army, then retreating slowly, and only under pressure from the allies.

But even if the Iron Curtain followed a boundary across Europe, de-

*Remarkably, Fulton was also the site of a lecture by Reinhold Niebuhr that led to his study of exceptionalism, *The Irony of American History*.

fined by Churchill as stretching "from Stettin in the Baltic to Trieste in the Adriatic," the Cold War was also a global contest from the outset. Many of the first sparks flew in Muslim regions. Iran had hosted a friendly meeting of the Big Three in December 1943, but already by the war's end it was a focal point of tension. The Red Army had occupied large sections of northern Iran at the request of Britain, which desperately needed to protect its petroleum interests in the region. But long after the collapse of Germany, there was no sign of a Russian departure, and not until well into 1946, after intricate negotiations, did the troops finally retreat. Russian ambitions also encompassed Turkey, and particularly the straits that Russian leaders had coveted for centuries, the Bosporus and Dardanelles. Stalin sought military bases and territorial concessions adjacent to the straits that would effectively have surrendered them to Soviet control. Further, he wanted a role in administering the former Italian empire in North Africa, which would have granted the Soviet Union a naval presence in the Mediterranean. Greece and Turkey—the same place-names that had caused American hearts to beat faster in the 1820s—were once again central to the United States and its worldwide struggle against tyranny (although it would take an artful argument to make the case that either Greece or Turkey was a bulwark of democracy).

The first few months of the Cold War revealed an inconstant, looking-glass world of shifting language and meaning, showing the former allies to be half conciliatory and half antagonistic. Any historian parsing the language of Stalin's and Truman's utterances in late 1945 and early 1946 can find plenty of evidence of a desire to cooperate—and equal evidence that cooperation was becoming impossible. With no remorse, Stalin broke the promise of free elections he had made at Yalta and refused to allow self-determination in what was clearly becoming a Soviet bloc in Eastern Europe. Yalta has become a code word for "appeasement," as if weak negotiation by Franklin Roosevelt gave away something precious that ought to have been retained by the United States. But it is extremely difficult to imagine how the United States could have prevented the Soviet bloc from coming into existence, short of invading Eastern Europe, for the Red Army was already in complete control of the territory it occupied. Furthermore, Stalin had reached a secret agreement about spheres of influence with Winston Churchill in October 1944 that gave percentages of Eastern Europe to Great Britain and the Soviet Union, a rather ugly resurgence of colonialism at a moment when FDR was doing his utmost to prevent a return to the prewar mentality. This fact is often forgotten by conservative ideologues who lionize Churchill and, by a conspicuous act of omission, fail to accord the same respect to his American partner.

The United States did not completely live up to its promises, either—and for good reason. FDR had promised Stalin at Tehran that U.S. troops would be home in two years. But as the dust settled and the new landscape of Soviet occupation became clear, Truman realized that the United States could not simply withdraw its troops. This in itself was a revolutionary decision, for the United States had traditionally refused to maintain a large army in peacetime and had certainly never left one deployed in Europe. Although powerful political pressures called for the return of American soldiers, Truman refused to yield, and so a new kind of American foreign policy emerged, in which the threat of force was always in the air. That essential fact, coupled with the atomic bomb, gave considerable weight to U.S. pronouncements on world affairs. But at the same time, there were glimmers of the idealism that had infused the deliberations to create the UN, growing rapidly amid, and to some degree because of, the new tensions. Truman trusted the United Nations enough in the early glow of 1946 that he proposed giving it control over American nuclear weapons (although, to be sure, under terms to be set by the United States). The offer was not accepted by the Soviet Union; still, it was remarkable that it was made at all.

But the clear trend during these early years was not toward reconciliation. Just as Russia was flexing its muscles in Europe and the Middle East, Truman's position became weaker by virtue of a number of unanticipated problems that showed some of the cracks inside democracy at exactly the moment the United States was trying to promote it as a durable model for the world. In Great Britain, Winston Churchill was shockingly voted out of office in July 1945, before the war was even over. In the United States, the election of a new Republican majority in 1946, highly critical of Truman's foreign policy but unwilling to offer any realistic alternative, placed new pressure on him as he struggled to find the right way to confront the rising Soviet threat. To make matters worse, the isolationist Republicans slashed his military budget at a critical moment of engagement with the world.

As a result, the language of American foreign policy changed, from the conciliatory way that FDR was speaking in the final months of war, setting the stage for his grand project of the United Nations, to a new and uncompromising vocabulary of confrontation. The shift affected Democrats and Republicans alike and undermined internationalists in both parties. Within a few months of the greatest military triumph in American history, the American people lost some of FDR's confidence and plunged into an older way of looking at the world as effectively divided between good and evil. And so we lapsed into something that was not exactly a war, though it was called one, and was far from short, though defined by a thousand temporary responses. When Walter Lippmann published a slender volume entitled *The Cold War* in 1947, the strange new conflict finally had a name.

I would like to take some time with the way American leaders described the situation they were confronted by, because the formula they found proved to be so durable that we have not entirely escaped its thrall, long after the Cold War has ended. To an amazing extent, presidents still talk of "the free world," containment, and even appeasement as if we are still fighting all of these wars simultaneously.

No document shaped the new vocabulary more than a telegram sent early in 1946, barely six months after the nominal end of hostilities. It was sent on Washington's birthday, and like his Farewell Address it shaped American foreign policy for a generation, even as it pointed toward the exact forms of intervention that Washington had warned against. On February 22, 1946, George Kennan, an analyst in the U.S. embassy in Moscow, drafted an eight-thousand-word telegram to the State Department, purportedly to answer a few questions about Soviet behavior. Appropriately, in an essay devoted to the topic of expansionism, he exceeded his word limit. The so-called Long Telegram explained in detail why the Soviet Union was determined to spread its influence around the world and urged a vigorous, global American response. It has been likened to a Puritan sermon for its shape (divided into five sections), its tone (attacking its enemy as a "malignant parasite which feeds only on diseased tissue"), and its call to total commitment. To be sure, it was a spiritual as well as a political summons (among other warnings, it urged that the Russian Orthodox Church not be allowed to expand). Like the eyewitness accounts of the Trinity Test, it, too, was a theological document in its way.

A year later, the telegram was expanded into an extremely influential article in *Foreign Affairs*, titled "The Sources of Soviet Conduct," famously signed with the mysterious letter X. (Walter Lippmann politely referred to the author as Mr. X.) The result of this subterfuge, of course, was that everyone in the world soon knew X's identity. In this piece, Kennan expounded the theme at great length, again likening the Soviet empire to a dangerous rival church with "mystical, Messianic" tendencies (he disliked its claim to "infallibility," a favorite complaint the Puritans had voiced about the Catholic Church), and calling upon Americans to develop their full "spiritual vitality" for the struggle. "Let us bring this apocalyptic vision down to earth," he urged, just before coining the word *containment* to explain America's new stance of resisting the Soviet Union in places around the world. He even ended his essay with an appeal to Providence and advanced the classic Puritan argument that this moral challenge was welcome, even necessary, if Americans wanted to live up to their potential.

In the looking-glass world of the early Cold War, every action demanded a mirror action, so Stalin ordered his ambassador to Washington, Nikolai Novikov, to issue an equally exhaustive document, explaining the sources of American conduct. Much of it was poppycock, but revealing for its equally dark view of the contest the Soviet Union and United States were beginning. Novikov began by asserting that the United States was "striving for world supremacy," propelled by its insatiable capitalistic appetite, and had reached a "secret agreement" with Britain to divide the planet. As evidence, he cited some impressive statistics that most Americans probably did not know, such as that the United States had built 228 military bases, points of support, and radio stations around the Atlantic Ocean and 258 in the Pacific. Or that the U.S. military budget was now 40 percent of its total budget, and ten times larger than it had been eight years earlier. Ironically, Novikov claimed that the Soviet Union, not the West, was working toward "democratic" reform, citing Eastern Europe in particular—an outrageous lie, but a tacit admission that the language of freedom was powerful indeed.

Kennan also had his American critics. Walter Lippmann found his theory of containment "a strategic monstrosity"; not only did Lippmann think Americans did not have the patience to wait out a prolonged contest without clear battles, but it was also uncharacteristic of a great power to be always responding to its rival at a series of "constantly shifting geographical and political points." Waiting for years with no goal other than the eventual "frustration" of the Soviet Union was almost sure to result in the eventual frustration of the American people themselves. Further, Lippmann felt an instinctive aversion to ideological crusades and doubted "that Mr. X has read the mind of Providence and that he knows what history has plainly intended." Everything Lippman said was correct. Yet for all the cogency of his critique, Kennan's theory was sensationally popular, and even enlarged by some of its acolytes into a kind of global military readiness beyond what its author had in mind.

The emerging binary view of the world received a great boost on March 12, 1947, when President Harry Truman went before the U.S. Congress to ask for $400 million in foreign aid for Greece and Turkey. Only two weeks earlier, British officials had explained that they could no longer sustain their commitments in those countries, and that they would fall into the Soviet sphere if the United States did not assume their burden. And so, nearly overnight, the United States inherited some of the responsibilities of the British empire, and a great deal of its baggage as well. In defining what would become known as the Truman Doctrine, Truman did his best to persuade hesitant legislators that the United States had no choice but to assume the British mantle of leadership in the eastern Mediterranean. To do so, he stressed the stark choice available to the peoples of the world between the American and Soviet models. Ironically, two former parts of the Ottoman empire, in one of the least black-and-white regions on earth, became the birthplace of a way of talking that described the world as divided into halves, each the opposite of the other. One was based on liberty, broadly defined, and FDR's set of freedoms and rights. The other, according to Truman, was exactly the opposite, dedicated to the suppression of those rights, relentless imperialism, and the "terror" that resulted from the loss of freedom. Meeting records from the State Department indicate that speech planners realized that the best way to persuade Americans was to describe the crisis as a threat to democracy itself.

Truman put the matter with characteristic bluntness: "I believe that it must be the policy of the United States to support free peoples who are resisting attempted subjugation by armed minorities or by outside pressures. I believe that we must assist free peoples to work out their own destinies in their own way." These two crisp sentences contained far more history than their epigrammatic delivery would indicate on the surface.

Generations of Americans had expressed thoughts along these lines, from the Greek excitement of the 1820s to Manifest Destiny, Kossuth, and beyond. But these aspirations had never been articulated so clearly as national policy before. If Truman's words were to be taken at face value, then the United States was now committed to providing financial and military support to all "free peoples" fighting against oppression. That could, of course, be construed to mean just about any people on earth. Truman's speech was clearly set in the narrow context of Soviet aims to topple a Greek government and control the Bosporus. But it set a broad precedent for the future.

This was not the only way in which centuries of tradition in American foreign policy were being overturned. For the first time, entanglement was precisely the goal as the United States created a welter of international institutions, ranging from the Bretton Woods institutions to the UN agencies to the organizations designed to implement the Marshall Plan, announced in June 1947, shortly after Truman's speech to Congress. That plan, with its extraordinary expenditures on behalf of Europe's economies (nearly 10 percent of U.S. government spending), deserved Churchill's praise as "one of the least sordid acts in history." The result was an astonishing success, as millions of Europeans escaped poverty and starvation—surely a form of liberation. True, this act of altruism was enmeshed in the growing competition between Russia and the United States, and the fear that European nations would join the Iron Curtain countries if not supported. And without doubt, it created millions of future customers for American goods. But it was splendid all the same.

The nation that had fought against every concentration of European power was now directing traffic, and building larger international organizations than Europe had ever before seen. Most important of all was NATO, the military alliance that undergirded all of the others. With the signing of the North Atlantic Treaty on April 4, 1949, the Western alliance was complete. It was the first peacetime alliance for the United States since the eighteenth century.

This new web of entanglements troubled some Americans, but reassured others, especially as the nation reeled from one foreign policy crisis to another. Contemplating the range and the profundity of the problems that afflicted the United States in the first five years of the postwar era, it is easy to understand the gloom that settled over many who simply wanted to return to normality. In a short compass the United States had finished the largest war in its history; begun another with almost no definition; overturned centuries of experience by creating a network of alliances; sponsored the United Nations; paid for European reconstruction; developed the most formidable weapons ever known, only to see those weapons developed by our chief adversary; witnessed the fall of a sympathetic government in a crucial nation (China); and blessed the creation of a new nation (Israel) whose very existence enraged allies in another historically friendly part of the world. Six decades later, we still deal with the aftershocks of these earthquakes in U.S. foreign policy.

With each of these events, tensions between the Soviet Union and the United States seemed to deepen. Russian actions exacerbated the divide, from the putsch that eliminated Czech independence (February 1948) to the isolation of Berlin (June 1948–May 1949), and the development of the Russian bomb (August 1949). The Chinese Revolution stunned Americans when Mao declared victory on October 1, 1949, and with the revelations of serious espionage failures in early 1950, the American mood grew dark indeed. After North Korea's invasion of South Korea in June, it was possible to say, as many did, that the United States had lost more ground to the communists than it had gained in the five years since the war ended.

As the United States was reeling from these revelations, it continued to issue public and private pronouncements seeking to impose order on the postwar world. On April 14, 1950, the U.S. government issued one of the most important documents of the Cold War. Presidential directive NSC-68 was shrouded in secrecy at the time, but has now become famous as a blueprint of the military strategy that would define policy for years to come. Responding to the rising Soviet military threat, and the atomic bomb in particular, NSC-68 resorted to some old language to advance its new message. Specifically, it argued that "freedom" was eternally opposed to "slavery," and that it was the historic role of the

United States to stand for liberty. *Freedom* was everything in this binary equation, the all-encompassing idea that justified any expenditure or new weapons system. It was nothing less than "the most contagious idea in human history." Its antonym, *slavery*, was "a degradation willed by the individual upon himself under the compulsion of a perverted faith." Clearly, this was yet another tortured expression of theology. Advocates of communism, "a fanatic faith," were odious because they believed that "the system becomes God." The rivalry between Russia and the United States had nothing to do with anything as mundane as international relations—it stemmed from a much larger contest between good and evil, and "the antipathy of slavery to freedom."

In effect, NSC-68 proposed a permanent war footing for a society at peace, and defense spending to go along with it. It was part of a wholesale reinvention of the way the government operated and complemented a parallel increase in the government's intelligence operations. The Central Intelligence Agency came into existence in 1947, and by its very nature redefined America's orientation toward the rest of the world. It was enormous, well funded, and by definition, difficult to monitor. Between 1949 and 1952, the number of CIA employees working on covert operations mushroomed from 302 to 2,812, with 3,142 "contract" employees working in foreign countries. The budget for covert practices increased from $4.7 million to $82 million in that same three-year span, while the number of overseas stations rose from seven to forty-seven.

The result was a government much more attuned to foreign threats than ever before in American history. But this government's left hand could be unaware of what its right hand was doing, and it was far less accountable to the American people. The CIA's tendency to act independently of, and occasionally against, the government's public positions made it difficult to think of U.S. foreign policy as a single, comprehensible set of views. By giving presidents a nearly limitless power to pursue private initiatives, far from sight, these new structures increased the executive's power to do both good and ill, with nearly none of the checks and balances the founders considered essential to responsible government. At its best, the CIA, with its sister agencies (the National Security Agency was also created by Truman), helped presidents stay alert to constantly changing problems in a dangerous world. At its worst, it deepened those problems, by acting precipitously, and with little supervision, to interfere in the way other peoples governed themselves. In practice, this often meant that the United States was subverting other governments while proclaiming its faith in democracy. This was hardly the first time that a government has contradicted itself, but the practice was troublesome to those who believed in the historic role of the United States as a provider of moral leadership to the rest of the world.

NSC-68 might have remained an ordinary memorandum, unsigned on Harry Truman's desk. But when North Korean troops, with Stalin's permission, overran much of the Korean peninsula in late June of 1950, all tensions deepened and the Cold War grew hot. Soviet and American pilots even engaged in dogfights over Korea—a fact not widely known at the time. Historians have generally approved of the way Truman handled that difficult conflict, but the combination of a new war with intense domestic political pressures made it difficult to talk about the communist threat without resorting to new demonology. To read Truman's State of the Union addresses from 1946 to 1951 is like watching a plant shrivel, as the idealistic tendrils of the immediate postwar period turned into the hardened statements of "freedom" vs. "tyranny" near the end of his presidency. His final State of the Union was not a State of the American Union at all—if anything, its theme was the State of the Soviet Union, and it dilated at considerable length on the remarkable fact that all evil seemed to be concentrated in that one location.

Roosevelt's vision was not entirely defunct—American leaders went to great lengths to claim that the Korean War was fought with UN approval, in fact fought under the official flag of the UN, a polite euphemism that would have been unthinkable later in American history. If subsequent wars were fought in spite of the UN, this one was fought to save it, and Truman justified America's entry by saying, "We can't let the UN down." But clearly, the peaceful world FDR believed himself to be glimpsing at the moment of his apotheosis, with his bags packed for San Francisco, was not going to be glimpsed by his generation or even the one to follow. Five years after its birth, the "Great Design" was in dire peril.

PERILOUS STEPS

As he was revising his seminal Long Telegram for publication, George Kennan added a rumination from an unusual source, Edward Gibbon, the great English historian of ancient Rome—whose book, by coincidence, had come out in 1776. Kennan was reflecting on the Soviet Union, but his interest in the rise and fall of empires also spoke to Americans about the precipitous rise of their own country to a new height of global influence: "From enthusiasm to imposture the step is perilous and slippery; the demon of Socrates affords a memorable instance of how a wise man may deceive himself, how a good man may deceive others, how the conscience may slumber in a mixed and middle state between self-illusion and voluntary fraud."

While the Russian threat was paramount, a second challenge, not clearly perceived at the time, was the simmering resentment of millions of people around the world, looking for freedom in their own way and furious at the old colonial powers—including, at times, the United States—for thwarting their desires. This challenge, dwarfed by the Soviet menace at the time, looms larger in retrospect. How was it possible that the United States, the historic champion of self-determination, could suddenly be cast as the villain blocking change in many parts of the world?

To get at that essential question, it helps to consider a place that could not have been more remote to most Americans—Indochina. Its very name conveyed some of the indeterminacy of the region, historically dominated by the two enormous civilizations to the north and the west, but home to the fiercely independent Vietnamese people, eager to throw off the chains of Japanese and French occupation. Franklin Roosevelt had been eager to support them and considered this particular example of French colonialism one of the most odious on earth. He promised to work "with all my might and main" against France's "imperialistic ambitions."

The Second World War was not yet finished when a young Vietnamese patriot began to send a series of appeals to the president of the United States, asking for support in the fight against colonialism, and drawing deeply from his knowledge of American history. The author was impressively steeped in that history. Ho Chi Minh had attended the

Paris peace talks as a young man in 1919, although few had given him the time of day. But Wilson's talk of self-determination had inspired him. Surprisingly, one of his first publications was a short essay on American history, although the topic he chose (the origin of the Ku Klux Klan) would not have impressed Woodrow Wilson. It would be the height of irony if Ho's detailed knowledge of guerrilla movements originated in his study of the Klan.

In the spring of 1945, Ho was still deeply involved in American history of a more recent vintage, for he was surrounded by friendly American agents of the Office of Strategic Services, working with him to fight against the Japanese occupiers of his country. Now sensing the approach of one of those rare moments, such as 1919, when borders become porous and the map of the world can be redrawn, he sent his pleas to the White House, hoping that America would help his country find the self-determination that had eluded it for the past century. No response ever came.

Despite being ignored, Ho pressed forward with his cause. When he composed the Vietnamese Declaration of Independence, it would have been hard to find a document more deferential to American history. He read it for the first time in Hanoi, before a jubilant throng of four hundred thousand, on September 2, 1945, the day that Japan formally surrendered. He began with three simple sentences: "All men are created equal. They are endowed by their Creator with certain inalienable rights, among these are Life, Liberty, and the pursuit of Happiness. This immortal statement was made in the Declaration of Independence of the United States of America in 1776." Near the end of his speech, the crowd saw an airplane circling the event, and they cheered wildly when they saw the flag of the United States painted on its side.

However, Vietnam was not on the radar of the Truman administration, preoccupied with Europe and the rising tensions with Russia. It is a pity that no one read Ho's Declaration more carefully, including its final sentence: "The entire Vietnamese people are determined to mobilize all their physical and mental strength, to sacrifice their lives and property in order to safeguard their independence and liberty." They were able to achieve both, at incalculable cost to themselves, and enormous cost to the United States as well.

Six decades later, and knowing the story of Vietnam and a dozen other battlefields of the Cold War, it is possible to reflect more clearly on the strangeness of America's position in the aftermath of its smashing victory in World War Two. Though at the height of its power, the United States was also in some ways unprepared for its new role. As the civil rights movement would show, Americans had not resolved their own internal contradictions regarding freedom, and those contradictions would be amply borne out in the inconsistencies of U.S. foreign policy. At times, when all of the pistons were correctly firing, the United States could and did appear as a beacon of hope for a postcolonial world desperate for models and material support. After all, it could be claimed that FDR had done more than anyone else to dismantle the British, French, and German imperial regimes, in effect liberating millions of people around the earth. The legacy of Woodrow Wilson was still alive as well, and had inspired many of the nationalistic struggles just reaching their crescendo in the aftermath of the war, from Ho to Gandhi to Syngman Rhee in Korea. As African nationalism stirred, it too cast a glance across the Atlantic. When Kwame Nkrumah proposed Ghana's independence by a "Motion of Destiny" in 1953, he did so in the full context of African and American history: "The eyes and ears of the world are upon you; yea, our oppressed brothers throughout this vast continent of Africa and the New World are looking to you with desperate hope."

Of course, the United States could also point to a spectacular example of anti-imperialism early in its own history, and the American Revolution was often cited by would-be revolutionaries in other lands. The speech that coined the phrase *the third world* was given on April 18, 1955, by Indonesia's President Sukarno, at a conference of nonaligned Asian and African nations eager to avoid the long shadow of the Cold War. If it's possible for a speech to be pro- and anti-American at the same time, then Sukarno offered a helpful example of how the world was thinking. He expanded at some length on how April 18 was the date on which Paul Revere rode to Concord in 1775, inaugurating the American Revolution, "the first anti-colonialist war in history," and a new era in human history. He added, "That battle which began 180 years ago is not yet completely won," and he cited Franklin D. Roosevelt as a still vivid inspiration for his efforts to eliminate poverty and build opportunity. But in the same speech, he attacked free trade as a new form of colonialism, criticized the world's disparities, and in almost every clause rejected the new binary world system that the United States had created, with no small help from the Soviet Union.

That tension seemed to dominate the world's reaction to every complex crisis that the United States was involved in during the early Cold War—and few were not complex. To be sure, altruistic policies such as the Marshall Plan and the Berlin Airlift inspired millions of bystanders and pointed out how much better the U.S. model was than the Soviet system. But the United States was increasingly perceived as an obstacle to the aspirations of the world's disenfranchised during the Cold War years, particularly in Africa, Asia, and the Middle East—a fact that the Soviet Union, and China (after 1949), used to great advantage. It was not simply that the United States was a wealthy nation entering a particularly materialistic phase of its existence. It was also a growing sense of the double standards that prevailed in American foreign policy. For starters, there was the evidence of racism at home (which the Russians spared no opportunity to mention). Eleanor Roosevelt called racial discrimination "the one point which can be attacked and to which the representatives of the United States have no answer." Then there was the heavy-handedness with which marginal countries were occasionally treated, and a feeling that all of the world's economic rules were being written from Washington—which was not exactly untrue. Many observers noticed that Washington did not hesitate to spend enormous amounts of money to rebuild Europe, while giving far more sparingly to the world's darker-skinned peoples. There were exceptions to this rule—Muslim Turkey received generous aid under the Marshall Plan, and Truman's Point Four program, which gave money to Asian and African nations, was an important forerunner to the kinds of foreign aid programs that routinely shower money on the developing world today. But still, the complaint was expressed, especially after the Eisenhower administration killed Point Four in 1953. Furthermore, doubts were growing about American complicity in foreign coups and U.S. support for neocolonial projects, such as the French attempt to retain Vietnam, which was paid for by the United States before we entered the struggle as a belligerent in our own right.

Much of this growing tide of criticism was unfair. But a perception can be as important as a fact. Even if the United States had historically opposed colonialism, it was simple to see why millions of young people around the world would now see it as the heir to the colonial apparatus that was still draped all around them, though sometimes veiled in new forms. In other words, America's very power made it vulnerable to criticism. For now it was not enough to voice aspirations for liberty, as Americans had been doing since time immemorial. A hundred years earlier, Lincoln had warned against the great peril of proclaiming a faith in freedom and not living up to it. In fact, he had identified Russia, which he considered the least free nation on earth, as a place he would rather live if Americans could not live up to their ideals: because at least the czar was honest about his refusal to grant freedom to anyone! He understood, as few of our leaders before or since have, that even a small gap between rhetoric and reality can undermine a government. Any builder knows that even the tiniest spider crack can ruin a foundation. Into this fissure poured all of the criticisms of America's rivals, and many of the frustrations of her allies.

The dawning realization that we were not as popular as we expected, or deserved to be, was a difficult new reality of the Cold War. After centuries of leading a world revolution of democracy, human rights, and the integrity of small nations, it was hard for Americans to adjust to a new world in which the champions of those ideals did not always admire the United States. Was there a French existentialist who didn't join the attack? Sartre wrote, with uncharacteristic clarity, "Beware! America is a mad dog." Frantz Fanon called the United States "a nation of lynchers" (though he was happy to come here for medical treatment). His ambivalence, loving liberty while disliking the United States, was a common condition in the 1950s.

One particular region where these mixed feelings grew conspicuous was the Middle East. Before the Second World War, it would have been difficult to find a region where Americans were better liked. The American educational tradition had left citadels of intellectual freedom in Istanbul, Cairo, and Beirut, all profoundly influential in their respective countries. American forebearance in the First World War had been greatly appreciated within the Ottoman empire, and the United States was generally admired by nearly all parties as the shattered empire was rebuilt into the modern nations that rose in its wake. The Second World War had only deepened these feelings. Americans fought in the

Middle East, they held prominent peace conferences there, and they were instrumental in disassembling the British and French regimes that had dominated the region since the nineteenth century.

But as the heir to the colonial system it dismantled, the United States also inherited some of the problems of leadership, and no problem was thornier than the creation of a Jewish state in Palestine. The British had increasingly advocated such an act, and worldwide sympathy for the Zionist cause increased exponentially as the full horror of the Holocaust became evident. But to say that there was resistance to such a dramatic step, both within the U.S. government and around the world, would be a considerable understatement. On October 27, 1945, in his first major speech outlining U.S. foreign policy, Truman had insisted that no nation could ever enact "territorial changes" that did not accord with "the freely expressed wishes of the people concerned." Now he was contemplating exactly that, through the creation of a new Jewish state that would dislodge huge numbers of Arab landowners and cause considerable violence to parties on all sides.

Truman's bold decision to recognize Israel in May 1948 was admirable in many ways, but it complicated the reputation of the United States as the protector of essential human liberties, including the right to be secure in one's home—a basic tenet of the American Revolution, enshrined in the Constitution. For a Palestinian forced to flee his ancestral village, the Fourth Amendment did not set a meaningful precedent. For a Jewish refugee family seeking to repeat the American dream of founding a new country, American history was inspiring indeed. How to resolve those hopes and disappointments was an enormous challenge in 1948, one that has not exactly vanished.

BEST TRADITIONS

A third major challenge for the United States in the aftermath of World War Two was the simple difficulty of living up to its own standards. George Kennan finished his famous article on the sources of Soviet conduct with a simple admonition: "To avoid destruction the United States needs only measure up to its own best traditions." Those were soothing words—but far easier said than done.

Traditionally, our domestic history has been seen as something separate from our foreign relations. That view is naive. No one would deny that the same human rights FDR had trumpeted to the world were applied somewhat indifferently at home, a fact that became increasingly obvious to all onlookers as the civil rights movement gathered momentum in the late 1940s and early 1950s. But to a degree unappreciated, each setback to the struggle was, in a way, a setback to American foreign policy, because it weakened the moral assumptions that lay at the core of that policy. NSC-68 celebrated the "diversity" that lay at the heart of freedom, but in practice the government of the United States was a bit circumspect about applying the full force of its might toward this end.

Some Americans were quick to grasp the dichotomy. An early defender of civil rights, Hubert Humphrey, instinctively fused the domestic and the foreign with his spontaneous remarks at the 1948 Democratic National Convention, when he asserted that civil rights and human rights were one and the same, and that Americans had to promote both if they expected to lead the "free world." Humphrey argued, with incontestable logic, that "our demands for democratic practices in other lands will be no more effective than the guarantee of those practices in our own country." The true path to American freedom lay in a bold confrontation of "the issue of the twentieth century." If resolved, the United States could finally fulfill Lincoln's promise and become "the last best hope of earth."

But again, our best hopes were maddeningly hard to live up to. The United States has always been divided between those who walk in "the sunlight of human rights," as Humphrey put it, and those who prefer to operate in the shadows. The flip side of our dreamy utopianism is a malevolent distrust of the outside world. Millions of Americans believed with every fiber of their being in the spread of democracy—but large numbers were not ready for the color-blind implications of the system they claimed to admire. Once again, the ark of the liberties contained a confusing hodgepodge of passengers, from those who embodied America's best possibilities, applying their optimism and inventiveness to the world's problems, to those who confirmed America's worst realities, distrusting different races and nationalities, and hoping that simplistic military solutions would make some of these inconsistencies disappear.

For an era that continues to inspire a kind of Kodachrome nostalgia, it is remarkable to probe how dark the 1950s truly were. From the agonies of the civil rights movement to the terror of nuclear apocalypse, the United States was obviously as complicated a nation then as now. The great historian Richard Hofstadter began to probe the fearful, paranoid tendencies of Americans in his writings on pseudoconservatives in the 1950s, which surprised readers who'd assumed they were living in one of the great periods of forward progress. If anything, Hofstadter underestimated the force of the counterreaction he was studying.

Who were the opponents of American foreign policy? It is difficult to know where to begin. Certainly they were related to the large numbers of Americans who hated Franklin D. Roosevelt, either because he forced the wealthy to pay more taxes, or because he urged a racial acceptance that was ahead of his time, or because he seemed to like urbanites. Undoubtedly many other Americans were afraid of the rest of the world for the simple reason that enormous weapons could now wipe out most of civilization. Fear was a recurring motif in the speeches of the era, palpable in the clenched-jaw orations of Cold Warriors and in those of contemporary observers. William Faulkner, accepting the Nobel Prize for Literature in 1950, put it well: "Our tragedy today is a general and universal physical fear so long sustained by now that we can even bear it. There are no longer problems of the spirit. There is only the question: When will I be blown up?"

These nuclear tensions were new, but they fit snugly inside old fears. One political fact of the 1950s was the rise of a bloc of evangelical voters who saw the large threats facing the United States and quickly denounced them as the work of Satan, or Antichrist, or both. Evangelicals have always been a part of American politics, of course, but they had previously cared more about domestic issues (temperance, Sunday mail delivery) than foreign policy, and they were arguably more Democratic than Republican (so William Jennings Bryan would have argued). By the early 1950s, with nuclear tensions run amok, and a high degree of expectation that the Apocalypse might be more imminent than most people cared to think, more Americans began to see dark sources behind every Soviet action, or UN debate, or civil rights march. When the Treaty of Rome was signed in 1957, creating the European Economic Community, some Americans were convinced that it was the work of the devil—that the treaty was signed at Rome proved it!

It is remarkable to consider the full range of people who hated Harry Truman for the new foreign policy he was creating for the United States. Liberals led by Henry Wallace found Truman a terrifying warmonger and were eager to calm tensions with the Russians. Southern Dixiecrats were distressed by the race-blind implications of Truman's insistence on civil rights. Republicans criticized him on every front they could conceive of, from being excessively interested in the rest of the world (the party was still the home of most isolationists) to being insufficiently eager to take the battle to the enemy. The chief factor explaining Truman's survival of these serial attacks is that because there were so many, coming from so many different directions, they sometimes canceled one another out.

Oddly, many of his critics used the same vocabulary, even when they had nothing in common. Henry Wallace, for example, attacked the "Truman-led, Wall Street–dominated, military-backed group" for "supporting Kings, fascists and reactionaries." But the growing right wing was equally terrified of a foreign plot emanating from Washington, and the new Republican congressional majority elected in 1946 skillfully fanned these fears. A revived House Un-American Activities Committee, led by J. Parnell Thomas of New Jersey, insisted that a "foreign-directed conspiracy" was sabotaging America. One representative of the U.S. Chamber of Commerce soberly announced, "We will have to set up some firing squads in every good-sized city . . . and liquidate Reds and Pink Benedict Arnolds." If this fear sometimes had the feeling of a religious crusade, it may be because church leaders were among the most active participants, including prominent Catholic spokesmen such as Francis Cardinal Spellman of New York.

One of the more remarkable amendments to the Constitution was proposed in this climate, introduced in 1951 by Senator John Bricker of Ohio, a leading conservative who was horrified by Truman's foreign policy in general and the rise of the UN in particular. The Bricker Amendment (which failed by a single vote in 1954) would have removed much of the executive's ability to make foreign policy and given it to Congress. The rebellion had begun in conservative legal circles, working through the American Bar Association, and particularly targeted the UN's Universal Declaration of Human Rights and Genocide

Convention as potentially invasive of American liberties—despite their foundation in American concepts of human rights. In other words, there was a fear that the United States would be forced to live up to its own ideals! The language used to criticize these charters was covertly racist, suggesting that white Americans might be deported to The Hague for car accidents in which the victims were African-American, and that international tribunals would soon control the federal government and its policies toward education and marriage. Though the Bricker Amendment began as a Republican insurgency, the Eisenhower administration, to its credit, broke with its party to fight hard against it. It is difficult to imagine conservatives leading a movement to reduce executive power today.

Given the swirling currents of disapproval flying around the Truman administration, it is unsurprising that a bitter form of recrimination began to blame the very culture of foreign policy, particularly after the twin shocks of the Russian bomb and the fall of China unmoored Americans in the fall of 1949. In the eighteenth century, the founders had eschewed the protocols between nations and monarchs. But now an extreme version of antidiplomacy appeared; a new cult evolved that accused the State Department's "elites" of communist tendencies, believed military solutions preferable to diplomacy, and considered the United Nations the particular locus of evil and irresolution, if evil can be said to be irresolute. Some of this thinking was sincere, while a great deal of it was manipulated by cynical politicians to advance their careers.

No one played the communist card more dramatically than Joseph McCarthy, the Republican senator from Wisconsin, who put a welter of meanings into the conveniently broad adjective *un-American* (for example, that Dean Acheson might be both a communist and a wealthy elitist). But the same strategy reaped even richer dividends for Richard Nixon of California, who won elections by deploying many of McCarthy's smears while remaining—just barely—within the bounds of respectability. His enemies were attacked on every ground he could think of, from communism to sympathy for the UN and the racial tolerance that it implied (he attacked his 1950 Senate opponent, Helen Gahagan Douglas, for her support of antilynching laws). Nixon made his reputation with his aggressive pursuit of Alger Hiss, a pursuit that was all the more tempting because of the important role that Hiss had played in the conference that created the UN. While Hiss may well have been guilty of espionage—the jury is still out, though leaning guilty—his internationalist background added fuel to the fire.

McCarthy's rise and fall are now treated as a kind of terrible anomaly of our history, which is not exactly untrue but understates the degree to which his entire career was encouraged by the majority leader who gave it his blessing, Senator Robert Taft of Ohio, "Mr. Republican." At one of the lowest moments of the Truman administration, in the immediate aftermath of China's fall and Russia's bomb, McCarthy entered the national limelight with a speech that he gave in Wheeling, West Virginia, on February 9, 1950. Famously, he described a "list" of communists in the State Department, a claim later derided both because he never produced the list and because he changed the numbers of people on it, from 205 to 81 to 57. But that easy dismissal of the speech prevents a full appreciation of a remarkable oration, powerful not so much for its inspiration as for its conjuring of old hobgoblins. Like an exorcist in reverse, McCarthy effortlessly produced all of the demons that had bedeviled America in the past.

Strangely, for a speech that would become so angry, it began with a simple celebration of Abraham Lincoln, and of the nostrums of Republican isolationism from earlier in the century, to wit, "peace in our time," the outlawing of war, and worldwide disarmament. But McCarthy worked himself into a snarl as he contemplated the privileged backgrounds of those making U.S. foreign policy, "born with silver spoons in their mouth" and endowed with the "the finest homes, the finest college educations." It was ironic to hear a Roman Catholic channeling the backwoods evangel of a couple centuries previous, but it is a testament to his political skill that he did it so well. No one angered McCarthy more than Truman's secretary of state Dean Acheson, the embodiment of an evil so great that it ventured well into sacrilege: "When this pompous diplomat in striped pants, with a phony British accent, proclaimed to the American people that Christ on the Mount endorsed communism, high treason, and betrayal of a sacred trust, the blasphemy was so great that it awakened the dormant indignation of the American people."

In McCarthy's black-and-white worldview, the fight was not simply between the United States and the Soviet Union, or capitalism and communism. It was nothing less than an epic battle between Christianity and atheism, or good and evil: "Today we are engaged in a final, all-out battle between communistic atheism and Christianity . . . He has lighted the spark which is resulting in a moral uprising and will end only when the whole sorry mess of twisted, warped thinkers are swept from the national scene so that we may have a new birth of national honesty and decency in government."

McCarthy was finally brought down by his own excesses as much as any great achievement of his enemies, and his poorly conceived assault on the U.S. Army was a particular disaster. That defeat allowed internationalists to feel for the moment that the viper in their midst had been strangled. But clearly a distrust of U.S. foreign policy was pervasive well after McCarthy's career went up in flames. The intense emotions aroused by the 1951 removal of Douglas MacArthur, who advocated using nuclear weapons against China, were related to this seething discontent. Even as that controversy flared, the bombs were becoming vastly more powerful. Although the Truman administration went out with a whimper, one loud bang occurred on November 1, 1952, when the first test of the hydrogen bomb completely vaporized a small island, Elugelab, in Eniwetok Atoll. Four hundred sixty years earlier, the discovery of the New World had made small islands visible for the first time. Now, America's purpose seemed to be the opposite.

As the Truman presidency rolled to a feeble halt, it was easy to fault him for the many ways in which America's place in the world seemed less secure than it had been when he inherited the presidency. But for the most part, a president with little training had adeptly managed the superhuman responsibilities that were placed on his shoulders. The United States had adopted a new strategy of containing a dangerous new rival, and it had acted bravely in diplomatic and military ways to advance the hopes of free peoples. There was a great deal to admire as well as to criticize in the early American response to the Cold War. But whether listening to its better angels or not, the United States had undergone an enormous transformation and become something at odds with its earlier history. It was indisputably true that American power had finally grown commensurate with American optimism, and the United States now possessed the ability to realize its oldest dreams. But it was also unclear what exactly those dreams were: the utopian reveries of a Jefferson, a Wilson, or an FDR; or the dystopian nightmares of a ranter awaiting the Last Days. That has always been the problem with the millennium: it prompts vivid extremes of expectation precisely because its acolytes have so little idea what to expect.

CHAPTER TEN

THE COLD WAR: TWILIGHT

EISENHOWER

If dawn characterized the beginning of the Cold War, then twilight aptly described its middle period, perfect for its moral ambiguities and misty indeterminacy. In 1961, John F. Kennedy likened the conflict to "a long twilight struggle," a lasting catchphrase that summarized the uncertainty that every presidency, whether Democratic or Republican, encountered as it struggled to come to terms with America's new role in the world.

Truman's successor, Dwight D. Eisenhower, was easily elected in 1952, in no small part because so many Americans were distressed by Truman's foreign policy. When Eisenhower was inaugurated, launching a new Republican era, many of his supporters expected a complete reversal of Truman's policies, and a return to the isolationism and religiosity that defined the party for so many of its faithful. One of the vehicles in Ike's inaugural parade was called God's Float. A religion writer compared it to "an oversized model of a deformed molar left over from some dental exhibit."

But Eisenhower maintained many of the programs that his predecessors had put into place. He vowed firm support for NATO and the UN and seemed determined to improve America's image in the world. He ended the Korean conflict, as he promised. He traveled overseas extensively (thirty-six times), including to nations that no president had ever been to, such as Turkey and Afghanistan. In Pakistan, he traveled in an open Cadillac, drawing large, friendly crowds. In India, people cheered, "Long live the king of America!" He also permitted reckless U.S. involvement in government coups that tarnished the reputation of the United States for decades. For all these reasons, he remains difficult to pigeonhole. Certainly, Eisenhower was no reactionary—in some ways he was notably progressive. One could almost call him an academic—he was the only president besides Wilson to come to the White House from a college presidency, and his egghead credentials were nearly as good as Adlai Stevenson's. A far more adroit politician than his nonpolitical background might have suggested, Eisenhower navigated many of the problems that came his way with superb skill. But at the same time, his long presidency coincided with the steady drumbeat of the Cold War and a far larger military presence around the world than the United States had ever known in peacetime. Tensions may not have increased during his administration, but they did not noticeably decline, either.

Again, the words used by a president can be tremendously useful in deciphering the history of the era. Eisenhower was skilled at speaking about the predicament of American leadership in a terrifying world—certainly more so than his secretary of state John Foster Dulles, who persistently invoked a righteous and unforgiving God in his black-and-white depictions of the world. Eisenhower knew how to invoke God—and did so beautifully on the eve of the D-day landings. But he could also speak in soothing tones about the virtues of restraint and, in so doing, speak against some of the more extremist voices in his own party. His second inaugural address not only pledged to honor and fortify the United Nations, it promised that "no nation can longer be a fortress, lone and strong and safe. And any people, seeking such shelter for themselves, can now build only their own prison." Eleanor Roosevelt could hardly have put it better.

But these soothing words concealed the severe challenges he was facing, both within and without his government. The Soviet threat hardly receded during his presidency, and nuclear tensions remained acute throughout the 1950s. In fact, they grew apace with the capacity of the weapons themselves—and the intercontinental missiles that could deliver them in minutes. Whatever sense of protection the two oceans had once afforded Americans was little more than a pleasant memory. Annihilation was only a quick rocket flight away—a fact that altered U.S. foreign policy forever.

That was only one of many challenges facing Eisenhower. As Truman learned, foreign peoples would not always support the United States merely because we were standing up to the Soviet Union, and it was not always easy to get the American people to agree on what form of liberty they wished to export to the world. The civil rights movement provoked a blistering right-wing critique of the federal government, nearly as devastating as McCarthy's attacks on Truman, and the world's ambivalence was increased by the rising level of American subterfuge abroad. Eisenhower's government, while powerful, was not always in control of itself, and it initiated a wide range of adventures around the world: direct interventions, secret coups, and a variety of small activities that could be described as a permanent state of low-level conflict.

The CIA had grown rapidly into an important instrument of foreign policy, but an instrument that was not always checked and never released its budget or its operations to the American public. While that was by design, and essential to its efficiency, this new arrangement raised questions about who exactly was in control of American foreign policy, especially when the CIA undertook to dislodge foreign governments perceived as unfriendly. We now know far more than we did about the covert activities of the U.S. government during the early Cold War, and clearly, what were perceived as necessary and successful operations at the time were not especially either. Worse, the aftershocks of these episodes left deep and lasting resentment against the United States that severely undermined American interests.

Of course, all wars require espionage. But generations of Americans had insisted that high moral standards were essential for democracy—a system predicated upon trust—to succeed. No group of leaders ever put a higher premium on civic virtue than the founding fathers, although they expected some degree of moral dry rot to enter the system now and then. But to a new degree, official documents of the United States allowed that it was acceptable to do anything, no matter how reprehensible, in the interest of fighting the Soviet Union. Nor was this ordinary espionage. NSC-68 said, "The integrity of our system will not be jeopardized by any measures, overt or covert, violent or non-violent, which serve the purposes of frustrating the Kremlin design," as long as they are not "so excessive or misdirected as to make us enemies of the people instead of the evil men who have enslaved them." The Doolittle Report, a 1954 confidential report on CIA operations, wrote simply,

"There are no rules in such a game." Eisenhower mused privately on the ethical predicament he found himself in, wanting to defend "truth, honor, justice, consideration for others, liberty for all," but aware that dubious acts were sometimes necessary to success.

In his defense, he was facing a threat that felt, in the word of the day, existential. By the late 1950s, the Soviet Union was capable of destroying the United States, although by doing so it would ensure its own destruction. The Soviet leaders were ruthless and violent and respected strong countermeasures more than polite phrases inserted into speeches. But again, they did not claim to be especially virtuous—or at least they did not claim so persuasively.

Two examples illustrate the conundrum of U.S. foreign policy with special clarity. In 1953 and 1954, the United States essentially removed the leaders of two very different nations, Iran and Guatemala. With a minimum of fuss, the United States, acting through the CIA, installed more sympathetic governments and seemed at the time to get away with it. But with the advantage of hindsight, each intervention was clearly a catastrophe for U.S. foreign policy, whether measured by hard strategic interests or the softer indices of the way people thought about the United States.

Iran could almost be argued to fit into earlier history, for yet another Roosevelt, Theodore Roosevelt's grandson Kermit, engineered the coup that removed Iran's prime minister, Mohammed Mossadegh. But things had grown more complicated since the days of the Rough Riders, and what seemed at first like a surgical strike had disastrous ramifications for the image of the United States in the Islamic world. As I have tried to stress at several junctures, that image was generally positive at the end of World War Two, since Americans had mainly stayed aloof from imperialist intrigue in the region, leaving that to the British and the French. Franklin Roosevelt's willingness to fly to Tehran near the end of the war uplifted this image further. But Iran was becoming a hot spot of the Cold War, thanks to its proximity to the Soviet Union and its enormous capacity to produce oil. When Mossadegh, a nationalistic prime minister, decided to assert more Iranian control over British petroleum interests, the CIA grew worried. Truman restrained the plotters while president, but Eisenhower granted them their liberty. Iran, where FDR had planned the UN and where Truman had resisted Soviet aggression, now became the birthplace of the CIA coup.

The short-term result was Mossadegh's forced removal and imprisonment, and the concentration of all political power with Shah Mohammad Reza Pahlavi. But close observers wondered how a nation trumpeting democratic ideals could have deposed a legitimately elected leader, only to elevate one of the world's most corrupt monarchies, which leaned heavily upon a brutal secret police to enforce its whims. The result was a long period of festering resentment toward the Shah and the United States, which deepened as American soldiers were given special exemptions from Iranian law and impoverished Iranians beheld the spectacle of the Shah's opulence. (In 1971, the Shah threw a two-week party in celebration of the twenty-five-hundredth anniversary of Iran's royal house and its original victory over the forces of Babylon. Nine kings were in attendance, with seventy tents outfitted with French crystal, china, chandeliers, and the finest food from Paris. The only Iranian food was the caviar used to stuff the quail eggs.) It does not take much imagination to see all that followed—the Iranian Revolution and takeover of the U.S. embassy, the Iran-funded bombing of the U.S. military barracks in Beirut in 1983, and the continued funding of Shi'ite groups in Iraq—as an unpleasant legacy of Kermit Roosevelt's operation.

A year after the overthrow of the Iranian government, history repeated itself in Guatemala, where the democratically elected government of Jacobo Árbenz Guzmán was deposed by the CIA because it was beginning to reform the feudal land policies that allowed a U.S. corporation, United Fruit, to own vast sections of the country without paying taxes. The flag of the CIA-sponsored rebels read, "God, Fatherland, and Liberty." For years, moderate democracy had been spreading in Latin America, thanks to FDR's Good Neighbor policies, the rise of unions, and the gradual spread of economic benefits. In one act, the United States shattered this progress, converting moderates to extremists and enraging a generation of intellectuals. The agency's seeming success had its own long chain of reactions, beginning with the disgust expressed by a young doctor from Argentina, Ernesto "Che" Guevara. His decision to join Fidel Castro and the other plotters of Cuban independence in Mexico City resulted directly from the Guatemalan coup. Widening the scope, it is possible to argue that this relatively small success for the CIA led not only to the Cuban Revolution but also the Cuban Missile Crisis, the most lethal threat to the United States in our history. Even if one does not accept that speculation, decades of seething frustration with the United States un-doubtedly resulted from the coup, and hundreds of thousands of Guatemalans suffered terribly at the hands of the corrupt governments that followed. The tendrils of Guatemala would stretch all the way to Watergate (thanks to E. Howard Hunt), a weed spoiling a garden.

In 1954, the United States also took ownership of the Vietnam War. For years, Americans had been paying the exorbitant costs of the war for the beleaguered French. But in the spring of that year, the battle of Dien Bien Phu, fought during the Geneva negotiations that attempted to settle the conflict, effectively ejected the French forever from Indochina. It was a major turning point, the first time that a colonial people had definitively beaten their colonizers on the field of battle, and a sign to many in the U.S. government that a deeper presence in Asia was required. As *The New York Times* put it, with more than a little euphemism, "In Dienbienphu the French are fighting heroically the battle of the free."

The accords that resulted seemed to point the way toward a solution based on the Wilsonian principle that the people of Vietnam ought to determine their own fate. But the United States, agitated over evidence of Chinese and Russian support for Ho Chi Minh, refused to abide by the accords, or to sanction the free elections that they promised. At a press conference that spring, Eisenhower voiced the domino theory for the first time: "You have a row of dominoes set up, you knock over the first one and . . . the last one will go over very quickly."

Understandably, this frustrated Ho Chi Minh, who expected to be voted into power, and the war continued and intensified. Once again, the CIA inserted itself, with mixed results. The agency helped to deepen the country's internal divisions by urging huge numbers of people in the north, mostly Catholics, to move to the south. They were told, "The Virgin Mary is moving south," in Operation Passage to Freedom. But freedom was elusive. The American puppet Ngo Dinh Diem never allowed an election, but did consent to a referendum. He won 133 percent of the vote.

All three of these cases—Iran, Guatemala, and Vietnam—were unique and not easily reduced to patriotic boilerplate about freedom and tyranny. If they were part of a global movement at all, it was the movement of small nations to assert themselves and throw off their colonial oppressors, as Woodrow Wilson had urged. The release of postcolonial energies around the world, from Ghana to Algeria to the Middle East, was one of the most obvious facts of the world in the mid-1950s. Nevertheless, senior figures in the Eisenhower administration addressed each of these different situations with the same old black-and-white language about freedom and tyranny. Elderly-seeming, conservative, and ill-disposed to hasty shifts in policy, they were uniquely unsuited to speak to these energies.

Richard Nixon was more rhetorically challenged than most and seems to have spent most of the decade defending freedom from anyone who took the time to notice him—which led Venezuelan students to nearly overturn his car during a visit to Caracas. The worst may have been John Foster Dulles. Secretary of State Dulles only deepened the divide he inherited, with his plodding, righteous speeches and his circling of the West's wagons into strange new acronyms (SEATO, the South East Asian Treaty Organization, began its not very illustrious career in 1954 under his aegis). After Dulles's death, the British ambassador to the United States found a historical precedent in the same religious wars that had impelled the English to America in the first place:

> Three or four centuries ago, when Reformation and Counter-Reformation divided Europe into armed camps, in an age of wars of religion, it was not so rare to encounter men of the type of Dulles. Like them . . . he came to unshakeable convictions of a religious and theological order. Like them, he saw the world as an arena in which the forces of good and evil were continuously at war.

The comparison of the Cold War to the Thirty Years' War was not without merit—for its length as well as its use of proxies. But a huge part of the world was beginning to reject the black-and-white dichotomies that were offered and to see the world in living color. Independent mavericks in both the East (Tito) and the West (De Gaulle) began to break away from their camps. A global movement toward "nonalignment" captured considerable attention in places ranging from the Arab world to Africa, India, Indonesia, and China.

But even as it suffered these setbacks, the United States remained a powerful symbol of liberation, even to those well to the left of center. Fidel Castro, no stranger to the language of political symbolism, eagerly seized the imagery of democracy in the early stages of his movement to topple Cuba's government. A prominent photograph was taken of the Cuban flag draped over the Statue of Liberty in 1955. In 1957, *The New York Times* scored a scoop when it interviewed Castro in hiding and reported that he was a thinker with "strong ideas of liberty, democracy and social justice." After winning power in 1959, and horrifying the U.S. government with his sweeping land reforms, he told a huge crowd, "This is pure democracy."

Behind the Iron Curtain, too, the United States was a real inspiration. But two moments in October 1956 showed both the strength and the limits of American power. Hungary had held center stage for Americans once before, in the middle of the nineteenth century, when Kossuth excited Congress enough that it contemplated sending troops to help him. Now, once again, the United States was deeply interested in a Hungarian revolution and did all that it could short of intervention to provoke one. Radio Free Europe broadcasts, sponsored by the CIA, strongly implied that American military aid would be forthcoming if Hungarians rose up against their Soviet oppressors. When they did just that, no aid came—a tragic example of the gap between rhetoric and reality. Their heroic revolution, in October and November, was fought with the ghosts of 1848 alongside them—it began under a statue of a hero of 1848, Józef Bem, and Hungary's radio station was rechristened Radio Free Kossuth. But those ghosts turned out not to have any weapons. The revolution was crushed by Soviet tanks as Hungarians were issuing desperate pleas to the West for assistance. The last representative of the short-lived government wrote a moving proclamation that declared they had fought for liberty, justice, and freedom from exploitation. Any American would have been proud to have written it.

Hard on the heels of that disaster, which shook the Eisenhower administration to its core, came another severe test of American influence. In November 1956, British, French, and Israeli troops tried to seize the Suez Canal in a bid to eliminate Egypt's Gamal Abdel Nasser, a charismatic spokesman of pan-Arab nationalism. Here was a foreign-policy crisis of the utmost delicacy, involving new and old allies, acute local sensitivities, Cold War ramifications, and serious national interest.

Eisenhower rose to the occasion. Outraged that he was not consulted, he forced an embarrassing withdrawal by the British, French, and Israelis by threatening severe economic sanctions. As he did so, he asked a remarkable question: "How could we possibly support Britain and France, if in doing so we lose the whole Arab world?" By merely asking the question, he was acting in the historical tradition of the United States as an honest broker in the Middle East, dismissive of colonial spoils, mandates, and special interests.

The Suez Crisis was a watershed of sorts. Not only had Eisenhower stared down three important allies, but he had placed the Middle East higher on the list of American priorities than it had ever previously been. After the crisis he issued the Eisenhower Doctrine, in January 1957, which promised American military and economic aid to any Middle Eastern nation coming under threat of attack. The language he used to announce the doctrine bears rereading. He stated categorically "the immense importance of the Middle East," reasserted his opposition to "International Communism" taking root there, and repeated "our dedication to the principle that force shall not be used internationally for any aggressive purpose and that the integrity and independence of the nations of the Middle East should be inviolate." It was a bold statement, and probably impossible to fulfill, but historic for the new centrality of the region to American interests.

Still, American power was far from paramount. In July 1958, following a coup in Iraq that removed a king sympathetic to the United States, Eisenhower sent the U.S. Marines to Lebanon, afraid once again of a domino effect. But having accomplished this theatrical gesture, he was wise enough to recognize he could do little more and ultimately pulled the marines out. Economic and military threats might work against Western allies, but they were less useful against local populations. "Since we are about to get thrown out," he reasoned wisely, "we might as well believe in Arab nationalism." But the United States did not entirely pull out. A year later, when the new Iraqi leader withdrew his country from the pro-Western Baghdad Pact, the CIA apparently authorized an assassination attempt. The plot failed, but it succeeded in placing one of the assassins on a road to high visibility. The young man's name was Saddam Hussein.

Despite these limits on America's ability to export liberty, the word was enjoying a renaissance at home, particularly among conservatives. Just as it had in the 1850s, and the 1930s, liberty became the mantra for a wide range of extremist right-wing groups, generally united by their loathing of the civil rights movement, the UN, and anything that smacked of international diplomacy. The Liberty Lobby, a white-supremacist, anti-Semitic organization, was founded in 1955. Three years later, the John Birch Society was created, founded by a radical visionary from the great conservative state of Massachusetts. Robert Welch spared no expense to get his message out to sympathizers, issuing a flood of publications, starting "American Opinion Libraries" around the country, attacking "communist sympathizers" ("Comsymps") at every opportunity, and reserving particular contempt for the way that American diplomacy had lost China (John Birch was a U.S. soldier killed by the Chinese). His writings spewed vitriol in the guise of ultrapatriotism and repeated the word *liberty* in every paragraph. Welch hated Eisenhower nearly as much as he hated the president who must not be named, Franklin D. Roosevelt. He and his followers were certain that an international conspiracy had reduced American influence in the world, and that the communists were linked to the Bavarian Illuminati, whom they believed had caused the French Revolution. And people say we Americans have no sense of history?

The John Birch Society was not always on target in its accusations—amazingly, Welch accused Barbara Bush's father, a magazine publisher, of being a communist because he was responsible for the women's magazine *Redbook*. But the society played a strong role in certain circles that would eventually form the core of the Republican Party, including the wealthy new suburbs forming outside cities, the growing populations of the Southwest and the West, and pockets of the South resisting the civil rights movement. Even for those who did not join the fringe, large numbers felt frustrated by the rapid changes of American life and our seeming inability to win the Cold War. Eisenhower had a difficult time balancing the concerns of these backers, who would come out into the open during the Goldwater campaign of 1964, with the more moderate Republicans he truly represented.

Ironically, these ardent proponents of liberty seemed most provoked by the efforts of black Americans to achieve their own civil liberties. A very real struggle over freedom was taking place in the United States, and to its credit, the federal government supported it, through Supreme Court decisions and army deployments when those decisions were put to the test in places like Little Rock. One might add Arkansas to the long list of interventions by the United States in the Eisenhower era.

The most casual glance through the literature of the extreme right reveals how agitated it was over civil rights, which it considered as serious a threat as the Red menace. It was no coincidence that the Liberty League was founded a year after *Brown v. Board of Education* (1954). Nearly every John Birch Society pamphlet attacked Earl Warren as a traitor and painted Martin Luther King Jr. as a secret Soviet agent, a canard that was repeated at high levels by J. Edgar Hoover, who monitored King's every move. Even progressive Republicans—the young Senate candidate George H. W. Bush, for example—would hint at these accusations. Some voiced them every chance they got. The Mormon leader Ezra Taft Benson, a cabinet member under Eisenhower, spoke for many when he called civil rights a "tool of communist deception." No slouch in the millennial department, Benson also believed that the Second Coming was imminent, that "God will interject himself," and that "the final and eternal victory shall be for free agency." Free agency for Mormons, that is.

Another sacred article of faith for the rising conservative movement was its seething hatred for the United Nations. It remains difficult to decipher this rage toward what was essentially a body of diplomatic specialists—a body whose weakness has been on display for several generations now—but several motives rose to the surface. Some of it was surely rooted in the historical distrust of foreign entanglements, and the more specific dislike of FDR's internationalism. Some came from what was perceived to be the UN's constraints upon U.S. sovereignty and military might—a fear that went back to the Korean War and Harry S. Truman's dismissal of General Douglas A. MacArthur from command of UN forces fighting in Korea (oddly, nostalgia for MacArthur's brinkmanship with China often displaced gratitude for Truman's preventing a war with that country). But plenty came from the UN's rising role as a tribunal for the world's colonial peoples, mostly dark-skinned, who were asserting their own rights to freedom as they overturned centuries of European colonization. The UN had always been an antiracist organization, as its charter demanded, and as Eleanor Roosevelt's devotion to it proved. But ironically, the charter, a document modeled on American precedents, caused great tension inside the United States. The John Birch Society even launched a campaign to get Americans to spurn United Airlines because of its possible connection to the UN.

These disparate groups may have possessed small significance at the time, but their loud and emotional contribution played a role in the ongoing and difficult debate over America's place in the postwar world. That contribution would only increase over time, as they spread their erratic beliefs in America's complete separation from the world and its destiny to utterly triumph over the world (a contradiction, of course). FDR had been an exceptionalist in his way, to the extent that he believed that American ideas about personal freedoms were in advance of other nations and might usefully be taught to the rest of humanity. But the new exceptionalism rejected every tenet of the FDR philosophy, and the very idea of an international order of any kind. Oddly, this was exactly the sort of irrational, emotional nationalism that FDR's vision was designed to counter. At times, it betrayed some of the same tendencies that historians have identified with the rise of fascism—a sense of grievous injury to the nation, an inflated perception of injury, a vague feeling that earlier eras were greater. In other words, rising numbers of Americans were attacking an international system, founded by the United States along principles inherent in our own founding charters, on the grounds that the new system was un-American.

That was not the only way in which the United States was losing its historical bearings. Extremists on right and left could unite now and then, and one point of concern was the sheer extent of the American military presence overseas. Obviously, America was no longer a simple republic and, if short of an empire, still commanded an extensive presence in the world. Throughout the 1950s, the number of overseas bases rose rapidly, along with the numbers of Americans stationed there. Where soldiers and airplanes could not go, new technologies provided a different kind of presence, watching and listening to enemy actions in the atmosphere, underwater, and in the world's most remote regions. The surly bonds of earth were no match for American engineers, as better and better airplanes and rockets were built to fly higher and faster. The first U-2 spy plane made its debut on July 4, 1956, flying high over Leningrad and Moscow, and taking photographs of everything its pilot beheld. Intercontinental ballistic missiles flew with extraordinary range, accuracy, and speed, in effect promising instant destruction to both the United States and the Soviet Union if diplomacy failed. Unfortunately, Russian engineers were also quite proficient, and they beat the United States into outer space when they launched the first satellite, *Sputnik*, in 1957.

Until then, Americans had been afraid that Soviet bombers might someday fly over the United States, and twenty-five thousand contractors had built one of the world's great construction projects, the Distant Early Warning (DEW) Line, in the frozen wastes of northern Canada between 1954 and 1957. It was opened on July 31, 1957. The next month, the Russians developed the ICBM, and the DEW Line became irrelevant. Still, the project would have made Charles Sumner and other northern expansionists of the nineteenth century happy—they had always longed for the day that American dominion would extend to the Arctic Circle.

As the unofficial boundary between the United States and the Soviet Union, the Arctic was also visited by a new kind of vessel as submarine technology improved by leaps and bounds. The USS *Nautilus* went under the north pole in 1958, rendering the old Northwest Passage irrelevant. Two years later, the USS *Triton* circumnavigated the world underwater. Not many places on the planet were out of the reach of American power, which became even more evident when U.S. subs were armed with nuclear weapons. Ironically, the earliest American submarines, invented early enough that the founding fathers could contemplate them, had been intended as a way to escape the tyranny of large and expensive navies.

The rate at which defense spending was increasing and new weapons were being developed only complicated the difficult balancing act that Eisenhower was trying to maintain, and near the end of his administration there was a palpable loss of focus. It was hardly simple to maintain the intensely alert posture that more than a decade of Cold War activity had generated for American political and military leaders, and mistakes would inevitably be made. A large one ensued when the Soviet Union trapped Eisenhower in a bald-faced lie in the spring of 1960. The U-2 planes had been gathering priceless intelligence for the United States and were considered invulnerable. When the Russians shot down one that had taken off from Pakistan and was flying over Russia, Eisenhower routinely denied that the plane was spying, thinking its pilot had been killed. When Nikita Khrushchev produced a living pilot who confessed to all of his charges, the world was legitimately shocked, at both the spying and the ease with which an American president had lied about it. The Cold War's moral ambiguities—its twilight—did not always bear up well in the broad daylight of public scrutiny. Though most understood Eisenhower's motives, it was a serious blow to American prestige and to the idealistic image the United States labored to project.

Still, for all of his lapses, Eisenhower brought an admirable restraint to the difficult job he had inherited, and his unassailable military credentials allowed him to take several daring risks for peace. In 1955, he had proposed that the Soviet Union and the United States draft an "open skies" agreement that would give each the right to fly over the other's territory, monitoring military activity. It was rejected, but in the fall of 1959, the two nations, along with other interested European parties, signed a treaty at Washington that the founding fathers would have approved. The Antarctic Treaty offered a new model for peaceful international relations, rejecting the idea that any nation might exercise sovereignty in that frozen continent and insisting that "Antarctica shall be used for peaceful purposes only."

Eisenhower also spoke out, as perhaps only he could, against the rising danger of a defense industry that was not always subject to the checks and balances that define a healthy federal system. In his farewell speech to the nation, in January 1961, he named the "military-industrial complex" for the first time and argued that a permanent industry of defense contracting—the exact lobby that had been so unpopular after World War One—was not in America's interest. Notably, he identified this new form of influence as something far beyond a military interest: it was "economic, political, even spiritual"; it was "new in American experience"; and it was the kind of looming threat that idealistic Americans should vigilantly guard against. It was a fitting farewell sermon from a leader who had led the United States during a difficult moment of transition.

JFK

> "New order of the ages" did they say?
> If it looks none too orderly today,
> 'Tis a confusion it was ours to start
> So in it have to take courageous part.
>
> —Robert Frost, "Dedication"

Robert Frost famously read his poem "The Gift Outright" at the inauguration of John F. Kennedy. What is not remembered as clearly is that he read that poem from memory because he could not read the one he had composed for the occasion, titled "Dedication." A far longer poem, tailored for the occasion, it meandered between slyly skeptical statements about America's purpose and the expected paeans to the greatness of the nation and event. From the earliest European encounters to the recent election, Frost outlined the national epic, concluding wisely that "Our venture in revolution and outlawry / has justified itself in freedom's story." Perhaps his inability to read the poem that day was divine retribution for a poet who questioned some of the providential assumptions at the heart of the American saga.

When Kennedy won the presidency in 1960, it was difficult to list all of the ways it seemed to mark a break with tradition—the first president born in the twentieth century, the first Roman Catholic president, the first Irish president, the youngest elected, and so forth. Yet for all of these departures, the Kennedy administration continued many of the traditions of its predecessors. To be sure, it was enmeshed in the Cold War, the contest begun and extended under Truman and Eisenhower. In fact, it experienced—and barely survived—what was probably the most apocalyptic single moment of history, the Cuban Missile Crisis. But in ways that are important to point out, Kennedy used his sense of bearing—a bearing that depended profoundly on his reading of history—to lead the United States effectively at a time when the smallest misstep might have led to Armageddon. His precise acts and words have occasionally been overlooked in the rush either to lionize him outside of all recognition of the person he was or, in the opposite impulse, to demonize him, but he generally found the correct response to the formidable array of challenges he faced in his three short years in office.

In fact, his Catholicism may ironically have been his saving grace, for just as the original Puritans felt a healthy skepticism toward the received dogma of their time, so JFK could express on occasion his own healthy remove from the sacred scripture of America's Protestant mission. To be sure, he believed in an aggressive defense of American interests around the world—but unlike, say, John Foster Dulles, he could see more than one angle to an argument and was impatient with dogmatic definitions of liberty that shortchanged the fullness of the American story.

Despite his youth—a youth that feels exaggerated by his abbreviated existence—Kennedy had traveled extensively before assuming office, and had a deeper experience than most of the power and the limitations of American idealism. Before World War Two, he had listened to the debates over the Munich Pact in the British Parliament. He had served in the war that followed, leading a PT boat through the same regions of the South Pacific that American sea captains had first penetrated in the middle of the nineteenth century. He had also experienced firsthand some of the idealism with which the United States hoped to rebuild the world, as a journalist covering the San Francisco conference that created the UN, although it is difficult to claim that idealism rubbed off on him in any tangible way.* As a young congressman and then a senator, he had traveled both behind the Iron Curtain and in the Middle East.

More than most presidents, he was conversant in history. His book, *Profiles in Courage*, had shown an abiding respect for those who sailed against prevailing winds. Whether he would be able to do so was very much up in the air, for he had run his campaign by attacking his opponent, Richard Nixon, and the Eisenhower administration for being soft on communism, and early in his career he had tolerated the attacks of Joseph McCarthy, which many of his colleagues had found objectionable.

On the night before he assumed the presidency and gave the most famous speech of his life, Kennedy gave a speech that was quieter, but equally full of meaning, before the Massachusetts General Court. In that speech, he more or less channeled John Winthrop, the original

*His first dispatch: "There is an impression that this is the conference to end war and introduce peace on earth and goodwill towards nations. Well, it's not going to do that."

New Frontiersman, returning to the city upon a hill and likening the United States to better parts of the Puritan expedition (specifically, to the founding of Boston). He quoted Pericles, of whom perhaps Winthrop himself had been mindful: "We do not imitate—for we are a model to others."

Foreign policy had played a large role in Kennedy's political formation, and a major step in his progress toward the Oval Office had been his appointment to the Senate Foreign Relations Committee in 1957. We now know that Lyndon Johnson appointed him to that post because of the great allure of Joseph P. Kennedy's patronage, but still, JFK had several impressive qualifications. As a senator, he had shown a willingness to take on difficult foreign problems—particularly problems concerning the developing world, which were precisely the problems that the Eisenhower administration had so much difficulty talking about.

We don't especially think of Kennedy as a Middle Eastern specialist, but in 1957 he gave a major speech in the Senate about Algeria and the ugly war France was fighting there to keep its power intact, a topic that almost no other American politician was willing to address, and one that had relatively little to do with the Cold War. In fact, his point was specifically that the Cold War was distorting American foreign policy in regions of the world that were not especially affected by Russia or the United States, and that America should return to its higher standards and help the nonaligned peoples of the earth achieve freedom in their own manner.

What made his speech unusual was that he explained that the average Algerian considered the Western powers nearly as imperialistic as the Soviet Union. Boldly, at a time of considerable sympathy for the beleaguered French (who were, after all, NATO allies), Kennedy ridiculed their efforts to impose their will on a different people. Fascinatingly, he dismissed those who simplistically denounced all opponents as "terrorists" and argued that every internal revolution, including our own, has seen "a rising temperature of terrorism and counterterrorism; but this does not of itself invalidate the legitimate goals that fired the original revolution." By accepting the legitimacy of Algeria's independence movement, and working constructively with its leaders and young people, he argued that the United States could help an Arab nation withstand "both the pull toward Arab feudalism and fanaticism and the pull toward Communist authoritarianism." He ended the speech with a call for the United States to truly work for the legitimate independence movements of the world, and to live up to "our traditional and deeply-felt philosophy of freedom and independence for all peoples everywhere." To say that this was an unusual position at the time would be an understatement. It showed prescience about the simmering struggles separating not only East from West, but North from South, and considered the Middle East more carefully than any speech until the time of Jimmy Carter.

In other words, before assuming office, Kennedy had shown impressive flexibility before a foreign policy establishment that was anything but. When running for office, he was as firm a hard-liner toward the Soviet Union as anyone; when left to his own devices, he could think in arresting ways. Like all presidents, he did not always live up to his finest articulations, and Kennedy was undoubtedly capable of aggression. The Bay of Pigs invasion of Cuba, in April 1961, was about as naked an invasion of a foreign country as one could imagine, despite elaborate attempts to dress it up as a Cuban internal matter (including firing gunshots into American airplanes before takeoff so that they could claim to have been fired upon). The Roosevelt Corollary was still within living memory of elderly Washington officials, and the invasion must have seemed like business as usual before it failed miserably. In fact, aspects of the operation went back even deeper into American history. A CIA secret radio station, Radio Swan, was located on the Swan Islands, a tiny chain off Honduras that had been claimed under the Guano Act of 1856. During the invasion, the station broadcast coded messages to insurgents. More than a few fishermen must have found it confusing to hear emissions such as:

> Alert! Alert!
> Look well at the rainbow.
> The first will rise very soon.
> Chico is in the house.

But the Cuban disaster may have been a blessing in disguise, for it solidified a commitment to diplomacy that was already latent and deepened as the Kennedy administration found its footing. Kennedy had given brave speeches throughout his career, expressing some distaste for the simplistic mind-set of American exceptionalism. His speech at the University of Washington, in 1961, was not then especially noted, but became so with the passage of time. "And we must face the fact that the United States is neither omnipotent nor omniscient—that we are only 6 per cent of the world's population and that we cannot impose our will upon the other 94 per cent of mankind—that we cannot right every wrong or reverse each adversity, and that, therefore, there cannot be an American solution to every world problem."

That Lincolnesque realism served Kennedy well in the most acute situation he encountered, and perhaps the worst ever encountered: the Cuban Missile Crisis. After all the years of brinkmanship, and the Bay of Pigs in particular, Nikita Khrushchev, who assumed leadership of the Soviet Union following Stalin's death in 1953, had privately recounted, "We had to think up some way of confronting America with more than words." The result was an insane plan to place Russian nuclear weapons on Cuba, in utter defiance of the Monroe Doctrine (which had originally checked czarist Russia's ambitions in the New World).

Kennedy's response was perfectly calibrated between clear demonstrations of American resolve when necessary and an equally critical willingness to step back from the abyss and listen to better angels. This was not easy to do given the useless advice of hard-line military advisers and the natural tendency of leaders to ratchet up tensions during confrontations, but Kennedy's skepticism toward received wisdom allowed him to craft a perfectly modulated response that gave Khrushchev just enough room to retreat. Once again, history was a helpful ally. Kennedy had just read Barbara Tuchman's *The Guns of August*, with its account of Europe's slide into World War One through rigid posturing, and he was determined not to repeat the calamity. Attorney General Robert Kennedy, listening to his own better angels, offered the compelling thought, at a crucial moment, that the United States could not initiate hostilities and stay true to its heritage. When a plan to bomb Cuba surfaced, he passed a note to his brother: "I now know how Tojo felt when he was planning Pearl Harbor." The motion failed, and humanity survived as a result.

Of course, the Kennedy administration had its imperfections, all well documented. The CIA continued its active schedule of destabilization and even assassination of foreign heads of state, and the number of military "advisers" in Vietnam increased steadily. But the Cuban Missile Crisis marked a high-water mark in the Cold War, from which both sides were happy to see the tide recede. Afterward, there is no doubt that Kennedy began to speak with a new kind of accent.

Eight months after the crisis, on June 10, 1963, Kennedy gave a speech at American University that may have been the greatest of his life. It completely recast the basic assumptions of the Cold War. He renounced the simplistic idea of a "Pax Americana," called for a cessation of nuclear weapons tests in the atmosphere, and tried earnestly to look at the Cold War from the other side, without dogma, because ultimately "we must deal with the world as it is." Not since Lincoln briefly considered the Confederate outlook on God in his second inaugural address had a president tried to question American assumptions so bracingly and refreshingly. "Let us reexamine our attitude toward the Soviet Union," Kennedy announced, and listed the ways in which the two sides had failed to understand each other over a generation.

Parts of the speech seemed to come from earlier in the century—he mentioned that Americans had once led the international movement toward disarmament, in the 1920s, and cited Woodrow Wilson both by name and by suggestion, implying that the United States should always protect the rights of the vulnerable, building a world "where the weak are safe and the strong are just." Emphatically, he reasserted something that Wilson would have said: "The United States, as the world knows, will never start a war."

Other parts were very much in the moment. Another daring aspect, besides the empathy with which he treated the Russian perspective, was his insistence that the United States could not persuasively argue on freedom's behalf around the world if it did not put its own house in order. Just as FDR had instinctively understood, Kennedy knew that the United States could not be an effective force for liberty if its own people were not treated equally. Arrestingly, Kennedy reminded his audience that "freedom is incomplete" in America. "Let us examine our attitude towards peace and freedom at home," he continued, because "the quality and spirit of our own society must justify our efforts abroad."

Appropriately, the next day, he delivered a nationwide address on civil rights that brought all of these thoughts to a forceful conclusion. To promote liberty abroad, we needed to protect it at home. Taken together, the two addresses offered an encouraging sign that the United States was finally about to achieve a form of integration, not only between the races, but among the various strands of freedom that politicians had been invoking since the dawn of the republic.

Of course, merely because Kennedy gave a good speech did not mean that the more extremist definitions of liberty would vanish. If it was possible for the John Birchers to hate someone more than Franklin D. Roosevelt and Dwight D. Eisenhower, Kennedy fitted the bill. That he was Catholic aroused considerable worry in evangelical precints and revived the Great Awakening fears of a Romish conspiracy. The quickening of the civil rights movement brought many of these misformed ideas out into the open again. When George Wallace was inaugurated as the governor of Alabama on January 14, 1963, he gave an emotionally charged address that summoned all of the ghosts of American history into a confused melee, borrowing from the founding fathers and the Confederates (who had renounced the founders), insisting on "liberty," denouncing "tyranny," and returning to the old black-and-white divide between those two words—in this case literally. His peroration:

> It is very appropriate then that from this Cradle of the Confederacy, this very Heart of the Great Anglo-Saxon Southland, that today we sound the drum for freedom as have our generations of forebears before us done, time and time again through history. Let us rise to the call of freedom-loving blood that is in us and send our answer to the tyranny that clanks its chains upon the South. In the name of the greatest people that have ever trod this earth, I draw the line in the dust and toss the gauntlet before the feet of tyranny . . . and I say . . . segregation today . . . segregation tomorrow . . . segregation forever.

Fortunately, he was not the only American with a deep interest in our history. Liberty has always offered a capacious house to those who choose to enter it, and it would have been difficult to answer Wallace's claim with more dignity than Martin Luther King Jr. did on the steps of the Lincoln Memorial. King proclaimed "a dream deeply rooted in the

American dream," and specifically in the Declaration of Independence, the great fountainhead of the rights—civil and human—that he was striving toward. He insisted that all Americans, white and black, were entitled to the same rights, and that white and black notions of freedom were "inextricably bound." As if that weren't enough to send the crowd into rapture, he rooted his dream even more deeply in the nation's subconscious by offering a snapshot of the millennial bliss that would ensue when these freedoms were achieved: "I have a dream that one day every valley shall be exalted, and every hill and mountain shall be made low, the rough places will be made plain, and the crooked places will be made straight; 'and the glory of the Lord shall be revealed and all flesh shall see it together.' "

To be sure, the United States was still confronted by danger, both without and within. All three of the orators of 1963 would be the target of assassination attempts, two of them successful. The world was still a dangerous place, and the United States was deeply extended across it, from the Berlin Wall to the artificial boundaries of Korea and Vietnam. As the Cuban Missile Crisis had shown, Armageddon was closer than anyone had truly realized—just an island away, in fact. But as Kennedy and King had found, the correct answer to the threats posed by history was simply to find more history—a better history of one's own choosing.

LBJ

From twilight, the ark would sail into nightfall before finding its way to morning again. At the 1964 Democratic National Convention, Robert Kennedy famously dismissed Lyndon Johnson in the most subtle way possible—by alluding to Shakespeare! How could Johnson possibly fight back? At the end of his remarks, RFK cited *Romeo and Juliet* to predict a time when "all the world will be in love with night, and pay no worship to the garish sun." No Cliff's Notes were needed to guess whom the "garish sun" referred to.

Night was indeed settling over American foreign policy in the 1960s and early 1970s, as the United States stepped with more and more of its weight into the quicksand of Indochina, and the presidency of Richard Nixon collapsed under a farrago of lies, evasions, and bluster about the national security interest. Watergate was of course a domestic melodrama, but it was deeply rooted in the story of Vietnam (the White House Special Investigation Union, a.k.a. "the plumbers," formed in response to the release of the Pentagon Papers), and a government's fury that a different version of its foreign policy story was being told than the one it preferred.

To be sure, 1974 was incomprehensibly far into the future in 1964, when Nixon seemed an ancient relic of the early Cold War and LBJ was master of all he surveyed. All, that is, except the Democratic National Convention, where Robert Kennedy's mere appearance loosed a twenty-minute ovation, simply because he symbolized the road not taken.

The tragedies of Dallas continue to proliferate, like the conspiracy theories that will not let the events of November 1963 fade into oblivion. No result was more catastrophic than the way that John F. Kennedy's martyrdom was turned into a justification to expand the Vietnam War at the very moment he appeared ready to reduce American involvement.

If the Cold War had lurched into existence erratically under Truman, Eisenhower, and Kennedy, it showed some signs of stabilizing in the summer of 1963, with the signing of the Limited Test Ban Treaty, and several public statements of Kennedy's desire to withdraw American advisers from Vietnam. After glimpsing the apocalypse over Cuba, Kennedy and Khrushchev appeared ready to settle into a long-term policy of mutually assured survival.

But the sudden removal of Kennedy and Khrushchev in 1963 and 1964 brought a new instability to the Cold War and revealed, once again, how precarious the destiny of a great nation can be. Kennedy's successor, Lyndon Johnson, could not have believed more ardently in the legacy of Franklin D. Roosevelt, his original political mentor. But lacking Roosevelt's mastery, and his no less impressive self-restraint, Johnson blundered into one of the worst foreign policy debacles in American history. Four presidents, from Eisenhower to Nixon, led the United States into Indochina—two Democrats and two Republicans. But Johnson stands out as the one who escalated the conflict, turning it from a proxy war on a distant side stage into the central drama of its time. The drama turned out to be a tragedy.

Vietnam, as I have mentioned, was a remote theater of the early Cold War, but one with a surprisingly durable cast of players. Ho Chi Minh was still very much alive as he confronted Johnson, his eighth U.S. president since Woodrow Wilson. The number of Americans in Vietnam had steadily ratcheted upward during the Eisenhower and Kennedy administrations, from six hundred in 1961 to sixteen thousand by end of the Kennedy administration, and the United States was implicated in the ghastly coup that killed the Diem brothers in November 1963.

But still, by the end of his administration, Kennedy showed signs that he intended to disengage, including the beginning of modest troop withdrawals. It is unlikely, in an election year, that he would have disengaged beyond this. But having won the election, it is inconceivable that he would have escalated the conflict as radically as his successor did. And there is mounting evidence, fueled by statements of former secretary of defense Robert McNamara, that the Kennedy administration planned to withdraw most U.S. advisers from Vietnam by the end of 1965.

That this point is still emotional, unresolved, and unresolvable can be discovered by anyone who enters the words *Kennedy* and *Vietnam* into a search engine. But the weight of the evidence suggests that Kennedy, having triumphed over both the Soviet Union and the lunacy of his own military advisers in the Cuban Missile Crisis, was moving to reduce involvement at the time of his death. So his closest advisers maintained, and so his language—a language consistent with his earlier criticisms of unwinnable wars—would indicate. Though he had publicly stated, many times, his support for a strong U.S. presence in Vietnam, from his 1957 Algeria speech onward he had also shown the most acute sensitivity to the problem of imperial overreach. When his aide George Ball predicted that three hundred thousand Americans would be in Vietnam in five years, Kennedy replied, "George, you're crazier than hell." He once stated with exasperation, "You know, Eisenhower never mentioned it, never uttered the word *Vietnam*," and one senses that he felt growing admiration for his predecessor's taciturnity regarding the war that dare not speak its name. Having won reelection, he would almost certainly have taken steps to ensure that he did not have to speak it too often.

But if Kennedy revealed a perpetual willingness to think anew, his successor showed no such flexibility. In the summer of 1964, in the middle of an election campaign, destiny—aided by Lyndon Johnson—took a hand. On August 2 and 4, the American public was led to believe that two U.S. naval vessels, the USS *Maddox* and USS *Turner Joy*, had been attacked by Vietnamese gunboats in the Gulf of Tonkin. Later information cast considerable doubt on the official version of the story, particularly the second attack, which probably did not occur.* Further, it is now known that the United States was engaged in covert harassment of the North Vietnamese prior to the incident. On the night the first attack occurred, American vessels were participating in a secret operation whose code name was DeSoto, after the Spanish explorer of the sixteenth century who tried to find a way to get from America to Asia. The U.S. flagship supporting the operation was the *Bon Homme Richard*, heir to the famous John Paul Jones ship. History was fully on patrol in Vietnam.

Following the incident, Johnson went to Congress with an impassioned address demanding retaliatory action. As a candidate for president, running against Barry Goldwater, a Republican who had ventured far to the right in his journey toward the center (and had refused to censure Joseph McCarthy), Johnson was certainly aware that his hardened edge would help him to win election. But he had shown this interest in deepening the war earlier, when he increased U.S. military support in the immediate wake of the Kennedy assassination, and he was now ready to extend it significantly further. The resulting resolution gave him free license to deploy American troops in Southeast Asia without a formal declaration of war—to help "the free nations of the area to defend their freedom." He argued, "This is not just a jungle war, but a struggle for freedom on every front of human activity." His lofty language was followed by a lofty commitment, as the United States began to bomb North Vietnam and then to send in huge waves of American soldiers. By the end of 1965, there were nearly two hundred thousand troops in Vietnam; a year later, twice that again; and by mid-1967, nearly half a million.

*In 2005, *The New York Times* reported that the National Security Agency had not only falsified the original account of the attacks, but had also falsified its falsification.

In some ways, the drama seemed a restaging. The Tonkin Gulf incident bore more than a passing resemblance to the murky beginning of the Mexican War, when James Polk asked Congress to sanction a U.S. invasion despite a lack of clear evidence that an attack on U.S. forces had occurred. But in other ways, Vietnam seemed to have nothing whatsoever to do with the American past. Saigon was 9,006 miles from Washington, a more remote location than any other major military theater in American history, farther away than Japan or the Philippines. And it became clear as the war escalated in 1965 that the traditional rhetoric of liberty and tyranny—the rhetoric that had moved so many Americans on so many previous occasions—was no longer accurate. The corrupt government of South Vietnam fell and was reconstituted seven times in 1964 alone.

Of course, that did not prevent Johnson from trying. With impressive tenacity, he pressed the case to Americans that their liberties were somehow contingent upon the successful outcome of a jungle war on the other side of the world. The war was fought with the most modern military hardware known to man, and with the oldest weapon in the American arsenal—the rhetoric of freedom.

We all sing the freedom we know, and no form of liberation had meant more to Johnson than the economic empowerment engineered by Franklin Roosevelt in the 1930s. And so he often couched his vision of the future that he was trying to build for Southeast Asia in the discordant language of a government planner, promising that the United States would turn the Mekong Delta into the Tennessee Valley Authority, and transforming a nasty conflict into a bit of New Deal forest-clearing. But LBJ also moved easily into the pomposity of larger statements about freedom, unmoored utterances so gaseous that they might have floated a fleet of weather-observation balloons. Johnson was never one to hold back, and his 1965 inaugural address announced that "the American Covenant" compels nothing less than "the liberation of man." In August 1965, he explained that the Vietnam conflict was part of a "war on tyranny," that America always fights for ideals and not for territory, and that we were especially motivated to fight for the "little nations" such as Greece, Turkey, and Iran. With Wilsonian solemnity, he asked, "If this little nation goes down the drain and can't maintain her independence, ask yourself, what's going to happen to all the other little nations?"

But the language of freedom became less and less persuasive as the United States failed to prevail. It was further undermined by the growing skepticism of America's allies, less convinced that freedom was on the line in Vietnam. And it was fatally compromised by the fact that the North Vietnamese spoke their own version of freedom, with better results. With an odd echo of a Jeffersonian insight, General Vo Nguyen Giap asserted, "The most correct path to be pursued by the people is to liberate themselves in revolutionary violence and revolutionary war." Unfortunately for Lyndon Johnson, Giap's views prevailed.

One of the fatal effects of the way Johnson wielded rhetoric is that his words became a self-fulfilling prophecy. Vietnam had not been essential to the liberties of American citizens, as became clear when the war ended in 1975 and those liberties were still intact (Cambodians were not so lucky). But by insisting at such a high volume that the cause of America was linked to the war, Johnson did in fact raise the stakes significantly, which led to a catastrophic setback for American prestige around the world when he failed to win. The war was a defeat in every sense, not only for the United States as a military force, but for the worldwide example of democracy. As the military effort bogged down, so did the political process at home, with results that were all too easy to see. The argument seemed to bring out the worst in both Democrats and Republicans. Democrats, with preponderant political majorities, emanated a kind of smugness that government expertise could solve any problem, including military crises. (Robert McNamara, for example, once said, "North Vietnam will never beat us. They can't even make ice cubes.") But the Republicans were not much better, shifting from head-in-the-sand isolation to immoderate calls for nuclear attack, divine retribution, or some combination of the above.

A culture of deceit pervaded the entire defense establishment during the war's prosecution. The costs of the war were routinely concealed from Congress and the American people, which hardly advanced democracy. And slowly, the language of democracy was degraded as well. Operations were routinely given grandiose titles such as Operation Certain Victory and Operation Resolve to Win, a sure sign that victory was uncertain and resolution was lacking.

Those swirling problems led the United States to be utterly hamstrung by a tiny nation halfway around the world. Worse, by being cast in the position of a large empire attacking a small nation fighting for its independence, the United States completely reversed its identity. It was a devastating setback to the nation's reputation around the world, calling all American actions into suspicion, and destroying for a generation and more the Democratic Party's reputation as a wise shaper of foreign policy. It was a disaster for the Democrats because they included both the militarists prosecuting the war and the antimilitarists resisting it—a fact the Republican Party made artful use of. Everything was turning topsy-turvy in the 1960s. A literal ark of the liberties, the USS *Liberty*, a naval vessel patrolling the Mediterranean, was attacked by an ally, Israel, on June 8, 1967, leaving thirty-four dead.

Most Americans felt that a valuable form of freedom would be liberation from the war itself. These feelings were particularly experienced by the young generation expected to fight it. They, too, spoke a language of freedom, quite different from Lyndon Johnson's, which was in turn different from the language of freedom spoken by the distant reaches of the right wing. The acrimony left by these competing visions still haunts American politics to this day. The extraordinary result of the Vietnam War—the United States unable to win despite overwhelming technological superiority—led to an ideological realignment that Americans are still recovering from. In later years, few would have dared to call this a war for freedom or any other worthwhile principle. When George Washington warned against entanglement, he could not have chosen a better word to describe the vinous foliage of Southeast Asia, which seemed to be extending all the way from Indochina to the United States itself.

The range of difficulties created by war and its tentacles now extended fully into American political life and dominated every twist and turn of the presidential election of 1968. First, the president disentangled himself by withdrawing from the race. Then a series of apocalyptic scenes unfolded. On the last day of March in 1968, Martin Luther King Jr., by now an outspoken opponent of the war, gave a landmark speech attacking it in Washington's National Cathedral that seemed to reach all the way back to the Puritans. Quoting the book of Revelation (21:5), he intoned, "Behold, I make all things new."

That turned out to be a forlorn hope—a week later he was killed. The chaos in black neighborhoods that ensued, and the conservative white reaction it provoked, were connected both to the disaster in Vietnam and to a growing sense that the foreign policy of the United States was foreign to its own people. In fact, that was one of the few opinions that America's splinter groups could agree upon. No theme was more passionately argued by Robert Kennedy, assassinated two months later, and the failure to articulate a new course in foreign policy doomed the campaign of Hubert Humphrey. The election of Richard Nixon, the former red-baiter, on a peace platform completed the circle of unlikelihoods that marked the 1968 campaign, which also marked the end of nearly four decades of Democratic hegemony, and a certain way of looking at the world.

NIXON

To his credit, Nixon seemed true to his words at first. He was clearly not the same Richard Nixon who had made his career by accusing his opponents of communism. In fact, Nixon seemed to get along well with communists when he needed to, and his chief achievements in foreign policy were his stunning initiative in opening up the United States to China and his durable détente with the Soviet Union. He worked toward a relaxing of tensions with North Vietnam, and if the war did not end under his watch, he still reduced America's commitment substantially.

He achieved these breakthroughs the old-fashioned way, through careful, plodding diplomacy and patient negotiation with people who were very different from Americans. Many voters were relieved that they no longer had to listen to LBJ's grandiose language of liberation, and Nixon generally refrained from promising freedom to all who asked. More than refreshing, that pose was honest as well—for the Republican Party did not especially intend to liberate anyone and had notably refrained from progressive statements on civil rights or South Africa as it began to gather in disaffected Southern Democrats who felt threatened by the civil rights movement. From Ronald Reagan to George H. W. Bush, it is difficult to find a leading Republican of the late twentieth century who did not express diffidence about civil rights at some point in the 1960s. Though not notably religious himself, Nixon also had the enthusiastic support of the evangelical community, enjoying a resurgence amid all of the Sodoms and Gomorrahs presented by the era. Many of these evangelical leaders, such as Jerry

Falwell, were outspoken critics of the civil rights movement. (Falwell called it "civil wrongs.")

The early months of Nixon's presidency nearly justified his supporters' faith in him. For all of its turmoil, America still had the capacity to astonish the world, and no single act of the 1960s may have inspired humanity more than the moon landing of July 20, 1969. Once again, Americans were rejecting precedent and venturing beyond the application of international law (in this case, the law of gravity), but few objected. The moon landing represented the best aspects of American idealism and know-how, at a time when the earth needed both badly.

Nixon made a great deal of progress on some important fronts. He concluded serious arms negotiations with the Soviet Union, brokered a period of détente, launched the all-volunteer army in 1973, and achieved the breakthrough for which he is most celebrated, the restoration of relations with China. All of these actions softened, though they did not entirely eliminate, the damage that Vietnam had inflicted on U.S. foreign policy. There, too, he made progress, agreeing to a cease-fire that essentially ended the serious involvement of the United States in the war, although it kept U.S. forces there until the collapse of South Vietnam in 1975.

But over time, something about the Nixon administration's language—perhaps the combination of Henry Kissinger's European style of diplomacy and Nixon's naked craftiness—struck observers as jarring. Kissinger was a lifelong admirer of Metternich, the great architect of European diplomacy. It would have been difficult to choose a hero less likely for Americans to latch on to—Metternich, after all, was the principal architect of the Holy Alliance, the great enemy that the Monroe Doctrine was designed to counter. Likewise, Nixon's refusal to speak in the reassuring language of Wilsonian morality, while honest, also left him open to charges of conducting a foreign policy that was amoral at best. Those charges, ultimately, proved to be quite true. He enraged Americans already angry over the Vietnam War when it was revealed that he had secretly bombed Cambodia, a neutral nation, and ordered the falsification of air force records to pretend that he had not done so. "Operation Menu" was later an article of impeachment, and contributed to the destabilization of a country that saw 1.7 million people killed through genocide.

For all his legendary foreign policy expertise, and for all the dramatic breakthroughs that he engineered, Nixon also pursued a number of cynical policies, favoring dictators and military strongmen, that hardly seemed likely to advance American ideals in the world. Over time, history, aided by the tape recorder, has revealed how precarious Nixon's commitment to genuine democracy was. His administration was implicated in the overthrow of yet another South American leader with leftist leanings, Salvador Allende, who had been elected president of Chile in 1970, despite aggressive CIA efforts to turn the election to another candidate. (Allende died in still-mysterious circumstances in September 1973.) The more information that comes out, the deeper that implication seems to be. Again, Latin American moderates were radicalized against the United States. Kissinger's lame justification was, "In the Eisenhower period, we would be heroes."

As the Watergate scandal paralyzed the U.S. government, it became clear that it was a foreign policy crisis in addition to everything else. For it eroded further whatever authority the White House had to speak out on the spread of freedom around the world and weakened Nixon to the point where he was more or less incapacitated by the fall of 1973, a year before he resigned. It is fortunate that the opening of China came when it did—later might have been too late.

One could argue that the entire mess stemmed from Nixon's obsessive desire to control the way that America's story was told to the world. For at the start of it all was the Nixon administration's hysterical response to the release of the Pentagon Papers, the secret history of the government's deliberations over Vietnam, going back to Ho Chi Minh's first letters at the end of the Second World War. The Pentagon Papers had been compiled by Robert McNamara and kept classified. One of the few who had seen them was a former Pentagon staffer, Daniel Ellsberg, who was shocked by the difference between the cynical way the government talked in private about its overseas business, more or less expecting the Vietnam effort to fail from the beginning, and the idealistic way it proclaimed its purposes in public. So in a way, Watergate can be traced to precisely a problem that I have been trying to address in this book—the disconnect between the ways Americans talk about the world and the way that they truly enter into it. Nixon did not want that disconnect to see the light of day. And so he entered a dark night of moral blindness, beginning with the decision to form a clandestine White House organization to deliberately violate the most sacred civil liberties in the interest of protecting the president.

The White House Special Investigations Unit, or Plumbers (their slogan: "We Stop Leaks"), was not a group of democracy activists. Their number included E. Howard Hunt, a veteran of the CIA who had been directly involved with the Guatemalan coup of 1954 and the Bay of Pigs, and G. Gordon Liddy, a former FBI agent who nicknamed the Plumbers "Odessa" (Organization Directed to Eliminate the Subversion of the Secrets of the Administration) because he was fascinated by the Nazi group of that name. That background was not exactly a ringing endorsement of freedom. The amateurish burglary of the Democratic Party's National Committee offices in Washington's Watergate Hotel was the logical consequence of years of covert overreach. Arguably, it set in motion the most successful regime change ever initiated by the Nixon administration.

After Vietnam and Watergate, enough was enough. Congress restrained Nixon with the War Powers Act of 1973, which prevented him and his successors from fighting without congressional consent. Nor were the Plumbers the worst of it. Private White House tapes revealed Nixon to be the most cynical practitioner of politics imaginable, contemptuous of religious and racial minorities, dismissive of those who dared to criticize him, and utterly opposed to the constitutional checks and balances created by the founders—the essence of our liberties. Throughout the congressional deliberations leading up to what would have been his impeachment, his argument was that of a king, asserting monarchical privileges from a republic ill-disposed to grant them.

When the Vietnam War finally ended in April 1975, amid heartrending scenes of Vietnamese trying to flee the U.S. embassy by helicopter, Nixon was no longer the president, having made his own helicopter escape eight months earlier. A certain image of the United States died that day—as the nation that could not lose in battle, and the nation that would never abandon its ideals. But we had obviously abandoned some of those ideals well before we abandoned Vietnam. And perhaps by losing our first war, as we surely did in Vietnam, Americans had taken an important step toward regaining a more realistic kind of moral authority. For now there was not the slightest doubt that we were, for all of our astounding capabilities, eminently human.

CHAPTER ELEVEN

MORNING IN AMERICA

CARTER

It would be difficult to find two presidents more different, on the surface, than Jimmy Carter and Ronald Reagan. One was said to be weak on foreign policy, despite knowing more about military matters, arguably, than any other president since Eisenhower. The other is perceived to have been so strong that he won the Cold War single-handedly, despite the inconvenient fact that the Cold War had not ended when he left office, and many Republicans were furious at him for making too many concessions to the Soviet Union in his final doddering years.

The need to claim "victory," while deeply rooted, has distorted the need to explore what truly happened as the Cold War neared its end. Certainly, Reagan's tough rhetoric and defense spending played a vital role in hastening that moment, although it's rather unsatisfying to claim that we simply outpurchased our enemies into submission. But Carter's unrelenting emphasis on human rights, combined with the Helsinki Accords (negotiated during Gerald Ford's brief presidency), also went a long way to destroy the fear that controlled the Soviet Union, and therefore all that the Soviet Union controlled. Reagan's "morning in America" began in some ways before his presidency, with several cheering developments in the immediate wake of Nixon's resignation and the collapse of South Vietnam. It is always darkest just before the dawn.

The final months of the Nixon presidency were a disaster for the Cold War mind-set, destroying every shred of credibility that a number of credible arguments still possessed, simply because Nixon was associated with them. The election to Congress of a young and very Democratic majority in 1974 accelerated the desire for change, a desire that only increased with the tragic final scenes in Saigon.

Still, we Americans have an amazing capacity to survive both the criticisms of our enemies and the damage we inflict upon ourselves. One of the many results of the 1974 Democratic rout in the elections was a new majority that wanted to clean house of the secret actors who had undercut American ideals in their pursuit of privately defined national security interests. In 1975, a new Senate committee began to investigate the excesses of the FBI and the CIA over the previous decades. Chaired by Frank Church of Idaho, it produced a remarkable litany of the misdeeds that had been performed in the name of the United States of America. Senator Church concluded that American intelligence agencies had become "rogue elephants" trampling over the rights of the American people, to say nothing of their conduct abroad. Reviewing American-initiated assassination attempts on foreign leaders, the Church Committee concluded them "aberrations" that "do not reflect the ideals which have given the people of this country and of the world hope for a better, fuller, fairer life." In 1978, Congress would try to rein in the agencies with the Foreign Intelligence Surveillance Act, which required warrants for domestic surveillance.

The media also provided new information. In late 1974, *The New York Times* revealed the existence of the "family jewels," a secret CIA history of the illegal acts it had performed on behalf of democracy since its inception—assassinations of foreign leaders, coup attempts, domestic surveillance, and other acts of subterfuge. The misdeeds were utterly bipartisan and may have been more pronounced under Democratic than Republican administrations. Either way, they shook all Americans.

The resulting pressure exerted a healthy influence on the way the United States conducted foreign policy. Gerald Ford continued the arms negotiations of his predecessor and generally defused tensions abroad, just as he did at home. He was so successful, in fact, that a rogue group inside his government began to drum up anxieties that the Soviet Union was far stronger than it was. "Team B," as it was called, was appointed by CIA director George H. W. Bush and concentrated the energies of a group of hawkish intellectuals, later to be known as neocons. Most of their conclusions were inaccurate, but they operated in a world of such monkishness and stealth that it remains difficult to debate their findings.

In 1975, the Helsinki Accords were signed by many nations, among them the United States and the Soviet Union. Included in the accords were a number of sentiments that seemed to have come straight from the textbook of Woodrow Wilson, including self-determination, freedom of expression, and obedience to international law. But this time the impetus for the accords came from Canadians and Europeans, not Americans. Still, the Ford administration approved the document, and miraculously, so did the Soviets. This treaty, which the Soviets desperately wanted in order to confirm the boundaries they had claimed since World War Two, included clear articulations of basic human rights for all Russians to read. It would prove to be a watershed, legitimizing forms of dissent that had been suppressed for decades, and opening up the Soviet Union to the kinds of criticism that, unlike a nuclear attack, it could not withstand. Woodrow Wilson's wimpy idealism was not so wimpy after all—it just had a long time-delay mechanism.

In this climate, it made sense that a purer idealist than usual would be elected president of the United States, and Jimmy Carter lived up to his billing as a man of character. A striking aspect of American history is how many idealists have come from the South, even if some of our least idealistic history has taken place there. Carter, a graduate of the Naval Academy, would likely have commanded a nuclear submarine if his father's death had not forced him to return to Georgia and take over the family business. In Georgia, he entered local politics, eventually winning the governorship in 1970. While conservative in many ways, and a devout Baptist, Carter was caught up in the winds of reform that swept across the country in the wake of Watergate and entered the presidential contest as a distant long shot. His ultimate victory proceeded in no small degree from his calming way of speaking about the moral responsibility of Americans—a rejoinder to both Nixon's amorality and Johnson's bloated ambitions. That many voters could hear religious undertones, even beneath arguments to the left of center, did not hurt his chances a bit.

Carter did not have extensive foreign policy experience when he entered office, with the possible exception of a UFO he claimed to have seen outside a VFW hall in Georgia in 1969. But he had a knack for saying the things that Americans wanted to hear in a chastened atmosphere. His inaugural offered the most modest projection of American power in many generations when he stated, "We have learned that more is not necessarily better, that even our great nation has its recognized limits, and that we can neither answer all questions nor solve all problems."

Given his Christian background, his experience fighting segregation in the South, and his legitimate claim to have served on the front lines of the Cold War, it made sense that he would begin to talk about human rights behind the Iron Curtain. What came as a surprise is how effective that talk would prove to be. Not only did Carter's words encourage activists around the globe, they went a considerable distance to restore America's shattered reputation for moral leadership in the world.

A few months into his presidency, Carter stated his new vision for American foreign policy in a commencement speech at Notre Dame. It was a breath of fresh air for a nation tired of cynical politics. Carter's point, which few could disagree with, was that the foreign policy of the United States should somehow connect with "our essential character as a nation." He also made the revolutionary argument that no policy could stand up to scrutiny for long if the American people did not both support it and, "for a change," understand it. Carter's disquisition seemed to take on the gray tones of the Cold War as well as the darker moments of Vietnam and Watergate: "For too many years, we've been willing to adopt the flawed and erroneous principles and tactics of our adversaries, sometimes abandoning our own values for theirs. We've fought fire with fire, never thinking that fire is better quenched with water." Nor did he stop there. In unflinching language, he called Vietnam "a profound moral crisis, sapping worldwide faith in our own policy and our system of life, a crisis of confidence made even more grave by the covert pessimism of some of our leaders."

He understood that the solution to these crises, promulgated in the name of freedom, was simply more freedom—but a freedom defined better, through clear rights, acceptance of diversity, and a pragmatic understanding that the world "will always be imperfect." Rigid moral maxims would not work in such a world, and neither would cold calculations of national interest. Rather, America's leaders should keep the discussion of freedom alive around the world, because "words are action," and Americans are good at forcing change through the eloquent statement of ideals.

In many ways Carter fulfilled that promise. No president ever worked harder to build peace in the Middle East, and his efforts toward the Camp David agreements between Israel and Egypt earned him worldwide acclaim. He criticized the racism of South Africa's apartheid regime, which previous presidents had tolerated because of Cold War pressures. He worked to lower nuclear tensions with the Soviet Union, while maintaining American defenses. And his repeated invocation of human rights had a ripple effect around the world, particularly in Eastern Europe, where events were unfolding rapidly, thanks to agitation by Polish steelworkers and the fortuitous selection of a Polish pope, whose visit to Poland in 1979 set off reactions that the communist government could not control.

But, needless to add, that is not the entire picture. The earnest expression of idealism is always followed by a healthy reality check, and Carter received more than his allotted share. Two events in particular stood out during his solitary term: the 1979 Iranian Revolution, which included the takeover of the U.S. embassy by hostile students, and the 1980 Soviet invasion of Afghanistan. Both events had a long background and left an equally long legacy.

The Iranian Revolution stemmed from decades of misrule by the Shah, and the widespread perception that his government was dominated by corrupt, pro-Western interests. The memory of the 1953 coup that had removed Mossadegh had been like a slow-burning ember through all of those years and had deepened as Iranians suffered from various internal problems, ranging from poorly distributed oil revenues to badly managed relations with Shi'a clergy. Carter may have accelerated the Revolution inadvertently by putting pressure on the Shah to support human rights, which led the Shah to release some political prisoners who added to the volatility of the moment. In 1979, the Shah fled the country, and his archrival, the Ayatollah Khomeini, returned from exile, leading to a radical form of Islamic government and a revolution that seemed to echo certain aspects of the American Revolution (it opposed corruption, colonialism, and the way great-power diplomacy was conducted). Interestingly, the new Iran was as anti-Soviet as it was anti-American, which was easy to forget as the ayatollah denounced the United States as "the great Satan," a term that was considerably different from the way Americans were used to being described. Iranian-American relations collapsed completely when the United States admitted the Shah for medical treatment in the fall, and students took over the U.S. embassy in Tehran, holding more than sixty employees hostage for 444 days. This may have been the worst insult ever inflicted upon American diplomacy, and led to Carter's defeat in the 1980 election.

But history had one last trick up its sleeve for the idealistic president. In December 1979, the Soviet Union returned to its tactics of old when it sent troops into Afghanistan to quell a revolt—in this case, another Islamic movement. As usual, the stated intent was to "liberate" the people of Aghanistan. The result, nine brutal years later, was that Afghan fighters liberated themselves from Russian influence. Carter's foreign policy team, including the CIA, was deeply involved in supporting the resistance movement from the beginning. To an extent, this tactical victory in the Cold War would alleviate some of the sting of the Iran disaster. But it would be difficult to call it a ringing success for the United States, for the Afghan resistance included Osama bin Laden and the other founders of what would become Al Qaeda. Furthermore, the bitterness of the struggles in the Middle East and neighboring regions was forcing policy-makers to rethink their priorities. For decades now, the Soviet Union and the United States had been engaged in a mortal contest, measuring victory in every category they could find. Now, in the aftermath of Iran and Afghanistan, they could reflect on which nation had been more clueless in its approach to the broad swath of the earth that followed Islam. Like so much of the Cold War, that contest was too close to call.

REAGAN

> We raised a banner of bold colors—no pale pastels. We proclaimed a dream of America that would be a shining city on a hill.
>
> —Ronald Reagan, 1984

The election of 1980 was inevitably a referendum on Jimmy Carter's foreign policy, and Carter, for all of his early promise, was found wanting. That result was attributable in some ways to bad luck, in some ways to political mistakes, and in a large degree to the extraordinary political appeal of his challenger, Ronald Reagan. Reagan was the antidote to Carter just as surely as Carter was the antidote to Ford and Nixon. After Carter tested the patience of the electorate with his penchant for self-criticism, Americans hungered for a more robust way of talking about the world (and their place in it). Reagan had an arsenal of words ready for them. With an engaging manner, a mellifluous voice, and an unflinching belief in the superiority of American institutions, Reagan rode American discontent to overwhelming victory in 1980.

As several biographers have complained, it is difficult to know who Reagan exactly was. It is simplistic to call this former FDR Democrat a conservative, though he remains a saint to the conservative movement—more so now than he did when he was president. He could certainly speak that language, but he was also skilled at calming tensions when he needed to, and at times his nostalgic bath of optimism made him seem less like a president of the 1980s and more like a radio announcer of the 1930s—which he had been. The journalist Frances FitzGerald wrote, "The national mythology is no dull centrist amalgam, but rather a sparkling collection of elements, which, if arrayed on a spectrum, could appeal to the political right, center or left. His range and suppleness as a politician came from his ability to move through that spectrum, combining and recombining the elements at will."

After all the disappointments of the late Carter presidency, Reagan's ease in asserting the classic verities of American power was greatly reassuring. The United States was simply the greatest force for good in the world, and the greatest military force as well, and the world would ultimately bend to those realities. There is a great virtue to simplicity, and Reagan's message, for all of its repetition, assuaged Americans who still felt anxious over the serial disappointments of Vietnam, Watergate, and Iran.

Reagan's message also clearly drew from precedents in both recent and not-so-recent history. To a wonderful extent, it included the bromides he had effortlessly picked up throughout a remarkable life as a young New Dealer, a Hollywood actor in the 1940s, and a pitchman for General Electric in the 1950s. These included the comforting asides that a veteran actor can effortlessly make, and some of the more ancient language woven into the American DNA—a particular fondness, for example, for John Winthrop's city upon a hill. Reagan used that line many times, adding the word *shining* for good effect.

Clearly, Reagan was inspired by a most powerful sense of American history, a presence in his life that was intense, immediate, and mystical. While drawing different conclusions, he regarded the founding in much the way that Woodrow Wilson did, or Abraham Lincoln, or Walt Whitman—as a unique moment in the history of the human species, not entirely unlike the Nativity, that had created a model for how people should live. He returned to that theme over and over in his long career as a speaker, re-creating the founding in rhapsodic language that does not entirely comport with his hawkish image. As president, Reagan would often joke about a conversation he had had with a founder—Jefferson, usually—but in ways that were profound and personal, he *was* communing with them. In 1974, he said, "We cannot escape our destiny, nor should we try to do so. The leadership of the free world was thrust upon us two centuries ago in that little hall of Philadelphia." It might have come as a surprise to many of the founders, or to Louis XVI or George III, that the United States had become the leader of the free world in 1776, but what matters more is that Reagan believed it, and believed it intensely.

Reagan also spoke a darker language, specifically crafted to appeal to the right wing of the Republican Party, which he had inhabited at least as far back as his political breakthrough, a televised speech he gave on behalf of Barry Goldwater in 1964. In fact, he had been speaking in these accents well before that. Reagan joked about his age to great effect, but it is striking to remember how old he truly was. In the first of several memoirs that he wrote, *Where's the Rest of Me?* (1965), he remembered the chilling effect of World War One upon his small-town utopia. He included a vivid and terrifying memory of the armistice celebrations, seen through a seven-year-old's eyes: "The parades, the torches, the bands, the shoutings and drunks, the burning of Kaiser Bill in effigy created in me an uneasy feeling of a world outside my own." From that moment forward, foreign policy seemed a slightly unpleasant place for Ronald Reagan, and he began to divide the world into halves, the shining city and the fiery pit.

It is surprising to reread some of his early writings and speeches and to see that someone who would become famous for talking about the morning spent so much time describing the stark high-noon differences between light and darkness. His messages were not always overt, but now and then a strident thought would emerge, flavoring his thinking like a red-hot chili pepper accidentally tossed into a salad. His first memoir includes one amusing anecdote after another about his charmed life, but then turns apoplectic when it awkwardly confronts the specter of communism. Yet unlike Richard Nixon, who understood clearly the military and political threat emanating from Moscow and Beijing, Reagan's "communism" was not Russian or Chinese at all—it was the insidious form of leftist thinking that he had encountered inside Hollywood, as the head of the Screen Actors Guild. There was almost no mention of any Cold War scenario whatsoever.

That slightly odd vision of the world, an unpleasant nightmare emanating from this most pleasant dreamer, was repeated in speech after speech. In 1952, at exactly the moment his film career and first marriage were foundering, he began to speak out against the unspeakable evil. In a commencement address that year at the University of Missouri, he told the students that America was less a place than an idea, buried "deep in the souls of man since man started his long trail from the swamps" (a passage that will not be cited by opponents of evolution). What was that idea?

> It is nothing but the inherent love of freedom in each one of us, and the great ideological struggle that we find ourselves engaged in today . . . It's the same old battle. We met it under the name of Hitlerism; we met it under the name of Kaiserism; and we have met it back through the ages in the name of every conqueror that has ever set upon a course of establishing his rule over mankind. It is simply the idea, the basis of this country and of our religion, the idea of the dignity of man, the idea that deep within the heart of each one of us is something so God-like and precious that no individual or group has a right to impose his or its will upon the people, that no group can decide for the people what is good for the people so well as they can decide for themselves.

The years went by, but it was always high noon. In 1961, before the Phoenix Chamber of Commerce, he predicted, "By 1970 the world will be all slave or all free." Three years later, he gave the speech on behalf of Barry Goldwater that launched his national career. He repeated many of Goldwater's doomsday scenarios, but in a context that seemed more relaxed. He began his remarks by worrying that America was in peril of losing its freedom, and that we were approaching "the last stand on earth." But through the balm of anecdotes, humor, and an easy immersion in American history, he managed to avoid Goldwater's clenched-jaw defense of extremism. In an impressive display of rhetorical dexterity, his peroration cited FDR, Lincoln, and the book of Revelation simultaneously: "You and I have a rendez-vous with destiny. We will preserve for our children this, the last best hope of man on earth, or we will sentence them to take the last step into a thousand years of darkness."

That was quite a choice. That darkness, of course, was the Soviet half of the earth, while the American side perpetually faced the sun. Reagan's famous aside about bombing the Soviet Union, made in jest into a live microphone in 1984, echoed Barry Goldwater's famous aspiration to lob a nuclear bomb into the men's room of the Kremlin. Another famous description, the "evil empire," which Reagan first tried out in a 1983 speech to evangelicals, effortlessly captured in two short words what Americans had been opposed to for centuries. At the time, both words were richly resonant for followers of the right. *Evil* was particularly so, drawing its force not only from evangelical language in the Bible, but from its heated use in right-wing publications, where it was applied as often to domestic enemies (Earl Warren, Martin Luther King Jr.) as it was to Russia and China. Reagan's early traffic with John Birch members was significant; he helped to raise funds for them, joined boards and organizations overflowing with them, and received extensive support from segregationist governors of the South. No racist language can be found in Reagan's speeches, and his early memoir contained a moving account of playing football with an African-American teammate; but at a time of intense debate in the United States over freedom and its availability to all citizens, Reagan was firmly planted in the camp that opposed it.

Reagan's actual views about foreign policy were harder to tease out because he did not express them often, except to denounce communism and to express his strong hope that America would not change in any way. In his rhetoric, Russia was more a counterpole—the antipode of liberty—than a recognizable entity unto itself. If not quite Antichrist, then it represented a source of dark energy that needed to be constantly resisted, in all parts of the world. His advisers considered it a major victory when they got him to stop using the phrase *totalitarian ant heap* to describe the Soviet Union.

One wonders how this genial man could form such a consuming hatred, and the answers are not easy to find, but signs of a fear of apocalypse were present in his life from a young age. Even if he was not conventionally observant, his mother, Nelle, believed deeply in the literal message of the Bible. Reagan seemed to as well, at times. When Israel bombed Iraq in 1981, he thought Armageddon might be near; after the 1986 Soviet nuclear reactor meltdown at Chernobyl, he told a journalist that he believed it to be the opening of the seventh seal in Revelation. His lifelong obsession with building a missile shield for the United States seems in many ways to have proceeded from his desire to protect Americans from apocalypse—although the form that protection was to take may have emanated from his experience acting in the 1940 film *Murder in the Air*, in which he plays an American spy trying to develop a secret weapon called an Inertia Protector that will shoot down enemy aircraft.

This bipolar view of the world was not apparently based on personal experience. Unlike other Cold Warriors—John F. Kennedy and Richard Nixon, for example—Reagan was not especially exposed to the rest of the world in the years that he was shaping his political career. When he became governor of California in 1967, he had been abroad once in his life, in 1947, when he made a movie in England. But seeing the world was in no way a requirement for his supporters, who subscribed to predictable far-right opinions about foreign policy—namely, that the loss of China was a travesty managed by State Department elites, that Chiang Kai-shek should be "unleashed," that Douglas MacArthur had been right to want to bomb China, that Europe and the UN were effete and irrelevant, and that the Soviet Union was evil incarnate. Reagan's great skill was to hint at these beliefs without quite bringing them to their conclusion, making his vision palatable to larger numbers of people than those who might agree that bombing the Soviet Union and China were wise policies, or who wanted to reverse the civil rights movement and resegregate America.

When he ran for president in 1976 to Ford's right, and then in 1980 as the nominee, his speeches stressed many of the concerns of the far right: its disdain for diplomacy, treaties, arms control, and the UN; its conviction that freedom was eroding, as Reagan said in his 1976 convention speech; and its obsession with Cuba and Central America (famously, Reagan accused Ford of wanting to give away the Panama Canal, insisting, "We bought it, we paid for it, it's ours, and we're going to keep it!"). Reagan failed to see the significance of the Helsinki Accords (which he hated) and pushed for "morality" planks in the GOP, calling for a theatrical end to tyranny, without quite going into details.

Through both his outbursts and his self-restraint, he became a formidable leader of the Republican Party and was easily elected. Needless to add, freedom and tyranny were essential notions in his oratory. His presidency was an orgy of liberty; it would be impossible to cite how many times the word was used in his speeches. But liberty means different things to different people, and Reagan's version of freedom seemed to offer more to some groups than to others. Notoriously, he launched his 1980 campaign with a speech defending states' rights in the tiny hamlet of Philadelphia, Mississippi—not exactly the city of brotherly love, but the site of the sickening murder of three civil rights workers in 1964. Throughout his 1980 campaign, he was helped by former segregationists in the South, such as George Wallace, Jerry Falwell, and Jesse Helms, and the rise of the Republican Party in the 1980s depended heavily on the former Democrats who had been alienated by the civil rights movement. These shadows never quite disappeared during his presidency—notably, he opposed naming a holiday after Martin Luther King Jr., declared Jefferson Davis his hero, and expressed sympathy for such institutions as Bob Jones University, which banned interracial dating. As they listened to his speeches about sending freedom around the world, many felt that he should begin right here at home.

The civil rights movement was over, but in the 1980s there was still a most visible way to measure one's commitment to building freedom in the world. For decades, South Africa had belligerently resisted the tidal pull away from racism, and while some American politicians had gone there in person (famously, Robert Kennedy), many refused to acknowledge this uncomfortable bit of reality. Apartheid was a mockery of freedom—it was a worse form of state-sanctioned racism than the preintegration South had inflicted upon American citizens. It was the simplest thing in the world to denounce "tyranny" and support "freedom," but quite another to use America's vast influence toward the admittedly difficult but eminently worthy cause of declaring apartheid unacceptable.

Unfortunately, the Reagan administration failed this test of freedom, and failed it badly, offering material and verbal support for the white regime throughout his tenure. In an interesting reversal of the religious rhetoric that the conservative movement found appealing, Bishop Desmond Tutu labeled Reagan's policy "immoral, evil, and totally un-Christian." Speaking before Congress, he continued, inverting all of the polarities, and giving the black-and-white language of the right a peculiar twist: "You are either for or against apartheid and not by rhetoric. You are either in favor of evil or you are in favor of good. You are either on the side of the oppressed or on the side of the oppressor. You can't be neutral."

South Africa was not the only place where observers found soft spots in Reagan's rhetoric. Idealism also bumped into hard reality in Central America, where a number of local guerrilla movements were undermining governments, with plenty of atrocities on all sides. The movements were confusing enough without the problem that they all, left and right, were for "freedom" and against "tyranny." Despite the rhetoric, this was not a shining moment for American democracy. Through various forms of intervention, we supported corrupt oligarchs who ran their governments with impunity, in many cases (Guatemala, for example) murdering hundreds of thousands of civilians with death squads. By supporting them and failing to heed the legitimate aspirations of the people, we were failing in our self-proclaimed mission. It should be added that there was no easy solution, and that the opponents of these regimes could also be brutal, but still, it was sickening to contemplate that American aid was propping up petty dictators in the name of freedom.

Perhaps the worst scandal was the Iran-contra mess, which involved nearly every taboo imaginable: executive overreach, lying to Congress, money-laundering, drug lords, Mafia kingpins, and dealing with terrorists while proclaiming that we would not. It was as if the lessons of Vietnam, Watergate, and the Church Committee had never happened. Many of the details of Iran-contra remain unknown. Among other setbacks, it empowered the Iranian government in particular (to whom we provided military hardware) and terrorists around the world, who now understood that the words of a president did not mean what they said. The most depressing aspect was the smallness of the goal in comparison to the magnitude of the crimes—the restoration of an oligarchy in Nicaragua.

One could recite an endless litany of failures in any administration, but these were particularly acute because of the great stock Americans placed in President Reagan's words. And in truth, his language did achieve greatness at times. He was gifted with an instinctive understanding of what the American people wanted to hear. So many of his speeches struck the right chords with his audiences. His Notre Dame speech in 1981 called communism "a bizarre chapter in human history whose last pages are even now being written." His Westminster address to Parliament in 1982 proclaimed "a crusade for freedom that will engage the faith and fortitude of the next generation." His rousing speech to evangelical leaders in 1983—odd for its inclusion of Thomas Paine, our least conservative founder—was about the need to oppose evil, including the evils of racism. His speech at the centennial of the Statue of Liberty, in 1986, brought out all the themes he had been celebrating for forty years on the stump: "Call it mysticism if you will, I have always believed there was some divine providence that placed this great land here between the two great oceans, to be found by a special kind of people from every corner of the world, who had a special love for freedom."

If these flights of fancy perplexed liberals, they, too, were capable of misunderstanding history, including the particular defect of under-estimating Reagan. For all of his conservative rhetoric, and the real lapses in his extension of freedom, considerable progress occurred in the Reagan administration. His robust challenge to Soviet imperialism—his speech in Berlin, for example—empowered those who were fighting to weaken Soviet control over their lives. In what seemed like a paradox at times—but also sprang from his vision of America as a prelapsarian paradise not to be tampered with—Reagan also negotiated a series of impressive arms agreements.

But another component of his vision for the world was less utopian in practice, though it was deeply utopian in principle. Technology promised to enable him to make his theology part of U.S. policy by fashioning a missile shield to protect the United States from nuclear attack. The argument was and is deeply flawed, like the system itself, which to this day has not once succeeded in destroying a target in a test resembling battle conditions. Furthermore, it encourages new systems of attack—the building of extra missiles, for example—that hardly increase security. But despite these facts, it has received billions of dollars in funding over the years and remains an article of faith among its supporters.

Near the end of Reagan's term, he became much weaker, despite the transformation accelerating around the world. In Russia, Mikhail Gorbachev proved likewise an extraordinary agent of change. One of the most moving expressions of freedom, because it was so surprising, came not from the United States but from the Soviet leader. In a 1988 speech to the UN, he announced that the Soviet Union was reducing its military presence in Europe, adding, "Freedom of choice is . . . a universal principle, and it should know no exceptions."

But Reagan, weakened by Iran-contra and internal divisions in his White House, was a spectator for most of these events. In fact, much of the White House's control over foreign policy had been reined in by Congress, which was eager to assert its own ideas about freedom, especially after the Democrats won control of the Senate in 1986. In 1982, the Boland Amendment demanded that the United States stop trying to overthrow Nicaragua's government with CIA-funded contra rebels. In 1986, Congress overrode Reagan's veto to order the first meaningful American boycott of South African business, a huge step toward undermining the apartheid regime. In the wake of the scandals and convictions that followed Iran-contra, Reagan's foreign policy limped toward the finish line.

When the Reagan administration ended, these events were still in flux, which inconveniences the hagiographers who would like to argue that Reagan won the Cold War, and all by himself. But any honest assessment of Russia's remarkable changes in the late 1980s and early 1990s would have to find more reasons than that an American president spent a great deal of money on armaments. This article of conservative scripture relies on a most unusual theology—that Reagan taxed-and-spent them into submission. In fact, the Russian economy never collapsed at all. Credit belongs to many, including not only Reagan but Russia's courageous reformers, beginning with Mikhail Gorbachev, who renounced war while helping his fellow Russians take control of their government from the hard-liners. That Russian revolution, the second in a century, was hardly perfect—no revolution is. But in its way, it was an essential act of self-determination, and as such, another fulfillment of Thomas Paine's urge to begin the world anew.

BUSH I

Reagan's departure suggested to some that a phase of history had ended, if not all of history itself. But history has a way of trumping that sort of prediction. The election of Reagan's vice president, George Herbert Walker Bush, was a historical aberration in one sense—he was the first vice president elected since Martin Van Buren in 1836. But this one-term presidency was fated to generate considerable history on its own. At least five events of enormous moment happened during Bush's brief tenure: the crushing of student protests in Tiananmen Square (June 1989), the fall of the Berlin Wall (November 1989), the release of Nelson Mandela from prison (February 1990), the first Gulf War in Iraq (August 1990–February 1991), and the collapse of the Soviet Union (December 1991). Some of those events were more victorious than others. All had profound consequences.

Bush came to office with a stronger interest in foreign policy than his predecessor. In fact, he had a stronger interest than just about any of his predecessors. It would have been difficult to find a candidate more deeply entrenched in the foreign policy establishment, for Bush had variously served as director of the CIA, ambassador to the UN, and emissary to China—the only president who has ever served in any of those posts. That sort of inheritance was nearly enough to derail his candidacy, for the UN was nearly as radioactive to the far right as the CIA was to the far left. Keeping his own counsel, Bush sailed toward the center, with rewarding results. Despite what seemed to be ordinary political skills, and a profound aversion to eloquence, Bush evolved, survived, and even flourished in Washington's Darwinian environment.

Those adaptive skills had been evident from early adulthood, when he moved from the protective cocoon of his New England upbringing to the frontier of west Texas. The oil company that he helped to found in the 1950s, Zapata Oil,* allowed him full entry into the wide range of economic and political activities joining the United States and the Caribbean during that turbulent decade, as the U.S. government was selling its offshore drilling rights, and Zapata may have played a support role during the failed Bay of Pigs invasion (also known as Operation Zapata). Whether true or not, Zapata was acting out several earlier chapters of American history by testing the limits of American sovereignty in the Caribbean, and creating islands of its own to explore. Its breakthrough technology, cultivated in the mid-1950s, was the offshore oil rig, which allowed an enormous man-made island to suck oil out of the ocean floor, far from the continental United States. In fact, one of Zapata's star rigs was only forty miles north of Cuba.

From these oleaginous beginnings, Bush fashioned a promising political career, winning the Republican nomination for the Senate in 1964 (he lost the election), and then a seat in Congress in 1966. Generally, he weaved between the far right (he attacked Martin Luther King Jr. and the Nuclear Test Ban Treaty) and the not-so-vital Republican center. Eventually he expressed regret for his far-right positions, explaining that he needed them to get elected.

Unlike most politicians, for whom public speaking is as natural as breathing—and often just as interesting—Bush was not a gifted orator. But his career did not seem to suffer from his taciturnity, and in some ways it advanced his prospects. Certainly it helped him when he was director of central intelligence under Gerald Ford, and serving in other sensitive diplomatic posts. Not talking can be as important a talent as talking, and for a generation, American politicians had been promising the moon (literally). In some ways, Bush's relatively modest oratorical scope came as a breath of fresh air after the grandiloquent promises of Reagan.

That talent even came in handy during Bush's first year in the

*Zapata's name, by one of those quirks of fate that enliven the study of history, came from the Marlon Brando film *Viva Zapata!*, about the Mexican revolutionary Emiliano Zapata, who fought for liberty, by which he meant land rights for Mexico's underclass. That peculiar definition of liberty would not be of much interest to Zapata Oil.

White House, when he faced some of the deepest crises any American president had encountered in a generation. The year 1989, like 1956, showed both the remarkable power of America's example and some of its limitations. In May, Chinese students began to gather in Tiananmen Square, the historic center of Chinese imperial authority—in other words, a shrine to one of the most arbitrary and despotic powers on the earth, whether dynastic or communist. In that hugely symbolic location, the students began to demonstrate in favor of democracy, and even to erect a thirty-three-foot Styrofoam and papier-mâché statue that resembled the Statue of Liberty, called the Goddess of Democracy (or the Goddess of Liberty). Could anything have been calculated more effectively to move American hearts?

But unlike American history, which always seems to be tending toward a cathartic culmination, the result of the protests was not a triumph for anyone—certainly not the Chinese, whose image was sullied by their violent suppression of the dissent, but not the Americans, either, who never responded vigorously to this literal assault on democracy. When Chinese troops were called in to disperse the students, they did so with brutal efficiency, killing hundreds, perhaps thousands, and imprisoning and scattering the rest. The United States reacted with feeble expressions of protest. In its defense, there was little that anyone could do, and China resented even the mild protests registered by the Bush administration. But a more ringing affirmation of human rights would still have had a salutary effect and left a better lasting impression than the compliant silence of June 1989. Like Hungary in 1956, it was an agonizing moment for a nation that had prided itself on its ability to project democracy abroad.

Several months later, an equally momentous disruption occurred in another hot spot of the Cold War, with far better results. On November 9, the Berlin Wall fell—or technically, it became irrelevant, as East German authorities announced that their citizens could travel to West Berlin with impunity. And like that, the imperial reach of the Soviet Union crumbled. On Christmas Day, an American, Leonard Bernstein, led a concert of Beethoven's Ninth Symphony in Berlin, with musicians from both Germanys and other nations. Fittingly, the words of Schiller's "Ode to Joy" were changed to become an international "Ode to Freedom." For centuries, millennial thinkers had been predicting the great day that would initiate the new heaven and the new earth—this may have been as close as we are ever likely to get.

A new version of the domino theory ensued, as all the nations of the Eastern Bloc undid their communist history by quickly dismantling their governments and installing leaders who more honestly represented the aspirations of their people. The process had begun earlier that fall in Poland and Hungary; now it continued to include Czechoslovakia, Bulgaria, and Romania. For all intents and purposes, the Cold War—whose deepest tensions had often stemmed from proxy states rather than any expectation that either the Soviet Union or the United States would be invaded—was over.

But plenty of tensions in other parts of the world signaled that the ramifications of the Cold War, and the long-term patterns it had engendered, were not entirely concluded. The glow of good feelings most Americans felt as the Soviet bloc disintegrated was diminished by the U.S. invasion of Panama in December 1989, which was a relatively simple military maneuver but awakened many unpleasant memories in the region. Certainly there was little sympathy for Panama's dictator, Manuel Noriega, awash in drugs and corruption, but nations throughout Latin America were skeptical of the American claim that it was promoting democracy by sending in troops. The American argument was not helped by Noriega's being widely known as a former CIA informer, wallowing in the kind of right-wing brutality that had tainted so many earlier American interventions in the region. Once again, the secret activities of the U.S. government had compromised a legitimate foreign-policy goal.

In February 1990 the world was astonished to see another change that it never thought possible, when Nelson Mandela emerged from the jail cell where he had spent twenty-seven years to literally walk in the bright sunshine of human rights. Throughout his long incarceration, Mandela and the African National Congress had been branded as communists and terrorists, and now that those words held less terror, they also held far less effect. Few moments of the twentieth century symbolized more perfectly man's unquenchable desire to be free, and the force a single focused person can wield against an illegitimate authority.

The United States was not directly involved in the internal events that led to Mandela's release and the creation of South Africa's first democracy—in fact, prominent members of the Bush administration, including his secretary of defense, Dick Cheney, had voted against resolutions critical of apartheid. In the 587-page memoir he wrote with his national security adviser, Brent Scowcroft, Bush mentioned Nelson Mandela a grand total of zero times. But in a higher sense, America was deeply involved the day that Mandela walked free. For his search for freedom—a word he used movingly throughout his career—had begun with the inspiration afforded by Gandhi, who was himself inspired by Woodrow Wilson. We tend to think of Wilson's end as a crushing failure, simply because the U.S. Senate rejected the League of Nations. But in fact, we have never reached Wilson's end, because the immensely complex legacy of self-determination is still determining itself.

In many ways, Bush could not have been less Wilsonian. Certainly, he was no intellectual, and he tended to distrust eloquence and lofty idealism. Yet time and time again, the echoes and thoughts of Wilson reverberated throughout the drafty chambers of his speeches. Foremost among these was his prediction that "the dream of a new world order" would arise out of the collapse of the Soviet bloc. The only problem with this dream was that it bore only an occasional relationship to reality. As usual, the Middle East failed to fit into the new order. When Iraq's dictator, Saddam Hussein, committed the un-Wilsonian act of invading Kuwait in August 1990, Bush was in a bind. Not only was Hussein, deeply odious, a former U.S. and CIA client, but his invasion threw cold water on all of the idealism that had gushed forth in 1989 and 1990. The result was the most significant American military action since Vietnam.

Operation Desert Storm produced an impressive triumph of American arms that overwhelmed Saddam Hussein and forced him to retreat from Kuwait and agree to a number of humiliating concessions. But that positive result never sat well with certain segments of the American public, from the far left, discomforted by the pyrotechnics of American military might, to the far right, where the failure to take out Saddam rankled as deeply as the failure to bomb China during the Korean War. The New World Order was slouching toward Bethlehem, waiting to be born—but as Yeats had predicted, no one had any idea what this creature would actually look like.

Perhaps the most shocking denouement of all was the final collapse of the evil empire itself. After the inevitable internal shocks that followed the end of Soviet influence over Eastern Europe, the pressures on the old system became impossible to bear, and in December 1991 the patient was taken off life support. It was as if the dose of freedom administered when the Berlin Wall fell was a poison in the bloodstream that the Soviet system simply could not overcome. It was more or less exactly what Ronald Reagan had been predicting, and Kennedy and Truman, and most of the others as well. The Soviet Union now became, for a time, the Commonwealth of Independent States, a name that might well have been chosen by America's founding fathers.

In the book that he coauthored with President Bush, Scowcroft defined the end of the Cold War as September 12, 1990, the day the Soviet Union officially accepted the principle of a united Germany in NATO. That is a very specific statement, and historians love specifics. But it seems far too narrow when one is considering a period that covered half a century, and whose ramifications we continue to see long after the fact. Just as the Cold War began in the murk of Russian-American relations near the end of World War Two, so it continued well after the apparent cessation of hostilities. German unification was a tremendous achievement for U.S. foreign policy, and for Bush personally (many European leaders opposed the idea). But long after the Bush administration itself had ended up on history's ash heap, lingering aftershocks of the breakup of the old system continued.

CLINTON

If Nelson Mandela's walking free and the brave actions of young people in Beijing and Berlin had signaled a different kind of new world emerging than simplistic celebrants of "victory" in the Cold War had announced, then that impression gained strength with the appearance of a formidable young candidate for the presidency in 1992, and the shocking defeat of George Bush.

Bill Clinton was not, at first blush, a strong foreign policy candidate. Bush achieved a rare success in one of the debates with a joke that accused Clinton of securing most of his foreign policy experience at the

International House of Pancakes. But Clinton's strong emphasis on domestic topics distracted most commentators from his deep interest in the rest of the world, based on long experience as the governor of a Southern state wrestling with real issues from the collision of foreign and domestic policies, through trade, jobs, immigration, and a host of other concerns. An acute reading of history also persuaded him not only that Bush was beatable, but that the United States needed a new kind of president at this transitional moment. Shrewdly, Clinton understood that there was far more to U.S. foreign policy than the Cold War's endgame (essentially about Europe), and that Americans wanted a leader capable of articulating something inspiring to the rest of humanity beyond that the Soviet Union had ceased to be a threat.

In fact, Bush was vulnerable on a number of fronts. He had never been sensitive to the plight of poor Americans or the developing world and had both tolerated and even advanced the kind of racism that passed for normal politics in Texas as he was launching his career. That indifference was easy to overlook while it was hidden beneath the urgent problems of the Cold War contest, but it became more evident as the Soviet threat receded. Clinton understood far more intuitively that the world was racing toward a new and more inclusive identity, and that the problems of the developing world were relevant to the United States in a way that they had not been for a long time. Nor were these ideals simply "Wilsonian," by which most modern commentators would mean theoretical and toothless—they were part of a new way of describing the world that had deep relevance to the interests of the United States.

During the 1992 campaign, and for years afterward, an article of faith of the enemies of Bill Clinton was that his foreign policy was deeply flawed. To be sure, he had missteps in the early years of his presidency, such as the awkward intervention in Haiti, the failure of American troops to do much to alleviate the crisis in Somalia, and the ineffectiveness of U.S. efforts to remake the Russian economy. Those were not shining cities on a hill, and the failure to prevent genocide in Rwanda was a tragedy. But Clinton was, in his way, a most adept steward of American foreign policy. Even by conventional terms, he scored impressive successes, from the Balkans to Northern Ireland to the Middle East, where Clinton enjoyed an unusual rapport with both Israelis and Palestinians. Building on traditions going back to Jimmy Carter, and even to Theodore Roosevelt, Clinton used the bully pulpit to get deeply involved in peace negotiations between hostile parties of the Old World, with generally favorable results. That was a use of American power that the founders would have admired. His integration of economic concerns into foreign policy was also widely perceived as an improvement, allowing rapid intervention in financial crises in Mexico and Asia, and contributing toward the prosperity enjoyed during the 1990s.

It is too soon, still, to know how historians will interpret all of the events of the late twentieth century. The Clinton years could easily be seen as an interregnum between two Bushes, a sort of Weimar Republic period of optimism and democracy (but with a much better economy), sandwiched between two administrations more comfortable with force than words. Or it could be described as the beginning of a new time of its own—which is certainly how it felt at the time. But a third argument is possible: conceivably, one could claim that, for all their differences, the administrations of George H. W. Bush and Bill Clinton had a fair amount in common—a desire to moderate the extremes of the Reagan years, a commitment to build peace in the Middle East (Clinton's successes built on the work of Bush and his secretary of state James Baker), an interest in free trade and hemispheric alliances (NAFTA), a deepening of European alliances (NATO expansion), and certain nagging problems (Somalia, Iraq) that frustrated both as each pursued his own vision of the new order coming into existence.

Certainly, Clinton worked toward such an order, even if he did not use the phrase. In general, Clinton had little interest in the Cold War paradigms that had trapped American presidents for decades. With the end of the Soviet threat, he began to speak expansively about what America and the world might offer each other. To an extent, it was a vision of economic liberation, in the tradition of LBJ and FDR, offering all peoples of the world a chance to embrace democracy and free markets. It was also a chance to use new alliances to tackle new problems, such as environmental degradation and the rise of international terror organizations. Clinton spoke a language that had not been heard for some time—that of an altruistic America ready to help people make better lives for themselves. It was the America of Kennedy's Alliance for

Progress, and Truman's Point Four, and FDR's promise of freedom for all people willing to go out and make it happen for themselves. Clearly, Clinton would go to extraordinary lengths to build peace, as his pertinacity in Northern Ireland revealed, or his marathon sessions toward an agreement in the Middle East, which proved tantalizingly near in the final months of his administration. Nor did he shy away from the displays of force that make American idealism that much more persuasive. The Dayton Accords in Bosnia were ordained by American firepower as much as by hard-nosed diplomacy, and it took bombing campaigns in Serbia and Iraq to restrain dictators. But the world understood that this was power with a purpose, and throughout the 1990s, the United States was generally admired, both for its power and its restraint. As a minor participant in the Clinton administration, I realize that my perspective is hardly objective. But still, it seemed at the time—and it still seems, a decade later—as if the best of U.S. foreign policy was working and the worst was held in check.

Of course, as the world knows, there was never a shortage of problems in the post–Cold War world, yet the era from 1989 to 2001 was a time of remarkable progress for the United States in the world. It was the fullest realization of Franklin Roosevelt's vision (realism, idealism, and great alliances) since FDR himself had put it forward. Clinton also deserved credit for addressing some of the tensions in American foreign policy that had gone unaddressed for most of the Cold War, with its singular focus on the Soviet threat. He was particularly gifted at speaking of American aspirations to the vast developing world. To some extent, this was the result of personal diplomacy—Clinton went on more trips, and longer trips, to Africa and Latin America and Asia than any of his predecessors (by my count, a staggering 133 foreign trips in all). But it also stemmed from the world's conviction that this was an exponent of freedom who believed in liberty, properly defined. Clinton's entire career had been devoted to opposing racism and discrimination, and his own rise over economic determinism gave that message added relevance. Like FDR, he intuitively grasped that America's domestic freedoms and its ability to export democracy were linked. The world's peoples are not easily bamboozled. Nothing has ever better sold the American message of international democracy than a commitment to work out American's internal contradictions, including our dilemmas concerning full racial equality. Roosevelt said, "Freedom means the supremacy of human rights everywhere." Near the Berlin Wall, John F. Kennedy insisted, "Freedom is indivisible, and when one man is enslaved, all are not free." Clinton did a lot to put meaning into those words, far from Newfoundland and Berlin, in places like Soweto and Guatemala and Hyderabad.

But if Clinton went far to repair the gap between America's stated ideals and its performance, he could not entirely solve America's own contradictions. A disturbing characteristic of the ebullient Clinton years was the terrible hatred—or set of hatreds—that roiled beneath the surface of an otherwise contented republic at the peak of its influence. For reasons that only occasionally had to do with foreign policy, homegrown terrorists attacked the government—and by extension, the American people themselves—at places far from foreign battlefields. In Waco, Texas, a cult of believers in the book of Revelation had a violent standoff with FBI agents. Their leader, David Koresh, called the U.S. government "Babylon" and spoke in the codes of the Last Things; a federal agent who overheard Koresh talking about the seven seals mistakenly wondered why there were performing animals in the compound. In Oklahoma City, a federal building was bombed, killing 168 people, the deadliest act of terrorism on U.S. soil before September 11, 2001. The bombers were retaliating against the government for its previous raids on cultists in Waco and Ruby Ridge, Idaho. A T-shirt worn by the principal planner, Timothy McVeigh, quoted Thomas Jefferson: "The tree of liberty must be refreshed from time to time with the blood of patriots and tyrants." History is never so dangerous as when it is selectively adopted.

A subtler form of criticism was the perpetual assault on Clinton and his foreign policy led by political opponents throughout his presidency. If a bipartisan consensus to unite behind a president's foreign policy had been a feature of much (though certainly not all) of the Cold War, then that truce was no longer apparent during the Clinton years. Throughout his presidency, Republicans were united in their opposition to any initiative proposed by Clinton, from Bosnia (which the Bush administration had avoided resolving), to his strenuous efforts in the Middle East, to his trips abroad (especially to Africa, which struck Republican leaders as unworthy of a presidential visit), to Kosovo, to

Clinton's military efforts to restrain terrorists such as Osama bin Laden and dictators such as Saddam Hussein. When Newt Gingrich wrote his "Contract with America," leading the GOP to victory in 1994, only a single plank had to do with foreign policy, and that was a call for a missile shield. It was as if House Republicans were living inside a bubble.

In the same breath the Republican opposition would criticize military intervention in some places while it was urging military action on a much grander scale in others. One group in particular had a vaguely millennial name: The Project for a New American Century. Composed of hawkish former members of the Bush, Reagan, Ford, and Nixon administrations, it released a widely publicized letter in January 1998 urging Clinton to conduct a ground war in Iraq to depose Saddam Hussein. Curiously, many of the signers of the letter (such as former secretaries of defense Richard Cheney and Donald Rumsfeld) had not availed themselves of the opportunity to remove Hussein when they had had much better opportunities to do so, but that degree of historical parsing struck most observers as unnecessary at the time. In fact, even more parsing might have been useful—the chief instigators of the letter, including Cheney, Rumsfeld, and other leading neocons, were the same Washington insiders who had built their early careers on overstating the Soviet threat to the United States in the 1970s. These habits of exaggeration would resurface.

Of course, it is a sacred American right to criticize presidents and their foreign policy. But what placed this particular vein of criticism apart from more traditional forms was its venom, its reflexiveness (to oppose Clinton was ipso facto correct), and its connection to darker currents flowing through American political life, traceable to the hatreds unleashed in the 1950s. The Project for a New American Century was paid for by foundations with deep ties to the John Birch Society, the Goldwater campaign of 1964, and the historically twinned causes of shrill anticommunism and racism. Many of those same foundations had also paid for the so-called Arkansas Project, an attempt to generate as much negative publicity as possible about Clinton, in effect preventing him from doing his job for the American people. Even in his undesired role as a lightning rod for conservative hatred, Clinton was immersed in residual Cold War tensions that went all the way back to its origins—origins so distant that they preceded Clinton himself, the first president born after the Cold War began.

Of course, occasional tremors of the traditional Cold War occurred even to the end of the Clinton administration. Russia's historic, convulsive reinvention of itself took many years to accomplish, if indeed it is finished, and there were still moments of confrontation. Throughout the Kosovo crisis, one of the biggest challenges was how to alleviate Russian frustrations that NATO was fighting in its backyard, a situation that Russia occasionally protested by sending troops menacingly close to Americans. On one day in particular—June 12, 1999—the onset of hostilities briefly appeared to be possible as Russian troops raced toward Kosovo in advance of NATO.

But that crisis passed, and most of the others as well. After Clinton's eight years—years that felt so busy every day that it was difficult to look at them with a long-term perspective—the Cold War was truly a thing of the past. There would always be problems in the world, and in the United States, but to a remarkable degree the plan floated off Newfoundland by Franklin Roosevelt and Winston Churchill had proved to be seaworthy.

Not far from the National Archives, where the great charters of freedom are preserved in something like perpetuity, the representatives of the NATO nations gathered to celebrate the alliance's fiftieth anniversary in 1999. Although NATO was at war for the first time in its history, the mood was upbeat, not only because victory in Kosovo was expected any day, but because so much of history had turned out the way NATO's founders had hoped it would. *Upbeat* is too small a word—tremendous optimism was in the room, because for once in European-American history, the predictors of doom had turned out to be wrong. With the end of the Cold War, who knew what limits there would be to human achievement in the years ahead?

Not long after that summit, after nearly a thousand years of inaccurate predictions, the millennium finally arrived, right on time. For generations, Americans had tried to accelerate its arrival, with breathless predictions, mountaintop revels, and forced readings of the book of Revelation. As usual, God proved to be much wiser than the human beings who claim to speak in His name. In the end, the United States and the rest of the world reached the millennium at exactly the same time. Ultimately, we achieved it in the most old-fashioned and unexpected way of all: by simply waiting for it to show up.

EPILOGUE

The end I know not,
it is all in thee
—Walt Whitman, "Prayer of Columbus"

The conquest of Babylon, prophesied for centuries, finally began on the first of April 2003. While there was no rain of toads, what did fall from the sky was suitably impressive, as precision-guided munitions softened up what little organized resistance there was to U.S. ground forces. The first Americans to enter the ancient city, sixty miles south of Baghdad, were Navy Seabees attached to the First Marine Expeditionary Force, which had secured the nearby town of Al-Hillah. Little did they appreciate that by the mere act of walking into the legendary city, so closely tied to the story of the great battle between good and evil in the book of Revelation, they were fulfilling the aspirations of generations of soothsayers, going all the way back to the original thrust that had brought Europeans to the new-found-land of America.

Considering how much anticipation had gone into it, the taking of Babylon was a bit anticlimactic. These were not, alas, the final events. In fact, there was nothing final about them at all. No angelic choirs were heard, no wo-joy trumpets sounded, and no particular military objectives were gained by seizing the legendary battle site. "Babylon is fallen, is fallen, that great city," proclaim the words of Revelation 14:8, and so indeed it was, even before the Seabees arrived to claim it. The city had already lost some of its allure in the previous decades, as it became one of the historical monuments that Saddam Hussein reconfigured into a celebration of his murderous reign. Over the original bricks, Saddam had had laid millions of new bricks, inscribed, "In the era of Saddam Hussein, protector of Iraq, who rebuilt civilization and rebuilt Babylon." They began to crack after a mere ten years. Then they were looted, along with much else, in the chaotic days of the early invasion.

To make matters worse, the Americans occupying Babylon soon turned it into a military base, with the rather unfortunate name "Camp Babylon," and built helicopter landing pads and parking lots for the immense amount of matériel they needed to transport around the region. The act of construction, ironically, was also an act of destruction, and much of Babylon's historic value was irreparably compromised. Several ancient structures collapsed during the frenzy of building, and many of the original bricks of the great processional route through the Ishtar Gate, 2,600 years old, were crushed by heavy military vehicles. In short, Babylon's ruins have been ruined. But perhaps all is not lost—there is now talk of Babylon finding a new and peculiarly American form of afterlife, as a theme park with hotels and a mall.

The fall of Babylon is only one of a thousand episodes that reveal how much history was in the air as the United States went to war with Iraq at the beginning of the twenty-first century. With little national security to gain, and a great deal to lose, the U.S. government committed hundreds of billions of dollars and even more precious prestige toward a poorly defined set of aims that it now seems unlikely to ever realize. There are shortages of many things in the Middle East, but history is not one of them, and the paradoxes unfold like tents in the desert. Iraq, where the world's first set of laws developed nearly four millennia ago, is now a place where laws apply indifferently. The same ancient valleys that witnessed the rise of writing and of civilization itself have lately seen something like the opposite, libraries pillaged and civilizations at each other's throats. Another biblical story set in Iraq—that of the Tower of Babel—recounts God's anger at human arrogance, and the pride of those who thought they could draw closer to heaven by the simple act of building a large and expensive platform to stand on. The division of humanity into thousands of warring tribes and irreconcilable languages was the consequence.

The final result of this adventure is not yet known, but it seems reasonable to predict that it will not be a ringing triumph for American arms. Once again, we have revealed that our desire to change the world has exceeded our capacity to do so. It is not so much that we lack the ability to project an immense military force—no one doubts that we do. It is rather that our aims in doing so have been contradictory and unclear. For all the progress of the last hundred years—FDR's Great Design, the successful conclusion of the Cold War, and the Pax Americana that prevailed in its aftermath—we still have an astonishing capacity to confuse ourselves. Indeed, the Bible tells us that the root word of *Babylon* means "confusion." The Puritans may have been right to spend so much energy warning their children against the place.

Time and again, we Americans have demonstrated a remarkable ability to learn from our mistakes and chart a new course. What better place to learn about the future than the past? In the rush to secure Baghdad, very few people took time to think much about history, and as the world knows, countless national treasures were looted from its museum and library. But American history was also pillaged by the simple act of deciding, against a great weight of tradition, to invade a small foreign nation that could not threaten the United States nearly as much as it aspired to. In ways large and small, we ignored the most noble of our foreign policy traditions and concentrated with great intensity on the worst. Altruism was replaced by bullying; common sense by zealotry; and our natural openness, the very essence of democracy, by an unprecedented emphasis on the clandestine and encoded. All this despite the fact that the threats posed by international terrorists, while significant, never added up to anything like the danger posed by Nazi Germany or, at certain moments, the Soviet Union.

No amount of patriotic drapery (and no administration has cited liberty quite as frantically as the one that launched this preemptive war) can conceal the now-apparent fact that the 2003 invasion of Iraq was a profound miscalculation, and that we are paying an exorbitant price for the temporary possession of a nation that is not, in the end, valuable to us. Not only have we rejected the better parts of our own history, we have in some ways reversed course, like a groggy commuter who accidentally gets on a train going in the wrong direction. Once a small nation, and always a defender of small nations, we are now derided as a superpower that pays no heed to the rights of others. Once a tiny military power and an opponent of unrestrained armaments sales, we have become by far the world's leading military power, both in our own right and as a vendor to others. Once the opponent of mercenary armies, we now provide them to other nations and to ourselves, where they act with seeming impunity. Once the opponent of secrecy in diplomacy and the creator of new forms of open interaction between nations, we now conduct our foreign relations in a more guarded manner than at any moment in our history. Once the driving force behind the UN, we are now its leading critic. Once the embodiment of the idea of human rights in a world that rarely recognized them, we are now perceived as a chief violator of those rights. Once the nation that, more than any, defined the aspiration toward meaningful standards of international conduct, we are now denounced as scofflaws, picking and choosing which rules we adhere to, and indifferent to both international tribunals and the court of world opinion.

Not all of these perceptions are fair, but they exist nonetheless, and their mere existence has created enormous problems in a world that conducts a lot of its foreign policy around the idea of consensus—an idea we had something to do with implementing. All of this has come about for the relatively specific reason that we launched a war that was not defensive, in violation of the UN Charter and much of our history. Rereading the Declaration of Independence can be an uncomfortable exercise in the early twenty-first century, for in a certain late afternoon light it can read like a declaration against ourselves.

Nor is that the only way America has failed to live up to its history. Well before the Declaration, the earliest settlers poured their intellectual energy into the denunciation of arbitrary authority—of popes, archbishops, and certain dark figures of the supernatural world. What were all those attacks on Antichrist if not a complaint against the untrammeled power of the executive? Have we, at long last, become our own worst enemy?

The answer, fortunately, is no. The United States will emerge from the current predicament chastened but intact, and we will have learned an important lesson as a result. But it is a haunting question all the same, and worthy of attention from a people who have rarely lacked the confidence to ask hard questions. Of course, we have never been quite as perfect as our rhetoric, as our critics are quick to point out, and as we should feel no shame in admitting. I have tried to show that we always had tendencies working against our best ideals, and that it was never accurate to see America as the embodiment of pure virtue. But I have also argued that, for all the setbacks, there was an extraordinary story unfolding across the centuries—an arc of liberty—and that the idealism of the founders was essential to America's modern greatness. Each generation built upon the sacrifice of its predecessors, and just as Lincoln deepened the meaning of liberty for all Americans, so Franklin D. Roosevelt deepened it for all humanity. It is that particular arc that is in jeopardy at the moment, thanks to poor planning, poor communication, and pure sanctimony concerning our errand into the Mesopotamian wilderness. In his 2006 State of the Union address, President George W. Bush stated the obvious when he said, "Sometimes it can seem that history is turning in a wide arc, toward an unknown shore."

Twice, the phrase *Babylonian Captivity* has described a nation's temporary departure from its true history—first, in Judaic history, when the Israelites were forced to remove to Babylon in the sixth century B.C., and second, in Christian history, when the papacy removed to Avignon, in France, during the fourteenth century. Perhaps the phrase can be borrowed a third time to describe the United States in the early twenty-first century, its history interrupted, wandering in the desert for clues that will lead us back home. Clearly, Americans and Iraqis will not be liberated from each other for a long time to come. Our ark of the liberties has beached itself on a rather nasty sandbar.

How could such a disaster have happened, at the beginning of a century that held so much promise? Americans will be asking that question for some time, now that the first presidential administration of the twenty-first century is drawing to a close, and we can begin to view its legacy with objectivity.

This is not a book about the Bush administration, which will soon fade into the very history that it worked so hard to separate itself from. But it is worth pausing for a moment to contemplate how a group of patriotic leaders could have inflicted so much harm, so quickly, on the world order that had been created by their own country. Perhaps there was a structural flaw in our democracy that we were unaware of until now—namely, that the ease of entry into American politics, combined with our vast military might, gives just about anyone a chance to rule the world.

At the end of the last century, this clique went to some lengths to define the "New American Century" approaching, with a blizzard of position papers and speeches, and a few particularly loud manifestos. To their credit, their views were candidly expressed. Perhaps historians should have paid more attention at the time.

These views are still worth parsing, if for no other reason than the fact that the best antidote to a structural flaw is a well-informed citizenry. All of the future members of the Bush team, assembling in the wings in the late 1990s, displayed the most ardent devotion to freedom and liberty, but it was a most selective kind of freedom. Not one of them, for example, had participated in the greatest struggle for freedom of their lifetimes, the civil rights movement, a victory over terror by any definition. Many had been downright hostile to it, or had opposed Nelson Mandela's long quest for liberation. Several opposed the human rights initiatives of the 1970s, including the Helsinki Accords, which did so much to bring down the Soviet Union. All had spoken out in favor of self-determination when discussing the oppressed nations of Eastern Europe under the Soviet Union; not one had supported the same principle of self-determination when the left-leaning nations of Central America were trying, in imperfect ways, to achieve an independent destiny of their own in the 1980s.

Throughout several administrations, as these Cold Warriors rose through the ranks, they learned that promoting an acute sense of danger overseas brought political rewards at home. In the 1970s, they wrote alarmist reports about the Soviet Union that turned out not to be true, and failed to understand that it was approaching collapse rather than triumph. They understood instinctively, in a succession of administrations from Nixon onward, that a strong and secretive foreign policy was a way to assert executive authority over Congress. They supported expensive weapons systems, especially those that offered the added advantage of weakening existing treaties. They felt a deep dislike for the United Nations, which they tried to portray as an alien organization, with some help from the UN itself. They generally pursued a very hard line with the Middle East, eventually helping to forge a coalition between the Christian right and the Israeli right. In all of these ways, and many others, they pursued a scorched-earth campaign, denouncing Democrats with more than usual vehemence, and internationalist Republicans as well.

Even by America's bullish standards, this was a uniquely disruptive way to enter the china shop of world diplomacy. It favored secrecy over dialogue, executive privilege over checks and balances, and force above everything. In extremely rare situations in our history—say, the beginning of the Civil War, or World War Two—those arguments held temporary merit. But there was nothing in the background of the Bush team to suggest a Churchillian sensitivity to history, or even the most minimal awareness of the world's likely trends. In fact, they had managed to get a surprising number of things wrong, from their tendency to blame Saddam Hussein for events he had nothing to do with (the first attack on the World Trade Center, and the 1995 Oklahoma City bombing), to their insistence that the Strategic Defense Initiative worked (it does not), to their indifference to the lethal danger posed by Osama bin Laden. In the blizzard of white papers, manifestos, and speeches generated by these self-proclaimed experts in the years leading up to the administration of George W. Bush, it is impossible to find a single report on Al Qaeda. Looking back, it is fair to ask the question: Could these so-called realists have been any more unrealistic?

Reflecting on this not-so-distant history, it comes as no surprise that the United States was plunged into a war, or that the war was poorly defined. Vaporous wars often follow vaporous ideas. Increasingly, Iraq is likened to Vietnam, a war it once had nothing in common with, but begins to resemble as the years tumble by without any clear resolution. That is only one of a thousand echoes from the past, more audible now that the sound and fury of the war's commencement are over and we are left with the drudgery of entrenched police work. It seems unsurprising, though still disturbing, that the same places of semi-sovereignty that we acquired in earlier efforts to enlarge our influence are exactly where we are now being accused of violating human rights. Guantánamo Bay, for example, our most tangible legacy of the Spanish-American War, will be forever linked in the world's mind with our extralegal treatment of enemy combatants.

In some ways, it even seems as if we have been moving backward. It takes an especially tortured logic to argue that we now depend on torture for information necessary to our security. For the last seventy years, statements obtained by torture were inadmissible, but today military panels are empowered to accept them. All American presidents have opposed this, including Ronald Reagan, who supported an international covenant opposing torture. Woodrow Wilson once said, "I would be ashamed of this flag if it ever did anything outside America that we would not permit it to do inside of America." But as we have learned, the United States has permitted a worldwide system of extradition and interrogation that not only violates treaties we negotiated, but models itself on our very enemies, even to the extent of using former Soviet prisons in Eastern Europe. Some particular techniques—waterboarding, for example—go back to the Spanish Inquisition, and to everything Columbus left behind.

Our disregard for the treaty process has also reversed a course that was clearly charted and served the United States well under many Republicans and Democrats. There was a time when one could make the argument that the ethical treaty was one of America's major contributions to diplomacy. But now, one could compile a long list of international agreements we have refused to honor, from curbs on climate change to international legal arrangements to standards of military conduct and restraints on weapons. In fact, after decades of suppressing nuclear activity, we are again contemplating test scenarios and new generations of offensive weapons that have the potential to ignite new arms races and to weaken our efforts to control nuclear proliferation in places such as Iran and North Korea.

No idea was more deeply out of sync with the American tradition than the notion that we were entitled to attack another nation in a preemptive strike without clear evidence of its intention to attack us. As Robert Kennedy reflected during a far graver situation, the Cuban Missile Crisis, the United States had to stay true to its ethics, even as it contemplated Armageddon. Nor did the successful invasion of Iraq promote the democracy we claimed, belatedly, to be promoting there. In truth, we hoped to avoid direct elections (which would bring in Shi'ites) and instead apportioned power through "caucuses." We paid journalists to write friendly stories. Perhaps worst of all, we offered meager rewards to our own soldiers, the brave Americans fighting this war. In previous generations, the act of fighting for freedom was itself a way of securing freedom, and veterans were given new kinds of rights (such as the right to attend college). Today, that particular right seems too expensive to offer the National Guard, which does not receive full military benefits despite its heavy responsibility in Iraq.

Slowly, Americans began to realize that these attacks in the name of liberty were harming our own liberties. We have always had realists and idealists in our midst; more often than not, our leaders have been combinations of the two. The men who led America into Iraq in 2003 were not quite either—perhaps *cynics* is the best word. What does one call an effort to spread democracy by people who do not seem to believe in the basic consensus of democracy? What does one call airy theories of perfect human behavior floated by people with no inclination to utopia? What does one call the interventionist yearnings of people who have shown very little interest in foreign cultures? So it has been with the rhetoric of the Bush administration; these were wolves in Wilsonian clothing.

There are many speeches to choose from, but none stated the case more reverberatingly than President Bush's second inaugural address, which mentioned liberty or its equivalent forty-nine times. To make sure his audience understood, President Bush proclaimed "the ultimate goal of ending tyranny in our world," despite the fact that it is completely unattainable outside of the world of comic-book superheroes. Strangely, a day later, the White House claimed that this was not, in fact, the goal of the United States; and the president's father said, "People want to read a lot into it. It's just a speech about freedom."

The more carefully one looked into the particular freedoms offered by this vision, the more difficult it became to ascertain what they were. One problem was the incendiary image President Bush offered: promising that "this untamed fire of freedom will reach the darkest corners of our world" was not, perhaps, the most welcoming metaphor, although it did echo some aspects of Revelation. Another was that the overuse of the words *freedom* and *liberty* dulled the senses to them. Now and then, a word choice can make a healthy difference (for example, "Operation Iraqi Freedom" was chosen to replace "Operation Iraqi Liberation" after someone noticed the acronym created by the latter). But choosing the same word over and over again can eliminate that word's best qualities. As Emerson once said, "When words lose all power to stimulate the understanding or the affections, the fraud is manifest." The more these liberty bells were struck, and clanged interchangeably, the more the feeling grew that there was a false note to them.

The trumpets of Revelation were audible in other ways as well.

Bush's speeches were strangely archaic in their intense expectation of a grand result in the future, pitting the forces of righteousness against his enemies. Effortlessly, they recycled the religious language that always murmured below the surface, like a secret mountain stream. He spoke often of the "transformational power of liberty," a way of speaking that would not have been entirely out of place during the Great Awakening. He said that he sensed a "Third Awakening" of religiosity in the United States, coinciding with the war on terrorism, a "confrontation between good and evil," and he told Bob Woodward that he was "casting his vision and that of the country in the grand vision of God's master plan."

For most of American history, genuine evangelicals were rather far from the levers of power, and to the extent that they approached the political stage, they were isolationist and devoted to peace (William Jennings Bryan, for example). In the early twenty-first century the opposite was true, and many of President Bush's religious advisers were among the most aggressive in supporting the invasion of Iraq, linking Saddam to Nebuchadnezzar or arguing that his overthrow would convert Muslims and hasten the Final Days. The viral theory of democracy expressed before the war was its odd parallel—namely, that a democracy in Iraq would magically lead to democracies in other countries—a sort of domino theory in reverse, and equally implausible. This particular combination of evangelicals and neoconservatives—a Holy Alliance of sorts—brought something new, a religious commitment to overthrowing regimes.

To be fair, in many ways the war that the Bush administration started does resemble the conflict described in Revelation. Our enemies are formless, and shapeless, and seemingly universal. Like the struggle against Antichrist, there is no clear field of battle. But to be equally fair, many of the particular descriptions of Antichrist—described as a huge invading power exercising terrifying military strength—apply just as accurately to the United States, a fact that our enemies have made good use of in their propaganda. Babylon is a confusing place, full of sandstorms. Words change their meaning; new alliances are made and then broken; and destiny seems anything but manifest. It is melancholy to reflect that for most of the last century, a loose commitment to American ideals was the glue that held the world together; today, the world increasingly rejects the United States and sees us as the chief opponent of those ideals. At long last, the United States has succeeded in uniting the world—against us.

Of course, we have always fought against ourselves, as I have tried to show in every chapter of this book. It could hardly be otherwise when a nation went so quickly from an idea to a fact to the world's controlling force. There were always pressures against our better angels, even as we were consistently deepening the meaning of freedom, generation after generation. Slavery's defenders advocated more land in defense of "liberty"; Douglas MacArthur promised a "victory" over China that was never going to come; furious backbenchers derided those who secured America's place in the new world order as agents of communism, or the devil, or, God forbid, both.

But an especially deep and Babylonish confusion seems to prevail at the beginning of what could still be a great American century. The administration has claimed to be at war (when that advanced the administration's "Freedom Agenda") and not at war (when the Geneva conventions have felt restrictive). It has raised emotions by insisting that a titanic struggle between good and evil is under way, but then has demanded no sacrifice, and postponed most payments until our children will have to make them. It has compared our difficulties to those suffered by Americans in World War Two, or the Civil War, or the American Revolution, which were entirely different conflicts, both from each other and from this one. It has predicted the broad liberation of the Middle East but invested little time in the peace process, which is the central problem of that region. It has expressed a desire to spread liberty like so much vinyl siding, but never defined what this liberty will look like, and balked at the hard work required. It has claimed victory when there is no victory in sight. To call on God to help us prevail in a war we cannot win is in effect to ask Him to join us on the losing sideline. And as countless generations of Americans have argued, God is no loser.

A few hundred feet from my office, in a library in Providence, there is a document that was once entitled, appropriately, "Meditation on Providence." But this piece of writing is not confined to a city, or even a great nation. It is universal—a philosopher's reflection on the natural limits that will always prevent human beings from becoming divine. In the middle of the Civil War, Abraham Lincoln wrote down, on a scrap of lined paper, his innermost thoughts about the war effort he was leading:

> The will of God prevails. In great contests each party claims to act in accordance with the will of God. Both may be, and one must be wrong. God cannot be for and against the same thing at the same time. In the present civil war it is quite possible that God's purpose is something different from the purpose of either party—and yet the human instrumentalities, working just as they do, are of the best adaptation to effect his purpose. I am almost ready to say this is probably true—that God wills this contest, and wills that it shall not end yet. By his mere quiet power, on the minds of the now contestants, He could have either saved or destroyed the Union without a human contest. Yet the contest began. And having begun He could give the final victory to either side any day. Yet the contest proceeds.

Lincoln seems to be saying that great lessons come from the conflicts we endure, including the essential lesson of humility and the self-knowledge that comes with suffering. It can be hoped that the current conflict will bring Americans of all stripes to a fuller understanding of our national history, and the values that brought us to the summit of influence that we felt as this new millennium began.

It is still too early to write the final epitaph of George W. Bush's administration, or of the equally American world order, created by Franklin Roosevelt, that it set itself against. Bush himself has persistently used the most grandiloquent language to describe his place in history, citing Churchill and Lincoln, or when things were not going so well, Harry Truman, the patron saint of embattled Republicans and Democrats alike. But that comparison is not for him to make. Historians will reckon with this presidency, as they have reckoned with all the others, at a time of their choosing.

If this sweeping look at the centuries has taught me anything, it is that no single event is capable of dominating the narrative, and that it is always darkest before the dawn. The ark of the liberties has shown a consistent ability to right its course, and we have every reason to expect it will do so again. Of course, the latest American century is barely under way, and a great deal of our history remains unspooled. The United States of America is still an extraordinary force for freedom, offering new beginnings to huge numbers of immigrants every year, generating new ideas and technologies, and providing, as it has for centuries, a relative tolerance in a world still shackled by a billion petty despotisms. Despite our manifest imperfection, no nation has ever stood more clearly for freedom, and no other nation will soon assume that particular mantle. Certainly no one is looking to China, Russia, or India as a shining beacon. In fact, "liberty" is a threatening enough concept to the Chinese government that it is one of the keywords that authorities use to shut down Internet sites.

By any standard, freedom is still on the march. In 2006, there were 123 electoral democracies, according to Freedom House, and the number of genuinely free countries has risen from roughly a quarter in 1972 to nearly half today. When all the countries that are either free or partly free are judged together, they add up to 148 nations, or 77 percent of the world's 194 polities. Liberty and democracy are such powerful political ideas that they are even embraced by their enemies. In a recent video message to the West, Osama bin Laden sounded almost Jeffersonian. "This is why I tell you: as you liberated yourselves from the slavery of monks, kings, and feudalism, you should liberate yourselves from the deception, shackles, and attrition of the capitalist system." Khalid Sheikh Mohammed, the architect of 9/11, cited our founder of founders as his "hero" when he told a military court, in broken English, "We consider we and George Washington doing same thing." That is not exactly reassuring, but the fact that our enemies feel compelled to speak of our ideals is a tribute to their universal appeal.

Where will our ark sail next? As I have tried to show, we will always have choices—for this ark, unlike Noah's, is driven by its passengers. It seems safe to predict that a peculiar mixture of realism and idealism will generally guide this most creative of recently created nations. At times, when threatened, we will revert to our insular identity and contemplate ourselves as the sequestered island that we first appeared to be on the earliest maps. At other times, when feeling inspired, or compassionate, or merely bored, we will lower the drawbridge and begin once again the eternal effort to remake the world. The combination will always be interesting.

Surely our future course will be made easier by a clear grasp of how far we have already come. And a celebration of our endless possibilities will not be diminished by the knowledge that we, like all peoples, have to live inside certain kinds of boundaries. Words also have boundaries, and I hope that we will not be dazzled by the mere mention of a word such as *liberty*, as we so often have been in the past. Like wise customers, we should examine the promises that our leaders make, as if they were so many unripe melons at the grocery store. Liberty can, in fact, be measured, and it should be. Will our policies give people around the world enhanced access to the political process and the information they need to make wise decisions? Will we support governments that are accountable to their people, with fair legal systems, minority rights, free media, transparent elections, and opposition parties? Will we build peace and international treaties and business agreements? Will our embassies reach out to people in foreign countries, or will they be enormous concrete fortresses located so far outside city centers that no one can visit them?

Nor should we be surprised if our own liberties continue to evolve. Near the end of his presidency, Franklin Roosevelt was teasing out the idea of new kinds of economic rights, such as the right to health care and education. Future Americans may clamor for the right to live on a planet that is not overheated, or they may decide, in concert with other nations, that all the world's children have the right to receive medicine that will protect them against easily curable diseases. That would be a liberty worth fighting for.

Of course, there is no guarantee that things will get better, despite the generally progressive trend of our history. Americans may be a famously confident people, capable of meeting just about any challenge, but at the same time, huge numbers believe that we are going to hell in a handbasket. Forty percent of us (and 71 percent of evangelical Protestants) think that the world will end with a battle at Armageddon between Jesus and Antichrist. As of this writing, the rapture index is at 159, which suggests "heavy prophetic activity" (160 means "fasten your seat belts").

In truth, the world *is* scary, with or without the aid of a prophetic speedometer. The mess in Iraq has dearly cost the United States in prestige and influence, which will make it that much harder to enforce international law during the crises of the future. China, India, and Russia have been more than happy to increase their leverage as we have wandered in the desert, and Revelation 16:12 predicts the arrival of "the kings from the east." If that is not unnerving enough, there is also the uncomfortable fact that the ancient Mayan calendar predicted the world would end on December 21, 2012. Rising seas and angry heavens are hardly biblical in places such as the Seychelles, the Maldives, or even New Orleans. If environmental catastrophes don't get us, there is an unusually high chance that an 850-foot-long asteroid, Apophis, will strike the earth on April 13, 2036, with apocalyptic consequences. Have a nice day.

But there is some comfort in the knowledge that every doomsday prediction that has ever been made has turned out to be wrong. No millennium is ever going to happen if, as is so often the case, a change in human nature is required. If American history is a guide, then there is no reason to believe that we will not dust ourselves off, correct our mistakes, and move on. The immediate temptation may be to pull up the drawbridges to our island fortress; we should do exactly the opposite. The best way to persuade the world of America's greatness is to display it. We need to deepen our influence, not parcel it out, and we need to be worthy of the immense power we still wield. Dean Acheson said that it should be U.S. policy to be "the first to attend international conferences and the last to retire." Americans should pay more attention to foreign news (the trend is the opposite) and put pressure on our leaders to form foreign policies that make sense for constituents. We cannot proclaim America's global destiny and refuse to pay attention at the same time. As always, we need to calibrate our desire to reshape the world with our capacity.

At our best moments, we have done just that. The Marshall Plan was an extraordinary investment in a better world, made by the only nation in history that could have afforded it, and it paid for itself a thousand times over. FDR's Grand Design of international architecture was idealistic in spirit, as it needed to be, but it was also grounded by the incontestable might of the American military and economy. Wilson offered the old world a glimpse of a new one when it desperately needed to believe that such a world was possible. Throughout the nineteenth century, American educators and statesmen gave other peoples around the globe, and particularly in the Middle East, the sense that international relations did not have to be colonial. The founders showed everyone that it was possible to lead a revolution based on law and human rights, and to build a responsible government in its wake. That's a lesson that most of humanity is still learning from.

We Americans are at our best, and our most truly world-shaping, when we reject the idea of special destiny and simply get to work. That's how Lincoln and Grant won the Civil War, defeating ideologues from both North and South who were convinced that God was on their side. That's how FDR defeated hunger and Hitler. He put it efficiently, and therefore well, when he said, "failure is not an American habit." That's how Truman and Marshall and Acheson convinced war-weary Americans that they had global responsibilities they could not walk away from in the early Cold War. All of those changes were agonizingly difficult at the time, and seem effortless only in the history books. But they were accomplished with the purposefulness of the American people, drawing from deep wellsprings of both idealism and realism, mixed in with plenty of elbow grease.

In the same passage in which Melville invoked the Ark of the Liberties, he wondered if the American people would ever find the "political Messiah" they had been waiting for. Startlingly, he announced that one had already been found, and that "he has come in *us*." To put it another way, there is nothing broken by the American people that cannot be fixed by the American people. By acknowledging our imperfections, remembering our strengths, and embracing our history in all of its richness, we can help this ark rediscover its true course.

T. S. Eliot may not seem like the most robustly American author to conclude with. In many ways, he was barely American at all, hiding his healthy St. Louis upbringing behind a bow tie and a British accent. But more than most, he knew the earliest history of the Europeans who came to the New World. In 1941, he remembered an unusual image from his boyhood, the Dry Salvages (or Three Savages), a group of rocks off Cape Ann, Massachusetts, in waters that were English before they were American, and French before they were English, and Spanish before they were French, and native before they were anything. The rocks rise out of the ocean like America itself, concealing more than they reveal, presenting both danger and opportunity; sometimes visible and sometimes not—a phantasm, but real enough to cause a shipwreck; an idea and a fact. That same year, in an equally terraqueous setting to the northeast, FDR was negotiating the Atlantic Charter, which grounded American aspirations to rebuild the world in real words and promises.

Even as he wrote about the beginning of American history, Eliot conveyed his feeling that it never really stops, despite all the boundaries we put around nations and stories. His Puritan ancestors might have been disappointed, for they had put a lot of energy into the end of the world. But perhaps we can take solace in the fact that we are here at all, even in our flawed and mortal condition. Eliot's words still speak to Americans struggling to learn from our history:

> you are the music
> While the music lasts. These are only hints and guesses,
> Hints followed by guesses; and the rest
> Is prayer, observance, discipline, thought and action.

In "Little Gidding," the final of his *Four Quartets*, Eliot renewed that call to arms, urging us to see America as the earliest adventurers did, a place of spectacular possibility. If, as he argued there, "the beginning is often the end," then the opposite is also true, and it is exciting to go back to the sources, a little wiser, ready to do it all over again:

> We will not cease from exploration
> And the end of all our exploring
> Will be to arrive where we started
> And know the place for the first time.

ACKNOWLEDGMENTS

One of the great pleasures of writing a book is to thank all the people who shaped it. In my case, the list is long and the names are numerous, but I will do my best to enumerate them. Many I will never be able to thank, because they wrote books that vanished into obscurity decades or even centuries before this book was written, but their influence was felt on every page.

I feel lucky, even if my readers do not, that I have always been interested in the widest possible definition of American history. Near the beginning of my undergraduate career, now a distant epoch in its own right, I had the good fortune to study with a colonial historian, Alan Heimert, who insisted that nearly everything contemporary was also present in the deep past. I always appreciated his skepticism toward the pieties of political correctness, then in abundance at Harvard University, and his insistence that his students think for themselves (while, if possible, agreeing with him). Since then, I have enjoyed wide friendships within the academic world, even while departing that world on occasion. I am especially grateful to my colleagues at the various universities where I have worked, from Harvard to Washington College to Brown University and the John Carter Brown Library. At the latter institution, I feel proud to be associated with an ever-expanding group of visiting scholars and fellows, from nations around the world, eager to deepen their knowledge of the New World and its origins. Their relentless research into the ancient mysteries gives me, paradoxically, great hope for the future. I would like to thank the JCB's board of governors and staff (particularly Maureen O'Donnell) for their constant support.

I, too, visited many libraries in my research. In *The Tempest*, Ariel says, "Where the bee sucks, there suck I"—not a bad summary of the way scholars float from one archive to the next, extracting nectar. I always profited from the collections of Brown University, Harvard University, and the New York Public Library. I also enjoyed the occasional random discovery in the Providence Athenaeum, where I have been an armchair explorer since my researches were confined to the Dr. Seuss collection. I should also thank a group that does not get thanked nearly enough: the owners of secondhand bookstores, purveyors of serendipities. In my case, it was a constant pleasure to go to Cellar Stories, where my son could read comic books and I could embark on long-forgotten voyages.

Every bee needs an infrastructure, and I was fortunate to receive several fellowships along the way. In New York, I was a fellow of the Gilder Lehrman Institute for American History (thanks to Lesley Hermann and Jim Basker). In Paris, I was a visiting scholar at Sciences Po (thanks to Richard Descoings, Pascal Deslisle, Béatrice de Clermont-Tonnerre, and Susannah Hunnewell). I also was invited to give talks in far-flung places, ranging from Bosphorus University in Istanbul to the École des Hautes Études en Sciences Sociales in Paris to the Rothermere Institute at Oxford University. I am particularly grateful to the New America Foundation and to the Center for American Progress for inviting me to affiliate with their excellent programs.

I spent considerable time gathering material for this book, without knowing that I was doing so, when I worked in the White House from 1997 to 2001. In that capacity I was primarily a foreign policy speechwriter, but I also read widely in the history of presidential oratory and traveled with the president of the United States as he undertook the essential work of explaining American policies—and by extension, democracy itself—to the world. The conclusions of this book are mine alone, but I want to express my gratitude to President Clinton and to Sandy Berger for the opportunity they gave me to serve in the White House. I also want to say what a privilege it was to work alongside the dedicated men and women of the National Security Council.

Many friends contributed toward this book through reading, writing, or simply talking. Two historians in particular, no longer with us, were essential in urging me forward: James Chace and Arthur Schlesinger Jr.

Their salty combination of skepticism and optimism continues to offer a most attractive path out of the wilderness. Clara, Emily, and Joan Bingham were always supportive listeners. The danger of listing a few friends is that one fails to list all the others, but I would like to add how much I have enjoyed my conversations with Dan Aaron, Leslie Dunton-Downer, Susan Morrison, Tony Horwitz, Max Kennedy, Big Mike McLaughlin, George Perkins, Polly Carpenter, Joel Rosenthal, Alex Chilton, Suzanne Despres, Marc Mazzarelli, Anthony Bevilacqua, Christina Bevilacqua, and all the members of the Rhinelander family.

This book was conceived in Maryland, when I worked at Washington College, and I'd like to thank all my friends there who made it such a pleasant place to teach—particularly Adam Goodheart, who saw several early drafts and whose passion for American history always restored my own. The late Townsend Hoopes set a constant example with his courage and eloquence, and I enjoyed several unforgettable interviews with a retired OSS agent who worked with Ho Chi Minh in the critical year 1945. I'd like to also thank Jay Griswold and Birch Bayh for their lively camaraderie, the McColls and the Blacks for their dinner parties, and the Maryland Historical Society for inviting me to give the talk that led to this book.

Jonathan Edwards once wrote, "When God's appointed time was come, his work went on with a swift and wonderful progress." Unfortunately, the same cannot be said for this book. But I thank Thomas LeBien for keeping the pressure on at exactly the right moments. I would say something effusive but he would strike it as a cliché. I could not have asked for a more conscientious editor. I am also grateful to Elisabeth Sifton for her early support, to Liz Maples for her heroic efforts to find images, and to Tina Bennett for her many dispensations of wise advice.

Though I had little to do with it, I was fortunate to be born into a family that cared intensely about foreign perspectives on the United States. I can hardly remember a day when there were not piles of foreign books lying around the house, nearly always in languages that I could not read. I'm grateful to my parents for the many overseas adventures they provided, from Taiwan (where I flunked out of an all-Chinese kindergarten) to Brazzaville, Khabarovsk, and beyond. I am particularly hopeful for King's Academy, a school that my father is working to build in the Middle East, with Meera Viswanathan and my brother Matt, and dozens of inspired young teachers. My late grandmother Carolyn Ladd Widmer was a lifelong traveler, and spent long stretches of her life in South America and Lebanon, working in public health and education. She seemed to never stop learning, and her overflowing rooms were another early source of inspiration. At some point in adolescence, I discovered that her grandfather Cyrus Hamlin was the founder of Robert College in Istanbul, a factoid that escaped much notice from me until I turned to the writing of this book. While striving to avoid the excesses of the missionary tradition, I have benefited greatly from this strangely insistent web of international influences.

Last, I want to acknowledge the two people who lived through this book more than anyone. To Mary Rhinelander and Freddy Widmer, I can never offer thanks enough.

INDEX

ILLUSTRATION CREDITS

Frontispiece:

Columbus, *De Insulis Inventis* (Basel, 1493), courtesy of the John Carter Brown Library.

Images from insert:

Map by Jan ze Stobnicy (Cracow, 1512), courtesy of the John Carter Brown Library.

Theodor de Bry, *Grands Voyages* (Frankfurt, 1590), courtesy of the John Carter Brown Library.

"Blemmyae," from Levinis Hulsius, *Die Fünffte Kurtze Wunderbare Beschreibung* (Nuremburg, 1603), courtesy of the John Carter Brown Library.

Cotton Mather's *The Fall of Babylon* (Boston, 1707), courtesy of the Massachusetts Historical Society.

"The Man of Sin," from *The New England Primer*, courtesy of the John Carter Brown Library.

George Whitefield, 1745, courtesy of the Brown University Library.

French print of Benjamin Franklin (Paris, 1778), courtesy of the John Carter Brown Library.

The French-English engagement off Brittany, July 27, 1778, courtesy of the John Carter Brown Library.

Albert Gallatin, courtesy of the Library of Congress.

Abraham Lincoln, courtesy of the Library of Congress.

D-Day, 1847, courtesy of the Brown University Library.

Robert College, Constantinople, author's collection.

Theodore Roosevelt seated with globe, National Photo Company Collection, copyright by F. B. Hyde, courtesy of the Library of Congress.

William Howard Taft, Governor-General of the Philippines, c. 1902, courtesy of the U.S. Army Military History Institute.

Poster of New York City aflame after an imagined aerial attack, by Joseph Pennell, c. 1917, courtesy of the National Archives and Records Administration.

Statue of Liberty replica in Paris, photograph by Arpingstone.

Statue of Liberty replica at Odaiba, Tokyo Bay, photograph by Rob Fahey.

The Goddess of Liberty during the 1989 protests in Tiananmen Square, Beijing, by Jeff Widener/AP Images.

Crowd welcoming Woodrow Wilson to Paris, December 1918, courtesy of the Princeton University Library (Woodrow Wilson Collection, Public Policy Papers, Department of Rare Book and Special Collections).

FDR and Churchill off Newfoundland, courtesy of the Franklin D. Roosevelt Presidential Library.

Eleanor Roosevelt in Paris, September 1948, courtesy of the Franklin D. Roosevelt Presidential Library.

John F. Kennedy in Ireland, June 1963, by Robert Knudsen, Office of the Naval Aide to the President/John F. Kennedy Presidential Library and Museum, Boston.

Lyndon Johnson listening to a tape sent from Vietnam by Captain Charles Robb, July 31, 1968, by Jack Kightlinger, courtesy of the Lyndon Baines Johnson Library.
Ronald Reagan at Pointe du Hoc, Normandy, courtesy of the Ronald Reagan Presidential Library.
President George W. Bush on the deck of the USS *Abraham Lincoln*, May 1, 2003, AP Images.